RuPedagogies of Realness

# RuPedagogies of Realness

*Essays on Teaching and Learning with* RuPaul's Drag Race

*Edited by* LINDSAY BRYDE *and* TOMMY MAYBERRY

McFarland & Company, Inc., Publishers
*Jefferson, North Carolina*

*This book has undergone peer review.*

ISBN (print) 978-1-4766-8183-2
ISBN (ebook) 978-1-4766-4606-0

LIBRARY OF CONGRESS AND BRITISH LIBRARY
CATALOGUING DATA ARE AVAILABLE

Library of Congress Control Number 2022001640

© 2022 Lindsay Bryde and Tommy Mayberry. All rights reserved

*No part of this book may be reproduced or transmitted in any form or by any means, electronic or mechanical, including photocopying or recording, or by any information storage and retrieval system, without permission in writing from the publisher.*

Front cover images: © 2022 Shutterstock

Printed in the United States of America

*McFarland & Company, Inc., Publishers
Box 611, Jefferson, North Carolina 28640
www.mcfarlandpub.com*

# *Halleloo!*
## Acknowledgments

**The Contributors would like to thank…**

David J. Fine: Jenna Lay and Emily Shreve. Ricarda Goetz-Preisner: Nina Heidorn. Phillip Joy: Troy Toole, Wallace, and Sizzle. Vicky Kampouridou: Dina Vaiou, Irene Micha, and Dr. Phevos Kallitsis. Russ Martin: Dr. Karen Fricker and Allysin Chaynes. Peter Piatkowski: Cole Robertson and Teresa Piatkowski. Maggie Ward: Lorraine York, Basmah Rahman, and Rebecca Salazar. Nathan Workman: the ODU family and cohort, the Society for Cinema and Media Studies, Popular Culture Association, Meghan Morris, Dr. Amy Milligan, Dr. Avi Santo, Cheryl Workman, and Catherine Parker.

**Lindsay would like to thank…**

The influential educators who informed my perspective on pedagogy and performance: Leslie Boritz, James Desmond, Antony Dudley, Kermit Frazier, Tom Loughlin, Christina Jarvis, and Shannon McRae. My dear friend, Patricia Feraldi, and the fiercest boss ever, Patrick Rochelau, who welcomed me to Fredonia and opened so many doors. I would like to recognize my former students Jennifer Brown, Evan Gerard, Vic Figlia, Ryan Harinski, Jenna McDonnell, and Andy Santos for always being present in everything they do; it was a joy to be your professor. The network of educators that I've had the privilege to work with throughout the years, particularly: Linda Chapilliquen, Orsete Dias, Tara Fagan, Joseph Gatti, Lisa Hamilton, Atiya Mandani, Saundra Monteiro, Jason Ramirez, Mohamed El Seginy (my work husband, not yours), and Isaiah Vianese.

My colleagues at SUNY Empire State College are wonderful for their encouragement and patience as this collection came together and for putting up with all of my *Drag Race* backgrounds on Microsoft Teams that I used for motivation over the last two years: Norana Cantrell, Sheryl

Coleman, Jon Easton, Michael Fortune, Shaun Hoppel, Carolina Kim de Salmanaca, Michael Panetta, and Nathan Whitely-Grassi.

For my dear friends and family for being a wonderful network of laughs and constant support: Luci Burkett, Anitra Butler, Amy Cicala, the Cicala-Harris-DeFrens, the Cole family, Dan Coniglio, Maria Cosenza, Jared Durham (re. my nemesis), James Emmett, Elliot Freeman, Dan Gerrish, Sarah and Vinny Lettieri, Frankie Marchiony, Megan Mitchell, Deanna Mordente-Rossi, Anna and Laura Naclario, Shannon O'Leary, the O'Rourkes, the Richard family, John, Noreen, and Patricia Rinaldi, George Russo and Ann Sestak, Alissa Steele-Pruitt, Helen Trougakos, the Werners, and Alexandra Zahakos. Thank you to Christopher Mandemaker and John Santosus for literally and metaphorically picking me up every time that I am down.

I'd like to remember the people I wish that I could share this with in person. William Bryde, Marie Naclario, Emily Russo, and George Russo, who each shaped a different part of who I am and how I approach my work. Jessica Werner, who jumped in feet first for our first drag show and so many other milestones.

My mother, Joanne Bryde, deserves all the credit in the world for encouraging her kid to be smart and own it (even when it drove her up more than one wall). This is why I went and got all those degrees; it was worth it.

Finally, I would like to thank Edward Richard for surviving the last nine years of insanity and partnership with me. You are my favorite companion to watch *Drag Race* (and everything else) with; it is a little scary and delightful sometimes how much you have immersed yourself in RuPedagogies.

**Tommy would like to thank…**

My educational development mentors, peers, and friends who either introduced me to pedagogy and to the scholarship of teaching and learning, supervised me in my writing journeys and teaching experiments, and/or supported me in and across my educational development work. Svitlana Taraban-Gordon, Monika Soczewinski, Trevor Holmes, Donna Ellis, Mark Morton, Dale Lackeyram, Janet Wolstenholme, Sara Fulmer, Aron Fazekas, Jenn Reniers, Madison Wright, and, of course, (kokum) Jennifer Winters Ward, I can't thank you all enough.

My academic mentors, peers, and friends who seem to have supervised me since Day One in undergrad and now into doctoral studies … and everything in between and beyond! You've been with me for drag days in Tokyo, drag nights at home, and many, many conversations as I've learned about and become the academic drag queen I am today. Tristanne Connolly and Sarah Tolmie, I can't thank you both enough.

My post-secondary mentor, peer, and friend who met me (dressed as Harry Potter) in the EDSS library on Hallowe'en all those years ago and recruited me to St. Jerome's University and who has been there with me through all my studies, my multiple declarings and redeclarings of majors, double-majors, minors, double-minors, etc., and who saw something in me and championed me before I knew how to champion myself. Sue Brubacher, I cannot thank you enough.

My parents who literally have been there for me since Day One, pushing me farther, picking me up, cheering me on, watching me grow and growing with me. Chris Mayberry and Ray Mayberry, I love you both, and I can't thank you both enough. (And for putting me in drag for the very first time ... and second time ... and third time ... thank you, Mom!)

And my Tommy. (With our Sam.) You've walked with me in drag and out of drag across this world, from Niagara Falls to Odaiba to Oʻahu and that highest peak at Kualoa. You're my best friend, and I never will believe you that my make-up is ever too much. Tommy Bourque, I could not—and would not want to—do any of this without you: I love you, and I thank you.

**The editors would like to thank...**

Layla Milholen and the entire McFarland team for taking a chance on our collection. We are indebted to each of our contributors and to the scholars who shared their work with us along this journey: Kyler Chittick, David J. Fine, Ricarda Goetz-Preisner, Nina Heidorn, Vicky Kamouridou, Meredith K. James, Brooke Malone, Marko Mandić, Russ Martin, Mandy Penney, Peter Piatkowski, Tanner Sebastian, Maggie Ward, Nathan Workman, and Florian Zitzelsberger. The Northeast Modern Language Association (NeMLA) hosted the conference panel that started this project, and they have continued to foster our scholarship, passion, and obsession with *RuPaul's Drag Race*, its paratextual cultures, and pedagogy.

# Table of Contents

*Halleloo! Acknowledgments* .... v

*Hieeeee: An Introduction to the Collection*
    LINDSAY BRYDE *and* TOMMY MAYBERRY .... 1

**Start Your Engines: Critical Context
of the Language and Influence of Drag** .... 13

*RuPaul's Drag Race* as a Heterotopic Learning Experience
    VICKY KAMPOURIDOU .... 15

The Influence of *RuPaul's Drag Race* on Pop Culture and
the Way We Talk: A Pop-Linguistic Analysis
    RICARDA GOETZ-PREISNER .... 37

Pedagogy of the Mother: Exploring Freire's Philosophy
of Co-Productive Learning
    PHILLIP JOY *and* JILL MARIE MCSWEENEY-FLAHERTY .... 59

"And where is the body?" Naked Drag and the Social
Construction of Anatomy as Sexed and Gendered
    TOMMY MAYBERRY .... 91

**She Already Done Had Herses:
When Drag Curates Culture** .... 115

Pop the Corn and Teach the Children: Drag Lessons in Gender,
Race, and Class Beyond RuPaul's Televised Curriculum
    RUSS MARTIN .... 117

"Cultural appropriation! That's what we never heard": Performing
Indigeneity on Reality Television and Beyond
    MAGGIE WARD .... 142

Table of Contents

RuPaulogetics: Assimilation, Backwash, and the Charisma
of Queer Pedagogy
    DAVID J. FINE      161

## May the Best Drag Queen Win: The Competitive Nature of Drag      183

Gay Super Bowl: Homonormative Authorization, Instruction, and Discipline Through Sports Media Borrowings
    NATHAN WORKMAN      185

Where Are the Jokes? Comedy as Pedagogy
    PETER PIATKOWSKI      205

Digital Drag and YouTube as Queer Space: Queens as Influencers from Performance to Pedagogy
    FLORIAN ZITZELSBERGER      228

Pedagogies, Praxis, and Privilege: RuPaulean Communities of Care
    MANDY PENNEY      252

*Sashay Away: Resources to Support Learners*      273
*Spilling the Tea: Glossary*      277
*Let's Have a KiKi: Discussion Questions for the Class*      279
*Very Special Guest Judge: Select Bibliography*      283
*Charisma, Uniqueness, Nerve and Talent:
About the Contributors*      299
*The Library Is Open: The Index*      303

# *Hieeeee*

## An Introduction to the Collection

LINDSAY BRYDE *and* TOMMY MAYBERRY

Drag as an art form has been in existence for generations. It has been a consistent part of cabaret culture and traditional theater (think back to Shakespeare's *Twelfth Night* and its first performance in 1602). Yet, its prominence saw an incredible rise in America's collective consciousness with the advent of ball culture and trailblazing performers, such as Crystal LaBeija, Divine, and Lady Bunny. As sixteenth-century English scholar and Senior Educational Developer Mark Morton writes, "In the 1940s, the term *drag queen* emerged," yet "[e]arlier on, dating back to the 1870s, the word *drag* denoted women's clothing worn on stage by a male actor, a word that inspired the familiar idiom *in drag*."[1] And before we had the words and language for drag that, in a Foucauldian sense, brought them into existence, we can see drag/trans- bodies across the centuries in heartwarming and heartbreaking history; for instance, in 1810 at The White Swan on Vere Street (popularly known as The Vere Street Coterie) the men who were arrested, convicted, pilloried, and/or hanged for crimes of sodomy and attempted sodomy were written about in historical records as "*equivocal gender customers*"[2] who would "assume feigned names, though not very appropriate to their calling in life ... for instance, Kitty Cambric is a Coal Merchant; Miss Selina, a Runner at a Police office."[3] (Other "feigned names"—i.e., pre-drag queen drag names—identified are: Black-eyed Leonora; Pretty Harriet; Lady Godina; The Duchess of Gloucester; The Duchess of Devonshire; and Miss Sweet Lips.[4])

"In its purest form," though, as drag historian Joe E. Jeffreys attempts to explain in a more concrete sense what the form entails, "drag is when a person goes into a dressing room, they put this thing on, they go out on stage and they perform, and [after the show] they take it off."[5] It is a very simple definition, yet the key to it is that it focuses on the act of performance over the matter of gender. There are no pronouns mentioned or styles of clothing inferred. Importantly, too, there is no mention of sexual orientation nor sexed anatomy. It can encompass as wide a spectrum of participants as would be feasible. Mind you, Jeffreys's quotation does go further to connect the practical form to the queer community because of its emphasis on performance and the significance of "playing" with gender. He is not diminishing nor dismissing any single group; everyone can participate, and everyone can learn from it. This is important for our collection because it reflects the assumption that there is more than one way of defining drag and of doing drag, which feels essential to bring to the fore of this conversation. Drag cannot be pigeon-holed into a single form; where is the fun in that? Not in a collection like ours.

Jeffreys's view of drag does stand in contrast to RuPaul Charles's vision of drag, at least in the context of Charles's show, *RuPaul's Drag Race* (*RPDR*). Charles and his show have come to define the art form of drag for a generation. This collection looks at the ways that we can learn through and from drag, as well as how *RPDR* is a looming part of that conversation. While Charles sets out to find "America's Next Drag Superstar," the answer we have gotten so far is more complex than that goal. Each queen who entered the workroom since the show's premiere over a decade ago in 2009 has challenged the narrative Charles attempts to control, allowing for a more complex story that is pedagogically relevant to a variety of fields, disciplines, and communities.

Drag has been a piece of (counter)culture for decades. It is a medium that allows for community and education. As Judith Butler writes in *Bodies That Matter* (1996), "[Drag queens] 'mother' one another, 'house' one another, 'rear' one another, and the resignification of the family through these terms is not a vain or useless imitation, but the social and discursive building of community, a community that binds, cares, and teaches, that shelters and enables."[6] While this quotation primarily looks at the insular drag community of performers, there is a broader audience of spectators and appreciators that can also be invited into the fold and learn from the form. Iconically, as Michael Lovelock points out in his discussions of *RPDR* and that immortal line from episode 5, season 7—"You know we, as gay people get to choose our families.… You know what I'm saying? I am your family. We are your family, I love you."[7]—in his book *Reality TV and Queer Identities* (2019), RuPaul and *Drag Race* invoke "a history of queer people taking up and reconfiguring the terms of the heterosexual family to forge their own kinship structures."[8] Lovelock specifically states, "When RuPaul asserts 'we love you' and 'we are a family,' this 'we' encompasses the production context of the programme itself, the groupings of queer people that this televisual context has brought into being and the kinship networks which are built around the practice of drag more generally."[9]

By engaging with a culture, we can learn more about ourselves, and society by extension. This is not a new idea, yet we argue that *RPDR* is a vehicle that has grown exponentially in the last decade to spread the reach and accessibility of drag culture (and by extension, queer culture/identity) to mainstream audiences. "The show [*RPDR*] has opened up and educated the minds of many people who were ignorant to the world of drag and has made equality and respect a possibility for those involved."[10] As a result, a broader-reaching conversation can take place about drag and queer culture in terms of the cultural touchstones that can be utilized for pedagogical purposes. Henry Giroux might refer to this as the power of public pedagogy, which he describes as the "performative practice embodied in the lived interactions among educators, audiences, texts, and institutional formations" through his challenging of "the presupposition that the classroom is the exclusive site in which pedagogy becomes a relevant object of analysis."[11]

Anna Hickey-Moody, Glenn C. Savage, and Joel Windle write that "Giroux's development of the term public pedagogy is based in his foundational view that culture *can* and *does* operate in pedagogical ways."[12] Giroux himself, then, says that popular media is "a powerful form of public pedagogy,"[13] and Jennifer A. Sandlin, Michael P. O'Malley, and Jake Burdick, in their study on mapping the complexities of public pedagogy across over a hundred years of public pedagogy scholarship, add to Giroux that other "informal education sites" and "extrainstitutional spaces and discourses" are part and parcel of the power of public pedagogy, too.[14] *RuPaul's Drag Race*, then, as popular media in an extrainstitutional space engendering extrainstitutional discourses and that thrives in the social construction of knowledge, values, and experiences through performative practices embodied in lived interactions, absolutely is, as we in this book together with our authors are arguing and exploring, publicly pedagogical. Through this lens of public pedagogy, we look at how the contestants, platform, and host have informed not just *what* we learn but, importantly, *the ways that we learn* as well. We consider how through the artistry of drag and the competition of the series, for all its good and for all its bad, we can learn and continue to achieve something better.

## *The Fandom and Reception Just Keep Growing*

Since 2015, the producers of the show have been producing the fan convention DragCon in LA; a New York off-shoot was launched in 2017;

a UK edition was staged in 2019. The conventions have sold out, and that success is attributable to the curation of the event as a celebration of the series, allowing viewers to interact *en masse* with former contestants and friends of the show in-person. It is a place for unique experiences (i.e., the wedding of a former contestant) and informative panels about drag, costuming, makeup, and performance as an extension of the series. Critically, the show has steadily gained recognition in recent years. Charles, personally, has won several distinctions including five consecutive Emmy Awards for Outstanding Host for a Reality or Reality-Competition Program for the mothership program from 2016 to 2020. The series as a whole won for Outstanding Reality-Competition Series from 2018 to 2020,[15] becoming only the fourth series to win in the category since the category's inception in 2003.

The show has expanded its scope and popularity in consistent leaps and strides from the hazy-filtered days of season one to its current incarnation (with international, all stars, and celebrity editions/spin-offs). At the center of it all is Charles, who has elevated his own career in pursuit of finding his successor (i.e., "America's Next Drag Superstar") and acting as the world's teacher of the medium. Whether a true successor has been found is arguable (as is whether Charles himself is America's inferred *first* drag superstar, since he is looking for the *next*), yet there have been several queens who will be featured in this collection who have made their voices known and have contributed to discourse on a range of issues. Some of their work has been in direct opposition to Charles's beliefs and expectations. As Charles once noted on-air, "I may be the host of this show, but you, all of you, are my teachers."[16] In devising this collection and working with the authors, this quotation has loomed large. With all respect to the body of his work, we need to consider Charles beyond the pedestal of being the titular host and icon that guides the ship. We need to challenge RuPaul's authority as, to borrow a phrase from teaching and learning cultures, the sage on the stage.

## *How We Conceived* RuPedagogies

Part of RuPaul's persona, as both a host and performer, is to constantly re-define ideas and concepts under her name/brand (i.e., using the "Ru" of her first name as a prefix to create self-endorsing puns, neologisms, and other brands, such "Ruveal yourself," "Rupologize" "RuVC").[17] This is what inspired part of the title for this collection, *RuPedagogies*, because there is a lot we can learn when we look at the world through the extended network of television series and personality that make up the *RPDR* now-global brand. Given the scope of the series, it presented a few editorial and pedagogical challenges that impacted how we structured the collection.

First, we knew from the outset that this needed to be an interdisciplinary collection because a major part of the appeal of *RPDR* is that its contestants, challenges, and commentary break the boundaries of reality television and drag. While the challenges in acting, costuming, and modeling can be found on shows like *America's Next Top Model* or *Project Runway*, these variations on a theme synthesize and act as a hybrid of all these other tropes through the lens of drag. It is part of the fun here. While the show has certain signature challenges at this point (e.g., Snatch Game, the Rusical, etc.), new twists are introduced each season to keep things fresh. In that spirit, we didn't want to look at our work strictly in terms of gender studies, television studies, pop culture studies, fandom studies, performance studies, *insert-your-discipline-here* studies, etc. While these categories can serve a purpose, we did not want to limit ourselves in showing the ways that the show can be educational and entertaining.

Second, the series is not widely available across regional and national borders, so we could not presume what seasons of the mothership or iterations of the spin-offs that readers would have access to. Part of our adventure was figuring out what seasons were available based on geography, streaming services, and/or paywalls. If you are looking at this collection for textbook adoption, that question can loom large since there are so many potential entry points. Viewers who are new to the world of drag face a trial by fire in many ways. Thankfully, the show is quick to immerse newcomers in the vernacular that accompanies the form by the contestants. This is something the writer Decca Aitkenhead points out in a profile of Charles: "Contestants are fluent in the vernacular of drag—'throwing shade' (criticizing), 'hog body' (an insufficiently hourglass figure), 'Judy' (good friend)—making the show feel like an invite to a private party on another planet."[18] Keeping this in mind, there is a glossary for *RuPedagogies*, and the first third of the collection can serve as a primer for students and audiences new(er) to the world of *RPDR* and/or drag.

Third, there were many ways of approaching a collection on *RPDR* and pedagogy. There were three key questions we kept getting asked. *Is it for super fans of the show?* Not really: it's great if you love the show (we do, too!), but it's not required. The show is celebrated, but this is not RuPaul's Best Friends' collection. *Is this for educators who like the show and want to find ways of bringing it into their class?* Absolutely: we include several lesson prompts, discussion questions, and resources for this very purpose. *Is this a textbook that can be adopted for a course?* Certainly, it is: there are many entry points for introductory to more advanced *RPDR* fans. For example, you can look at the full collection for an upper-level gender studies or education course. Yet, there are individual essays that we could see adopted for an introductory composition or communication course, too. It all depends on the learning outcomes and student demographics that you are working with.

## A Little Bit About Our Journey

For context about the collection ahead, there is a timeline to establish. In some ways, this work came together very rapidly. The coeditors met in-person for the first time to present at a panel on *Drag Race* and pedagogy at the April 2019 Northeast Modern Language Association (NeMLA) conference. Lindsay had proposed and chaired the panel. She knew Tommy took this topic very seriously and embodied it intimately and deeply when they arrived in drag for the panel to perform their paper. We parted two hours later with the goal of proposing this collection. The logistics be damned, and there were quite a few to work through with Lindsay in the United States and Tommy in Canada. We should probably acknowledge our dear friend "the cloud" at some point…. At least we knew early on how challenging it would be for readers to have access to all the seasons and series, which are distributed in sharply contrasting ways depending on where you are on a map. We have a lot of practical experience not spoiling each other, that is for sure. It also helped us to set some ground rules for each other and for our contributors.

The contributing writers started their work on their respective essays just after season 11 of the mothership (2019) and season 4 of *All Stars* (2018–2019) were completed. A series of events in and out of the world of drag would take place that would further inform the work that you hold in your hands: *RuPaul's Drag Race U.K.* season 1, season 12 of the mothership, the launch of *RuPaul's Secret Celebrity Drag's Race*, and *All Stars* season 5 all aired. *Canada's Drag Race* season 1 was just on the horizon, too. While there are a few allusions to these seasons, spin-offs, and series herewith, they were not required nor expected (with two notable exceptions). We make no assumption that a reader is well-versed in drag and/or the series.

Given the evolution of the series' fan base and tenuous availability of some seasons at times, depending on your access to streaming services and the country you live in, this was a priority as we attempted to look at pedagogical approaches within the series in tandem to critical analyses effectively. The contributors were encouraged to explore the series critically, yet asked to avoid any major spoilers about a given season (i.e., how contestants placed, particularly in the most recent seasons) unless it was imperative to their respective analysis.

Another layer of the story is that the coeditors did reunite for only one more in-person meeting, at the March 2020 NeMLA conference, to plan out the final stages of this collection's development and to quite simply spill the tea. This fateful meeting was the same day that the producers of *RPDR* announced the disqualification of Sherry Pie for misconduct prior to her casting,[19] which has been widely reported on in entertainment media. The implications of the disqualification would only become more apparent in the months to come as the twelfth season unfolded (with disclaimers abounding for context and ominous reminders that something ran amiss this season).

The other looming story beginning to take shape in North America was the COVID-19 outbreak that, just days after the coeditors returned home from NeMLA 2020, the World Health Organization classified as a global pandemic. While the former story is certainly relevant to the fandom since it affected production of the show(s), the latter would alter the development process for some of our contributors in the final phases of the publication process of *RuPedagogies*. It posed challenges and barriers that speak to their passion and dedication to produce the final collection that lies ahead. Unfortunately, not all the authors we started this collection with were able to finish their work due to personal and professional hardships, and most of the final drafts were submitted before our authors could address how the pandemic informed creative choices in season 12's final two episodes. We were fortunate enough to have a couple of new authors join us to round out the collection—chances are you will notice who came in at this point because their essays are the only ones that had the opportunity to address season 12 of *RPDR* and *Canada's Drag Race* season 1. The COVID-19 global pandemic also impacted the peer-review process of *RuPedagogies* and the editorial timeline for getting the manuscript to press. We know with the nature of scholarship, culture moves much faster, and so we respectfully clock *scholarly* time of completion for this book, which was August 2020. As such, many of the lessons learned from this time in herstory—including even more developments and franchising off the *RPDR* mothership!—will have to wait for another day, a new collection, and many more wonderful, robust scholarly contributions.

## *What Will You Find in this Collection?*

To bring you into our process, we sought inspiration from the pedagogical approaches that inform our courses as course designers and teaching-and-learning practitioners and tried to bring an *RPDR* twist to it. We admit, we may have gone a bit wild with the puns; we do not RuPologize.

The collection has been divided into three categories:

- Start Your Engines: Critical Context of the Language and Influence of Drag
- She Already Done Had Herses: When Drag Curates Culture
- May the Best Drag Queen Win: The Competitive Nature of Drag

Drawing from Bloom's Taxonomy, each section begins with a set of learning outcomes that we feel guide and connect these essays. This helped us consider how readers might be processing the work and developing their understanding with each section's respective focus.

In "Start Your Engines: Critical Context of the Language and Influence of Drag," we begin with the primers, essays that look at the fundamental aspects of the series. Starting us off is Vicky Kampouridou with her essay "*RuPaul's Drag Race* as a Heterotopic Learning Experience" where she looks at how the show depicts binaries of masculinity and femininity. What makes her essay a good gateway is that it really confronts many of our assumptions about drag and its performative nature. If you're relatively new to the world of the show or to looking at the show critically/pedagogically (rather than just as a form of entertainment), this can be an important hurdle to cross. Once we get the presumptions out of the way, it is time to consider the language of both drag as a whole and within the show. This is where we come to the essay "The Influence of *RuPaul's Drag Race* on Pop Culture and the Way We Talk: A Pop-Linguistic Analysis" by Ricarda Goetz-Preisner. In her work, Goetz-Preisner examines how the early years of the show were translating drag culture for a widespread audience. Yet, as the show has gone on and reached greater prominence, it has shaped its own vernacular, based on quotations and events within the series that define how the terms are used (i.e., "Back rolls" or "Halleloo"). This is what Goetz-Preisner uncovers and peels back the layers on, showing exactly why there is even an entire Wiki to help catch-up newcomers to the series.[20]

Next is Phillip Joy and Jill Marie McSweeney-Flaherty's piece, "Pedagogy of the Mother: Exploring Freire's Philosophy of Co-Productive Learning." Together, they strike an interesting cross-section of the personal and professional: an exploration of their own respective journeys with drag culture and a broader perspective of health and community within Freire's critical lens. It really does dive into a broader conversation about the lines that the series has drawn and since blurred when it comes to activism, and how the queens have driven that narrative. Rounding out this section is Tommy Mayberry with their piece, "'And where is the body?' Naked Drag and the Social Construction of Anatomy as Sexed and Gendered." Here, they look at the importance of the body as a type of canvas for clothing (or lack thereof), makeup, shoes, and properties to be placed and curated in drag. Mayberry deconstructs some classic queens and moments of the series, and broader cultural touchstones that defined some of the early seasons and are still applicable today.

The second section, "She Already Done Had Herses: When Drag Curates Culture," begins with "Pop the Corn and Teach the Children: Drag Lessons in Gender, Race, and Class Beyond RuPaul's Televised Curriculum" by Russ Martin. He takes a leap when it comes to looking at the true reality of drag. He presents a number of topics that the queens on *RPDR* have discussed on the show, yet these do take on a different dimension when Martin interviews a collective of Canadian queens (including two contestants on *Canada's Drag Race* season 1), many of whom have not (yet) broken into the echelons of "racers." (Or at least, none that we know of at this moment. If any queens are appearing on future seasons of any World of Wonder series, we are delighted for them, but we do not have any type of insider track on casting.) Their struggles and passion for the form are informative and pose some sincerely challenging questions about how society views drag when the lights and cameras are turned off. This piece really acts as a bit of a launching pad into the middle third of the collection. Next, there is a slap of reality (of reality *television*, that is … no contributors, editors, or participants were injured during the making of this collection) with Maggie Ward's "'Cultural appropriation! That's what we never heard': Performing Indigeneity on Reality Television and Beyond." Where Martin addresses issues that the series does not truly capture/address, Ward presents some of the more overt missteps of the series when it comes to the matter of race and how we can and need to do better. In hindsight, some of the choices made during challenges by contestants and judges can be understandable; the things said and their implications may not be appreciated fully in the heat of the moment. Yet, the choices of the editors and producers about how to present these problematic decisions are another matter to contend with. To close this section of the collection, David J. Fine develops a strong case for looking at RuPaul as both teacher and student in "RuPaulogetics: Assimilation, Backwash, and the Charisma of Queer Pedagogy." He does a remarkable job of showing us how RuPaul (the mother, the character, and the queen) may fight for love and self-worth, yet stand apart from Charles's own feelings on drag.

The final third of the collection, "May the Best Drag Queen Win: The Competitive Nature of Drag," seeks to explore *RPDR*'s sub-genre, as a reality-competition series and what happens when a queen's season ends. They are not really done with the show, but they do face a challenge when they need to figure out "what's next?" Nathan Workman's "Gay Super Bowl: Homonormative Authorization, Instruction, and Discipline Through Sports Media Borrowings" provides a look at how the show has adopted (and co-opted) some of the trappings of sports culture within the series. How does our perception of drag and performance change when the performers are packaged and promoted as players to be drafted? There are many different types of drag and queens being presented throughout the collection, yet there was a key form that was heavily underrepresented: comedy. Enter "Where Are the Jokes? Comedy as Pedagogy" by Peter Piatkowski. He presents us with a deep dive into how the comedy queens have dominated certain challenges within the competition, yet have received blow back for their unique set of skills as being "less than" to other types of queens (i.e., the rivalry of Jinkx Monsoon and Roxxxy Andrews in season 5). "Digital Drag and YouTube as Queer Space: Queens as Influencers from Performance to Pedagogy," by Florian Zitzelsberger, looks at the paratexts that have launched out of *RPDR* (i.e., *UNHhhh* and *Violet Chachki's Digital Drag*) and the influencers who have been inspired by the series. It is quite fascinating to see how YouTube has acted as a platform that supplements and complements the work of the mothership and provides a space for former contestants to begin striking their own path forward. The anchor of "race" is Mandy Penney's "Pedagogies, Praxis, and Privilege: RuPaulean Communities of Care." She provides a piece that is at times personal narrative and professional critique of how we can learn about digital spaces through season 12 of *RPDR*. Ultimately, it is a bit of a love letter to these queens, yet it also highlights the charisma, uniqueness, nerve, and talent that is needed by all the contestants to survive, and hopefully to thrive, on (and after) *RPDR*.

At the end of each essay, you will find mini- and maxi-challenges, which are our way of describing formative and summative assessment examples to guide how the arguments and research presented can promote critical thinking and inquiry pedagogically. After Penney's essay, we also provide supplemental resources to promote extended dialogue. There is a broader range of discussion questions for those looking to have a more holistic conversation regarding the collection. For those who may be new to *RPDR*, there is a glossary that breaks down some of the inside ball/jargon that recurs throughout the series and collection (e.g., Back rolls, the Porkchop). For educators and learners seeking more resources regarding the LGBTQ+ community, we include a list of organizations and readings for further research and support that we have provided our own learners in our classrooms and our teaching and learning work. Hopefully, these extension opportunities benefit you and anyone that you share this collection with.

## *Lip Sync for Your Life/Legacy*

Given how many new seasons are being commissioned and the plethora of spinoffs getting announced every few months, *RPDR* is not going away any time soon. It will continue to keep producing new lessons and "lewks" for us to learn from and critique. And it will keep teaching us … for good and for bad. We do not know what the "legacy" ultimately will be, yet that term does loom large each season, whether it's the mothership, *All Stars*, etc. How long will we spend our Fridays (or any night, thanks to streaming) with RuPaul, Michelle Visage, and let the music play? Will we ever see a true successor take up that mantle of America's Next Drag Superstar? Does it really matter? At this point, it is a little bit like *Waiting for Godot*: we are not actually waiting for drag's next superstar.… Everyone is going to see it in someone else, and thus constantly be looking elsewhere. We are caught in an existential trap, yet it is one with some fantastic innovators, assassins, queens, and yes, teachers.

## Notes

1. Morton, Mark. *The Lover's Tongue: A Merry Romp Through the Language of Love and Sex*. Insomniac Press, 2003, p. 204.

2. Holloway, Robert. *The Phoenix of Sodom, or The Vere Street Coterie: Being an Exhibition of the Gambols Practised by the Ancient Lechers or Sodom and Gomorrah, Embellished and Improved with the Modern Refinements in Sodomitical Practices, by the Members of the Vere Street Coterie, of detestable memory*. 1813. Facsimile edition, Sodomy Trials: Seven Documents, edited by Randolph Trumbach, Garland Press, 1986, Section 7, p. 50—italics original.

3. *Ibid.*, pp. 12–13.

4. *Ibid.*, p. 13. Earlier, too, in roughly 1788, in another arrest similar to Vere Street, historical records note that "so well did they [the arrested men] perform the characters they assumed, that one miscreant escaped the vigilance of the officers and the examining magistrate, and was discharged as a woman!" (Holloway 28).

5. Davies, Wilder. "RuPaul's Drag Race and What People Get Wrong About the History of Drag." *Time*, 9 Mar. 2018, time.com/5188791/rupauls-drag-race-history/.

6. Butler, Judith. *Bodies That Matter: On the Discursive Limits of Sex*, Routledge, 2011, p. 137.

7. "RuPaul Roast." *RuPaul's Drag Race*, season 5, episode 7, LogoTV, 11 March 2013, Amazon, www.amazon.com/RuPauls-Drag-Race-Season-5/dp/B00B45B4X2.

8. Lovelock, Michael. *Reality TV and Queer Identities: Sexuality, Authenticity, Celebrity*. Palgrave Macmillan, 2019, p. 156.

9. *Ibid.*

10. Carrera, Carmen (@carmencarrerafans). "Some of you guys asked me.…" Facebook, 31 Mar. 2014, www.facebook.com/carmencarrerafans/posts/679959392050537. Accessed 14 Jan. 2019.

11. Giroux, Henry A. "Cultural Studies, Public Pedagogy, and the Responsibility of Intellectuals." *Communications and Critical/Cultural Studies*, vol. 1, iss. 1, 2004, p. 59–79: 61.

12. Hickey-Moody, Anna, Glenn C. Savage, & Joel Windle. "Pedagogy Writ Large: Public, Popular and Cultural Pedagogies in Motion." *Critical Studies in Education*, vol. 51, no. 3, 2010, p. 227.

13. *Ibid.*, p. 228.

14. Sandlin, Jennifer A., Michael P. O'Malley, & Jake Burdick. "Mapping the Complexity of Public Pedagogy Scholarship: 1894–2010." *Review of Educational Research*, vol. 81, no. 3, 2011 p. 336.

15. "RuPaul's Drag Race (2009- ) Awards." *IMDB*, 2020, www.imdb.com/title/tt1353056/awards?ref_=tt_awd.

16. "Queens Reunited." *RuPaul's Drag Race,* season 10, episode 13, VH1, 21 June 2018, *Amazon,* www.amazon.com/RuPauls-Drag-Race-Season-10/dp/B07B6B9MDY.

17. "*RuPaul's Drag Race* Dictionary." Fandom.com, 2020, https://rupaulsdragrace.fandom.com/wiki/RuPaul%27s_Drag_Race_Dictionary.

18. Aitkinhead, Decca. "RuPaul: 'Drag is a big f-you to male-dominated culture.'" *The Guardian,* 3 Mar. 2018, https://www.theguardian.com/tv-and-radio/2018/mar/03/rupaul-drag-race-big-f-you-to-male-dominated-culture.

19. Nolfi, Joey. "*RuPaul's Drag Race* Disqualifies Sherry Pie Over Catfishing Allegations." *EW,* 6 Mar. 2020. https://ew.com/tv/rupauls-drag-race-disqualifies-sherry-pie-catfishing-allegations/#:~:text=%E2%80%9CIn%20light%20of%20recent%20developments,air%20the%20season%20as%20planned.

20. "*RuPaul's Drag Race* Dictionary." Fandom.com, 2020, https://rupaulsdragrace.fandom.com/wiki/RuPaul%27s_Drag_Race_Dictionary.

# Start Your Engines
## *Critical Context of the Language and Influence of Drag*

> "I'm not here to make **best** buddies, bitch! This is not **RuPaul's Best Friend Race!**"
> —Lashauwn Beyond, season 4 contestant[1]

## *Learning Outcomes:*

By the end of this section, we should be able to…

- Recognize the ways that drag impacts culture, language, and performance.
- Interpret the jargon and aesthetic choices within *RPDR* and the broader drag scene.
- Discover the cornerstones of critical race, gender, television, and pedagogical theory that guide a reading of this collection.
- Question *RPDR*'s effectiveness and ability to reflect the history of the LGBTQ+ community and what the landscape looks like today.
- Critique the gender and social constructs of drag.
- Facilitate a conversation regarding the intersections of drag, reality television, and socio-cultural discourse for audiences new to the discipline(s).

### Note

1. "RuPocalypse Now." *RuPaul's Drag Race: Untucked*, season 4, episode 1, Logo TV, 30 Jan. 2012, *Amazon*, https://www.amazon.com/gp/video/detail/B0073PR0VW/ref=atv_dp_season_select_s4.

# *RuPaul's Drag Race* as a Heterotopic Learning Experience

## Vicky Kampouridou

*RuPaul's Drag Race* (*RPDR*) is a unique example that provides an opportunity for peeping into the procedure of social gender change simultaneously as a subject for academic research but also accessible to the vast public, and it offers great fields of exploration on how cultural products of/by/for marginalized bodies provide indirect experiences that can mold human culture. In this essay, I will argue that *RPDR* comprises a heterotopia and that because of its public exposure, it can provide powerful tools for understanding the prevailing gender and body norms and for learning to reevaluate them.

The reality talent show *RPDR* started broadcasting on American television in February 2009, and it is still airing. The game follows a challenge-evaluation pattern, common to reality talent shows, with its purpose being to produce a winner at the end of each season who will receive, amongst other prizes, a large sum of money and the title of America's Next Drag Superstar until they pass it off to the next winner. Mentor and host of the show is RuPaul Charles, an emblematic, (somehow) underground figure who has built the whole show around her persona.

The show is, first and foremost, a spectacle. RuPaul himself,[1] among many others, shows business-recognized accomplishments, and she recently got her star on the Hollywood Walk of Fame. *Time Magazine* also included him in the list of The 100 Most Influential People for the year 2017; he and *RPDR* have been awarded several EMMYs; and Warner Bros. has produced a television series featuring her portraying the role of a traveling drag queen accompanying a child, which was originally broadcast by Netflix. Nevertheless, RuPaul declares that the purpose of the show is social acceptance for the drag and queer community as well as the creation of a platform that launches drag queens' talents and showcases them to the world. The show's viewpoint about success is described by fame, money, and recognition through hard work and goal setting. *RPDR* displays gender representations that disrupt the solid binary frame of general acceptance by inserting the new image of Otherness into the everyday lives of a large number of people, and not as a *freak show* image anymore. Instead, it includes drag queens in the norms of contemporary culture by taming the Otherness and partially undressing it from the unfamiliar. *RPDR* is a catwalk of deviation, where beyond the drag stars and queer personas strut other excluded bodies (like persons with disabilities and more) alongside a growing list of show business superstars. The show's representation of Other bodies[2] comes in direct contradiction with underworldly images of social marginalization and/or economic desperation that the general public is used to associating with queer people, especially queer performers and even more so drag queens.

This essay will examine three makeover episodes featured on *RPDR* where cisgender women and men get transformed into drag queens. Through the process of getting people into drag and the vast specter of their reactions, which vary from repulsion to genuine connection and to pure excitement, the show draws out the participants' and the audience's beliefs and ideas about body and gender norms. The presentation of these transitions is revolutionary both for the understanding of the acquired solid gender notions and the establishment of different narrations of embodied performance in the public sphere.

## Introduction

In this essay, I will be attempting to analyze three makeover episodes of the show from three different seasons of production: "Drag My Wedding" (season 6, episode 10); "Wizards of Drag" (season 8, episode 6); and "Social Media Kings Into Queens" (season 10, episode 10). Makeover episodes are a rare teaching and learning tool because they provide a way of an indirect experience of alternative gender performance, one that the viewers cannot easily attain for themselves. Almost every season features a makeover episode; however, these three were specifically selected because of the correlations they present between contestants and guests as well as the explicit depictions of Otherness they feature. "Wizards of Drag" interlaces multiple types of not-accepted bodies and identities and presents an example of the intersectionality of the human situation. "Drag My Wedding" presents to the TV screen a vivid description of the social pressure to conform and fit in, and it raises the discussion of expected masculinities. "Social Media Kings Into Queens" provides two loud examples of a reality shift on the perception of gender. Data for this research has been collected by viewing and analyzing twelve seasons of episodes of the show, its spin-off series, published interviews by the participants, and public opinions as exposed on social media. The episodes will be presented not in chronological order, but in an order serving the argument at hand. Content analysis consists of identification and summary of the episode, descriptive analysis, and theoretical analysis.

Television reality shows are infamous for being overly scripted and edited for the sake of *good TV*. This possibility will be kept under constant consideration through the discussion below. However, I will be choosing to analyze reactions as though they are authentic based on the arguments that they must be considered true until proven otherwise, but also and more importantly because these events, truthful or fake, were the ones broadcast and presented to the public; ergo, they are the ones registering as representations to the public eye. Furthermore, the supposed decision of the production to construct or air any of the following could be by itself a subject of discussion.

Experience is identified as a major factor of adult learning.[3] So, the chasm of gender conceptualization between a binary gendered body and a queer/questioning body could partially be attributed to the lack of experience. However, the queer/questioning body has been demanded to present "normal" while the "normal" body has been praised for not questioning and for never having a different gender experience. A potential breakthrough could be achieved by an exchange of social gender identities where bodies experience the concept of being another self and being perceived as another person. This is not an easily achieved nor accepted experiment; however, the easily accessible public representation of the makeover experiences provides a channel for people coming from different standpoints to share an experience that they otherwise would have no means of accessing. Although persons arrive at an experience through different pathways, I am arguing that these representations consist a means of learning for the public understanding by indirectly experiencing the bodily transformations. However, not every experience translates to understanding or knowledge; experiential learning happens when the experience is deliberately utilized as a learning procedure.[4] It is up to the academy, among others, to utilize experiences of the everyday and of pop culture to produce knowledge, which is a task that I will be attempting.

In the physical and virtual space of *RPDR*, normality is dictated by very different social contracts. *RPDR* comprises a heterotopia of social order where rules and norms are dictated by alternative authorities and values. Heterotopias have been firstly described by Foucault[5] as places differentiated by the normal space, simultaneously isolated and not from the normal space, in the sense that they work both independently and in synergy with the spaces that remain. Heterotopic spaces, Foucault argues, have been existent in every human society because they are necessary, and they serve a purpose to the normal space. Heterotopias are spaces, physical or virtual, that refer to and reflect the spaces that remain through a mutated lens and a different rule system. As a result, heterotopic spaces can function as laboratories of knowledge through which new descriptions of reality can emerge.[6] The perception of *RPDR* as a Heterotopia and a heterotopic experience is weaved in this essay as an underlying concurrent basis.

*RPDR* and other popular shows featuring deviating bodies are one of the ways that marginalized bodies may exercise their right to visibility. James Baldwin wrote in his unfinished manuscript of *Remember This House* (as featured in the 2016 documentary *I Am Not Your Negro*[7]) that growing up, he had a breakthrough experience when he realized that in spaghetti western movies,[8] a genre that he particularly enjoyed, the *good guy* was the white guy who was chasing down and killing the *bad guys* who were the people of color like him. The shift of reality Baldwin experienced describes a traumatic distancing of the person from their idols. Baldwin was referring mainly to skin color and race and not so much to his identity as a gay man, but the need of experiencing visibility for queer people as well as the access to a different type of role model for younger persons have been stated by other queer people, too, like Jonathan Van Ness[9] and Tan France,[10] both co-hosts of the TV show *Queer Eye*. Since show business is the matrix that generates social models due to its prominence in pop culture, the existence of a TV competition of pariahs is socially necessary; but it is also a catalytic agent for changes in culture. Other bodies need access to visibility for the represented-Other body but also for any possible viewing-Other body. Furthermore, the exposure of Otherness and its invasion into normality teaches inclusivity and acceptance of norm-conforming bodies, both for others and themselves. Pop culture is a product of humanity's progression and indicates the sub-existent values of human culture. It is necessary for the academy to (re)invent ways to analyze this significant source of endemic data if it wishes to be relevant to the sphere of the everyday and promote adult learning in realistic ways.

Human culture has adopted Descartes' Cartesian dualistic split in dialectics, strictly separating and giving dominance to the mind over the body, the logic over the emotion, the male over the female, with the dominant poles of each binary being linked together and describing the identity of the optimal person under today's social guidelines. This binary celebrates the reflecting mind and expels the experiencing body to the pit of invalidity as something to be overcome and dominated. However, many thinkers like Judith Butler, Elizabeth Grosz, and E. Michelson have been discussing that there is an embodied knowledge that should not be overlooked and that there is a necessity for the binary model of dialectics to be reevaluated.[11] Different cultures in space and time have held very different standards on gender and body, contradicting the narration of the naturality of the dominant roles, and many of them subvert binarity. Feminist and gender studies have been arguing that the performance of gender we are taught by one particular dominant Western culture bears little connection to any natural pre-existents and that there is a necessity for a new model of dialectics capable of discussing human complexity to its extent. *RPDR*, by rendering the Other bodies (hyper)visible, instead of accepting the "normal" rite of binary bodily expression of gender, actively produces new visual registrations in the norm, mutating the image of the social gender and body that is agreed and promoted by the dominant discourse.

"Teach the children" is a very common phrase in the drag lingo and is very commonly used by RuPaul during airtime. The quotation's basic meaning is to educate the ignorant, but it bears many secondary meanings as well. It may also be used after a very successful performance, meaning that through a performance or a particular success, someone may provide experience and knowledge to the viewers of this performance/success. Additionally, it has also been used during airtime after a pro-social-justice or pro–LGBTQ+ rights opinion has been expressed as a way of acknowledging a successful argument against hostile opinions on those matters. In the following text, I will be discussing that *RPDR* is succeeding in doing that: it displays an alternative possibility of gender and body reality that by its representation and loud presentation educates on the validity of its existence.

## *Any Type of Different "Wizards of Drag"—The Other Bodies of Another Otherness*

The sixth episode of the eighth season of *RPDR* aired in 2016, and it was titled "Wizards of Drag." It featured the casting group of the reality show *Little Women L.A.* who were being made over into drag queens under the thematic of *The Wizard of Oz*. Each little woman[12] was portraying a character of the plot and got to choose the drag queen with whom she would be paired, and together the pair would create a performance based on this character. Drag queen and little woman had to deliberate, conceptualize, and perform together. These two groups of marginalized bodies were displayed by the show to instantly find a connection under the umbrella of social ostracism. The little women took the role of the dominant of the pair having already gained a level of fame and recognition because of their appearance on their TV show. In discussing this episode, I will be focusing on specific pairs that raise the subject of social disadvantage, and I also comment on the whole representation of two groups of Other bodies being merged in a primetime TV show.

Chi Chi DeVayne is a Black drag queen who had given herself the nickname "The Broke Queen" and had many times raised the issue of class stratification among the drag queens. She was chosen by a Black little woman, Tonya, who appeared dynamic, positive, and outgoing. Chi Chi discussed with Tonya the difficulties that come with the lack of resources or financial safety. Tonya, on the other hand, gave a supportive speech of positive reinforcement and empowerment for any person in a disadvantaged group by providing the argument that if she could do it, anyone could do it, and ending with the phrase "Don't think small."[13]

The viewer is presented with the narration of the underdog's success, a recurrent theme in *RPDR*. As I commented earlier, *RPDR* strongly supports the belief that through goal setting and hard work, socially disadvantaged people can succeed, and the show presents itself as a platform for this as well. It is inescapable to comment upon the routes of this argument that are deeply embedded in the culture of modern capitalism that on some level is persuading people into believing that the poor are lazy or at least not working hard enough. This narration is being used against BIPOC, immigrants, poor people and citizens of poor countries, women and other Others, and it suggests that their situation is in a way their own doing, veiling the reality of an unjust human society. The large amounts of money that *RPDR* contestants had to borrow to be able to prepare themselves and their drag for the show is a recurrent joke and subject of conversation among them—for examples, Trinity the Tuck,[14] Trixie Mattel,[15] and more. During the many years of the show's airing, there has also been talk about the subject of race between the drag queens, with many queens of color publicly stating that the opportunities given to them after their participation on the show are not equivalent to those of their white-presenting peers.[16]

This raises complex combinations of marginalized identities, such as being a poor Black gay man working as a drag queen, hinting to the intersectionality[17] of the human identity. According to Crenshaw, different human identities attributed to a person intersect, thus creating a specific identity with a specific social status that is more/different than each of the statuses of the component identities and of them combined.

Later on in the "Wizards of Drag" episode, more little women shared their experiences of being ridiculed and excluded from social normality because of their bodily anatomy. Jasmine, paired with drag queen Naomi Smalls, shared her thoughts on the used terminology[18] and her experience of being treated as an exotic anomaly in public spaces, saying, "I get personally offended by the word 'midget.' Because 'midget' doesn't necessarily mean, like, a person. It just means something small. It's such a derogatory, ugly word. It, like, makes me cringe when I hear it. […] You know what trips me out? Is if I'm literally at the mall walking, and somebody's like 'Oh, my gosh! Look at that midget!' I am like, 'Are you serious?,'" to which Naomi Smalls responded by saying, "People have a long way to come."[19] Christy, paired with drag queen Robbie Turner, confessed her connection with queer people saying, "I think that's why I feel so comfortable around gay people, 'cause they get how I feel because, you know, they get treated the same way."[20] The pair engaged in a small conversation, where they expressed the connection they share being the recipients of social marginalization and judgment because of something that is beyond their choice—

> **ROBBIE TURNER**: "You can't stop being the height that you are, you know? It's like who you are."
> **CHRISTY**: "And you love who you love."
> **ROBBIE TURNER**: "At the end of the day everybody just wants to be loved. Everybody just wants to fit in."
> **CHRISTY**: "Exactly."[21]

The Other body, or the body of the Stranger, as it is described by Sara Ahmed, is not a body unknown. On the contrary, it is a very specifically recognized body[22] that does not resemble or not abide by the social contract; a well-known body deemed not belonging in the pure, right, and valid social space, and thus one that has to be outcasted. Our culture's violent desire for the pure, right, and able body derives from a fictional nostalgic desire for a pure space, a pure humanity.[23] This distorted notion of body derives from the Western human's distance from their body as socially existent. Dominant discourses teach the penalization of bodily experiences, neglecting, under-recognizing, ridiculing, and shaming bodies and their function through a variety of social contracts. There is knowledge being registered on the bodies and originated by the bodies. The combined experiences of several intersectional types of alternative bodies represented in pop culture firstly validate their existence to the public realm and secondly unveil the image of the optimal human, the fictionality of its narration, and the violence it collectively administrates.

    As commented before, people born into and those who choose to remain inside the limits of the social norm have been persuaded to accept these descriptions of the human body as *natural* and rarely question them as humanly constructed and contingent, even though human history has been registering otherwise, and this changes normality and beauty standards depending on political, economic, environmental, and other factors. Chi Chi DeVayne and Tonya, while conversing and mixing multiple intersecting identities of being excluded, portray to the everyday viewer the existence of a cruel social front of discrimination against any type of difference and actively suggest communication and solidarity as a means of educating oneself and overcoming it. Bodies born in or choosing to come out of the structure of normality unsettle the paradigms of naturality and present the universal need of humans to be accepted for and to experience through their physical and social body, as Robbie and Christy's conversation suggests. Ultimately, the "Wizards of Drag" episode's representations inform the viewer on the fragmented and deficient depiction of human bodies and identities in dominant culture. Additionally, it tames the dehumanizing descriptions of the Others and teaches human connection.

## *Male Social Genders to Female Appearances*

In the following sections, I will be discussing two episodes that display different outcomes of experimentations in gender performativity. For the situations featuring makeovers of cishet men, I will be using two tool-phrases—the "Mirror Moment" and the "Presentation Moment"—that signify two significant points in the makeover procedure, respectively. The Mirror Moment is the moment when the self-identifying male person sees themself in the mirror as a female presence for the first time. The Presentation Moment is the moment when the self-identifying male person has to present this newfound female identity to the public eye for the first time. I am grouping the following episodes in an attempt to juxtapose different realities of points of view regarding gender as experienced by men, and I am arguing that in comparison, they can be pedagogically valuable.

For many decades, most of the positions of power have been personed by men, and thus official and unofficial narrations of *good* and *bad* have been being constructed by male hands and minds.[24] In consequence, we as the human race have to agree that nowadays culture is a construct of the *culture of patriarchy*. However, taking into account the omnipresent point of intersectionality,[25] we have to examine the different realities of the situation of "being a man." We have to admit that not all assigned-male-at-birth men have been deemed worthy and have qualified to be regarded as the dominants of this binary. In recent years, there has been a constantly growing wave of bodies assigned male that condemn the male archetype, and a tendency to reject the standards of the dominant performance of manhood has made its appearance in a variety of ways. The basis of the feminist discourse has been trying to find a way to describe gender alongside and despite of the oppression of patriarchy. Yet, as Elizabeth Grosz (and many more) argue, duality is a patriarchal concept, and in order to describe gender adequately, we need to establish a new way of dialectics.[26] The rigid binary guidelines that attribute very specific and finite characteristics to each of the two binary genders is violence imposed both ways and confine every body behind one or the other side of a fictional wall.

## "Drag My Wedding"—The Expected Masculinities Experience

The tenth episode of the sixth season of *RPDR* aired in 2014, and it was titled, "Drag My Wedding." In this episode, heterosexual couples were featured as guests in the show and would conduct their wedding ceremonies in the studio in front of the TV cameras. The weddings would be performed by RuPaul herself, but the couples would exchange binary gender roles, with the woman dressed as the groom and the man being made over by a drag queen as the bride.

The subject of gay marriage is a dominant subject in the LGBTQ+ community and among social discourses. However, the discussion of the idea of marriage, in general, is a socially fixed point. The way that marriage is handled in this episode through the role exchange procedure provides another way of addressing the subject, one that disrupts its rigid and untouchable quality given by tradition and norm. In the episode, the drag queens and the straight men engaged in conversations about marriage rights, and the editing featured positive opinions coming from straight men pro to gay marriage being received with contentment and some surprise by the drag queens. Cishet man Alex had a conversation with his challenge partner, Bianca del Rio, about gay marriage, saying, "I'm from Holland, the most liberal country probably in world, and it's very normal, you know, gay couples be married. […] People are free to do what they want, you know?" after which Bianca commented to the camera, "It's really refreshing to hang around someone who's straight without any hang-ups. […] Look, I actually made a friend today."[27]

Most couples looked excited and very well-receiving of the role exchange at their weddings. However, I will be focusing on the one couple that had a dysfunctional experience. Joslyn Fox, a bubbly effeminate white drag queen who in real life was engaged to be married with his partner, was paired up with Brittany and Brandon, a cishet Black couple. While Brittany appeared very excited, and by her admission, she was the one who had signed the couple up to be guests of the show, her spouse-to-be appeared a lot more hesitant. Brandon kept looking uncomfortable and making nods of disapproval when hearing the drag lingo in the workroom. While Joslyn was expressing her excitement by giggling and displaying girl-attributed body language, she declared that Brandon was going to look so "purrty," a purposeful mispronunciation of the word "pretty" in order for it to sound more girly and flirtier. Brandon replied by repeating the word in its generally accepted pronunciation, both in an attempt to correct Joslyn but also to express doubt and to question how the word could possibly be describing him.[28] Being a professional basketball player, he stated that he was devastatingly afraid of the reaction he would receive from his peers. During the pair's consultation with RuPaul, he imagined scenarios of possible public humiliation and questioning of his sexual orientation.[29]

During the makeover, Brandon engaged with Joslyn in conversation on the same subject, and guest spouse-to-be Ryan and competing drag queen Courtney Act joined them—

> **Brandon**: "I just don't want my teammates to see me with hips on."
> **Joslyn Fox**: "What do you really think your teammates are gonna say when they see you in drag?"
> **Brandon**: "Oh, man, it will be posted all over Facebook. You know the locker room chat that we have, it's gonna be a disaster, man. Like, it's gonna be some serious questioning."
> **Ryan**: "You just gotta be secure with yourself, Brandon."
> **Brandon**: "No, I'm very secure with myself. I just.... In my profession, it's not funny for a gay person to, you know, come in the locker room. I'd rather someone be straightforward and say, you know, 'I'm gay' you know, if they're in the locker room with me. I don't want them, like, checking me out either."
> **Courtney Act**: "If your intent is that a gay man in a locker room should be open as gay because everybody should be able to express their sexuality freely, then that works for me, but if it's 'I want him to let me know I'm gay so that I know that he's not looking at me' or 'I feel uncomfortable because of that,' then I feel like the intent's a bit different. Doesn't entirely make sense to me."
> **Joslyn Fox**: "I get your concerns, but I think what you're doing is gonna change people's minds, especially your teammates."
> **Brandon**: "You think so?"
> **Joslyn Fox**: "I know so."[30]

Brandon's locker room statement was argued against and frowned upon in the conversation. Despite drag queen Joslyn's positive reinforcement and socially unifying speeches about him setting an example, Brandon's standpoint did not seem to change.

At the Mirror Moment, Brandon looked terrified by the result. He seemed unable and unwilling to connect his identity with his feminine appearance. Furthermore, at his Presentation Moment, he showed great discomfort and, in contrast with the other contestants and his own spouse-to-be, he was not enjoying the process or experience at all. Later on, during the critiques from the show's judging panel, he admitted that he was afraid of his *"manlihood being questioned"* by the world outside *RPDR*—

> RuPaul: "So, Brandonna [the drag name Brandon was given], was there anything you were uncomfortable with?"
> Brandon: "Just my manlihood being questioned."
> RuPaul: "And who was questioning it?"
> Brandon: "No one here, but it will be questioned."
> Michelle Visage: "That's yet to come."[31]

Many of the cast, guests, and judges appeared to be laughing, and laughter sounds of them were played. Brandon continued looking horrified and eventually got physically sick and left the stage.

The "Drag My Wedding" episode displays a typical example of experiencing social pressure to conform to the dominant gender behavior. I am referencing here the *expected masculinities* as described by Wellard,[32] specifically but not exclusively in the sports realm where very rigid rules of bodily appearance, behavior, and kinesiology are expected to be obeyed by men. In the culture of binarity, males (and females) are expected and demanded to perform gender in very specific ways, and all other behaviors and characteristics are deemed at best weird and at worst can situate the person outside of or opposite to the male (or even the sane and good) identity. Brandon, as a male-identifying cishet Black person who is a professional athlete, experienced the terror of pre-assuming being judged and ostracized by his peers, his group, and his identity because he appeared to the public tragically not abiding by the rules of the pack. Brandon seemed unwilling to communicate and was rejecting the rules of the heterotopic reality of *RPDR* because the set of rules he was abiding by in the real world were ruthlessly forcing him to be excluding of any different opinion. However, the dominant gender identification of being a man (and a woman) is a live acting role that involves everyday labor to ensure optimal performance in order to prove one's masculine (and feminine) identity. The Man archetype is strongly supported as well by tradition but also by repetition, and its function is not solely that of a written contract to be obeyed; on the contrary, it strongly depends on maintenance and complicity. Hegemonic masculinity is constantly being built on everyday practices through actions of both affirmation and continuation of its performance and also damnation towards alternative or subordinated masculinities and other social groups that are being oppressed by its performance.[33]

If we were to examine Brandon's reaction in comparison to the real world, it would be graded as normal, expected, and logical. In the context of the show, though, Brandon placed himself on the margin of the *RPDR* group/space, the active group as we watch the show. He experienced a situation where everything was opposite to normal, with him being the stranger, the one who does not conform. Whether he was comfortable in his gender role exchange or not, he experienced the role exchange being a social pariah in the heterotopic space of *RPDR* as he was deemed a social outcast by a gender choice. I am not trying to depict a bullying situation like the ones that many Othered bodies have experienced and are experiencing every day. However, even without any type of violence, Brandon was set aside from a group of "Normals" because of his choice not to accept a specific gender identity for himself. I am not trying to equalize situations, but what I am trying to say is that Brandon indeed exchanged roles, not with his wife-to-be, but with gender-queer people.

Indirectly experiencing the makeover, the viewer is confronted with question(s) very rarely encountered in the everyday. The viewer inside normality is confronted by the contingency of normality and accepted behavior, and they indirectly have to place themself in the position of the outcast of a social group and experience the individual's profound need to be accepted. By indirectly experiencing Brandon's anguish and terror, the viewer feels uncomfortable with the social contract that has put him in this position and may start learning to question and stop reproducing its rigidness.

I also find significant some other points displayed by the couples who succeeded in the role exchange of the "Drag My Wedding" episode. After the wedding ceremonies had been performed and while waiting for the judges' verdict, the editing featured scenes of the newly wedded couples waiting for the results. The persons, being still in their exchanged gender appearances, are displayed to have adopted some behavioralisms from the *opposite* gender. The viewer witnesses drag queen BenDeLaCreme's couple, Kevin and Amy, waiting for the verdict. Kevin (a man with large body anatomy, being drag-named Suzette à la Mode and dressed in a wedding gown with pink rosettes) was leaning on his anatomically smaller wife Amy's shoulder after hearing some good news, instead of the commonly seen opposite of wife-leaning-on-husband's-shoulder. I could not be familiar with Kevin's bodily expressions in his everyday life, and also in being aware that the scenes could very well have been directed, I want to argue that this scene still works disruptively to the fabric of macho masculinity. Especially if put in comparison with Brandon's experience of agony, the positively colored moments of joy publicly unravel the learnt rite of masculinity and teach that regarding masculinity as one unique performance as implied and taught by the dominant performance of gender gravely overlooks and oppresses the full prism of human experience.

Regarding the editing of the show, the production distanced itself from the actual reason for the dysfunctionality of the Joslyn-Brandon challenge pair, redirecting the situation with humor. Additionally, there has been talk about how the production emphasized and even played on the situation with viewers suggesting that the makeover result was sabotaged by lighting and montage to appear more strange-looking. I should also comment on the fact that since that episode (that aired in April 2014), there has been no similar incident. This could signify many things. The episode aired before the show had grown into its popularity of today. Since then, its deviant images are included in a variety of pop culture media and thus are more widely accepted by the public perception, or at least by the show's target group. However, it may be a choice of the production after a possibly not desirable outcome in the episode to have decided to be more vigilant and controlling in choosing its participants.

## "Social Media Kings Into Queens" Mini Challenge— A Shift of Normality

The tenth episode of the tenth season of *RPDR* aired in 2018, and it was titled, "Social Media Kings Into Queens." In addition to the main challenge, it featured a mini challenge in the beginning, which is a very common script in *RPDR*. This episode's mini challenge asked of the contestants to perform male gender stereotypes. The drag queens were challenged to portray "a super macho character"[34] and pose chopping wood and fixing plumbing for an advertisement of a supposed body spray called *Trade* that was *"made from essential oils found exclusively at truck stop restrooms."*[35] RuPaul satirically announced the challenge in a stereotypically manly manner, intentionally deepening his vocal tone, changing his kinesiology, and extinguishing any emotional expression from his face.

The contestants seemed to find the challenge amusing. Their appearances were changed with body hair, manly clothing, vocal tone, and kinesiology. There were nods to poor body hygiene and a tendency towards the over-presentation of masculine sexuality via suggestive movements of the mouth and the genital areas. Differentiation in lingo orbited around sexuality, vulgarity, and some commonly used male-attributed phrases. The interactions were kept short and limited to a few words per question or answer—

> RuPaul: "Been chopping wood?"
> Kameron Michaels: "Chopping wood."
> [...]
> RuPaul: "Can you get a deeper voice there?"
> Aquaria: "Trade." [he snorts]
> RuPaul: [he laughs]
> Aquaria: "You like that?"

RuPaul: "All right, bro."
[…]
RuPaul: "Can you put a hand on—between-me-down-there?"
Monét X Change: "Down here? It's really long."
RuPaul: "All right." [he laughs]
[…]
Eureka O'Hara: "I don't think y'all are ready for this smell. Trade."
RuPaul: "Nice." [he laughs]
Eureka O'Hara: "Yeah, you like that?"
RuPaul: "Yeah, that's nice."
Eureka O'Hara: "Yeah, the wife likes it too."
[all laugh]
[…]
RuPaul: "Say it sexier."
Asia O'Hara: "Trade. Can you smell me?"
RuPaul: "Yeah. Lick your lips like LL Cool J."
[…]
Asia O'Hara: "So I got the job or what?"
RuPaul: "We'll call you."
Asia O'Hara: "All right, I ain't got no phone, though."[36]

The created stereotypically masculine characters may seem extravagant and over-acted, but were they to be placed in a different social contexts than that of a pink brick-wall studio, I argue that they would actually not appear so excessive. There are countless examples of advertising campaigns for products targeted to men that could be referenced here. I will only reference the Dr. Squatch advertisement of soap for men, the company's active campaign today, because it is so extravagant that it features every stereotype of being a Man despite its attempt to disguise them with humor. The two commercial videos feature symbols like manly dirty work, strong pickle-jar-opening hands, wood work, lumberjacks, the navy, sperm count, not being told by a woman what to do, outdoorsy surrounding, full beards, being deemed sexy by women, arm wrestling, hard rock music, flannel shirts, topless muscular male bodies, meat eating, whiskey, and even Sasquatch himself by name and appearance in the videos. The advertisement also states publicly that their team is "made up of strong dads, sensitive lumberjacks and buff therapists" attempting to display macho sensitivity.[37]

In the context of the "Social Media King Into Queens" episode mini-challenge, the feminine appearance of the drag queen named Aquaria is presented as the normal against the James-Dean-resembling persona she created for the mini-challenge who snorted and picked his nose. Drag queen Eureka O'Hara's performance as a dirty, hairy man who makes vulgar jokes about his body scent and his wife's sexual preferences does not fall far from the actual real-world advertisements. The juxtaposing effect of this mini challenge could be used as a powerful tool in gender understanding and evolution. I argue that the viewer of this episode would indeed recognize the unrealistic and rigid depiction of masculinity in dominant pop culture were they presented with an actual advertisement targeted to men when zapping to the next channel.

This mini challenge creates the space for a shift of normality for the viewer and a suspension of the expected. The viewer watches the transformation of bodies from *their* normal (the queer person's normal) to *their* abnormal. We witness the procedure of ab-normal, feminized bodies being transformed into more normal bodily performances—an opposite procedure to that of the drag transformation. It is important to underline here that the viewer does not witness the transformation of a drag queen into a macho character, but the transformation of the contestants' everyday bodily gender performance to a macho character. The differentiation is significant because it tells the story of a real queer body that has been ostracized by the normal community because of its effeminate gender performativity, ridiculing the masculine archetype and offering to the queer body empowerment against the system of their oppression. Yet again, the viewer is being made part of a heterotopic experience. The alternative rule system of *RPDR* satirizes macho performativity and normalizes queer bodies, as opposed to dominant representations of masculinity in TV culture. As viewers, we are overly used to the images of ideally depicted binary bodies because their continual reproduction persuades us of their validity. The scenes displayed in this episode's mini challenge unsettle the learned narration of what is expected from a body for it to be valued. This argues to the necessity of the existence of pop culture products that register the image of the Other bodies in the collective perception. The viewer, being part of the heterotopic experience of the mini challenge, is taught a shift of their beliefs on normality and given a chance to actively compare the two rites; through this, I argue they would re-evaluate the dominant representation of masculinity.

## *"Social Media Kings Into Queens" Maxi Challenge— A Suspension of Naturality*

The same episode's maxi challenge (season 10, episode 10: "Social Media Kings Into Queens") featured six cismen popular as social media influencers. Each drag queen was paired with a social media star and was to be responsible for his makeover into a drag queen. Four of the guests were gay cismen, and two of them were straight cismen. My analysis will be gravitating towards the makeovers of straight cismen because of the longer perceived distance between their gender expression with that of a drag queen, and I will specifically focus on the pair of drag queen Miz Cracker and social media king Chester See because of their exceptional and unique outcome.

Chester See is a heterosexual, cis-, white-appearing male musician and YouTuber. Miz Cracker is a brainy Jewish comedy drag queen and has a Black drag mother, Bob the Drag Queen. Soon enough in their conversation, it was brought up that Chester See is heterosexual, a statement that was humorously accepted by Miz Cracker who suitably adapted the common saying about queer people and told the straight Chester, "This is a safe space, and we accept your life choices."[38] Chester See looked hesitant and timid and admitted to having never watched the show. He added that he only knew of it from his ex-girlfriend, but he declared being excited and wanting to know all about drag from Miz Cracker. Miz Cracker confessed to the TV camera that she felt like she had a bigger challenge than most of the other competing queen because of her shy heterosexual challenge-mate. Later on, RuPaul consulted with the pairs and advised Chester See to try on some high heels even though he was scared of them and suggested that he should select the ones that he felt would bring out the woman in him, saying, "Drag allows you to be that free. You'll learn who you are, you'll see the other side of Chester."[39]

Chester See's Mirror Moment is iconic and very much commented on by contestants, judges, and viewers. Upon gazing on his drag alter ego (named Miz Cookie) in the mirror, Chester See seemed ecstatic. He seemed not only amazed by the transformation and fully embraced his new female identity, but she was also brightly enthusiastic about her appearance, exclaiming, "Mother, I look beautiful."[40] At her Presentation Moment, Miz Cookie bore no resemblance to her male straight identity and instead fully embodied a female, sexually liberated, *wild* young woman with big blond hair who was twerking in a satin pink dress with butterflies and flirtatiously waving at the judges. Miz Cracker's and Miz Cookie's joined performance was praised by the judges who underlined that Miz Cookie was "*living*" with her makeover and that Miz Cracker was the one who walked her through this.[41]

The Miz Cookie experience is unique viewing material. It portrays and presents in prime-time TV a heterosexual, famous, perfectly "normal"-looking man discovering a new version of their identity through a different bodily expression of gender. Even if such a reaction could be scripted and produced by the show, it still presents to the public the possibility and reality of such an embrace of alternate gender expression being valid for any body. Chester See as Miz Cookie distanced himself from the expected gender role and rejected the dominant performance not only of masculinity but of the binary gender, and as a result, he even got praised for it—not only by the heterotopia that is *RPDR* but by the show's and his own fandom as well.[42] The significance of the Miz Cookie experience as an image to be registered in pop culture lies in its very opaque contradiction. The Chester See/Miz Cookie transformation deconstructs the fiction of the naturality of gender because if a masculine, heterosexual man can find a part of his identity that is capable of such womanly behaviors, then female-categorized behaviors are not naturally attributed. Furthermore, if a masculine man can "*pass*" as a woman solely by adapting some behavioral patterns, gender *is* a social contract, a role performed in the social stage. These arguments exist for drag practice in general but get another level of validity when the person in question is not a queer person.[43]

According to Judith Butler, by mimicking sex, drag practice indirectly reveals the mimetic structure of gender-body.[44] Persons/bodies follow and present to the public (space) an acquired, recurrent sequence of embodied practices of everyday life such as looks, kinesiology, or vocal tone, adhering to the social set of rules that generate the fiction of "normal" gender expression. Bodies inside the norm rarely question their given gender identity and regard the repetition of these behavioral rules not as a choice, but as intrinsic elements of their gender/identity. The culture of binarity is unfamiliar with differentiated bodily performances to the extent that it resorts to extreme violence to secure its narration. This duality has been serving as a cornerstone to society. Were the naturality of gender differentiation to be challenged, the basis of the everyday would start to deconstruct.[45] The procedure during which a body moves reciprocally back and forth between (and around) the two binary sexes reprograms categorizations of "male" and "female" performances and questions the ample network of images and mediated experiences, which instruct their repetition. The Miz Cookie experience is a great tool in the task of educating humanity about the gendered body because it deconstructs the rite of binarity but additionally presents this with joy. Chester See's transformation is not displayed by the show as a struggle but as a bright expression of something existent that brought a successful performance and a fun experience. What I am arguing is that the viewer, indirectly experiencing the joy and acceptance of Miz Cookie, is taught a valuable lesson in regarding body and gender not as a rulebook but as a means of experiencing life.

## *Conclusion*

Drag may have gained unprecedented visibility and a loyal and passionate fandom, but outside the group of its supporters, drag can still be a terrifying deviation. Even amongst the drag fandom, there have been many examples of non-inclusiveness and of discrimination. Furthermore, the acceptance of the show's narration gravely varies depending on demographics and geography. There is an advantage at this moment of human culture where drag practice is on the verge of social acceptance and is viewed as a deviation but situated right beside normality. Building on the ideas that Space is socially produced, and social knowledge is created and recreated in the personal knowledge of the learner, I argue that drag practice, as gender practice beyond and outside the norm, constitutes a valuable heterotopia of knowledge. Utilizing *RPDR* and its laboratory-like nature, which intrinsically experiments with and alters gender norms, new social contracts emerge when its narration questions the binary separation of bodies because of their embodied expression in the public space. *RPDR* inserts the heterotopic Otherness to the Everyday and generates virtual and physical space that subverts norms and becomes a learning medium of unsettlement and reevaluation of gender identity structures. Its uniqueness as a product of the phantasmagoria of deviation can offer to gender studies a new standpoint on discussing and teaching the fluidity of gender and body.

The significance the existence of Other-body pop culture produces exceeds any possible flaws or misconceptions presented since their necessity lies in redirecting pop culture towards discussions for a more inclusive concept of body and gender identity and performativity. One of RuPaul's catchphrases is, "We are all born naked and the rest is drag."[46] According to him, the meaning of this phrase is that drag practice is about portraying a role but that is not a practice limited to drag, for everyone acts according to roles in their everyday performances of self. This phrase is continuously featured during any RuPaul associated airtime and proposes one among many media for a different type of discourse. While the dominant belief argues about strict identities, the *RPDR* sphere of normality suggests that most social identities are acquired and only a matter of choice.

In June 2020, in the midst of our current time's social situation, Peppermint, a Black political trans woman, drag queen, and alum of *RPDR* posted on her YouTube channel a conversation she had with another *RPDR* alum (and winner, season 9), Sasha Velour, a scholarly, conceptual, Jewish drag queen and genderqueer person. Among other topics, they underlined the role of drag queens as educators of the human community, especially for the more prominent ones, with Sasha Velour saying, "I do think drag is supposed to be an escape from the homophobia, an escape from the racism and the transphobia, and, like, a place where queer people or femme people, people of color are important and empowered and have a voice but I don't think it's meant to be an escape from, like, reality to the degree that people with privilege don't ever need to feel bad at a drag show."[47] Peppermint responded that she views informing and educating almost as her responsibility. Marginalized groups have been put in a position of teaching human society about inclusivity and Otherness. We could say that bodies inside the norm need to learn a whole different way to address the subject of gender in order to accept the constantly growing social need for non-binarity, but it goes further than this. "Normal" bodies need to learn a very different way to address and understand the gendered body as a whole, not only for the sake of acceptance and social solidarity, but because these heterotopic Other bodies suggest a totality of bodily experience intentionally hidden from and unknown to the *Normals*. "Other" bodies with intersecting identities can teach "Normal" bodies an attempt of achieving the wholeness of the human identity by representing their very existences.

## Mini Challenge: Discussion Questions

- To what extent do you find representations of your own intersectional body/identity in pop culture? How do you feel about such existent representation, if any?
- What were your thoughts and feelings watching the role exchange experiences as they unfolded? (Especially regarding the "Drag My Wedding" grooms-into-brides episode.)
- What do you think being made over into a drag queen would have to offer to you personally? (This question could be addressed to the group twice, once before the class and once after. The group can then discuss their possible changes in viewpoints.)

## Maxi Challenge: Activities and Assignments

The essay itself delves into the experience of changing social roles, so a collaborative learning strategy that engages the group would be role-playing discussions that can amplify the experience of the learners. Some potential role-play scenarios would be:

- A conversation about one person's choice to participate on a reality television show and another's query as to why
- One friend suggests to another to consider changing their dress to be more [feminine, masculine, culturally appropriate, etc.].
- A peer is considering trying drag for the first time and another is [a drag queen, a drag fan, seen *Drag Race*, doesn't know about drag, etc.].

- Co-workers are seeking help/advice with [plastic surgery, makeup, new clothes, a makeover, etc.].

Lastly, since the essay calls for the readers to reevaluate and reassess the dominant viewpoints, a Socrative circle approach would be another layer to add. Have the students conducting the role-play at the center of the circle, and students on the outer circle take notes and conduct their own discussion after the role play. This can best allow for an inclusive-of-all-opinions discussion.

## Notes

1. RuPaul has publicly declared that he does not care about the pronouns anyone might use referring to him and that he accepts both *she* and *he*. For the cis male drag queens, I will be using the *he*-series of pronouns when describing situations where the person presents their everyday identity or uses their everyday name and the *she*-series of pronouns when describing situations where the person presents their drag identity or uses their drag name.
It is significant to note that drag might be performed by other genders as well, although this has been a point of disagreement among the LGBTQ+ community. Trans women drag queens appearing in this essay will be referred to by the *she*-series pronouns.
2. Ahmed, Sara. *Strange Encounters: Embodied Others in Post-Coloniality*. Routledge, 2000.
3. Knowles, Malcolm. *The Adult Learner: A Neglected Species*, 4th edition, Gulf Publishing Company, 1990.
4. Beard, Colin, & John P. Wilson. *Experiential Learning: A Practical Guide for Training, Coaching and Education*. Kogan Page Publishers, 2018.
5. Foucault, Michel. "Of Other Spaces: Utopias and Heterotopias" Translated by Jay Miskowiec. *Architecture /Mouvement/ Continuité*, no. 5, October 1984.
6. Stavrides, Stavros. *Towards the City of Thresholds*. Ellinika Grammata, 2002.
7. Peck, Raoul. *I Am Not Your Negro*. Magnolia Pictures, 2016.
8. The spaghetti western genre is a popular subgenre of the Western film genre. The term originated in the 1960s because of the box office success of Western films that were produced and directed by Italian people at Cinecittà Studios.
9. "David Letterman and Jonathan Van Ness on Beard Trims, Self Care, Gender and LGBTQ Rights." *YouTube*, uploaded by Netflix, 27 Jun. 2019. https://www.youtube.com/watch?v=v_dHWI4CzUU. See also, Van Ness, Jonathan and Cho, Margaret. Interviewed by Kaitlin Reilly. *REFINERY29*, 15 Jun. 2018, https://www.refinery29.com/en-us/2018/06/201908/margaret-cho-jonathan-van-ness-gay-pride-month. Accessed 10 Jun 2020.
10. "Netflix's Queer Eye in Conversation." *YouTube*, uploaded by 92nd Street Y, 21 Jun. 2018, https://www.youtube.com/watch?v=noRolBwYkYQ.
11. Grosz, Elizabeth. "Bodies and Knowledges: Feminism and the Crisis of Reason." *Space, Time, and Perversion: Essays on the Politics of Bodie*s. Routledge, 1995.
12. According to the website of Little People of America, "… terms as dwarf, little person, LP, and person of short stature are all acceptable, but most people would rather be referred to by their name than by a label." https://www.lpaonline.org/faq-#Midget.
13. "Wizards of Drag." *RuPaul's Drag Race*, season 8, episode 6, Logo TV, 11 Apr. 2016, https://www.amazon.com/gp/video/detail/B01BZGNENC/ref=atv_dp_season_select_s8.
14. Trinity the Tuck. Interviewed by Bianca Guzzo. *IN MAGAZINE*, 17 Apr. 2019, http://inmagazine.ca/2019/04/interview-catching-up-with-trinity-the-tuck/. Accessed 10 Jun. 2020.
15. Trixie Mattel. "The Most Powerful Drag Queens in America. Ranking the new

establishment." By the editors. *Vulture*, 10 Jun. 2019, https://www.vulture.com/2019/06/most-powerful-drag-queens-in-america-ranked.html. Accessed 5 Jun. 2020.

16. "Shangela, Shea Couleé, & Aja Discuss Racism in the 'Drag Race' Fandom." Mikelle Street. *Billboard*, 4 May 2018, https://www.billboard.com/articles/news/pride/8289680/shangela-shea-coulee-aja-racism-drag-race-fandom. Accessed 20 May 2020.

17. Crenshaw, Kimberlé. *Mapping the Margins: Intersectionality, Identity Politics, and Violence against Women of Color*. Stanford Law Review, vol. 43, 1993.

18. See "Wizards of Drag."

19. *Ibid*.

20. *Ibid*.

21. *Ibid*.

22. See Ahmed.

23. Haver, William. *The Body of This Death. Historicity and Sociality in the Time of AIDS*. Stanford University Press, 1996.

24. Spender, Dale. *Man Made Language*. London: Routledge & Kegan Paul, 1980.

25. See Crenshaw.

26. See Grosz.

27. "Drag My Wedding." *RuPaul's Drag Race*, season 6, episode 10, Logo TV, 21 April 2014, https://www.amazon.com/gp/video/detail/B00ICGYECE/ref=atv_dp_season_select_s6.

28. *Ibid*.

29. *Ibid*.

30. *Ibid*.

31. *Ibid.*—emphasis added.

32. Wellard, Ian. *Sport, Masculinities and the Body*, Routledge, 2009.

33. Connell, Raewyn W. *Masculinities*. Cambridge, Polity Press, 1995.

34. "Social Media Kings Into Queens." *RuPaul's Drag Race*, season 10, episode 10, VH1, 24 May 2018, Netflix app.

35. *Ibid.*—italics added.

36. *Ibid*.

37. "100% All Natural Soap for Men—Dr. Squatch" *YouTube*, uploaded by Dr. Squatch Soap Company, 18 Sep. 2019, https://www.youtube.com/watch?v=m_mF9MvksTU and "Dr. Squatch—Natural Soap for Men" *YouTube*, uploaded by Dr. Squatch Soap Company, 21 May 2018, https://www.youtube.com/watch?v=cjEK7qQKRDY.

38. "Social Media Kings into Queens." *RuPaul's Drag Race*, season 10, episode 10, VH1, 24 May 2018, https://www.amazon.com/gp/video/detail/B07B68P55J/ref=atv_dp_season_select_s10.

39. *Ibid*.

40. *Ibid*.

41. *Ibid*.

42. @chestersee (Chester See). "Hi," pinned tweet. Twitter, 30 May 2018, 1:13 a.m. https://twitter.com/chestersee/status/1001587237836898306.

chestersee. "We present to you... Miz Cookie!" Instagram, 25 May 2018, https://www.instagram.com/p/BjLNFWcHahs/?hl=en.

"The way Miz cookie was so effortlessly prancing in those heels really was a gag," posted by u/RVulcanz. Reddit, 25 May 2018, 21.05. https://www.reddit.com/r/rupaulsdragrace/comments/8m3tzf/the_way_miz_cookie_was_so_effortlessly_prancing/.

43. It is important to note that since Chester See in the tenth season, more situations of cishet men having very positive experiences being made over as drag queens have been featured in *RPDR*'s spin-off mini-series, *RuPaul's Secret Celebrity Drag Race*: notably, *RuPaul's Secret Celebrity Drag Race*, season 1, episode 1, VH1, 24 Apr. 2020, https://www.amazon.com/RuPauls-Secret-Celebrity-Drag-Season/dp/B087MW4ZY7 and *RuPaul's Secret Celebrity Drag Race*, season 1, episode 3, VH1, 15 May 2020, https://www.amazon.com/RuPauls-Secret-Celebrity-Drag-Season/dp/B087MW4ZY7.

44. Butler, Judith. *Gender Trouble: Feminism and the Subversion of Identity*. Routledge, 1990.

45. Lorber, Judith. "Chapter 36: The social construction of gender" *The Inequality Reader:*

*Contemporary and Foundational Readings in Race, Class and Gender.* Edited by D. Gusky and S. Szelenyi, Routledge, 1994.

    46. RuPaul. *Workin' It: RuPaul's Guide to Life, Liberty, and the Pursuit of Style.* It Books, 2 Feb. 2010.

    47. "Conversation: Peppermint & Sasha Velour" *YouTube,* uploaded by Miss Peppermint, 15 Jun. 2020. https://www.youtube.com/watch?v=WWjBnDT9iQk.

# The Influence of *RuPaul's Drag Race* on Pop Culture and the Way We Talk
## *A Pop-Linguistic Analysis*
### Ricarda Goetz-Preisner

## The Importance of Popular Culture on Linguistic Usage

"The library is open!" If you understand the meaning of that sentence, there is a big chance you have seen at least one episode of the show *RuPaul's Drag Race (RPDR)*. An "open library" refers to a mini challenge in *RPDR* where contestants are getting "read" by fellow peers like an open book, which means a person will be made fun of by other contestants when referring to looks, manners, and character traits. *RPDR* teaches you new words; and at the same time, it also teaches you changed meanings for existing words like "reading." "Reading" is closely related to its use in the 1990 documentary about the New York ballroom scene, *Paris Is Burning*. RuPaul Charles, creator of and genius behind *RPDR*, starts the reading mini challenge by referencing something like, "In the great tradition of *Paris Is Burning*, break out your Library Cards!"

*RPDR* has sparked a great interest on a global scale, as is the power of pop culture. The viewers are interested in both the glamorous and humorous drag culture and the sharp and poignant ways RuPaul and the drag queen contestants speak. Especially young people, and in this regard women, seem to be the most accommodating group to so-called drag linguistics. "The term pop culture is used here to mean 'culture that is widely favored or well liked by many people'[1] as it is conveyed by movies, TV programs, music, novels and magazines."[2] Today, expressions become coined more and more by their references to popular audio-visual texts. The saying "Winter is coming," deriving from the books and fantasy TV show *Game of Thrones*, has been heard and used in private, public, and cultural conversations. Since the show *RPDR* aired in 2009, the language used within the pop-cultural canon has influenced the way we talk, has taught us new vocabulary, and has also changed the meanings of certain words. Having an "extravaganza" is a so-called festivity where the glitz and the glam are at the center, where the "girls" (i.e., drag queens) are "serving their looks" (i.e., presenting their drag artwork). The term "extravaganza," however, is again strongly tied to the ballroom scene and the House of Xtravaganza therein whose members were at the forefront in *Paris Is Burning*.

Popular culture influences not only the way we speak but also what we know. A survey in 2006 found that while only one in five U.S.-Americans could name more than one of the five fundamental freedoms protected by the First Amendment, more than half could name at least two characters of the TV show *The Simpsons*.[3] *The Simpsons* is one of the longest running popular shows of all time, with a history of more than 30 years. That show, as well as other very popular formats like *Friends* or *Southpark*, has provided audiences around the world with various references that can be understood globally by respective viewers. Studies and research over the years have shown that the then-television shows from the '70s and '80s were strongly influential in transmitting information and awareness as well as influencing speech patterns, especially to young audiences.[4] Also, today shows like *The Daily Show* are a primary source of news for younger audiences, whereas Baumgartner and Morris call it "soft news."[5] The term *infotainment*—a portmanteau of the words "information" and "entertainment"—has been coined in that regard.[6] Kellner refers to certain pop texts like *The Simpsons* as a "media spectacle" in the way contemporary culture puts dreams, nightmares, fantasies, and values on display. *RPDR*, from that perspective, functions in a similar way. It is a media spectacle in the way it shows the values, nightmares, and dreams of the drag community. In that sense, it also fights underlying bias against gay men and drag queens. *RPDR* is *infotaining* us—or with another analogous portmanteau, *edutaining* us—with regard to its language use, and it is educating by using references to queer history and ongoing challenges (such as discrimination).

Recent research is focused on the online global availability of popular cultural texts.[7] The canon of pop texts also builds on one another as a global market does. As Weldes and Rowley put it: "Most forms of popular culture are produced and consumed in industrial form, and these industries, their inputs (raw materials, labor, technology), practices (of production and consumption), and outputs (films, clothing, toys, etc.) transcend state boundaries."[8] Within this research question, Murray, for example, did a study on Japanese language learners who have attained advanced levels of English from strongly relying on U.S.-American movies and television programs for both language input and information.[9] And while pop culture was an important source of language input for the learners in that study, their stories illustrate how the cultural knowledge of what is being spoken is an essential component of both comprehension and output.[10]

The power and influence of popular culture on its audience also has a lot to do with empathy. Pop texts create the possibility to walk in somebody else's shoes and also raise awareness to different lifestyles of various communities from different parts of the world. Media and popular culture in that way should represent different realities, for it plays a big part in reproducing or challenging bias as different research on the portrayal of women in film has shown. Fleischmann, for instance, says that the imbalance of power between women and men in the patriarchal system is reproduced especially in mainstream films. One reason for this is that since the twentieth century, the production of films (and of TV shows) was made by men, for men. That is why certain representation systems, so called codes, were established that are characterized by a heteronormative male view.[11] There is also a continuous shortage of women in film, numerically and with regard to their roles. If more than one women has a part, as Alison Bechdel already showed with the "Bechdel Test," they rarely talk to other women about anything else than men.[12] Movies and TV shows have the influence to change deadlocked audio-visual systems with the goal of a more diverse and equal representation.

## *Drag—Gender, Performance, and Visibility*

Drag is about many things: it is a performance of queerness and femininity, but it is also about community and its marginalization.[13] This translates to a specific use of words that can be seen as political statements and/or that have an eclectic history of counter-cultural linguistics, political demands, or societal exclusions behind them. In that regard, drag lingo can be used as a pedagogic means. However, the viewer also needs to follow off on their historic knowledge to completely understand certain expressions for what they relate to.

Drag itself has a colorful history and is formed as a mosaic of different cultural expressions; it can critique and ridicule, but at the same time, it can make its audience laugh. A drag performance can include humorous stand-up comedy, lip-synching or outperforming other queens with different skills, and dancing, too, which is a cherished one in *RPDR*. A drag persona usually embodies the portrayal of a physically realistic and exaggerated imagery of a woman[14] by mostly gay men. The "success" of a performance can be measured in the disguise of every hint of masculinity in the appearance. For this reason, drag queens rely on heavy makeup, wigs, extravagant clothes, fake breasts, and/or pads for a round shape of the hips.[15] Some might argue that this display solidifies the sexist demands of women's appearances or even misogyny. RuPaul Charles himself once answered a comment by Mary Cheney, who compared drag to black face. In a 2015 *YouTube* video, he then gave a little "herstory lesson" and described drag as being "underground," "over the top," "political," "politically incorrect," "camp," "couture," "mainstream," and declared that "It can start a revolution." He concluded overall that "Drag is never having to say I'm sorry," and "It is whatever you want it to be."[16]

However, Judith Butler says that the true and deeper essence of drag acts is the representation of a particular gender performance and not the superficial mockery and impression of women.[17] In her book *Gender Trouble* (1990), Butler introduced her famous statement that gender is a performance and of the connection between identity and performativity. According to Butler, the performative nature of gender is exactly exposed in the drag performance. Butler proposes the practice of drag as a "parody" in the way it destabilizes and makes apparent the invisible assumptions about gender identity and the inhabitability of such "ontological locales."[18] Barrett also says that the "queer identity of those who perform drag is evident in the exposed disunity between performed and true biographical identity."[19] She says a drag queen's identity constantly shifts from one form to another, creating a "multi-voiced and heteroglossic form of communication" that, rather than just imitating "the female," it is purely connected to the drag queen community and goes beyond the female/male categorization.[20] The result is the creation of a unique visual and speech with a constantly changing creative lexicon representative of the drag queen culture, used and understood within the community.

The drag community has long been a more or less secretive queer subculture. Through *RPDR*, it has become globally accessible to all viewers. Yet, *RPDR* is not the only popular cultural text about drag culture that has influenced the knowledge, perception, and language use of and in drag culture. In fact, the widely used term "yas" (instead of "yes") in *RPDR* and other pop texts was already used in the beloved, but at the same time contested, 1990 documentary *Paris Is Burning*, directed by Jennie Livingston. Filmed in the '80s, the documentary shows the ball culture of queer New York City. The documentary is cherished by many as an important piece of drag legacy and as an essential source for drag language. González and Cavazos list other U.S.-American films where the concept of doing drag has been portrayed, such as *Some Like It Hot* (1959), *La Cage aux Folles* (film,

1973), *Victor/Victoria* (1982), *The Adventures of Priscilla, Queen of the Desert* (1994), *To Wong Foo, Thanks for Everything! Julie Newmar* (1995), and *The Birdcage* (1996).[21] However, it has to be mentioned that the documentary also sparked critique due to the perspective of the director as a white, Yale-educated woman depicting drag, queer, and trans spaces of color. This line of criticizing documentaries and films about "othering" the filmed subjects has been getting more dominant in recent years. In that regard, it is also necessary to mention that the majority of films, TV shows, and documentaries are still directed by men and are still depicting women and their environments in stereotypical and sexist ways.

Three years after the release of *Paris Is Burning*, RuPaul Charles, the creator and mother of all *RuPaul's Drag Race* formats across the franchise, became famous with his hit song "Supermodel (You Better Work)." Today, almost three decades later, the sentence, "You better work" from the song is used on a daily basis: "We want to make it work."[22] RuPaul Charles never stopped referencing and borrowing from *Paris Is Burning*, making drag culture accessible around the world. This is the power of popular culture, and in that regard, *RPDR*: something that was once niche to a society, something misunderstood and/or biased against, gets showcased globally and representing actual people who tell their own stories.

"'There's something positive about normalizing something that was once seen as shameful,' says Calder, a drag performer. 'On the other hand, it can erase the origin. Misappropriation comes when people lose sight of its history, and when it becomes a commodity that the originators don't benefit from.'"[23] Drag culture, similar to feminism, both fights and welcomes its capitalization at the same time. It is a question whether or not the widespread knowledge of certain communal realities and desires counteracts the political projects of that same group. Still, *RPDR* has been vital for teaching audiences about the herstory and queerstory of drag in all its political contexts, similar to other shows like the animated *Big Mouth* does in edutaining about sexual education (Netflix, 2017– ) or *House of Cards* on the U.S.-American electoral system (Netflix, 2013–2018).

## *The Power of RuPaul as a TV Show*

*RuPaul's Drag Race* is a reality television format, which operates within American queer culture. *RPDR* started when social media was already a part of everyday lives, so the show received a lot of feedback by other media formats and on platforms such as *Twitter* or *Facebook*, which helped to make *RPDR* and the language they use popular on a global scale. *RPDR* is a combination of a drag casting show and reality program, paired with queer infotainment. The effect of the now-online availability of the show is that not only queer America is watching *RPDR* but a global, diverse audience, which spreads *RPDR* contents and lexical items.

Each episode of *RPDR* lasts for about 45–60 minutes, and it is structured into different challenges that change from episode to episode but are also repeated throughout different seasons: continuity devices are used throughout the series to get a cohesive image of the show, like "various catch-phrases, mottes [*sic*] and trademark linguistic constructions at specific points of the show."[24] Two omnipresent catchphrases from RuPaul Charles are: "If you can't love yourself, how in the hell are you gonna love somebody else?" and "Sashay away"/"Shantay, you stay" before a final elimination.

Even though the concepts of performance and entertainment play a fundamental role, drag queens have strongly contributed to the queer community in their activism for social justice against homophobia and racism.[25] Next to entertainment, *RPDR* also functions as a means to educate the viewership about queer history and ongoing challenges. Topics like gay pride, HIV/AIDS awareness and education, providing pieces of information about historically significant gay- and drag-related issues are also part of each episode. The queens provide personal narratives and experiences in that regard; talking about the challenges they witnessed doing drag or growing up in difficult areas or with a migration background. The contestants convey that getting to the point of being the proud, beautiful queen they are today always entailed many hardships and the overcoming of stereotypes. González and Cavazos mention "that through televisual media, drag queens have been given an opportunity to be normalized in heteronormative American society."[26] As many of the *RPDR* contestants and RuPaul Charles himself are queer, not only is the diversity of drag depicted, but normalization, acceptance of same-sex relationships, and different forms of expressing yourself are highlighted. However, *RPDR* does not miss pointing out that still in today's societies growing up gay, or being different from any gender norm, is an experience filled with fear and anxiety because of repercussions people face from their families, friends, and/or employers. *RPDR* provides a means for addressing these topics and at the same time gives a glimpse into the glamorous and hilarious world of drag queens.

Research about the show focuses a lot on its role for the drag community as well as on its subversive value, the performativity (keyword, *camp*) of the contestants, and the language as well as aesthetics of the show. Schottmiller looks closely into *RPDR* by analyzing the concept and usage of "camp." He shows how RuPaul's profound knowledge of gay, queer, and drag history is used in a form of pedagogy for viewers in the way RuPaul references different facts through the usage of certain words and information.[27]

Moore, for example, has also completed research into the language used in *RPDR*,[28] whereas theories by Butler, Bourdieu, and Derrida are used to analyze how contestants use language for "radical agency." Simmons' work is important for this essay, analyzing how contestants use speech codes to (de)construct, reinforce, and perpetuate cultural values.[29] Anthony also focuses on the language in *RPDR*, analyzing the portrayal of Puerto Rican contestants in *RPDR* seasons 1–4.[30] She analyses the significance of the standard of U.S.-American English in the show by using a "trans lingual lens." One of her findings is that Puerto Rican contestants are at a disadvantage for winning the show because of their accent. Goldmark also focuses on how the underlying demand for a high proficiency of English troubles the show's narrative of "upward mobility" and global understanding. He says that especially through language and respective moments of "miscommunication, witticisms and puns," *RPDR* creates inequality.[31]

Fine and Shreve's study shows how *RPDR* creates pedagogy through intertextual allusions. They argue that RuPaul uses various allusions to the 1961 novel *The Prime of Miss Jean Brodie* by Muriel Spark as a way to build a working pedagogy.[32] The book and 1969 movie tell the story of an unconventional teacher at an all-women's boarding school. In the movie, Jean Brodie is played by Dame Maggie Smith. Fine and Shreve analyze how RuPaul constantly alludes to Miss Jean Brodie on *RPDR* (and on *Drag U*, a short-lived spin off show by RuPaul). These references include direct quotations and imitations of Maggie Smith's performance. For Fine and Shreve, these allusions allow RuPaul to build his "radical pedagogy" where he is the educator both to the audience and the queen contestants—whom RuPaul often calls "my girls," which is an allusion to what Miss Jean Brodie calls her students.[33]

Other research, too, focuses on the concepts of race, gender, and heteronormativity.[34] Another way to assess the impact made by *RPDR* on its audience is to examine the thriving online fan communities for the show.

## *The Relationship Between Queer Culture and Language Use*

*RPDR* is in some way a phenomenon, which attracts a large interest on the Internet, especially the way the drag queen contestants and their host RuPaul Charles are talking to each other. Drag queens have become linguistic role models, but even before *RPDR* became popular, the English language has been shaped by both the language use of queer culture and of women. There is no extensive research regarding the influence of drag queens' vocabulary on the English language, but there are different authors focusing on how the culture of women and queer people has influenced language.

One of the few is a study by Paul Baker, who focused on the influence gay subcultures in the mid-twentieth had on the English language.[35] According to Baker, there are various words used in today's English that were influenced by the vocabulary used among gay Londoners, which is called Polari (a loanword from the Italian "parlare," which means "to talk"). Examples of that influence are words like "dish," which refers to an attractive backside, or the term "bevvy," indicating a drink.[36] A lot of the words are shortened in Polari, which was used from the 1930s to the 1970s. We can see strong similarities here to drag vocabulary today. Words get shortened or get a new meaning, and sometimes old words are revived. As Peter Gilliver, editor of the *Oxford English Dictionary*, said in an interview: "What people are doing with Polari is less about inventing new words and more about reviving ones that have fallen out of fashion."[37] Baker also stated that the language of (gay) subcultures is "constantly changing and evolving as any 'secret' language must to avoid being sucked into the swamp of the mainstream."[38]

Barrett also analyzes the lexical influence of "gay speech" on contemporary English. He describes foremost that the different cultural aspects that make up the eclectic lifestyles of the LGBTQ+ community coin certain linguistic terms.[39] Drag and (in Barrett's research) homosexuality are not connected to one particular ethnic group, country, or in that regards language. The gay subculture is a melting pot of various backgrounds and cultures.[40] Because of this, there is a lot of "code-switching" between different audiences that queer people speak in; secondly, there are numerous borrowed words between speakers of different backgrounds within the gay community.[41] Due to this intermixing of language between many cultures, the likelihood for language to spread outward from queer subculture to the mainstream language is very high. It is even higher nowadays with the means of the Internet and globally available pop formats.

Simmons says that especially marginalized groups like drag queens have unique ways of using language, with the goal of creating a shared reality.[42] Drag vocabulary can offer a glimpse into cultural ideologies, racial discrimination, and the challenging of traditional gender roles. Speaking like a queen originates from a complex relationship between linguistic forms and different identities.[43] Drag lingo draws from a rich history of Latinx and Black communities as well as different queer spaces. It mixes and changes meanings, creates new words, and is also used differently by different queens. A queen's way of speaking and the words used differ from one drag queen to the other, using one's own experiences, background, and knowledge in an individualistic style. The language of each queen also makes it part of the queen's allure. "America's Next Drag Superstar" of season 9, Sasha Velour, embodies that individuality perfectly. Sasha Velour is of Russian-Jewish descent and makes a bald head glamorous, which she wears in honor of her mother who had lost her hair during chemotherapy. Sasha calls herself an "intellectual queen" and she mixes her knowledge, language skills, and sharp wit in her performances. Quoting Sasha Velour: "*Drag Race* has made a lot more people into fans of drag, and that's allowed local communities to grow and flourish, but it's up to individual queens to share the spotlight with their communities. I definitely want to be one of the people who does that."[44]

## Women and Drag Vocabulary

We have focused so far on research that shows gay and queer culture has a profound effect on coining a secret, sub- or underground language. However, also the language use of young women seems to be a big part in spreading queer lingo. According to Blankenship, the influence of the vocabulary in *RPDR* on mainstream English is at par with the linguistic influence of young, mostly straight, girls. He notes that this is one of the strengths of *RPDR*: it mesmerizes straight audiences as well as queer ones, which also supports the mainstream use of drag vocabulary.[45] These words also get picked up by the pop cultural canon. We hear phrases like "Yas queen" in popular television shows like *Broad City*, *Queer Eye*, and from bloggers as well as celebrities. Pandell, however, says that *Yas*, "the word of the moment, has undergone the most scrutiny, it has become synonymous with hetero women."[46] She quotes the current definition for "Yas" from the *Urban Dictionary* as "An annoying expression used by girls expressing extreme liking."[47] Carmen Fought, a professor of linguistics at Pitzer College in Claremont, California, states: "If women do something like uptalk or vocal fry, it's immediately interpreted as insecure, emotional or even stupid […] The truth is this: Young women take linguistic features and use them as power tools for building relationships."[48] Next to the omnipresent "yas," other expressions have been circulated in the wild fire that is popular lingo, like "throwing shade," which means ridiculing someone in a non-aggressive way. Closely following in the footsteps of "yas," we can hear "okurrr" uttered from various televised celebrities, too. Singer Cardi B. even tried to trademark the term "okurrr," which in the end was shown to be used by many before her—the Kardashian sisters before her; and before them, it was made popular in *RPDR* season 6 by contestant Laganja Estranja. RuPaul Charles, however, credits Broadway actress Laura Bell Bundy for using the phrase even before. Bundy herself doesn't think she invented the utterance "okurrr" either. It was already used on a *Nickelodeon* show *All That* before, and even more so, as the author believes, the inspiration of "okurrr" lies in the actual vernacular of African American women.[49]

There are different theories about why women are so eager to pick up "drag lingo." Quenqua says that some linguists suggest "[t]hat women are more sensitive to social interactions and hence more likely to adopt subtle vocal cues."[50] Another perspective is that women use language "to assert their power in a culture that, at least in days gone by, asked them to be sedate and decorous."[51] Robin Lakoff elaborated the concept of "women's language" in 1975 in her book *Language and Woman's Place*. She focused particularly on the "linguistic discrimination" experienced by women in society.[52] Lakoff divides this discrimination into two main types: first, the way women are taught to use language; and second, the way general language use treats women; and both of them function to degrade women to a submissive position in society—i.e., "that of sex object, or servant."[53] The language of women in this regard had nine features, exclusive of the female speech, whose main common ground is their association with an "out of power" identity. Three examples of these features are the usage of empty adjectives, intensifiers, and tag questions, which problematically contribute to the oppression of the "woman's personal identity, by denying her the means of expressing herself strongly."[54] Lakoff proposes the hypothesis that gay men also use these nine features to distance themselves from the image of power traditionally associated with heterosexual men.[55] We can clearly see the profound use of the given examples—empty adjectives, intensifiers, and tag questions—in *RPDR*. A drag performance, as mentioned, generally includes different strategies to present an over-feminized look, accompanied by "female speech patterns" that can be strategically interrupted by a masculine voice, evident in "throwing shade" and using swear words.[56] All these strategies are mixed purposefully to create an ambiguous performed identity, the core of every drag performance.[57]

The heteronormativity of language has been criticized thoroughly in recent years, especially in languages like German, where nouns also have a specific gender and the linguistic possibility to "feminize" professions seems to be a never-ending scientific and public discussion.[58] The English syntax with its rather neutral use of articles and professions has the possibility to be more inclusive.[59] However, there are a variety of words in English that are still discriminatory and sexist, especially when considering the underlying history behind them—like the word *hysteria* or *hysterical*. When we consider that most popular cultural texts are still produced by men in the U.S., the power of language, and vice-versa, the need for its criticism within popular and mainstream culture, is undeniable.

## Drag Lingo in RPDR

Many of the popular words in *RPDR* as well as other popular texts derive from the social hierarchy we live in. Women, people of color, and queer people, for examples, have always had to fight for their acknowledgment in that hierarchy and against derogatory terms describing them. That is one of the reasons that reclaiming derogatory words is a common strategy. Linguistic re-appropriation as a cultural process can then be defined as a group reclaiming certain terms that were previously used in a derogatory way to describe traits of that same group. Michel Foucault discusses the idea of reclaimed words as a "reverse discourse": he provides, for example, that the terms used to describe sexual "perverts" (like people who practiced same-sex love and especially sex between two men as being called "sodomy") changed according to new categorization systems of "perverts" to new "species" like the term "homosexual."[60] Reclaimed words have often had a provocative nature. Reclaimed words with now-positive meanings are used within specific circles of communities. Outside these, such reclamations are contestable. In that sense, the use of some reclaimed terms by outside parties are mostly viewed as derogatory.

For some terms, even reclaimed usage by community representatives is a subject of discussion. For example, there is an ongoing debate within transgender and drag communities over attempts to reclaim the insulting term "tranny." RuPaul Charles, for example, defends using the word "tranny": "I've been a 'tranny' for 32 years. The word tranny has never just meant transsexual."[61] L.H. Stallings explains that the word "tranny" is specifically linked within the history of sex work that excludes transgender people.[62] Defining words for others or self-defining is, however, strongly linked to class and ethnicity. Stallings stresses that the means by which Black and transracial transgender and transsexual subjects define themselves can be as important as the definition of identity itself.[63] The possibility to describe and define one's gender or identity differs from every upbringing and subjective experience. The latter influence how each person is able to voice their own identity. Societal and political realities also influence how a term is defined, which is also open to critique and change. The challenges "to naming and being named by others are a form of unnaming practiced in racialized communities that changes with the politics of the time."[64]

Oppressed and marginalized groups have been fighting for their recognition socially, politically, and for what I'll call "linguistic respect." A means for this was and still is the initiative to reclaim derogatory words. Linguistic re-appropriation or reclamation is a specific form of a semantic change. This process can have wider implications in the fields of discourse and has been described in terms of personal and/or socio-political empowerment:

In the cases of oppressed groups, then, internal interlocutors may most often be engaged in confirming self-constructing narratives of humiliation, powerlessness, weakness, and diminished status. The oppression of a patriarchal system is effective precisely because the stories that dominant Others tell about us so easily and so often become the stories we tell about ourselves. Silent assent is the method by which these stories take root, allowing the voices of the external Others to echo within and giving epistemic authority to the stories they tell, leading to the distressed (often unacknowledged) perception of the self as inferior.[65]

The oppression of heteronormative patriarchy as well as the inwards struggle as a queer person with one's family creates a means for the linguistic re-appropriation of terms describing family members. As a marginalized group, the concept of family and "sisterhood" is present strongly in the queer and drag queen community.[66] In reality, as in *RPDR*, belonging to a minority creates a strong desire for solidarity and enables strong feelings of supporting each other and the drag community. For this reason, such terms as "family," "mother," and "sisters" are frequent,[67] as well as terms of affection like "honey" and "darling" when referring to one another. In that regard, even these family terms are reclaimed. "Contestants discussed being linked together which demonstrates how each member's behavior essentially affects, influences, and provides potential to honor or dishonor the collective. Throughout their talk, members revealed a sense of loyalty and comfort which are freely offered to members of the drag sisterhood."[68]

Simmons quoted Hymes's "speech codes theory" in researching how particular communication (de)constitutes collective drag queen group identity within *RPDR*.[69] Charisma, uniqueness, nerve, and talent (which creates the acronym "C.U.N.T.") are four characteristics RuPaul argues that "America's Next Drag Queen Superstar" must possess and how "such a C.U.N.T. should speak."[70] The way the contestants and RuPaul himself speak "revealed appropriate patterns of behavior which are acceptable and unacceptable."[71] These specific drag cultural codes reveal "what it means to speak, and act, like a drag queen."[72] As discussed, drag lingo mixes reclaimed words from many subcultures and draws from other popular texts and historic circumstances, so which terms have which origin and the answer on how they have developed into today's understanding is an interesting research project—some examples shall be mentioned; however, an in-depth analysis in the heritage of terms will not be made at this point. *RPDR* uses different challenges and speech patterns, like the "reading challenge." "'Reading' for example, can be traced back to African American women in the 1950s."[73] "Reading," in the context of *RPDR*, can also be "shady," which means that one queen is talking behind another's back or also overstep some boundaries. "Shady reads" are often taken more personally and hurtful as opposed to being witty and funny. "Throwing shade" means, then, to openly criticize another queen.

Many other words used in the drag community, as mentioned above, derive from the documentary and respective queer and trans culture of the '80s with *Paris Is Burning*. The word "Extravaganza," which is used in *RPDR* when there is a festivity happening where the queens wear their finest garments, can also be traced back to the documentary, where "Xtravaganza" is the name of a famous drag house. Hunger or the act of "being hungry" within the drag community and *RPDR* "refers to the act of being too competitive or having a 'cutthroat' attitude which disregards drag sister bonds which are expected to be maintained at all times even during competition."[74] Schottmiller uses Stuart Hall's theory of encoding and decoding to research *RPDR* and how RuPaul is referencing queer history in his language. He says that to "fully understand how RuPaul complexly stitches together (encodes) Camp references" the audience must possess an extensive knowledge of queer history—Schottmiller calls this "queer cultural capital."[75] "The majority of audiences will not be able to decode every single encoded camp reference in RuPaul's performances or reality television show. Most viewers will need help to unstitch (decode) the extensive references."[76]

*RPDR* and its community of international fans have mastered linguistic reclamation and camp references going as far as to introduce new words like "flazéda." There is even a "Drag Race online dictionary" for the viewership to keep up. It defines "flazéda" as: "feeling fierce or otherwise (the word is used differently by almost everyone). The term was coined by Pearl on Season 7 of *RuPaul's Drag Race*. It's a hashtag and it's spreading like wildfire. Pearl may have been trying to say 'laissez faire' but invented a new word instead."[77]

## *Euphemism Treadmill or* Geusenwort?

Words that are used to negatively describe supposed character traits of queer people, women, people of color, and/or those who do not meet certain psychological or physical demands of the powerful, have been used for such a time long in a subversive way by exactly these people in order to "own" those derogatory terms. The German word *Geusenwort* describes the same effect as linguistic reclamation or re-appropriation of a term that was (and still is) used as an insult against a marginalized group and is later used with agency by the same group.

The term *Geusenwort* goes back to Dutch freedom fighters that were called "Geusen," which translates to "beggars," who later reclaimed the word as their own and proudly called themselves *Geusen*.[78] There are many examples for this "Geusen-effect," in which people use former derogatory terms to describe themselves. Especially words used to describe people from specific groups or with distinguished traits can sometimes be seen as a *Geusenwort*.

Skinner uses the "Geusenwort-theory" to trace the historical linguistic change of the designation of homosexual people. Firstly, the term *homosexual* was used adversely, although it had already replaced terms like *sodomite*.[79] Furthermore, *homosexual* was a term to qualify homosexuality as a mental disorder in medicine and science and was used to demonize homosexual people, in particular men. Women who loved women were mostly ignored, though, until the nineteenth century when they were sometimes referred to as "Tribades."

The word *gay*, which followed the term *homosexual*, has also undergone much change. *Gay* was first part of the language used in the eighteenth century by criminals and referred to prostitution and cleverly muddling through life. As a positive term, *gay* was then used by the Gay and Lesbian Liberation Movement at the end of the 1980s; now it describes mostly gay men as the term "lesbian" is used as a counterpart.[80] In the tradition of the *Geusenwort*, both *homosexual* and *gay* are now used widely positively by people of the LGBTQ+ community, even though the term *homosexual* is an official term of othering. However, using it in the abbreviated form as an insult (i.e., "homo") has unfortunately not changed today, similar to other terms used to describe the "otherness" of people.

Another example used in *RPDR* is *fishy*: (*Fishy* is still used outside of the drag community as an insult for women, referring to reputed vaginal smell.) As a re-appropriated term in the realm of drag and *RPDR*, it functions as a compliment if one drag queen credits another one that she is "looking fishy today" because being called "fishy" is credited to looking very "female," which in the context of drag means hiding all male-coded traits convincingly. "To be 'fishy' is another way of saying, like a girl,"[81] meaning it complementary rather than condescending in the way the expression "like a girl" is normally used to degrade someone displaying not enough "manly" characteristics. The term *fishy* is used abundantly in *RPDR*. Gonzalés and Cavazos see the desire for drag queens to be as "fishy" as possible rather skeptically:

> From the beginning of *RPDR*, the audience is presented with a formal position that fishiness is valued over butchness with regards to the presentation of gender among the drag queen contestants. In the drag community, fishiness refers to the presentation of hyper-femininity and a consistent portrayal of physiological femaleness. On *RPDR*, queens are expected to reinforce the valorization of fishiness as well as heteronormative binaries of gender and sexuality.[82]

The *RPDR* Dictionary describes *fishy* as: "A term used to describe a drag queen who looks extremely feminine, or one who convincingly resembles a cis woman. The term is a reference to the scent of a vagina, which is colloquially likened to the smell of fish. Although the term is considered to be a compliment among Drag Queens, it is often considered to be an insult among non-drag women."[83] Occasionally, the use of the word *fishy* in *RPDR* is paired with a queen mimicking smelling something in the air by waving their hand in front of their nose and having a disgusted or pleased expression. Especially with the word *fishy*, it seems to be used only in the drag community and gets less used in the mainstream language. A specific example of "fishiness" can also show how many layers of puns drag queens work with in their language: drag queen (and now trans woman) Gia Gunn in season 6 of *RPDR* refers to herself as a "fresh Tilapia" upon first entering the workroom.[84] In order to understand the complexity of what Gia is saying here, first the audience has to know that Tilapia is a fish; more over, they have to know Tilapia is a type of fish with very white meat. As Gia Gunn is of Japanese-American descent, the pun is even more powerful because in this nuanced understanding, she is saying of herself that she is even serving *white woman realness*.

Even though the widespread use of former insults against women like *bitch*, *fishy*, or *cunt* seem to change traditional associations, caution should be exercised. Steven Pinker shows in his linguistic hypothesis, the "euphemism treadmill," that concepts, not words, are primary in people's minds.[85] He supported that theory by discussing that the terms "biology versus culture, nature versus society, matter versus mind, and the sciences versus the arts and humanities survive."[86] Considering the term *bitch*, the euphemism treadmill goes both ways. *Bitch* is used in almost every *RPDR* episode, most of the time as an endearing replacement for one's name. It can also be used in the same episode as an insult, dependent entirely on the context used. When two contestants have a serious argument, then *bitch* will still be used in a derogatory way. The difference of usage becomes also clear in the body language, facial expressions, and linguistically what kind of language follows after the word *bitch* (i.e., "Bitch, you are fabulous"). So, *bitch* can be a claimed word by the drag community and not really a *Geusenwort* because that entails the group using it in a positive way was confronted with the same word as a derogatory term. However, *bitch* can also be a "euphemism treadmill" in the way it (still) expresses an insult.

Pinker says that even though the euphemism treadmill can signal a new, positive use of a former negative word and seems to herald change, the hypothesis implies that every euphemism will sooner or later adopt the negative connotation of the predecessor expression as long as the actual social and political circumstances with regard to the word do not change.[87] One example shall be mentioned here where the attempt to politically correct a term used for people who are not able-bodied always ends up becoming offensive itself: "Retard[ation]" was once an accepted and professional term for a person with mental or developmental disabilities, and it first replaced insulting terms like "idiot," "moron," "imbecile," "feeble-minded," or "cretin."[88] *Retard*, however, quickly became a derogatory again—foremost on the playground and among youth, similar to the derogatory use of the term *gay*. Nowadays, official terms vary from "handicapped," "impaired," "challenged," "disabled" to words from representatives of the community like "able-bodied." Wehmeyer, director at the Beach Center on Disability at the University of Kansas, says in that regard: "It often doesn't matter what the word is [...] It's that people associate that word with what their perceptions of these people are—as broken, or as defective, or as something else."[89] Most of the ongoing criticisms surround the othering of people—a specific norm is created, a prototype, and everyone who deviates has to deviate linguistically from the norm with a certain designation.[90] The danger herein is that the differing properties become a stigma for people marked as "other" which leads to discrimination.[91]

Another example for a term that is racially, politically, and symbolically a *very* charged word that can—and also maybe shall—*not* be described as a *Geusenwort* is the n-word. Unfortunately, it is still widely used as a disgusting, derogatory term by racists around the world. On the other side, especially in the U.S., Black (mostly male) singers and rappers use the n-word frequently in their songs and/or speaking about other Black friends or colleagues. Deborah Cameron explains that Black people may call themselves the n-word in "friendship," without eliminating the racism of the word when white people use it.[92]

Pinker uses the term "image" to describe how words go hand-in-hand with a perceived mental picture of the spoken word and how they have an insidious power over our consciousness, presumably because they are inscribed directly onto a "blank slate."[93] These underlying images shape our view of reality, or they become reality themselves. This is especially true of images representing celebrities, politicians, women, queer people, and people of color.[94] An image may thus be tied to an imposed stereotype or cultural identity, often conveyed in popular media texts:

> Media images become mental images: people cannot help but think that women or politicians or African Americans conform to the depictions in movies and advertisements. [...] The study of ... stereotypes of women [and every group of people] can be reinforced, parodied, or actively contested through critical analysis, alternative histories, or creative work in writing and the media committed to the production of positive counter-images.[95]

## *The Legacy of Drag and* RuPaul's Drag Race

Pinker's hypothesis of the euphemism treadmill can be used in looking at the endeavor to find non-derogatory terms in both English and

German for Roma and Sinti people by also educating younger generations what definitions of former terms like "gypsy" entailed and in which cultural, societal, and political context they were coined. Pinker says that in this context, similar to criticizing other historic and racially loaded artifacts, it is important to teach the individual history of certain facts and constantly challenge the status quo:

> Far from being empty receptacles or universal learners, children are equipped with a toolbox of implements for reasoning and learning in particular ways, and those implements must be cleverly recruited to master problems for which they were not designed. That requires not just inserting new facts and skills in children's minds but debugging and disabling old ones.[96]

Teaching about the history of words and their uses throughout history can be pedagogically important, for students learn how oppressed people were treated and what kind of images were created around different identities and how they (still) influence us today.

At DragCon 2015, RuPaul gave an important keynote about his gay experience and the need to "educate the children."[97] In it, RuPaul mentions the importance of *Drag Race* as an educational tool and articulates the need for younger viewers to understand LGBTQ+ history. RuPaul addresses the toxic social media behavior directly, which refers also to their language use, and respective drag lingo that is used in a condescending way without understanding the heritage of that language:

> …through social media, we've noticed that younger fans who don't know the history of the gay experience where there are certain double entendres, certain speech if spoken out of school can be perceived as, um, I don't know, just like misunderstood, right. But they've taken that part of the language without understanding. […] We have lived through [the pain]. You know, a lot of us, a lot of the language that we talk about in the gay experience was a secret language.[98]

*RPDR* uses references to drag and queer culture, these camp references, in order to build the show's queer cultural legacy. Schottmiller draws from Paul Connerton's theories of social memory, who seeks to understand how social groups convey and sustain collective memories.[99] Connerton argues that participants in any collective social group share common memories that construct the group's identity. These shared images of the past often serve as collective, historical justifications that legitimate how the group's present social order operates. However, because social groups have multiple generations with different experiences of the past, the same social group can develop diverse, and often contradictory, sets of social memories.[100] The same can be said about the words used to tell these collective memories—terms and concepts along with the experiences people from these collectives have changed. Rather than a singular "truth" that is passed down, social memory produces multiple understandings of the present through acts of transfer.[101]

## Conclusion

*RuPaul's Drag Race* is an influential audio-visual format in many regards. It has the power to influence society rather than simply being a product of the material conditions of society.[102] The TV show not only influences drag culture itself but American society as well as other popular media formats. *RPDR* provides the drag scene and their drag queens a platform to represent themselves. It shows what it means to be a drag queen and how the queens' personal lives and experiences differ and at the same time have a common narrative for people who do drag. It educates viewers to what drag means, what language is used, and what concepts and challenges lay behind the history of queer expression. *RPDR* gives drag queens a voice to speak within the mainstream culture and the possibility to use, coin, and own their specific form of language.

If we take on Steven Pinker's theory (that concepts, not words, are primary in people's minds), the re-appropriation of words doesn't work for a long time. To change the meanings of insulting words permanently in a positive way, the images behind them also have to change. Having a strong awareness when using drag lingo is key to overcoming the euphemism treadmill. The idea that young women serve as gatekeepers of linguistic trends for the online and offline culture at large has different roots in linguistics. Whether a *Geusenwort* that is used by women really changes the meanings of its former derogatory meaning (like the term *cunt*) remains an open question.

The change in language and importance of certain words is in no way a patent solution to solve societal problems; language critique aims at pointing out the underlying images of derogatory words and is trying to constructively create alternatives. Going alongside movements like the Civil Rights, Gay and Lesbian Liberation, or the Women's Rights Movement, the public discussion about societal norms and conventions, as well as the language we use to describe reality, plays a big part in raising consciousness and awareness.

As we also heard, it is nonetheless important to consider that identities, class, and ethnic backgrounds play an important part for which words are used with what meaning and how we define ourselves and others with the help of language. Godrej sums it up perfectly:

> We reclaim words and phrases so that we alter their meanings to correspond to our particular realities. We rescue or salvage them from their earlier derogative

meanings so that we have the authority of our ownership behind them. Thus, the immediate target of reclamation is our discourse with one another. This specifically linguistic reclamation is a tool for disarming the power of a dominant group to control one's own and others' views of oneself, to categorize oneself or one's group in a totalizing way.[103]

## Mini Challenge: Discussion Questions

- What terms can you think of describing a group of people that have changed their meaning or usage over time? (Examples might include *pirate*, *punk*, *nerd*, *gay*, *queen*; and does this also work with words like *bitch*, *queer*, the n-word, etc.)
- What terms/words do you notice are used frequently in *RPDR*, and in what context?
- Analyze some of the terms used in *RPDR* with regard to their presumed meaning (from a historical, political, and/or linguistic point of view). Are these words really reclaimed, or reappropriated?

## Maxi Challenge: Activities and Assignments

1. Have students create a class Wiki focusing on new language, specifically used in popular culture, subcultures, and queer culture.
2. Develop a Jeopardy game. Instructors might focus on etymology, specifically philological (historical) linguistic analysis from building on main works in this field by Ferdinand de Saussure, Noam Chomsky up to linguistic reappropriation, reclamation, or resignification.

## Notes

1. Quoted in Murray's article is John Story, *An Introduction to Cultural Theory and Popular Culture* (2nd edn). Athens: University of Georgia Press, 1998.
2. Murray, Garold. *Pop Culture and Language Learning: Learners' Stories Informing EFL, Innovation in Language Learning and Teaching*, 2:1, 2–17, first published 2008, Akita International University, Japan, 2014. http://dx.doi.org/10.1080/17501220802158792.
3. McCormick Tribune Freedom Museum. "D'oh! More know Simpsons than Constitution. Study: America more familiar with cartoon family than First Amendment," *Associated Press*, Mar. 2006, http://www.nbcnews.com/id/11611015/ns/us_news-life/t/doh-more-know-simpsons-constitution/. Accessed April 1, 2020.
4. Iyengar, Shanto, & Kinder, Donald R. *News That Matters: Television and American Opinion*. Chicago, Chicago University Press, 1987.

5. Baumgartner, Jody, & Morris, Jonathan S. "The Daily Show Effect: Candidate Evaluations, Efficacy, and American Youth." *American Politics Research*, vol. 34, no. 3, May 2006, pp. 341–367. doi:10.1177/1532673X05280074.
6. Kellner, Douglas. *Media Spectacle*. Routledge, 2002.
7. Bimber, Bruce, & Davis, Richard. *Campaigning Online: The Internet in U.S. Elections*. New York: Oxford University Press, 2003.
8. Weldes, Jutta, & Rowley, Christina. "So, How Does Popular Culture Relate to World Politics?" *Popular Culture and World Politics: Theories, Methods, Pedagogies. E-international Relations Publishing*, edited by Frederica Caso and Caitlin Hamilton, Bristol, 2005, p. 15.
9. See Murray, p. 9.
10. *Ibid.*, p. 11.
11. Fleischmann, Alice. *Frauenfiguren des zeitgenössischen Mainstreamfilms*, Springer Fachmedien Wiesbaden, 2016.
12. Bechdel, Alison. *Dykes to Watch Out For*, 1983, https://dykestowatchoutfor.com/. Accessed 8 April 2020.
13. Pandell, Lexi. "How RuPaul's Drag Race Fueled Pop Culture's Dominant Slang Engine." *Wired*, 2018, https://www.wired.com/story/rupauls-drag-race-slang/. Accessed 17 Mar. 2020.
14. Barrett, Rusty. "Indexing Polyphonous Identity in the Speech of African American Drag Queens." *Reinventing Identities: The Gendered Self in Discourse*, edited by Mary Bucholtz, A. C. Liang, and Laurel A. Sutton, Oxford University Press, 1999, pp. 313–331; p. 314.
15. *Ibid.*, p. 315.
16. Charles, RuPaul. "A message to Mary Cheney from *RuPaul´s Drag Race*." *YouTube*, 2015. https://www.youtube.com/watch?v=5G4-oatHs3A. Accessed 9 July 2020.
17. Butler, Judith. *Gender Trouble: Feminism and the Subversion of Identity*, Routledge, 1990, p. 140.
18. *Ibid.*, p. 146.
19. Barrett, p. 316.
20. *Ibid.*, p. 318.
21. González, Jorge, & Cavazos, Kameron. "Serving Fishy Realness: Representations of Gender Equity on *RuPaul's Drag Race*." *Continuum: Journal of Media & Cultural Studies*, vol. 30, no. 6, 2009, pp. 659–669.
22. RuPaul. "Supermodel (You Better Work)." *Supermodel of the World*, Tommy Boy Records, 1993
23. Pandell.
24. Zabbialini, Giulia. "'*Girl, we are serving looks!*': the influence of drag queens' language on the 'beauty gurus' channels on YouTube." *Academia.edu*, p. 6. https://www.academia.edu/39236240/_Girl_we_are_serving_looks_the_influence_of_drag_queen_s_language_on_the_beauty_gurus_channels_on_YouTube.
25. Simmons, Nathaniel. "Speaking like a Queen in RuPaul's Drag Race. Sexuality & Culture." *Sexuality & Culture*, 18, New York, 7 Dec. 2013, p. 631.
26. Gonzalez & Cavazos, p. 8.
27. Schottmiller, Carl. "Reading RuPaul's Drag Race: Queer Memory, Camp Capitalism, and RuPaul's Drag Empire." Dissertation, University of California, Los Angeles, 2017, https://escholarship.org/uc/item/0245q9h9.
28. See Moore.
29. See Simmons.
30. Anthony, Libby. "Dragging with an Accent: Linguistic Stereotypes, Language Barriers and Translingualism." *The Makeup of RuPaul's Drag Race: Essays on the Queen of Reality Shows*, edited by Jim Daems, McFarland, 2014, pp. 49–66.
31. Goldmark, Matthew. "National Drag: The Language of Inclusion in RuPaul's Drag Race." *GLQ: A Journal of Lesbian and Gay Studies*, vol. 21, no. 4, October 2015, pp. 501–520.
32. Fine, David, & Shreve, Emily. "The Prime of Miss RuPaul Charles: Allusion, Betrayal, and Charismatic Pedagogy." *The Makeup of RuPaul's Drag Race: Essays on the Queen of Reality Shows*, edited by Jim Daems, McFarland, 2014, p. 168.

33. *Ibid.*, p. 180.
34. Morrison, Josh. "'Draguating' to Normal: Camp and Homonormative Politics." *The Makeup of RuPaul's Drag Race: Essays on the Queen of Reality Shows*, edited by Jim Daems, McFarland, 2014, pp. 124–147.
35. Baker, Paul. "Polari: The Lost Language of Gay Men," 2002, https://www.lancaster.ac.uk/staff/bakerjp/polari/home.htm. Accessed 8 April 2020.
36. *Ibid.*
37. D'Silva, Beverley. "Mind Your Language." *The Observer*, Guardian News and Media, 9 Dec. 2000, https://www.theguardian.com/theobserver/2000/dec/10/life1.lifemagazine3. Accessed 17 Mar. 2020.
38. *Ibid.*
39. Barrett, p. 186.
40. *Ibid.*
41. *Ibid.*, p. 196.
42. Simmons, p. 631.
43. Barrett, p. 318.
44. "Sasha Velour Quotes." *BrainyQuote.com*, BrainyMedia Inc, 2020, https://www.brainyquote.com/quotes/sasha_velour_940546. Accessed 9 July 2020.
45. Blankenship, Mark. "Mopping Drag Slang." *Out*, Here Media, 23 Apr. 2012, https://www.out.com/entertainment/2012/04/23/drag-queen-rupaul-race-language-slang. Accessed 1 April 2020.
46. Pandell.
47. *Ibid.*
48. Quenqua, Douglas. "They're, Like, Way Ahead of the Linguistic Currrrve." *New York Times*, 28 February 2012, https://www.nytimes.com/2012/02/28/science/young-women-often-trendsetters-in-vocal-patterns.html?pagewanted=all. Accessed 12 April 2020.
49. Munzenrieder, Kyle. "Cardi B Will Trademark 'Okurrr'—Even if the Phrase Has a Long History Before Her." *W*, 21 Mar. 2019, https://www.wmagazine.com/story/cardi-b-trademark-okurrr-phrase-origin-rupal/. Accessed 9 July 2020.
50. Quenqua.
51. *Ibid.*
52. Lakoff, Robin. *Language and Woman's Place*, New York, Oxford University Press, 22 July 2004, p. 4.
53. *Ibid.*, p. 53.
54. *Ibid.*
55. *Ibid.*, p. 7.
56. Barrett, p. 320.
57. *Ibid.*
58. In German, for example, even words that describe similar incidents like a fight, which has a male article—*der Kampf*—and a battle, which has a female one—*die Schlacht*—have different articles. Also, other words can have a "gender." This is the same as in French. Most German speakers would generally, when speaking in plural or using an example, use the male word as the neutral one (the word "citizens" can be spelled *Bürger*—which actually just refers to men; whereas *Buergerinnen* would refer to only women, and *BuergerInnen* tries to incorporate both women and men but at the same time is difficult in spoken language).
59. In recent years, there have been more discussions also with regard to the English language to make it more inclusive—words like *humankind* are used more frequently instead of *mankind*, and gendered phrases like "Hey guys" get used less when referring to a mixed-gender group. The question about whether prefixed terms like "Madam Mayor" are less derogatory than Mayoress or the creation of a new term for a woman who is mayor remains.
60. Foucault, Michel. *The History of Sexuality Volume 1: An Introduction*. London, Allen Lane, 1976, p. 37.
61. TransvestiteHerstoryLesson tweet, May 24, 2014, qtd. in L. H. Stallings, *Funk the Erotic: Transaesthetics and Black Sexual Cultures*, University of Illinois Press, 2015, p. 232.
62. Stallings, L. H. *Funk the Erotic: Transaesthetics and Black Sexual Cultures*, University of Illinois Press, 2015, p. 232.

63. *Ibid.*, p. 234.
64. *Ibid.*
65. Godrej, Farah. "Spaces for Counter-Narratives: The Phenomenology of Reclamation." *Frontiers: A Journal of Women Studies,* vol. 32, no. 3, Sept. 2011, p. 114, https://muse.jhu.edu/article/461367. Accessed 14 April 2020.
66. Simmons, p. 631.
67. *Ibid.*, p. 641.
68. *Ibid.*
69. *Ibid.*, p. 633.
70. *Ibid.*, p. 635.
71. *Ibid.*, p. 636.
72. *Ibid.*
73. Pandell.
74. Simmons, p. 637.
75. Schottmiller, p. 100.
76. *Ibid.*
77. "*RuPaul's Drag Race* Dictionary." *Fandom.com*, 2020. https://rupaulsdragrace.fandom.com/wiki/RuPaul%27s_Drag_Race_Dictionary.
78. Wierlemann, Sabine. "Political Correctness in den USA und in Deutschland." *Philologische Studien und Quellen, Band 175*, Erich Schmidt Verlag, 1 Sept. 2002, p. 72.
79. *Ibid.*
80. *Ibid.*
81. Simmons, p. 66.
82. González and Cavazos, p. 6.
83. "*RuPaul's Drag Race* Dictionary."
84. "RuPaul's Big Opening." *RuPaul's Drag Race*, season 6, episode 1, Logo TV, 24 Feb. 2014. *Amazon*, https://www.amazon.com/gp/video/detail/B00ICGYECE/ref=atv_dp_season_select_s6.
85. Pinker, Steven. *The Blank Slate*. Penguin Book, 2002, p. 190.
86. *Ibid.*, p. 182.
87. *Ibid.*
88. Barry, Dan. "Giving a Name, and Dignity, to a Disability." *New York Times*. 8 May 2016. https://www.nytimes.com/2016/05/08/sunday-review/giving-a-name-and-dignity-to-a-disability.html. Access 17 April 2020.
89. *Ibid.*
90. Wierlemann, p. 178.
91. *Ibid.*
92. *Ibid.*, p. 78.
93. See Pinker, p. 178.
94. *Ibid.*
95. *Ibid.*, p. 192.
96. *Ibid.*, p. 198.
97. See Schottmiller, p. 209.
98. *Ibid.*
99. *Ibid.*, p. 62.
100. *Ibid.*
101. *Ibid.*
102. González and Cavazos, p. 9
103. Godrej, p. 111.

# Pedagogy of the Mother

*Exploring Freire's Philosophy of Co-Productive Learning*

PHILLIP JOY *and* JILL MARIE MCSWEENEY-FLAHERTY

> **Drag mother** (n.): Also drag daughter, drag family. An experienced drag performer who acts as a mentor and guide to someone who wants to learn the art of drag. Often, the new drag queen, who is referred to as the drag mother's drag daughter, takes the last name of her drag mother to pay homage to her. A drag family is made up of a drag mother and all of her drag daughters.
> —Jackie Huba & Shelly Stewart Kronbergs[1]

RuPaul, star of the hit reality television show *RuPaul's Drag Race* (*RPDR*), is known as the Mother of Drag or "Mother Ru" to both contestants and viewers. As the Mother of the series, RuPaul is both a teacher and a learner. Mother Ru, through pedagogical practices, co-produces knowledge about queer culture and politics in ways that can cause both her girls and the wider audience to radically alter their understandings and perceptions about the lives and well-being of the LGBTQ+ people—much like a threshold concept.[2] *RPDR*, through political and cultural commentary, works to transform society by revealing and creating knowledge about the lives of LGTBQ+ individuals. While *RPDR* is often framed as a humorous and fun reality show, at the same time it has provided contestants with the platform to tell viewers of their personal stories with gender transitioning, being HIV-positive, and/or of deeply tumultuous homophobia from family members. Over the last decade, Mother Ru has used *RPDR* as a means to take the intimate and subversive experience of drag, traditionally housed within nightclubs, and strategically transform it into an award winning, top-rated, international reality TV show by applying fundamental aspects of Freirean[3] critical pedagogy, where both contestants and viewers learn about and reflect upon the systemic societal hegemonies faced by much of the LGBTQ+ communities.

*RPDR* regularly teaches contestants and audiences of historic milestones of LGBTQ+ history, such as the Stonewall Riots of 1969, the ground-breaking documentary by Jennie Livingston called *Paris Is Burning*, and the right for same-sex couples to marry. In the autoethnographic piece, Colin Whitworth notes, "RuPaul was, in many ways, my classroom for queer history. It taught me about gay men of the present and the past."[4] Like Whitworth, for many the show is a window into the lineage of LGBTQ+ identities and social disruption of heteronormative concepts. *RPDR* is an open space to learn about LGBTQ+ communities by providing an intimate look into the many political, social, and cultural factors that create barriers to the physical, social, and mental well-being of many LGBTQ+ people. Intentional or not, *RPDR* has potentially become one of the largest social learning environments of our generation by making drag culture available in living rooms across the globe.

This essay explores how *RPDR* creates opportunities for political, social, and cultural change through critical pedagogy and transformative experiential learning. The essay begins by providing context on the current state of political and social issues in Canada that influence the health and well-being of LGBTQ+ communities. We then provide a brief overview of the philosophies of critical consciousness and co-learning[5] and how the workspace and main stage of *RPDR* are pedagogical spaces in which Mother Ru and contestants participate in the co-production of knowledge and learning on the marginalization and stigmatization of LGBTQ+ individuals and communities. Then, through Mother Ru's walk-throughs and maxi challenges, we comment on how these activities mimic pedagogy that encourages the development of a critical consciousness[6] in contestants, by asking them to express how tensions and barriers in the real world have shaped their lived experiences and the art they perform, and ultimately provides an opportunity for Mother Ru to be both a teacher and learner in this co-production of knowledge. We discuss how the show has become a living classroom that teaches about the culture and lived experiences of the LGBTQ+ communities and can be a transformative teaching tool for viewers. The essay concludes with an exploration on how the pedagogical strategies found in *RPDR* should be mirrored by educators within health and medical programs. The use of these strategies can help train students to become be competent, confident, and empathetic professionals when working within LGBTQ+ communities.

## *Beating the Mug and Setting the Stage*

We believe that *RPDR* mirrors effective teaching strategies that enable students to explore moments of deep and profound learning and encourages the contestants to transform into critical agents of change through purposeful challenges that require them to examine structural barriers and personal experiences. The authors of this essay have experienced drag and *RPDR* in different ways, and in the following first-person brief interludes, we share our own reflections and connections that have helped frame our essay's exploration into Mother Ru, *RPDR*, and pedagogy.

## *The Boy Who Couldn't Keep the Heels On [Phillip]*

*I remember watching the first season of* RPDR *and being disappointed when Nina Flowers sashayed away. I was drawn to her fierceness and glamour, and over the years, I have continued to be captivated by the queens on the show. My first memories of what I would eventually come to understand as transgressing gender constructs are me in my mother's high heel shoes tiptoeing secretly (well, actually not-so-secretly as my mother noticed her heels missing many times) around the house when everyone was gone, pulling my t-shirt up over my head to give myself long sweeping hair that I could flip back and forth. My mother did not wear make-up, so to my regret I never got to beat my mug in my gender transgressions. I remember the feelings of shame within myself after playing in my mother's heels and the fear of being found out. Looking back on these feelings as an adult, I have more appreciation of how those experiences influenced my well-being and the way I view things. As a little boy growing up in rural Nova Scotia, I did not know there was a community of people blurring the boundaries of gender binaries through the art of drag. But now, through the community of* RDPR, *I have come to understand how important gender and its transgression can be to the experiences and health of LGBTQ+ individuals.*

*Drag, as Mother Ru often says, is a political act. Drag is also a transformative act, and I believe that drag can be transformative to the health of people. Health, like drag, is political. Health experiences are (re)produced through social institutions and cultural norms. Health inequalities exist as systematic gaps in the health of different groups of people. These gaps in health outcomes are a result of many social determinants that include, but are not limited to, education, income, social cohesion, political empowerment, and gender equality.*[7] *The World Health Organization in its Ottawa Charter calls for mobilization for social and political change to improve health outcomes for all "people*[8]. *The call" specifically seeks to raise awareness about the determinants of health through education of both health professionals and the public and to address social injustices and systems of power imbalances.*[9] *I believe that the queens on* RPDR *are doing more than living their fantasies: they* are co-creating knowledge on a variety of topics, including the determinants of health. The process of co-creation occurs when people share their existing knowledge in a collaborative way to produce new knowledge.[10] Many of the queens on RPDR co-create knowledge on the ever-changing political, cultural, and social systems that influence the health of LGBTQ+ peoples.

## The Girl Who Found Strength in Drag [Jill]

I can still remember my first drag show and how it made me feel. It was over a decade ago in a small local club: the floors were sticky from the nights of spilled alcohol, and while it was only filled to half capacity, it still felt stuffy. Myself—white, cis, and straight—giggled next to my white, cis, straight girlfriends. We were taking the night to rebel against the narrative that as young single women, we needed to spend our Friday making ourselves up for the male strangers that we should want to impress. We watched in awe of the queens, who looked better than we could ever look in makeup and gowns, as they sashayed to a soundtrack that we still danced to in our underwear within the safe privacy of our homes. In that moment, I felt internally warm and part of a community as I watched the performers push back against what society said men should be, but I also felt sad that I, a strong liberal woman, never felt as liberated as they seemed to feel in that moment. Since my first drag show, drag has represented the pinnacle of strength and freedom for me, but it wasn't until I found RPDR that I realized it was a platform to teach others about the internal strength one has to transform themself and the world around them.

Over the last few years, I have connected to RPDR through a pedagogical lens. As an Educational Developer, I work with faculty and graduate students to develop their own teaching skills and grow as teachers—or as agents of change. On many levels, I see my teaching mirror the process and goals of RPDR and drag. From the thoughtful student-centered assessments that embed deep self-reflection and critical introspection, through the community I build within a learning space to allow for safe and vulnerable dialogue, to transparent openness of the challenges and barriers I've experienced during my own professional and personal growth. Mother Ru enacts much of the same pedagogical principles I use in my own teaching. But most of all, I've used the strength and freedom I've learned from RPDR and drag to be a model of critical transformation, one that works to support a similar growth and awareness in students so that they too can be individuals who disrupt systems of power in their own teaching. In many ways, I feel the strongest, most powerful, and free when I am teaching others. As Mother Ru works to empower queens, I work to empower my students.

## Current Political, Social, and Health Issues for LGBTQ+ Peoples

"Health is wealth. You'll get to a certain age
and realize the valuable currency is good health."
—RuPaul[11]

This essay explores the pedagogical strategies of *RPDR* within a health context. Mother Ru, as noted in the above quotation, views good health as important in one's life, and we follow her perspective in our analysis by exploring the pedagogical strategies of *RPDR* within a health context. The queens on *RPDR*, over the course of many seasons, have talked about their own health issues and the associated social, physical, and mental stigmas that they have experienced. Ongina in season 1 was one of the first reality stars to come out as being HIV-positive; Katya in season 7 opened up about her substance use and mental health concerns; and Kim Chi in season 8 talked about her struggles with body image. Over the seasons, *RPDR* has provided a space to learn collaboratively about the health and well-being of the LGBTQ+ communities. Dominant and heteronormative social and cultural views of sexuality and gender marginalize, stigmatize, and negatively affect the health of LGBTQ+ individuals. Mother Ru often creates opportunities for the queens of *RPDR* to learn about the social forces that impact their health experiences, and these pedagogical strategies can be explored and utilized by educators, particularly health educators. As such, *RPDR* becomes a vehicle for co-learning about stigmatizing norms with the potential to transform society and positively influence the health and lives of all people by bringing awareness to future health professionals.

While the global shift in the acceptance of LGBTQ+ people has been happening over the last few decades, the Organization for Economic Cooperation and Development (OECD)[12] still strongly recommends the need for LGBTQ+ activism in many countries. Within Canada and other OECD countries, nearly one in three individuals identifying as LGBTQ+ report experiencing discrimination. The report also notes that social acceptance of sexual and gender minorities by Canadian citizens is approximately half the population surveyed. In addition, only 44 percent of respondents said they would accept a child who expressed themself differently from their assigned gender.[13] These numbers, considering the historic strides in LGBTQ+ rights within Canada, are surprising and staggering.

In 1969, the Canadian government decriminalized same-sex sexual activity between two consenting adults over the age of 21, but despite these reforms to the law, the persecution of LGBTQ+ individuals continued over the following decades. For example, thousands of civil servants and military personnel were surveilled, interrogated, and removed from their jobs due to their sexual orientation or gender identity.[14] In 2005, Canada legalized same-sex marriage and continued to be progressive in relation to the rights of LGBTQ+ individuals. In 2017, the Canadian Prime Minister Justin Trudeau apologized to the LGBTQ+ civil servants who were oppressed and criminalized by the previous governments.[15] The apology acknowledges the past discrimination of the Canadian government towards LGBTQ+ peoples, but as McDonald notes, there is still much work left to be done within the Canadian government to improve the legal standing of LGBTQ+ individuals.[16]

Health, like drag, is political. The health of LGBTQ+ people is continually being (re)shaped through political discourse that is deeply ingrained with notions of heteronormativity,[17] and some current discourses still position LGBTQ+ people as deviants, pathological, and othered, which further marginalize and stigmatize.[18] For example, the legal age of consent for same-sex experiences is higher than the legal age for heterosexual experiences, highlighting the continued stigmatization of gay sex. Men who have sex with men are still banned from donating blood due to dominant discourses of the potential pathological nature of their blood if allowed into the national blood supply.[19] LGBTQ+ people experience health disparities because of these political and normative systems, policies, and narratives, and this results in stigma, prejudice, and discrimination that creates adverse and stressful environments and influences the mental and emotional health of many LGBTQ+ people.[20] LGBTQ+ youth are at increased risk for depression, anxiety disorders, self-harm, suicidal thoughts and attempts, and suicide mortality.[21] Other health disparities in relation to rates of cigarette smoking, alcohol and recreational drug use, body image issues, sexual health, HIV and AIDS, and physical violence also exist for LGBTQ+ communities.[22]

The statistics are sobering. Gay and bisexual students (when compared to the general school population) are up to five times more likely to miss school because of the fear of violence against them, eight times more likely to require medical help because of suicide attempts, and more than nine times more likely to use heroin or other drugs.[23] These health disparities need to be addressed through political, social, and cultural transformation. Transformations that can result from teaching within a social justice framework.

Much of the progress addressing the health inequalities within LGBTQ+ communities has been achieved through activism and grassroot social movements, such as the AIDS activists movements.[24] Movements that have often involved drag activists.[25] *RPDR* provides opportunities and spaces for people to co-create knowledge about various social and cultural considerations of health of the LGBTQ+ communities. The show, despite its lack of in-depth exploration of the complex political, social, and cultural factors that influence the health of LGBTQ+ peoples, does give glimpses to the struggles that many sexually diverse and gender diverse people experience. The show alludes to how their struggles influence many areas of their lives, including their emotional and mental well-being. As Mama Ru said, "Health is wealth." The next sections of this essay continue to thread the concept of health within the context of *RPDR* and its pedagogy. At the end, we provide a discussion on how *RPDR* and its pedagogical practices may inform health education.

## *Philosophy Is Fundamental*

"First learn the rules, then break them." —RuPaul[26]

For meaningful change within society that can improve the lives and well-being of LGBTQ+ individuals, we must, in the words of Mother Ru, know and then break the rules; or as the Brazilian educator Paulo Freire (1921–1997) would argue, know the social structures that keep people oppressed and use education to transform them.[27] The philosophies of Freire are critical in understanding the transformative nature of *RPDR* at an individual and audience level. Freire explores how pedagogical practices can be a means to transfer knowledge from one person to another, often a structure referred to as the banking system of education,[28] where an expert dispenses their knowledge to the "vessel" or student. However, Freire sees this as a problematic system that often perpetuates marginalization experienced through social and cultural norms embedded in everyday lives. Freire believes that critical pedagogy could work to dismantle and replace the traditional capitalistic model of education and move to a concept of praxis where educators and learners are viewed as interchangeable and collaborative roles that result in the co-production of knowledge.[29] In this system, pedagogy is used to shift relations and perceptions of power within broader cultural and societal contexts and work to transform fundamental beliefs of the learner.[30] Whereas a structure of education that resembles the commodification of banking and (re)produces systems of oppression, the movement of praxis seeks to tear down systems that have shaped the narrative of our lives and facilitate transformative learning between teacher and student.[31]

Engagement in this praxis has allowed Mother Ru to develop into what Henry Giroux[32] would describe as a "transformative intellectual" in her role as teacher, for she has taken a critical stance on the show's goal of educating and disrupting misconceptions and biases towards the LGBTQ+ communities. Through the workroom walkthroughs, performance critiques, and more importantly, choice of competitions, Mother Ru actively translates her convictions and beliefs into her practice as host, mentor, and mother in *RPDR*. In this way, Mother Ru uses the structure of the show to engage both contestants and viewers in her agenda to be a social agent of change and encourages others to engage in the deconstruction of harmful systems of marginalization and disenfranchisement. From a pedagogical perspective, the *RPDR* praxis requires Mother Ru, contestants, and viewers all to reflect critically on their own assumptions, biases, and values, shifting their focus from themselves to the broader conditions and systems of the world that imposes injustice and inequity to others.[33]

The transformative nature of *RPDR* has developed over the seasons, and fundamental to the praxis is the positionality of contestants. In earlier seasons, contestants were viewed as objects to be changed and transformed by the judges,[34] whereas in later seasons, we see them shifting to be an active and critical subject undergoing their own individual transformation within the workroom. Using storytelling, viewers watch as contestants struggle to own their drag and strive for something greater than themselves. This praxis shift has equally transformed Mother Ru's role in the show, where she was once a judge of drag performance, she is now a teacher critical to the transformative process who helps liberate contestants from the systemic structures limiting their drag and challenges them to develop as individual and intellectual characters within the space of *RPDR*.

Fundamental in the facilitation of transformation is how *RPDR* creates a space for the learning of both contestants and viewers. Learning environments are critical to the transformative process of learning, for they are places where social and cultural norms are either (re)produced to maintain systems of power that marginalize or are where such systems of power are challenged to disrupt and shift relations for a more equitable society.[35] It has been suggested that television reality shows are designed to only superficially explore the political, social, and cultural systems that shape our lives and consequently our health and well-being.[36] From the television producers' viewpoint, this may be done to elicit sympathy for contestants and to provide an emotional storyline, but much as in a classroom, this discourse is a way to begin challenging our own pre-conceived notions and biases and to begin the process of a critical consciousness.[37]

*RPDR* is a pedagogical space, a learning environment comprised of the workroom and the main stage in which Mother Ru, the contestants, and viewers co-create the knowledge and learning in order to dismantle the broader structures that disenfranchise the LGBTQ+ communities.

Contestants, through the mini and maxi challenges, Mother Ru's visits to the workroom, and shared moments while applying make-up and donning wigs, reveal their authentic selves to the audiences and provide a window into the personal transformation they go through every episode. We believe that through the seemingly unintentional use of critical pedagogy, *RPDR* has enabled itself to become a global learning space that continuously transforms itself, Mother Ru, contestants, and viewers and encourages us all to reflect on broader systems of oppression through key conversations and challenges that represent the political and social barriers experienced by the LGBTQ+ communities.

## *An Example of Mother Ru Teaching for Social Change*

Mother Ru has learned to use the *RPDR* platform for greater political advocacy, which can begin to transform society and structures, including the health institutions and the health policies that directly impact LGBTQ+ communities. There are critiques that suggest *RPDR* is more aligned with corporate profits, selling wigs and make-up, and branding celebrities than with advancing LGBTQ+ rights and transforming society,[38] but the show has always had threads of political activism running through it. *RPDR* often highlights the stories of queens known for their community and political advocacy, such as fan favorites season 8 alum Bob the Drag Queen, who is known for community action, and season 11 alum Nina West, who has advocated and raised millions of dollars for issues such as HIV/AIDS testing and treatment, marriage equality, and trans rights.[39] *RPDR* also has a tradition of challenging the queens to debate each other in a run to make *herstory* by becoming America's First Drag President. Coinciding with the American election years (i.e., season 4 in 2012, season 8 in 2016, and season 12 in 2020), this encourages the queens to think about the broader systemic issues facing the LGBTQ+ communities, and it demonstrates to the audience through the use of satire how political platforms are often missing the voices, perspectives, and concerns of the LGBTQ+ communities.

In season 4, episode 9, entitled "Frock the Vote!," the guest judge was Dan Savage, a well-known sex columnist and political pundit. In this episode, the competing queens Sharon Needles, Phi Phi O'Hara, Chad Michaels, Latrice Royale, and Dida Ritz were asked to campaign and take part in a round table political debate to become the first Drag Queen President in herstory. As Mother Ru and Dan Savage walk through the workroom checking in with each drag queen, they ask Dida Ritz if she votes. Dida tells us, "I do, I do, I vote… politics is kind of something that's hard for me to discuss because it can get personal. It can get very ugly and I hate that." Savage calls her out. "Which is why it's important for us to pay attention," he says, "because politicians are gonna demonize sexual minorities and if they can count on us checking out, they're likelier to win and then get into office where they can really do us harm."[40] Sharing his reflection, Savage calls attention to the impact that politics have on the LGBTQ+ communities and the harm that can unfold when queens and individual viewers check out or remove themselves from the political landscape.

After the political debate, the queens gather in the workroom to talk about their performances and the place of politics in drag. "I know yesterday was a drag competition," begins Sharon Needles, "but I kind of wish we could've used it a little more as a platform to talk about things that, you know, we really wish we could see changed."[41] Sharon shares that they should have focused more on real issues instead of going for pure entertainment. Disagreeing with Sharon, Chad Michaels explains that "this is *Drag Race*… it's always been my policy especially like when I'm working at shows, you don't mix drag and politics." The show cuts to his confessional where he explains, "I'm out to entertain people and make them feel good and not to spread my political beliefs at the gay bar." Sharon ends the conversation saying, "…we are given an opportunity that no other drag queen is given, and that's a platform to actually talk about things."[42] That platform is *RPDR*.

Years later, in season 12, episode 9 entitled "Choices 2020," many queens echo Sharon's 2012 sentiments and feel it is even more important to talk about politics in the Trump era. In the workroom as they prepare for their main political challenge, they discuss their experiences with overt racism in America, such as the Muslim ban, and how Trump's presidency has created a divide in their country. In 2017, President Donald Trump signed an Executive Order that became known as a Muslim ban. The order banned foreign nationals from seven predominantly Muslim countries from visiting the country for 90 days, suspended entry to the country of all Syrian refugees indefinitely and prohibited any other refugees from coming into the country for 120 days.[43] Widespread condemnation and protests resulted from this order and divided the country. The ban was temporarily blocked by a federal court but, in 2018, the American Supreme Court upheld an amended version of it. In 2020, six African countries were added to the list.[44] Iranian-Canadian drag queen Jackie Cox, the first contestant in *RDPR* herstory to dress in a Muslim-inspired runway look, shares the personal impact of the Muslim ban that separated her family and the long-term and emotional impacts. "I'm just so angry this is America," she confesses.[45] The queens provide support and agree that it is time for action, a time for change, and a time to encourage people to vote. As the queen Widow Von'Du says, "…all the stuff Trump and the republicans have put this country through, have put people of color through, queer people, LGBTQ+, we need to be on the front lines fighting every day."[46] It is a rallying call from the queens to change America through democratic action, and an opportunity for viewers to hear the lived experiences of people directly impacted by the current political climate in America. In an article in *The New Yorker*, RuPaul discussions the importance of the USA presidential election and how he is using his platform to bring attention to how politics influence the lives of all people, but especially the LGBTQ+ communities. He tells the reporter that he understands "what it is we must do.... We're going to mobilize young people who have never been mobilized, through our love of music, our love of love, our love of bright colors."[47] For example, by giving the queens a "Go Vote" sign to hold up, point at, and dance with on the main stage as the episodes' end-credits music plays, *RPDR* emphasizes throughout the season the importance of voting and being politically involved for LGBTQ+ issues and beyond.

In the twelfth season, episode 7 features guest judge Alexandria Ocasio-Cortez, an American congresswoman serving as the Representative for New York's 14th district. In the *Untucked* episode, Alexandria Ocasio-Cortez (AOC) reflects on the nature of politics with the queens as she says, "The people who change what people think are artists, drag queens, and let's not forget who threw that first brick at Stonewall. That is what led to us passing the equality act in the house, marriage equality. It starts with you."[48] Unfortunately, in her talk presented on the episode, AOC does not name or identify the people "who threw that first brick" and the subsequent bottles that ignited the Stonewall movement.[49] These leaders were Marsha P. Johnson and Sylvia Rivera, who were two trans women of color who were also drag queens.[50] In season 4, episode 6, "Float Your Boat," Mother Ru enters the workroom: "It's time for a little *herstory* lesson," she says, "Back in 1969 at the Stonewall riots, it was a drag queen who had the charisma, uniqueness, nerve and talent to dig her heels in and start a revolution. And every year since, drag queens have been the shining stars of pride celebrations around the world."[51] Although Mother Ru also does not specifically name Marsha P. Johnson and Sylvia Rivera during the herstory lesson, it is important to recognize and celebrate these leaders. These examples are just a few of the herstory lessons Mother Ru gives us about the impact that drag queens have had on LGBTQ+ equality and rights. Drag queens are, as Mother Ru says, the stars of pride.[52] *RPDR*, through such lessons, *ruveals* the importance of becoming involved in political processes, and that the social changes that AOC referred to start with educating people about the forces that shape their lives and their role in making change.

While Mother Ru has spent much effort politicizing *RPDR* during election years, her teaching for social change does span all seasons. For example, "Trump: The Rusical" of season 11 creates an opportunity for the contestants and viewers to learn about the impact of politics, and the previous election, on the lives and well-being of LGBTQ+ individuals. The Trump Rusical is a musical parody of *Grease* and takes place in the "worst" high school in America—"Trump High." The lyrics of the Trump Rusical mock American President Donald Trump and the people he appointed to various positions of power within his government. In the Rusical, season 11 queens Shuga Cain, Vanessa Vanjie Mateo, and A'Keria Davenport (impersonating Hillary Clinton, Rosie O'Donnell, and Stormy Daniels, respectively) sing that Trump is "screwing our democracy."[53] In this one line, the musical highlights Mother Ru's views that the policies of Trump's administration create social injustices for all Americans, in particular, social injustices for LGBTQ+ communities. The Trump Rusical challenge continues Mother's Ru commitment to teach about the need for LGBTQ+ people to recognize the influence that politics has on their lives and to become active agents working for change.

One of the major discourses threading through "Trump: The Rusical" is gender. All the queens impersonate a woman in the life of the American President Donald Trump, including women of his republican cabinet (such as drag queen Scarlett Envy as current American Secretary of Education, Betsy DeVos, who has "never been inside a school before"[54]) as well as the prominent women of the democratic party. The Rusical calls for more women to be involved in political action, as the lyrics of the closing number ruveal:

> Ladies, gather 'round (Pow!)
> Women have had enough
> The glass ceiling shatters now
> Ladies I've found (Pow! Pow!)
> Powerful and tough
> Join with me and make a sound
> I can't believe what I am saying right now, but listen to this
> Let's all start marching together! Haha!
> Together we march
> Fair treatment, equal pay
> Remembered forever as
> Pussy power, nasty women, radical feminists
> Change, change
> We need more women to run.[55]

The lyrics draw attention to the gender inequality that exists in American politics and advocates the need for radical feminists to change and transform social systems that keep people impoverished and marginalized. The Rusical calls for fair treatment and equal pay, better education, social justice, and equality—or, as identified within the Ottawa Charter, broad social determinants of health[56] that directly and distally impact the well-being of all. At the heart of the Rusical is a call for the empowerment of the American people to take control and ownership of their lives and, as we suggest, control and ownership of their health. Improvements in health can only happen through knowledge and learning opportunities.

The teachings of Mother Ru in this challenge are political and have the power to help viewers understand the need for change, and these teachings ultimately call viewers to mobilize for social action, which is a Freirean practice of social justice. Like many challenges in the show, "Trump: The Rusical" creates a space for Mother Ru and the other drag queens to share their experiences of and reflections on living as part of the LGBTQ+ communities. The stars of the show, as well as viewers, are taken on a journey that focuses on developing a communal critical consciousness to be used for political, social, and cultural subversion.

Throughout *RPDR*, we see Mother Ru working to teach about social and systemic change by encouraging and teaching contestants to "transgress" against political, sexual, racial, cultural, and classist boundaries,[57] but *RPDR* is also about individual and holistic growth of the contestants through caring for the person behind the drag and developing a relationship and environment where learning can occur in a deep and intimate setting. As Brennan and Gudelunas note, through the use of storytelling in one-on-one confessionals, pre-runway "tucking," and individual speeches with judges, contestants share with each other and viewers their "personal histories of marginalization and disenfranchisement"[58] and often deconstruct the social, cultural, political, and health structures that have led to these experiences. This process, paired with action and disruption from Mother Ru herself and the contestants, is core to the co-construction of a critical consciousness, and with it comes the creation of a space where traditional roles, relationships, and identities of power are examined, critiqued, and interrogated.[59] While this form of teaching has been viewed as "one of the most dynamic and controversial educational schools of thought of the past 30 years,"[60] it has also been a fundamental approach in developing contestants' story arcs in *RPDR* and building the global viewership of the show.

## *Lessons from the Runway: Teaching Tools of Mother Ru*

> "I feel at my core that I am a teacher.
> I am here to be a conduit. I know how to make magic.
> I have the ability to help people cross over
> to their greatness and realize their potential."
> —RuPaul[61]

If we conceptualize Mother Ru as a teacher and the contestants and viewers as learners, then *RPDR* becomes the collective course that we have enrolled in. Within *RPDR*, pedagogical strategies that align with the paradigms of co-production of knowledge and transformative learning exist. We have critically reviewed seasons 8 through 11 for moments of transformative co-learning within a health and well-being context. Moments that involved Mother Ru and the contestants collaborating and sharing their knowledge about political, social, and cultural discourses of stigmatization and marginalization and that shape their lives and health as well as the lives and health of LGBTQ+ communities and the viewers. These moments, as Freire would argue, allow for learners to come to a greater understanding on the social and cultural forces that oppress people. These moments are transformative in nature in that they ruveal new ways of being and living, and they provide opportunities of political, social, and cultural change by building avenues of resistance. In our review, we identified three types of pedagogical strategies aligned with transformative learning, including: learning through dialogue; learning through vulnerability; and learning through reflection. The following section explore each of these strategies in greater depth, providing examples from the show.

## *Learning Through Dialogue*

> "Busting through fear has been a constant challenge. Finding places in my consciousness where I feel stuck or unwilling to change is a real downer, but not insurmountable. I can also learn from the experiences of others."
> —RuPaul[62]

In her book *GuRu* (2018), Mother Ru discusses her capacity to be both a teacher and learner and the transformative learning strategies that she ultimately incorporates into *RPDR*.[63] She believes that learning is through sharing experiences with others, engaging in dialogues about critical moments of change, as well as being vulnerable and examining and reflecting on our own fears and the places where we feel stuck. Learning for Mother Ru is a praxis of dialogue, reflection, and action and is reflected through her interactions with the other queens/learners on her show.

Fundamental to such a praxis shift is the use of dialogue between teacher-learner and between learner-learner. In *RPDR*, the workroom is a place where the contestants spend much of their time; it becomes a space where they not only learn about the challenges and what they need to do to become the next drag superstar, but it is also a space for critical reflection. Ru often asks the contestants to think about their lives and artform during his workroom walk-throughs. During these interactions, Ru becomes the Girouxian "transformative intellect," asking contestants to critically reflect on how their drag, relationships, and lives have been shaped by political, social, and cultural systems, ultimately mentoring them to push outside any constructed boundaries and find their own unique identity. Together, they create knowledge and possibilities for new ways of performing their art and sharing their lives with an audience.

An example of this shift can be seen during the Book Ball challenge of season 8 where Ru challenges the contestants to design three outfits, one of which is a tribute to their biological mothers.[64] The contestants in this episode all share personal stories of the relationships with their mothers, and for some, this is a window into the cultural tensions of gender and sexuality that they have experienced within this relationship. Through dialogue in the workroom, the viewers learn about the influence of heteronormativity and binary concepts of gender on family relationships that the contestants have experienced and have often left lasting feelings of hurt, sadness, and disappointment. In this regard, the contestants take on the role of co-producers of knowledge with the viewers as they share, reflect, and discuss their personal family experiences with each other and with Ru during the creative processes of designing, sewing and "tucking" their runway looks. In particular, Kim Chi speaks about the cultural norms that have created barriers in the relationship with her mother, for she taught her to be proud of her South Korean heritage, which is grounded within heteronormative values. As the dialogue in the workroom unfolds, viewers learn that while there is a strong cultural bond with her mother, Kim Chi has not shared with her mother that she is a successful drag performer or that she is even on the show. When Mother Ru hears this, she asks Kim Chi if she is afraid her mother will find out. In reply, Kim Chi says, "I am a bit afraid that she might see all of this, as like a waste of time."[65] After a slight pause, she confesses that "I just want my mom to be able to be proud of everything that I do. You know the person that I am today."[66] As the critical teacher, Mother Ru seeks Kim Chi to reflect and asks, "[D]o you think she doesn't know that already?" to which Kim Chi replies, "I don't think so, no."[67] Kim Chi fears her mother would view her drag, her vulnerability, as a sign of weakness and that her mother would be ashamed. In this moment, Kim Chi becomes both a learner and a teacher as she shares what it is like for her within her South Korean culture and how she feels she must balance her drag life with her family life.

For many gay men, heteronormativity negatively influences the relationships they have with their families. In the same episode, Derrick Barry shares his coming out story, and we learn that this vulnerable moment in his life changed his relationship fundamentally with his mother. "When I came out to my mom," Derrick recounts, "I thought she would embrace me with open arms, and I got the complete opposite reaction."[68] His experience, however, created empathy, compassion, and shared understanding with the other contestants, and it built an environment safe to explore deep-seeded memories of pain and family conflict. "That's why I have empathy for Kim Chi," Derrick tells us, "because I know when a kid feels broken down by their parents, it will always be at the back of their mind. I feel that my mom broke me, and I just never got put back together."[69] Strategically, *RPDR* created an "assignment" for its contestants/learners to explore family bonds within the context of drag and built a space for the queens and viewers to understand how gender, sexuality, culture, and family can shape their individual performance.

Mothers, whether biological or drag mothers, can be very significant. Nina Flowers in season 1, episode 6, in one of the show's more spontaneous moments, tells us that "mothers are very influential to drag queens."[70] Although many contestants (like Derrick Barry, and Dusty Ray Bottoms of season 10) talk about the struggles they experienced with their own families, other contestants have notably shared the positive ways family can shape drag. Nina Flowers shares with us how her mother influenced her drag, even after she passed away five years prior: "[S]he's still with me all the way. She was not really my mom, she was my best friend and she always encouraged me to go for the things that I wanted in life, so she's a big part of this."[71] Nina honors her mother and their relationship through her drag and her time on the show. While the show often uncovers the deeply difficult relationships between the queens and their family, it is moments like this with Nina where viewers are able to see the profound positive impact family can have on the career and growth of the queens. Similar challenges throughout the seasons (such as episode 7 of *All Stars* season 2 and *Drag Race UK* season 1, where family members were brought to the show to receive a makeover from the queens) allow the queens and audience to explore these family dynamics and allow the audience to consider their own family relationships. While likely unintentional, *RPDR* uses a student-centered approach to allow the contestants to reflect on how constructs of heteronormativity and family relationships, both positive and negative experiences, have shaped their art and their lives. It is a way for the contestants to share with each other their own experiences, and it can be potentially liberating to those dealing with difficult histories. For educators, such approaches can be used in the classroom to bring about reflections in their students and may create understanding and compassion to the lives of LGBTQ+ people.

The format of *RPDR* is designed to maximize dialogue that either elicits sympathies for contestants or produces conflicts that are ideal for dramatic television.[72] Many examples of both types of dialogues are present in the show; for example, in season 10, a conversation between Dusty Ray Bottoms and the other girls reveals her coming out story and how she and her family do not talk now because of the negative way being gay is viewed in their religion. She says that "when I came out to my family, the night before it happened, I was literally at my breaking point, like I was at my lowest low with everything," and as Dusty continues, she tells us, "I like literally cried out to God and was like, I need a change in my life. Like I need something to happen and to be different for me."[73] The other girls in the room listen to Dusty as she continues her story about her parents discovering she is gay. Dusty confesses that "they lost it. They took me to church. The got me exorcised because they thought I was possessed by a gay demon."[74] The scene cuts to Monét X Change's shocked expression as she listens to Dusty continue to share her story of her family's reaction to her sexuality. "I had to go through therapy," Dusty continues, "and I was on a track to go to straight camp. I was meeting with these pastors, and he was like 'in a homosexual relationship, you are never gonna find success. You'll never find love.' It was the most humiliating and awful thing of my life."[75] As Dusty breaks down in tears, she finishes her story by telling us that she did find happiness within a relationship with another man, a relationship that is fulfilling and loving. This dialogue ruveals the traumatic experiences that Dusty went through with her family and gives the audience the opportunity to learn more about the damaging responses that many LGBTQ+ individuals face when sharing their identity with family. Her story allows us to learn about the stigma many people in the LGBTQ+ communities face within their families, contemporary society, and modern religions, and the long-term impact of these reactions. The story creates dialogue through which experiential learning can occur and allows for the audience to reflect on their own reactions to the LGBTQ+ communities. The audience learns that LGBTQ+ people are not possessed by demons that religion needs to save but rather that they can live a life with loving, caring, and accepting relationships. Even more importantly, we learn that we, as LGBTQ+ people, can be loved and find healing and happiness rather than believing we need to be fixed.

The Vixen in season 10 is at the center of many dialogues that are used to produce conflict, as opposed to used to elicit sympathy, in the season. Such tension-filled and confrontational conversations not only create drama within the show but are also a pedagogical space for the other queens, as well as the viewers, to learn about the systematic discrimination of minorities that shape people's identities. Born in Chicago, The Vixen is famous for her drag that blends political activism and queer advocacy into her performances. In episode 7 of her season, The Vixen tells us that "a lot of people say drag should only be an escape from reality but drag can also help us face reality and deal with it."[76] For The Vixen, drag is political activism that can make the lives of people better by being a transformative force within society. Her commentary on *RPDR* is known for creating dialogues about the experiences of Black, gay drag queens in America. In episode 7, she shares more of her story with us: "It is hard being a Black person in America," she says, "it is hard being a Black gay person in America. It is impossible being a Black gay drag queen in America."[77] The Vixen continues to reflect on how her experiences as a Black gay drag queen has shaped the way she often interacts with people, saying, "I spend so much time keeping my mouth shut to get ahead that when I feel attacked, it all comes out."[78] Through these dialogues, *RPDR* frames The Vixen as a confrontational political drag queen who is able to speak about the systematic discrimination and homophobia that shapes her personal experiences and identity.

The dialogues within the show create emotional authenticity and relatability between the contestants and the audience that is a means through which the show teaches.[79] The audience begins to understand the political, social, and cultural systems that marginalize and stigmatize LGBTQ+ individuals. Viewers can begin to critically think about how topics such as sexuality, gender, ethnicity, body standards, heteronormativity, and stigma can negatively influence the lives, health, and well-being of the contestants and other LGBTQ+ individuals. This approach is similar to how an instructor might unpack difficult topics in the classroom—i.e., by presenting a variety of lived experiences, by creating a space where students can critically reflect and challenge their own assumptions, and by safely exploring personal experiences and broad topics of system oppression, all of which are foundational to facilitating transformative learning experiences.

## *Learning Through Vulnerability*

Mother Ru, throughout *RPDR*, uses the vulnerability of contestants to facilitate a deep and transformative reflective process to reveal their authentic drag selves. It is this authentic self that the viewers connect with and root for to win, and thus contestants are encouraged to actively embrace being vulnerable and to share in this process in the workroom. Vulnerability is a concept that Mother Ru believes is critical for drag, and it is often a significant pedagogical tool in transformative learning. As bell hooks argues, "[A] holistic model of learning will also be a place where teachers grow, and are empowered by the process. That empowerment cannot happen if we refuse to be vulnerable while encouraging students to take risks.... In my classrooms, I do not expect students to take any risks that I would not take, to share in any way that I would not share."[80] In creating an environment where Ru and contestants are free to share, co-learn, and be vulnerable, the workroom becomes a space that facilitates deep learning and self-growth.

In season 10, episode 11, entitled "Evil Twins," Ru enters the workroom in a bright and colorful suit of tropical design and reveals to the queens the nature of the maxi challenge: the contestants are to confront their evil twins. "Ladies," Ru opens, "we all have negative voices in our head. The inner saboteur that tells us we can't do it, or we are not good enough. I know I fight them off every single day, but if you can't beat them ... put them in drag."[81] As he describes the challenge, Ru reveals his own inner struggles and provides advice to overcome self-doubts that he has also experienced. His advice is to overcome inner negativity through drag, and he tasks the queens with presenting two distinct drag characters, one at their best and one, as he ruveals, "a dark-sided bitch that oozes negativity."[82] In other words, Mother Ru tasks the queens with creating a good twin and a bad twin. In this moment, Ru shares his own experience of self-learning and growth, and the workroom is once again transformed into a pedagogical space as the queens reflect on their own evil twins and are empowered by Ru's story. The contestants realize that the challenge calls for them to ruveal parts of themselves that they may otherwise not wish to see or even address. This, as Asia O'Hara notes, makes everyone feel "very vulnerable because there is nothing to hide behind in this challenge."[83] Mother Ru wants them to be open and vulnerable, to hide nothing of themselves.

During this episode, the queens decide to discuss the good and bad qualities of each other and their drag, being vulnerable with their peers and to viewers. The use of the workroom in this context is critical, for our peers are often key in the facilitation of change and helping us reflect and make new meanings from our lives and experiences,[84] and in this moment, the contestants co-learn together about being vulnerable. Aquaria notes how Miz Cracker "really beats herself up"[85] and is too hard on herself. Asia O'Hara and Eureka agree, stating that Miz Cracker refuses to show emotion. When Ru re-enters the workroom to check-in with his girls, he again speaks to the importance of reflecting on their drag and identities, and he again becomes the vulnerable teacher, sharing more of his own personal story: "This challenge is so important because we have to look at those things," Ru says. "I always see my saboteur in my peripheral vision and I always like to say, 'You can look, Ru: but just don't stare.'"[86] In essence, he asks the queens to further develop their critical consciousnesses[87] by critically examining what they fear.

When Ru confronts Miz Cracker about her inner saboteur, he tells her it's about balance and not giving the inner saboteur attention. Miz Cracker confesses that the inner saboteur is "sucking the life out" of her and how she always feels the need to over-explain her drag for validation.[88] She reflects further that this ensures that she has a sense of control over how other people see her but ultimately limits her ability to connect and be vulnerable with others. Miz Cracker ruveals that the "hardest part of this challenge is letting go of control and opening up. I've been through so much in my life. I am still learning to trust people. When Ru asks me to open up and to be vulnerable, I really want to do it because I want this so bad."[89] Miz Cracker, through the reflective process of designing her character, learns how challenges in her life have shaped her inner saboteur and prevented her from trusting others. By encouraging vulnerability and developing an authentic self, Ru engages in a relationship with Miz Cracker that is built on trust, respect, and empathy and that allows her to imagine things differently, which can be a catalyst for change.[90] This allows the audience to see her authentically and partake in her learning, for many of us can see ourselves reflected in her vulnerable self. At this moment, Miz Cracker becomes both the teacher and the learner, a co-producer of knowledge, when she explores and learns about her inability to be vulnerable in her personal and drag life, and how it has been detrimental to her emotional and mental health. Miz Cracker, through reflection on her inner saboteur, also teaches viewers about the private experiences of drag queens who may look strong and free on stage but also struggle with doubt, fear, and imposter syndrome. In discussing her inner saboteur with Ru, she opens up, and becomes vulnerable, creating a perception of authenticity and an emotional connection with viewers.

At the heart of teaching is a sense of vulnerability and authenticity,[91] which are critical components to support intentional transformative learning for students.[92] When we can create a space where our learners are able to explore, take risks, and open themselves up to critique and challenge, we increase the impact of their learning.[93] Even more importantly, when we build a space for our learners to be vulnerable with us, their teachers, we create a personal connection and an environment of trust that is critical for transformation. By Mother Ru sharing her own struggles, both in his drag self on the main stage and in his non-drag self in the workroom, Mother Ru demonstrates her own growth and learning and that failure is not a barrier to success, and he uses it as a connection with the contestants/learners, mirroring many interactions teachers experience in their own classrooms. Ultimately, this vulnerability and trust produces an environment—or, a learning space—that is safe and enables self-reflection and deep learning to take place.[94]

## Learning Through Reflection

The aims of teaching and learning should be transformative, both at an individual level and a societal level,[95] and *RPDR* as a pedagogical tool works on both. Reflection has long been viewed as a transformational teaching tool that encourages students to engage in deep and purposeful thinking about their lives, learning, and personal growth.[96] By engaging in reflection, learners are encouraged to make important and complex connections between their past and present to ultimately transform their future. Mother Ru incorporates many opportunities for learning through critical and personal reflections for contestants, which is pivotal in the process of transforming their drag and personal self. Mother Ru and the other judges actively seek to see the queens transform during their time on the show. They often ask the queens to talk about what they have learned about themselves, others, and drag through the competition, either through one-to-one conversations and/or on the runway. When speaking about the journeys of the contestants, Mother Ru has said:

> I always get very emotional, because I know, I know the struggle. I know what you all had to do to get here, not just in this competition but in your lives. You should be very, very proud of yourselves. You really should. Now so many of our younger viewers watch this show to find their tribe. That's why I ask each of you to take a moment to look back and reflect.[97]

Mother Ru recognizes that the queens have been through many struggles not only during the competition but in their lives as drag artists and as part of the LGBTQ+ communities. Mother Ru employs learning through reflection to share the journeys of the queens with the intent to help and connect with viewers who may be struggling and feeling alone and acknowledges how detrimental being outside heteronormative norms can be to person's well-being. She seeks to use pedagogical practices centered on reflection to help people find their community, friends that become like family, and hopefully to end the isolation that many LGBTQ+ people feel because of stigmatization and social marginalization. The show has become a way to build communities of support for fans and queens and is an integral part of Freire's[98] process of critical consciousness.

Mother Ru often challenges her girls to reflect on the main stage as part of the final race to the finish line of the competition. She often asks the final four contestants to share advice with their younger selves and engage in a final moment of deep self-reflection to be shared with viewers and themselves. Through this act of sharing and providing a life lesson, contestants actively become teachers to viewers and demonstrate the lessons they've learned during Mother Ru's reflective process. Many of the contestants emphasize the importance of embracing oneself and the characteristics within themselves that society has deemed inappropriate, especially for many little boys. They often talk about how they should not be ashamed of the things that made them different or the things that made them feel like outsiders, as this is critical to their individuality and power as a person and drag queen. For example, in season 8, episode 9, Chi Chi DeVanye advises herself, and in turn viewers, to "never be ashamed of how you walk or talk because that will be the key to your success."[99] Naomi Smalls in the same episode tells her younger self, and us, to embrace your looks and mannerisms and to "be proud that you are not like all the other boys."[100] And Kim Chi shares an emotional moment with her younger self, the judges, and viewers about the lessons she learned. She says,

> People might shame you for being too different and not fitting in with the rest of the culture. At times you are gonna feel like you are trapped in the wrong body and trapped in a place where you feel you can't get out, and at times you are gonna want to think about harming yourself or running away. But I just want to let you know that it will all get better; and once you grow up, the things you are ashamed of, are gonna be the traits others will love you for and you will be able to embrace them, and you are gonna find a group of friends that will love you, and you are not gonna feel lonely anymore—life will get better.[101]

In her speech, Kim Chi embraces being vulnerable and exposes how she felt isolated and alone growing up, and this ultimately creates an authentic and shared connection with viewers who may experience similar isolation and marginalization. She talks about how her experiences of being an outsider create feelings of shame and thoughts of hurting herself, which brings awareness of the influence of stigma based on gender, sexuality, and bodies on the mental and emotional health of many LGBTQ+ individuals. Lastly, like Mother Ru often does in the workroom, Kim Chi provides a message of hope for others. *RPDR* provided Kim Chi with a platform to teach others about her struggles and to learn from her experiences.

Mother Ru awards, much like a grade, and deems successful those queens who find their voice and when they accept those qualities that isolated them. The show's transformative message is to embrace vulnerability and to be true to oneself, and as Mother Ru says, to *love yourself*. Perhaps this is best emphasized with season 10's Aquaria's response when Mother Ru asks her what she learned about herself through the competition. Aquaria, whose off-stage name is Giovanni, says, "I've learned so much about needing to take care of Giovanni well as Aquaria ... being in the competition, I've learned to communicate with people and warm up to people and let them warm up to me."[102] Aquaria speaks to how her participation in the show has led to her reflection on the importance of not only taking care of her mental and emotional health, both in and out of drag, but also the importance of communities for support for people who are often marginalized within society.

RuPaul often refers to herself as a teacher and as a mentor for younger people,[103] but she is also the learner. From the very first episode of *RPDR*, she recognized the importance of her role as a learner and of growing from the experiences of the contestants on the show:

> The biggest revelation for me happened during the very first show we shot, when I realized that our little TV show was really about the tenacity of the human spirit: how these bullied little kids turned the tables on society and found their power in being whatever the hell they want to be.[104]

RuPaul learns about the stories and the struggles of the drag queens who walk across the main stage and how the contestants as performers use their drag to ease the tensions of stigma they often experience as gay, trans, non-binary, gender fluid, and queer humans. In doing this, she learns about how the queens use drag to turn the tables on society by shifting and challenging power relations within it, and this further allows the show's transformational agenda to adapt and grow.

*RPDR* itself has gone through its own journey of self-exploration and transformation, as many contestants and viewers have voiced critiques of reinforcing the broader systemic barriers of gender, race, and class experienced by the LGBTQ+ communities,[105] often misrepresenting the progressive nature of drag culture,[106] and Mother Ru has been criticized for some of her personal views of drag.[107] Ru notes that his drag is a force for social subversion of gender and suggests that his drag is a means to disrupt hegemonic masculinity that teaches boys to hide their emotions. "I feel bad for men in our culture," he says. "I think we do everyone a disservice by hiding our emotions."[108] While his drag attempts to challenge hegemonic masculinity so that boys and men are not limited in the expression of their emotions, others suggest that this reinforces strict notions about who can perform drag and why, ultimately limiting, excluding, and harming others within the LGBTQ+ communities, especially those who identify as transgender.[109] Reflecting on these critiques, Ru has publicly admitted the harm that her strict rules about drag have done to the LGBTQ+ communities, especially to the trans community who have been the leaders of equality movements, like Marsha P. Johnson and Sylvia Rivera. According to Brown,[110] Ru admitted in a tweet that she has come to understand and regret the hurt she has caused to the trans community. Ru continued her reflection in the tweet by saying that "the trans community are heroes of our shared LGBTQ+ movement. You are my teachers."[111] In acknowledging the teachers in the trans communities, Mother Ru accepts her own role as a learner. Learning is still taking place as the show, and as Mother Ru, continue to redefine themselves among diverse audiences.[112] The show is slowly shifting views of drag as a reflection of this learning, but it ultimately still adheres to Mother Ru's vision of drag on *RPDR* as a means for social transformation and as a means to teach. To teach the queens, and the audience, about the lived experiences of the LGBTQ+ people and their personal power to positively influence themselves and their broader communities in which they live through the process of dialogue, vulnerability, and self-reflection. To teach Mother Ru's vision that drag queens can be agents of change. The discourses that the show creates about those who are excluded in drag, and the strict gender rules of drag, creates another opportunity for growth, transformation, and the sharing of knowledge linked to the lived experiences of those who have been marginalized. Therefore, the show is expanding the voices of drag and is opening possibilities for expression and is challenging how drag is defined, who can engage in drag, and the message that is conveyed through this art; all of this is resulting in a more inclusive environment for those who have traditionally been left out of drag discourse and practice.

*RPDR* uses reflection as the primary means to facilitate discourse and vulnerability and to encourage contestants and viewers to engage in transformational learning. This method of pedagogy requires full engagement of teacher and learner in the process of meaning making, and throughout *RPDR*, viewers watch as Mother Ru and contestants become co-learners and co-facilitators of the reflective process.

## *Implications for Teaching Practice: An Example for Health Education*

Health, like drag, is political. *RPDR* has always in some ways addressed issues that impact the health and lives of the people within the LGBTQ+ communities. In the very first season, the fourth episode is entirely devoted to the topic of HIV/AIDS awareness. The competing queens, including Rebecca Glasscock, Bebe Zahara Benet, and Ongina, are challenged to showcase their glamorous selves in an ad for the MAC Viva Glam campaign. As Mother Ru introduces the challenge to her girls, she tells us that, "MAC donates 100% of the sales of this product [the MAC Viva Glam lipstick] to help people living with HIV and AIDS"[113] and that the winner of the challenge will be the next face of the campaign. The queens take this challenge to heart and reflect on the meaning of the task at hand and how they can work to improve the health of their communities. "This is not just make-up or lipstick," says Rebecca Glasscock, "this is make-up with a purpose, and that's when it really hit me. It wasn't a challenge. It was personal."[114] Bebe Zahara tells us, "Where I came from in Cameroon, HIV/AIDS is such a big issue and I have born a witness to it, and I'm a very spiritual person. And to me, this was just a way to really, really create an awareness."[115] But it was not just awareness about this health issues the show fostered for the queens, but also a personal celebration of life and compassion for people living with it. The campaign slogan created by Ongina, another competing queen, embodies these sentiments in its message to "Educate, donate, and celebrate because life is a celebration."[116] Resonating with the judges and Mother Ru, Ongina's message wins her the challenges, and as she is crowned, Ongina breaks down emotionally and confesses that she was "always so afraid to say it, that I have been living with HIV for the last 2 years of my life, and this means so much to me. I didn't want to say it on national TV because my parents don't know. You have to celebrate life. You have to keep going and I keep going."[117] Her vulnerability and sharing becomes a message of hope for people living with HIV/AIDS, a message of bravery in facing stigma, and a message of the resiliency of the LGBTQ+ communities in the face of serious epidemics. Mother Ru ends the episode reminding us that "we are all family. And if one of us is in pain, we are all in pain. We are all in trouble so let's be joyous so that we can all be joyous."[118] With these examples, we suggest that *RPDR* not only inherently creates knowledge about major health issues but also has transformative potential in the lives, health, and well-being of people, through its integration of critical pedagogy.

Currently, health education relies heavily on didactic forms of teaching and, historically, LGBTQ+ individuals have been pathologized medically within it.[119] This is slowly changing, but there remain gaps and tensions. For example, the Diagnostic and Statistical Manual of Mental Disorders (DSM) recently changed the term *gender identity disorder* to *gender dysphoria* in the attempt to reduce stigma for trans and gender diverse people. Others have argued that the term *gender dysphoria* is itself pathological, and that there is no need to medically classify gender diversity.[120] As previously mentioned, in Canada, men who have sex are banned from donating blood, meaning they must abstain from sex for three months before being allowed to donate blood. The three-month period is a recent change.[121] Prior to 2019, the period of abstaining for men who have sex with men was one year. In a survey of gay, bisexual, queer, and other men who have sex with men, it was found that most men thought this policy was unfair and needed to be updated.[122] It seems progress is still needed within health education, and *RPDR* might be able to provide some lessons for educators.

Many health and medical training programs do not adequately nor comprehensively address LGBTQ+ health issues in their curricula. For example, in undergraduate medical programs within the United States of

America and Canada, only an average of five hours is allotted for teaching LGBTQ+ content,[123] only an average of zero to three hours of LGBTQ+ content is provided in pharmacy curricula,[124] and in Canada, nutritional and dietetic training programs are overall lacking in LGBTQ+ content.[125] The absence of LGBTQ+ curriculum leads to health care professionals that have little understanding and confidence to work within LGBTQ+ communities. Numerous studies have found that health professionals, such as nurses,[126] doctors,[127] and social workers,[128] do not feel confident to adequately work with LGBTQ+ populations due to the lack of knowledge and training. The actual curricula of health programs need to be reevaluated and revamped to consider the needs of LGBTQ+ communities. Health curricula must recognize and fully teach their students about the social determinants of health that directly impact the health of LGBTQ+ individuals and their access to healthcare. A survey from Trans Pulse Canada[129] shows that 12 percent of trans and non-binary people in Canada avoid seeking emergency care despite their needs. Studies have shown that LGBTQ+ people often experience heteronormative and homophobic incidents in healthcare, ranging from verbal abuse, refusal to recognize partners, and unwanted physical contact.[130] Curricula that acknowledge these incidents and that equip medical and health professionals to understand and address health disparities in the LGBTQ+ communities is fundamental and similarly provide needed insight into the lived experiences of these communities.

The strategies of Mother Ru that we identified in our analysis of *RPDR* may be used within health education to address the gap in the training of LGBTQ+ culturally competent healthcare providers. Studies have shown that experiential learning strategies can improve the confidence of medical students to work with LGBTQ+ patients.[131] We suggest that health educators need to creatively include learning through dialogue, learning through vulnerability, and learning through reflection within their courses and programs. The integration of these strategies work on different levels to be transformative. For example, learning through dialogue may allow students to challenge and disrupt heteronormative discourses and binary notions of gender; while learning through vulnerability may provide students with opportunities to authentically learn about the divergent lives of LGBTQ+ people and their communities. Lastly, learning through introspection supports students in reflecting and discussing their biases, attitudes, beliefs, and behaviors towards LGBTQ+ individuals. We believe a Freirean approach to health education and the use of the pedagogical strategies of *RPDR* can help to reframe political, social, and cultural factors that shape the health of LGBTQ+ individuals. This may in turn lead to more positive improvements to the health inequalities faced by LGBTQ+ communities.

## Conclusion

Drag is not only art, glamour, and fantasy. It is also a pedagogical tool that can be used for political, social, and cultural transformation. Television is a critical site for pedagogy and learning about the forces that shape the identities and the experiences of people.[132] We suggest that *RPDR* unknowingly uses effective pedagogy and teaching methods to transform political, social, and cultural discourses that influence the lives and well-being of LGBTQ+ communities. Mother Ru and her competing queens, through workroom discussions, main challenges, and critical reflections, explore important structures of marginalization and hegemony that impact their personal lives and drag performance. In using three important pedagogical strategies—learning through dialogue, learning through vulnerability, and learning through reflection—Mother Ru brings awareness and engages in an educational praxis on the political and social structures that continue to discriminate and stigmatize LGBTQ+ people and create health inequalities for the LGBTQ+ communities. These strategies can be mirrored and utilized by health educators to train competent and confident healthcare professionals able to effectively work in our communities.

## Mini Challenge: Discussion Questions

- What are tangible ways that you can move from being a learner in your discipline to an agent of change in your discipline? What specific changes in social beliefs or stereotypes about the LGBTQ+ community could you address?
- How would you create learning environments and/or pedagogical spaces that support moments of vulnerability, deep reflection, and personal critique in your discipline, work, and/or personal life?
- Reflect upon your personal values, beliefs, and political principles towards the LGBTQ+ community. What are some examples of how these have informed or been enacted in your own teaching or curriculum development?

## Maxi Challenge: Activities and Assignments

- To embrace vulnerability in your teaching, one should regularly practice reflecting on and critiquing how your personal convictions and beliefs inform your own pedagogical practices, values, and

curriculum development. Examples of this may be through the use of pronouns, awareness of binary concepts of gender and sexuality and moments of intersectionality, and incorporating diverse voices in the course content and scholarly literature provided to students.
- Invite LGBTQ+ members into your classroom to speak to your students and engage in active learning that guides students in disrupting, critiquing, and critically reflecting on cultural, political, and social systems and norms within the discipline.
- Purposefully and thoughtfully build in and create safer spaces for students to engage in deep reflection and critical discourse of/on their own positionality and implicit biases.

## Notes

1. Huba, Jackie, & Stewart Kronbergs, Shelly. *Fiercely You: Be Fabulous and Confident by Thinking Like a Drag Queen*. Berrett-Koehler Publishers, 2016, p. 169.
2. Threshold concepts encourage an ontological shift in the learner that result in a new way of thinking, perceiving, or beliefs about the subject of inquiry. See Jan Meyer and Ray Land, *Threshold Concepts and Troublesome Knowledge: Linkages to Ways of Thinking and Practising within the Disciplines*, University of Edinburgh, Edinburgh, 2003.
3. Freire, Paulo. *Pedagogy of the Oppressed: New Revised 20th-Anniversary Edition*. The Continuum Publishing Company, 1993.
4. Whitworth, Colin. "Sissy That Performance Script! The Queer Pedagogy of RuPaul's Drag Race." *RuPaul's Drag Race and the Shifting Visibility of Drag Culture*, Springer, 2017, p. 148.
5. See Freire.
6. See Freire.
7. Mogford, Elizabeth et al. "Teaching Critical Health Literacy in the U.S. as a Means to Action on the Social Determinants of Health." *Health Promotion International*, vol. 26, no. 1, Oxford University Press, 2011, pp. 4–13.
8. "WHO | The Ottawa Charter for Health Promotion." *WHO*, World Health Organization. www.who.int, http://www.who.int/healthpromotion/conferences/previous/ottawa/en/. Accessed 12 Apr. 2020.
9. *Ibid.*; and Mogford et al.
10. Bagayogo, Fatou et al. "Co-Creation of Knowledge in Healthcare: A Study of Social Media Usage." *2014 47th Hawaii International Conference on System Sciences*, IEEE, 2014, pp. 626–635.
11. RuPaul. *GuRu*. Dey Street Books, 2018.
12. Organisation for Economic, and Co-operation and Development. *Society at a Glance 2019—OECD Social Indicators—En—OECD*. 2019, http://www.oecd.org/social/society-at-a-glance-19991290.htm.
13. *Ibid.*
14. McDonald, Michael David. *When the Government Apologizes: Understanding the Origins and Implications of the Apology to LGBTQ+2+ Communities in Canada*. 2019; and Smith, Miriam. "Homophobia and Homonationalism: LGBTQ+ Law Reform in Canada." *Social & Legal Studies*, vol. 29, no. 1, 2020, pp. 65–84.
15. See McDonald; see Smith.
16. See McDonald.
17. Crath, Rory, & Rangel, Cristian. "Paradoxes of an Assimilation Politics: Media Production of Gay Male Belonging in the Canadian 'Vital Public' from the Tainted Blood

Scandal to the Present." *Culture, Health & Sexuality*, vol. 19, no. 7, Taylor & Francis, 2017, pp. 796–810.

18. Epstein, Steven. "Sexualizing Governance and Medicalizing Identities: The Emergence Of State-Centered' LGBT Health Politics in the United States." *Sexualities*, vol. 6, no. 2, Sage Publications, 2003, pp. 131–171.

19. See Crath & Rangel.

20. de Vries, Elma et al. "Debate: Why Should Gender-Affirming Health Care Be Included in Health Science Curricula?" *BMC Medical Education*, vol. 20, no. 1, Springer, 2020, pp. 1–10.

21. Denny, Simon et al. "The Association between Supportive High School Environments and Depressive Symptoms and Suicidality among Sexual Minority Students." *Journal of Clinical Child & Adolescent Psychology*, vol. 45, no. 3, Taylor & Francis, 2016, pp. 248–261; Ferlatte, Olivier, et al. "Using Photovoice to Understand Suicidality among Gay, Bisexual, and Two-Spirit Men." *Archives of Sexual Behavior*, vol. 48, no. 5, Springer, 2019, pp. 1529–1541; Reisner, Sari L. et al. "Mental Health of Transgender Youth in Care at an Adolescent Urban Community Health Center: A Matched Retrospective Cohort Study." *Journal of Adolescent Health*, vol. 56, no. 3, Elsevier, 2015, pp. 274–279; Russell, Stephen T., & Fish, Jessica N. "Mental Health in Lesbian, Gay, Bisexual, and Transgender (LGBT) Youth." *Annual Review of Clinical Psychology*, vol. 12, Annual Reviews, 2016, pp. 465–487.

22. Connolly, Michael P., & Lynch, Kathleen. "Is Being Gay Bad for Your Health and Wellbeing? Cultural Issues Affecting Gay Men Accessing and Using Health Services in the Republic of Ireland." *Journal of Research in Nursing*, vol. 21, no. 3, May 2016, pp. 177–96. CrossRef, doi:10.1177/1744987115622807.

23. Massachusetts Commission on Lesbian, Gay, Bisexual, Transgender, Queer, and Questioning Youth. *Massachusetts High School Students and Sexual Orientation Results of the 2013 Youth Risk Behavior Survey*. 2013, http://www.mass.gov/cgly/YRBS13_FactsheetUpdated.pdf.

24. See Epstein.

25. Bennett, Jeffrey, & West, Isaac. "'United We Stand, Divided We Fall': AIDS, Armorettes, and the Tactical Repertoires of Drag." *Southern Communication Journal*, vol. 74, no. 3, Taylor & Francis, 2009, pp. 300–313.

26. See RuPaul.

27. See Freire.

28. *Ibid.*

29. *Ibid.*

30. *Ibid.*

31. Cahill, Caitlin. "The Personal Is Political: Developing New Subjectivities through Participatory Action Research." *Gender, Place and Culture*, vol. 14, no. 3, 2007, pp. 267–292.

32. Giroux, Henry A. "Teachers as Transformative Intellectuals." *Social Education*, vol. 49, no. 5. 1985, pp. 376–79.

33. hooks, bell. *Teaching to Transgress: Education as the Practice Of Freedom*. Routledge, 1994; Kumagai, Arno K., & Lypson, Monica L. "Beyond Cultural Competence: Critical Consciousness, Social Justice, and Multicultural Education." *Academic Medicine*, vol. 84, no. 6, 2009, pp. 782–787.

34. Yudelman, Julia. "The 'RuPaulitics' of Subjectification in RuPaul's Drag Race." *RuPaul's Drag Race and the Shifting Visibility of Drag Culture*, Springer, 2017, pp. 15–28.

35. See Freire; Snipes, Jeremy T., & LePeau, Lucy A. "Becoming a Scholar: A Duoethnography of Transformative Learning Spaces." *International Journal of Qualitative Studies in Education*, vol. 30, no. 6, Taylor & Francis, 2017, pp. 576–595.

36. Dewey, John. *How We Think. A Restatement of the Relation of Reflective Thinking to the Educative Process, Boston Etc. (DC Heath and Company) 1933*. 1933; Parsemain, Ava Laure. *The Pedagogy of Queer TV*. Springer, 2019.

37. Scott, Lindsay D. "Prisons, Pedagogy, and Possibilities: An Application of Freire and Hooks' Educational Philosophies." *Dialogues in Social Justice: An Adult Education Journal*, vol. 2, no. 2, 2017.

38. Brennan, Niall, & Gudelunas, David. *RuPaul's Drag Race and the Shifting Visibility of Drag Culture: The Boundaries of Reality TV*. Springer, 2017; see Parsemain.

39. Sega, Lauren. "The Philanthropy of Nina West—ColumbusUnderground.Com." *Columbus Underground*, 3 Oct. 2017, https://www.columbusunderground.com/the-philanthropy-of-nina-west-ls1.

40. "Frock the Vote!" *RuPaul's Drag Race*, season 4, episode 9, Logo TV, 30 Mar. 2012. *Amazon*, https://www.amazon.com/gp/video/detail/B007142CFE/ref=atv_dp_season_select_s4.

41. Ibid.

42. Ibid.

43. Kight, Stef W. "The Evolution of Trump's Muslim Ban." *Axios*, 2 Feb. 2020, https://www.axios.com/trump-muslim-travel-ban-immigration-6ce8554f-05bd-467b-b3c2-ea4876f7773a.html. Accessed 1 Jun. 2020.

44. See Kight.

45. "Choices 2020." *RuPaul's Drag Race*, season 12, episode 9, Logo TV, 24 Apr. 2020. *Amazon*, https://www.amazon.com/gp/video/detail/B08528GRKX/ref=atv_dp_season_select_s12.

46. Ibid.

47. Widdicombe, Lizzie. "Can "RuPaul's Drag Race" Save Us from Donald Trump?" *The New Yorker*, 4 Mar. 2020, https://www.newyorker.com/culture/culture-desk/can-rupauls-drag-race-save-us-from-donald-trump. Accessed 21 March 2020.

48. "Madonna: The Unauthorized Rusical." *Untucked*, season 12, episode 7, Logo TV. 12 Apr. 2020. *Amazon*, https://www.amazon.com/gp/video/detail/B0859PL9Z5/ref=atv_dp_season_select_s12

49. Ibid.

50. Maxouris, Christina. "Marsha P. Johnson, a [B]lack, transgender woman, was a central figure in the gay liberation movement." *CNN*, 26 June 2019. https://www.cnn.com/2019/06/26/us/marsha-p-johnson-biography/index.html. Accessed 4 June 2020.

51. "Float Your Boat." *RuPaul's Drag Race*, season 4, episode 6, Logo TV, 5 Mar. 2012. *Amazon*, https://www.amazon.com/gp/video/detail/B007142CFE/ref=atv_dp_season_select_s4.

52. Ibid.

53. "Trump: The Rusical." *RuPaul's Drag Race*, season 11, episode 4, Logo TV, 21 Mar. 2019, *Amazon*, https://www.amazon.com/gp/video/detail/B07P5GN25J/ref=atv_dp_season_select_s11.

54. Ibid.

55. Ibid.

56. See "WHO | The Ottawa Charter for Health Promotion."

57. See hooks.

58. See Brennan & Gudelunas, p. 3.

59. See hooks; Van Sluys, Katie et al. "Researching Critical Literacy: A Critical Study of Analysis of Classroom Discourse." *Journal of Literacy Research*, vol. 38, no. 2, SAGE Publications: Los Angeles, CA, 2006, pp. 197–233.

60. Fischman, Gustavo E., & McLaren, Peter. "Rethinking Critical Pedagogy and the Gramscian and Freirean Legacies: From Organic to Committed Intellectuals or Critical Pedagogy, Commitment, and Praxis." *Cultural Studies ↔ Critical Methodologies (CSCM)*, vol. 5, no. 4, SAGE Publications: Thousand Oaks, CA, 2005, p. 426.

61. RuPaul. *GuRu*.

62. Ibid.

63. Ibid.

64. "RuPaul Book Ball." *RuPaul's Drag Race*, season 8, episode 8, Logo TV, 25 Apr. 2016, *Amazon*, https://www.amazon.com/gp/video/detail/B01BZGNENC/ref=atv_dp_season_select_s8.

65. Ibid.

66. Ibid.

67. Ibid.

68. Ibid.

69. Ibid.

70. "Absolut Drag Ball." *RuPaul's Drag Race*, season 1, episode 6, Logo TV, 9

Mar. 2009. *Amazon*, https://www.amazon.com/gp/video/detail/B001RGOIWW/ref=atv_dp_season_select_s1.
   71. *Ibid.*
   72. See Scott.
   73. "Tap That App." *RuPaul's Drag Race*, season 10, episode 3, Logo TV, 5 Apr. 2018. *Amazon*, https://www.amazon.com/gp/video/detail/B07B68P55J/ref=atv_dp_season_select_s10.
   74. *Ibid.*
   75. *Ibid.*
   76. "Snatch Game." *RuPaul's Drag Race*, season 10, episode 7, Logo TV, 3 May 2018. *Amazon*, https://www.amazon.com/gp/video/detail/B07B68P55J/ref=atv_dp_season_select_s10.
   77. *Ibid.*
   78. *Ibid.*
   79. See Parsemain.
   80. hooks, p. 84.
   81. "Evil Twins." *RuPaul's Drag Race*, season 10, episode 11, Logo TV, 7 June 2018. *Amazon*, https://www.amazon.com/gp/video/detail/B07B68P55J/ref=atv_dp_season_select_s10.
   82. *Ibid.*
   83. *Ibid.*
   84. Molloy, Elizabeth, & Bearman, Margaret. "Learning Practices Embracing the Tension between Vulnerability and Credibility: 'Intellectual Candour' in Health Professions Education." *Medical Education*, vol. 53, iss. 1, 2019, pp. 32–41.
   85. "Evil Twins."
   86. *Ibid.*
   87. See Freire.
   88. "Evil Twins."
   89. *Ibid.*
   90. Mezirow, Jack. "Transformative Learning: Theory to Practice." *New Directions for Adult and Continuing Education*, vol. 1997, no. 74, Wiley Online Library, 1997, pp. 5–12.
   91. See hooks.
   92. Bullough, Robert V., Jr. "Teacher Vulnerability and Teachability: A Case Study of a Mentor and Two Interns." *Teacher Education Quarterly*, JSTOR, 2005, pp. 23–39.
   93. Vaughn, Lisa M., & Baker Raymond C. "Psychological Size and Distance: Emphasising the Interpersonal Relationship as a Pathway to Optimal Teaching and Learning Conditions." *Medical Education*, vol. 38, no. 10, Wiley Online Library, 2004, pp. 1053–1060.
   94. Rogers, Russell R. "Reflection in Higher Education: A Concept Analysis." *Innovative Higher Education*, vol. 26, no. 1, Springer, 2001, pp. 37–57.
   95. See Freire.
   96. See Dewey; see Rogers.
   97. "American." *RuPaul's Drag Race*, Season 10, episode 12, Logo TV, 14 June 2018. *Amazon*, https://www.amazon.com/gp/video/detail/B07B68P55J/ref=atv_dp_season_select_s10.
   98. See Freire.
   99. "The Realness." *RuPaul's Drag Race*, season 8 episode 9, Logo TV, 2 May 2016. *Amazon*, https://www.amazon.com/gp/video/detail/B01BZGNENC/ref=atv_dp_season_select_s8.
   100. *Ibid.*
   101. *Ibid.*
   102. "American." *RuPaul's Drag Race*, season 10, episode 12, Logo TV, 14 June 2018. *Amazon*, https://www.amazon.com/gp/video/detail/B07B68P55J/ref=atv_dp_season_select_s10.
   103. See RuPaul, *GuRu*.
   104. "RuPaul's Recipe for Success: Be Fabulous, Sing and Bring People Together (Guest Column)." *The Hollywood Reporter*, 15 June 2018, https://www.hollywoodreporter.com/news/rupaul-his-recipe-success-guest-column-1119261.
   105. Strings, Sabrina, & Bui, Long T. "'She Is Not Acting, She Is' The Conflict between Gender and Racial Realness on RuPaul's Drag Race." *Feminist Media Studies*, vol. 14, no. 5, Taylor & Francis, 2014, pp. 822–836.
   106. See Yudelman; Edgar, Eir-Anne. "Xtravaganza!": Drag Representation and

Articulation in "RuPaul's Drag Race." *Studies in Popular Culture*, vol. 34, no. 1, JSTOR, 2011, pp. 133–146.

107. Brown, Alexis. "Being and Performance in RuPaul's Drag Race." *Critical Quarterly*, vol. 60, no. 4, 2018, pp. 62–73.

108. See RuPaul, *GuRu*.

109. See Brown.

110. *Ibid.*, p. 65.

111. RuPaul, "Each morning I pray to set aside everything I THINK I know, so I may have an open mind and a new experience. I understand and regret the hurt I have caused. The trans community are heroes of our shared LGBTQ movement. You are my teachers," 5 Mar. 2018, 3:57 pm. Tweet.

112. See Brown.

113. "MAC/Viva Glam Challenge." *RuPaul's Drag Race*, season 1, episode 4, Logo TV, 23 Feb. 2009. *Amazon*, https://www.amazon.com/gp/video/detail/B001RGOIWW/ref=atv_dp_season_select_s1. For more information about this product, you can go to their website: https://www.maccosmetics.ca/product/13854/966/products/makeup/lips/lipstick/viva-glam-lipstick?gclid=CjwKCAjwzMeFBhBwEiwAzwS8zFok7gacd2ih8HwqqbW6oYK4pQli yFTzCV5gqRrzsrU1WjxzDJ-cyRoCC4kQAvD_BwE&gclsrc=aw.ds#!/shade/Viva_Glam_I.

114. See "MAC/Viva Glam Challenge."

115. *Ibid.*

116. *Ibid.*

117. *Ibid.*

118. *Ibid.*

119. DasGupta, S., Fornari, A., Geer, K., et al. "Medical education for social justice: Paulo Freire revisited." *Journal of Medical Humanities*, vol. 27, no. 4, Springer, 2006, pp. 245–251.

120. See de Vries et al.

121. Grace, D., Gaspar, M., Lessard, D., et al. "Gay and bisexual men's views on reforming blood donation policy in Canada: a qualitative study." *BMC Public Health*, vo. 19, no. 1, Springer, 2019, p. 772.

122. *Ibid.*

123. Lim, F., Brown, D.V., and Jones, H. "Lesbian, gay, bisexual, and transgender health: fundamentals for nursing education." *Journal of Nursing Education*, vol. 52, no. 4, 2013, pp. 198–203.

124. Llayton, C.K., & Caldas, L.M. "Strategies for inclusion of lesbian, gay, bisexual, transgender, queer, intersex, and asexual (LGBTQIA+) education throughout pharmacy school curricula." *Pharmacy Practice*, 2013, pp. 1862–1862.

125. Joy, Phillip, & Numer, Matthew. "Queering educational practices in dietetics training: A critical review of LGBTQ inclusion strategies." *Canadian Journal of Dietetic Practice and Research*, vol. 79, no. 1, 2018, pp. 1–6.

126. Stewart, Kate, & O'Reilly, Pauline. "Exploring the Attitudes, Knowledge and Beliefs of Nurses and Midwives of the Healthcare Needs of the LGBTQ+ Population: An Integrative Review." *Nurse Education Today*, vol. 53, Elsevier, 2017, pp. 67–77.

127. Parameshwaran, Vishnu, et al. "Is the Lack of Specific Lesbian, Gay, Bisexual, Transgender and Queer/Questioning (LGBTQ+) Health Care Education in Medical School a Cause for Concern? Evidence from a Survey of Knowledge and Practice among UK Medical Students." *Journal of Homosexuality*, vol. 64, no. 3, Taylor & Francis, 2017, pp. 367–381.

128. Craig, Shelley L., et al. "Educational Determinants of Readiness to Practise with LGBTQ+ Clients: Social Work Students Speak Out." *The British Journal of Social Work*, vol. 46, no. 1, British Association of Social Workers, 2014, pp. 115–134.

129. Report—Health and health care access for trans and non-binary people in Canada—Trans PULSE Canada, n.d.

130. See Craig et al.

131. Morris, Matthew, et al. "Training to Reduce LGBTQ+-Related Bias among Medical, Nursing, and Dental Students and Providers: A Systematic Review." *BMC Medical Education*, vol. 19, no. 1, Springer, 2019, p. 325.

132. See hooks; see Whitworth.

# "And where is the body?"

## Naked Drag and the Social Construction of Anatomy as Sexed and Gendered[1]

### Tommy Mayberry

In an episode of the third season (2011) of *RuPaul's Drag Race* (*RPDR*), RuPaul has the competing queens participate in a mini challenge photoshoot ... naked! In this episode (titled, "Face, Face, Face of Cakes"), RuPaul sets up the mini challenge by declaring,

> Now a drag superstar needs to be able to serve *womana* even when she's stripped of her wigs and padding and things of that nature. Now I posed [nude] for a photograph in my book *Workin' it!* and I did it without compromising my Christianity. I found the experience so liberating, I wanted to share it with you. Now for today's mini challenge, you'll be posing for a tasteful, intimate, feminine portrait, and you'll be doing it in the nude.[2]

While the queens are allowed "light makeup," as RuPaul establishes, as well as the artistic crutch of "a piece of fabric that [they could] use a little," as photographer Deborah Anderson, renowned for her artful nude portraits, directs them, the competing queens of season 3 are posing as their drag personae with nothing else on to aid in their respective transformations.[3] This is the first time that *RPDR* enters into a discussion of just what a drag body is and/or can be—especially/including when, as RuPaul says, "she's stripped of her wigs and padding and things of that nature." These discussions of what a drag body is and/or can be are not the forefront cruxes of what makes the show *werk*, but they are, absolutely and undeniably, essential to its narrative and success with viewers—indeed, one of the most iconically unprecedented things about *RPDR* is that it shows and showcases the transformations happening backstage in the workroom, which is a glimpse into the world of drag not often or even usually seen. And other than those visual moments we as viewers of the show see, there is not much discussion heard aurally around drag bodies and their construction and constitution. If we listen carefully, though, and analyze the language and devices used across the seasons, we can locate a script, a lesson plan, for teaching us just what a drag body is and can be. And the outcome of this lesson comes from the oxymoronic concept of "naked drag" that has the potential to shift the paradigm of understandings of human anatomy.

The naked drag body, as RuPaul and *RPDR* show and tell us, allows us to see and to know that gender and sex for our human bodies are both social constructs, right at the level of our very anatomy. And *RPDR* has the power to do this, and to begin effecting change, because of its power not just as a cultural platform but as a pedagogical platform as well. Anna Hickey-Moody, Glenn C. Savage, and Joel Windle, in their article, "Pedagogy Writ Large: Public, Popular and Cultural Pedagogies in Motion," write that "[Henry] Giroux's development of the term public pedagogy is based in his foundational view that culture *can* and *does* operate in pedagogical ways."[4] Giroux himself says that popular media is "a powerful form of public pedagogy,"[5] and Jennifer A. Sandlin, Michael P. O'Malley, and Jake Burdick, in their study on mapping the complexities of public pedagogy across over a hundred years of public pedagogy scholarship, add to Giroux that other "informal education sites" and "extrainstitutional spaces and discourses" are part and parcel of the power of public pedagogy, too.[6] *RPDR*, then, as popular media in an extrainstitutional space engendering extrainstitutional discourses and that thrives in the social construction of knowledge, values, and experiences through performative practices embodied in lived interactions, absolutely is publicly pedagogical.

This essay takes us through three key lessons (or, "RuPrimers," as I call them) across the mothership of *RPDR* that together teach us that anatomy is not destiny and that anatomy as sexed and gendered is a social construct. First, I set up discussions of naked drag in the show and what it means to be naked in/as drag before moving to the design and construction of the drag body with definitions of clothing and particular foci on footwear, underwear, and hair. Finally, we look at rhetoric and anatomy together, specifically via the figure of the antimetabole, to locate drag/trans- embodiment and to see it ultimately as human embodiment.

## *RuPrimer 1: Drag Bodies Before the Clothes*

"Jesus, take the wheel," Alexis Mateo exclaims when RuPaul issues the naked photoshoot challenge in season 3: "I have been single for a reason, and now America is going to find out why."[7] Stacy Layne Matthews even shouts in her talking head interview, "Are you fucking serious? My fat ass has got to take off these clothes? Y'all bitches is crazy!" before, mere moments in the episode later when she meets Anderson, blurting out, "Let's get naked!" as she throws her covering robe aside.[8] "All of a sudden," Stacy says, "I had this spiritual awakening that happened to me, and I fell into it."[9] Not every queen, though, was as quick as Stacy to fall into it, nor as keen to understand themselves as coming out the other side of their naked drag photoshoot as spiritually awakened. Delta Work's "heart just dropped" when RuPaul issued the mini challenge: "You know," she discloses, "I don't even like to have sex naked."[10] Delta is one of season 3's proud and fabulous plus-size queens (or "big girls," as Delta says of herself in the first episode of the season[11]), and she further shares that she felt incredibly afraid and that "all I can think is that this lady's [Deborah Anderson's] gonna freaking laugh at me."[12] But, after RuPaul offers her the piece of fabric and Delta says, "I want to use every yard of it," Delta, too, gets into it; so much so, in fact, that she doesn't realize when her time is up and the photoshoot is over: "Darling, we are done," Anderson says, "Oh? Cool!" replies Delta, visibly snapping out of her comfortable, and confident, reverie.[13] "My biggest fear was met today. I met it head on. I felt so liberated, I would love to do it again," Delta says.[14] RuPaul even jokes as Delta readies to leave the shoot, "We won't be able to get you to put clothes on anymore," and Delta agrees: "No, I don't think so. Carmen Carrera better watch out!"[15]

Carmen Carrera, of course, is no stranger to nakedness (whether it be artful nakedness, just plain nakedness, and/or even drag/trans- nakedness!): not only does she set the stage for who and how she is in her drag/trans- body by "runnin' around the dressing room all day completely naked. Just naked," as Shangela says of her in the first episode of season three,[16] but other queens, obviously, can't help but notice and take note either. "Carmen, you always naked," Venus D–Lite says,[17] and Alexis Mateo simply states, "Miss Carmen, you gotta be naked."[18] In Carmen's talking head interview, apparently asked about her nakedness and the other queens' comments on it, she says, "Girl, I don't even see it as naked. I don't know what these queens are talkin' about. I'm sorry, you know, I feel comfortable with my body."[19] And yes, absolutely she does: Carmen wins the naked photoshoot mini-challenge in the "Face, Face, Face of Cakes" episode, and she also continues past her time as a naked drag queen going about the workroom on season 3 to display her own naked trans-beauty in her Adam and Eve Life Ball posters with David LaChapelle in 2014—another naked photoshoot.

Four seasons of *RPDR* later in season 7 (2015), the premiere main stage runway challenge itself is absolutely naked drag, fittingly titled, "Born Naked."[20] RuPaul establishes this challenge by saying, "[F]or the first time in *Drag Race* herstory, you'll be making your mainstage debut ... naked.

And afraid! You need to create a resort wear look that tears away to reveal a nude illusion. Because you were what? Hashtag-Born-Naked and the rest is drag."[21] Those two words—*born* and *naked*—together have become a sloganic synecdoche of RuPaul's entire legacy, empire, and philosophy, very similar to Lady Gaga's use and branding of the phrase "born this way" for her legacy, empire, and philosophy: Not only does RuPaul have an album with an eponymous song and single, too, but the saying operates as the crux of his entire outlook from its first appearance in his autobiography/style guide *Workin' It!* (2010) when he wrote, "You're born naked and the rest is drag"[22] through season 7's cornerstone establishment of it (2015) and into (if not even more so) today. "I don't differentiate drag from dressing up or dressing down," RuPaul continues to write, "Whatever you put on after you get out of the shower is your drag."[23]

Canadian poet and novelist Daphne Marlatt seems to think so as well, for she discusses the speciousness of that little word *up* in her 1990 essay "Self-Representation and Fictionalysis" when she writes, "Children learn that dressing themselves is an achievement but dressing up is only play, child's play as they say of something easy. Yet as children we know that play is not only easy, it is also absorbing and immensely serious, that play is the actual practice (not factual but act-ual) of who else we might be."[24] "A powerful put-down, that word 'up,'" she says, "Does it imply we're trying to imitate the gods and have no business reaching a notch higher on the scale of creation, especially when it comes to creating ourselves?"[25] RuPaul's idea of "born naked," with the rest being drag, is absolutely about reaching for that higher notch on the scale of creation, as Marlatt wonders, because this philosophy for RuPaul appears to be adapted from twentieth-century French Spiritualism and Christian Philosophy—both RuPaul, in his 2010 book, and Oprah, in her 2018 podcast interview, link the idea of being "born naked and the rest is [just] drag" to the famous antimetabole, "We are not human beings having a spiritual experience; we are spiritual beings having a human experience" (popularly and culturally attributed to the Rev. Pierre Teilhard de Chardin, although historically of unknown/disputed origin). The specific quotation I give here I quote from Oprah in her podcast interview with RuPaul, "RuPaul Charles: We're All In Drag," that she says is her "favorite quote [by] Pierre Teilhard de Chardin."[26] What RuPaul says in *Workin' It!* is not actually a quotation or reference to anyone; he uses the sense of it as a framework to surround his quotation, "You're born naked and the rest is drag": "The truth is you are a spiritual being having a human experience"[27] and "We take on roles that become our identity … we believe we literally are the characters we are portraying, forgetting who we really are—spiritual beings having human experiences."[28]

Regardless of its origins, however, the sentiment rings true for RuPaul and his teaching about the human body before clothes/drag—as RuPaul sings in his song "Born Naked":

> Who do you think you are?
> I'm *telling the truth* now
> We're all born naked
> And the rest is drag.[29]

This entire conversation and philosophy can be seen as part of RuPaul's pedagogic motivation behind tasking the season 3 queens with their nude photoshoot in the "Face, Face, Face of Cakes" episode to share his liberating experience with them of being fully at home in their bodies—and of, in a deeper layer, "not compromising my Christianity" in the naked birthfulness that is RuPaul's spiritual truth based in his own, and queens' own, interpretation and embodiment of Christian philosophy. What RuPaul is starting to teach his queens here—and, by extension, starting to teach viewers of *RPDR*, is the sociality imbued in human bodies and human embodiment. And, even more so, a sociality of nakedness.

In season 7 in "the first ever naked runway," as RuPaul calls it, the queens are, though, not actually *sans* clothing like the season 3 queens were for their nude shoot with Deborah Anderson, like Carmen Carrerra was for much of the workroom readying but never (fully) for the main stage runways, nor even like the models are at the end of Robert Altman's 1994 satirical film *Prêt-à-Porter* set during Paris Fashion Week in the *real* first ever naked runway just over two decades before RuPaul hosts his own.[30] Instead of being *naked* naked, the season 7 queens are serving nude illusion in the wearing of clothing that needs to *appear* naked. (The models in *Prêt-à-Porter* had not even a shred of fabric or covering on them—they were walking the runway categorically, undeniably, and literally naked.) To heighten the realness of RuPaul's naked runway and push it (however campily) toward categorical, undeniable, and literal naked, the queens' runway footage is campily edited with blurring censored effects no matter the skill or depth of the "nude illusion": for examples, competing queen Katya is wearing boots, a wig, and hat, with her male-coded body's nipples showing, which are clearly identifiable though blurred out, and other queens, such as Trixie Mattel, Pearl, and Max, are wearing flesh-colored body suits, shapewear, and underwear, while queen Jaidynn Diore Fierce is wearing flesh-colored heels. Competing queen Violet Chachki (winner of both this first challenge and of the entire seventh season) says of her nude illusion runway look in this episode, "I feel great. I love being naked. I love my body. I'm comfortable with just a piece of duct tape on and a smile."[31] She is not lying when she says "just a piece of duct tape on," for the entire illusionistic appeal of Violet's nude illusion look resides solely in that piece of duct tape: her look is almost entirely her own naked male-coded body with a duct tape tuck, black heels, and a black wig; she did not use any makeup to sculpt the illusion of breasts on her chest, nor did she pad, stuff, or corset/cinch her frame. (Violet's male-coded body's nipples were, of course, campily censored in alignment with the overall theme of these fourteen new queens pummeling the runway scandalously *sans* clothing.)

Violet Chachki's naked body here is absolutely a naked drag body because of that duct tape tuck and the calculated decision to wear that duct tape as clothing—and nothing else but "a smile." The naked runway challenge of season 7 in tandem with the naked photoshoot mini challenge of season 3 institute a kind of curricular approach to establishing the way that RuPaul and *RPDR* teach their viewers about the drag body. While the mini-challenge nude photoshoot with Deborah Anderson was a serious project with learning outcomes for the queens around liberating themselves and becoming closer to themselves as themselves, the naked runway opening maxi-challenge was campy, playful, at times downright absurd, and not decidedly pedagogical. Yet together, we start to see in and across *RPDR* how bodies take on meaning and how they do this overarchingly through both clothing and lack thereof.

## RuPrimer 2: Drag Bodies as Wigs, Heels, and Undergarments

Specific moments of *RPDR* runways and challenges aside, there is an overarching theme in the trajectory of the show that suggests quite strongly that there is a look, an aesthetic, a design/construct to the body of a drag queen under her clothes, that reveals what a drag queen would really look like naked. In the seemingly perpetually-dreaded sewing challenges on *RPDR*, the ones for which the competing queens must create their entire runway looks from clothing and materials provided by a fabric merchant, a thrift store, the dollar store, or once even the dumpster,[32] RuPaul always states the rules of the challenge are that they must build their looks from the provided materials but that "you can wear your own wigs, heels, and undergarments."[33] These three items of (almost) every drag queen's drag bag—and I say *almost* here because some queens have made icons of themselves by decidedly not wearing wigs in their drag: season 9 winner Sasha Velour self-brands her look as "crazy bald club kid,"[34] and season 1 fan-favorite and *All Stars* season 5 returning queen Ongina "do[esn't] usually wear wigs"[35]—are what RuPaul grants the queens access to from their respective wardrobes for the building, sculpting, and maintaining of their own unique drag performances. Their own unique bodies that they have come to know and understand as the space between their naked male-coded bodies and their clothed female-coded bodies.[36] Their naked drag bodies. And these three categories of items together become an implicit instruction by RuPaul to the competing queens and to the viewing audiences of what we have learned is a constructed human body.

The line demarcating what clothes are, though, is debatable even outside the drag/trans- contexts. And perhaps it is more a continuum of nakedness than a definite line between clothing and nakedness—i.e., having no clothes on at all could mean being in your undies or in a state of undress not traditionally suitable for public viewing (such as a housecoat or pajamas), and not everyone would consider duct tape clothing. Nevertheless, the word *clothing* has impressively not changed its definitional meaning since it was first used, according to the *Oxford English Dictionary* (*OED*), around the 1200s when it meant "[t]he action of covering or providing with clothes; dressing" (*n.* 1.a.) as well as simply, "Clothes collectively, apparel, dress" (*n.* 2.a.). As an adjective, the *OED* cites *clothing* as meaning "That clothes, investing, enveloping," and it dates it to 1483 in its first use. *Clothes* as a noun is "Covering for the person; wearing apparel; dress, raiment, vesture" (*n.* 1.a.), and *apparel*, of course, is one's "Personal outfit or attire" (*n.* 5) with the definitions for *dress, raiment,* and *vesture* being essentially synonymous, according to the *OED*. So clothes, clothing, and even/especially having clothes *on*, in the definitional context, *would* include undies, housecoats, and pajamas (even if not suitable for public viewing) and, yes, duct tape (a something that is "covering" and "that clothes") as one's "[p]ersonal outfit or attire." That space between a drag queen's naked male-coded body and their clothed female-coded body, then, is a liminal space, and it is a liminal space that I am arguing is constitutive of the *naked* drag body. A *body* crafted from wigs, heels, and undergarments, as RuPaul first established and continues to establish across his platforms. And we can see parallels to this naked drag aesthetic with transgender (specifically transsexual) individuals who do not identify as part of the drag community through the "variety of technologies" that they use, as Trish Salah discusses in her entries in Lorraine Code's *Encyclopedia of Feminist Theories* (2000),[37] to bring their bodies into congruity with their selves.[38] A naked trans-body of course exists—Carmen Carrera shows hers off in The Life Ball posters, and transgender woman, actress, and activist Laverne Cox, for a perhaps more popular example, proudly shows off hers (in episode three "Lesbian Request Denied" of Netflix's series *Orange Is the New Black*) which exists through implants, surgeries, and/or wigs, weaves, and hair technologies.[39]

Undergarments for drag queens can be very elaborate and constructive of the culturally feminine—such as corsets, stuffed and/or push-up bras, Spanx™ or similar non-brand shapewear, and/or even (for the more industrious and perhaps "old school"–inspired queen) duct tape—or they can be very simple and so-called "naturally feminine"—such as (tucking) panties, pantyhose, and a bra, the latter two of which are really more just lower-level torture devices than corsets and duct tape, and the former of which are neither natural nor universal.[40] Undergarments, too, can also be an entire (drag) wardrobe. Raven, for example, in the finale of *All Stars* season 1, wears a classy, yet sexy, black bra, black panties, and black heels with a black lace-fringed mesh night shawl over her shoulders, and Extra Special Guest Judge Cheri Oteri wants to call her look "Donatella-You-A-Bedtime-Story Versace" with Raven herself saying of her boudoir look that it is "quintessential Raven."[41] Naomi Smalls (runner-up of season 8 and returning queen on *All Stars* season 4) wears for her Madonna-inspired look on season 8 a red bra with red panties unashamedly showing underneath an airy red kimono-like shawl. This is, as Naomi Smalls calls it, her "Kimono Madonna" look.[42] Extra Special Guest Judge Gigi Hadid calls it "the Victoria's Secret section of Madonna," punning on this idea of underwear and lingerie.[43] In these instances of drag queen clothing and performance, the body shown is either simultaneously clothed *and* naked (if we subscribe to my idea, through RuPaul's implicit idea, of what constitutes a naked drag body—i.e., wigs, heels, undergarments) or it is a naked male-coded body clothed in drag to give the illusion of a naked female-coded body that is not really there underneath, for the "underneath" is the naked man-coded body itself again.[44] Although, to be sure, even if the only clothing that a Victoria's Secret™-clad drag queen is wearing is the lingerie, there still perhaps would be tucking and maybe even stuffing/padding to accentuate further the female-coded body sculpted out of the male-coded body—accentuating further, or as Jack Halberstam might say, *editing* some part of the gender that currently defines the body.[45]

Heels are similar to undergarments in this instance, too, for they are absolutely a clothing item in being footwear, a something that is put on to cover, protect, embellish, and even adorn—as the *OED* defines *raiment* as importantly encompassing in being "an article of clothing *or adornment*" (*n.* 2—emphasis added). High heels themselves also serve a practical and embodied function: that of increasing height and of supporting posture. But heels also radically alter the way the body holds itself and are a body-morphing technology that has the power to change the very shape of the body that stands on them—visually, as we see with the synecdochic shoe in the 1995 film *To Wong Foo, Thanks for Everything! Julie Newmar*[46] and, yes, physically. Posture becomes focused, muscles tighten, height is added, and chests puff out. Elizabeth Semmelhack in her *Heights of Fashion* (2008) states that "the high heel [i]s essential to the … hourglass figure…[b]y reconfiguring the stance of the body and emphasizing the breasts and buttocks,"[47] and she specifically illustrates this with the example of Marilyn Monroe whose "hourglass figure is enhanced by her corset and high heels."[48] Every queen has differently and uniquely sized and shaped feet—and while RuPaul expects his queens to at least know their way around a needle (if not be straight up seamstresses themselves), he does not expect them to cobble a shoe. Heels for RuPaul are a necessary piece of the drag body *qua* drag body. Perhaps this is why drag queens read each other so fiercely when they remove their shoes before a Lip Sync for Your Life: removing your heels pushes your body back toward male-coded and away from female-coded. In the second episode of the fourth season of *RPDR* (2012), competing queen Lashauwn Beyond immediately kicks off her heels after RuPaul announces the start of the lip-sync, and the camera actually rests for a moment on RuPaul glancing downward at Lashauwn's feet with an unimpressed look of disdain on her face just as the music begins. Fellow competing queen Willam even shadily comments, "To do the whole song with no shoes, in close-toed pantyhose, like a web-footed duck…. Lashauwn's drag mother is going to read him for not even starting the song in shoes."[49] (Notice, too, Willam's use of the male-gendered pronoun "him" here while speaking about Lashauwn.)

2016's eighth season of *RPDR* sees this footwear-*faux-pas* taken to whole new levels when competing queen Laila McQueen strolls into the workroom for the very first time wearing flats instead of heels. Upon seeing them, fellow queen Thorgy Thor ironically comments to Laila, "These are a smart idea," and in a talking head interview, fellow queen Robbie Turner jokes, "I'm going to tell you a story about flats…. NO!"[50] Taking the shade even further in person with Laila, Thorgy continues her read on the flats through an extended pun of the *race* in "Drag Race" to say (mock-painfully falling down), "Fourteen hours from now, we're all like 'UNGH!'" and Bob the Drag Queen brings home the punchline by finishing (and mock-sprinting), "And she's [Laila's] like, 'Skechers, it's the end!'"[51] If taking your shoes off to perform pushes the drag queen body back toward male-coded and away from female-coded, then performing in flats rather than heels has a similar, albeit more pronounced and even detrimental, effect—i.e., the flats foreclose the full transformation and/or illusion, just as removing the heels fissures the full transformation and/or illusion. Not having/wearing heels is too boy-ish, and RuPaul specifically instructs to "[n]ever wear men's attire while in drag … sneakers, or flats,"[52] and she explicitly teaches in her "Ru-dimentary Suggestions" for drag, "Don't ever take your heels off in public and walk around barefoot while carrying them."[53] "Quite frankly," she spells out, "it makes you look trashy."[54] While heels would be there in the pile on the floor for sure when all the clothing comes off,[55] they would stay on to be naked in drag before (re)turning to the floor pile to be naked out of drag. Moreover, they would *have* to stay on to be naked in drag.

Wigs, obviously, have the same function from toe to tits-and-head for transforming the male-coded body into the female-coded body, for they add that supernatural dimension to the head and frame the face. RuPaul, to be sure, has ideas and dictums on hair and gender as well. RuPaul also interestingly outlines, similar to his *Ru-dimentary* suggestion on sustainable footwear, that queens should "[n]ever wear [their] own hair."[56] This suggests rather strongly that having hair is more feminine that masculine. Of course, the man-bun to man-braid to merman hairstyles of 2015–16 would beg to differ, and so would drag/trans- individuals such as Ongina and Sasha Velour who prefer a wigless aesthetic over a culturally sanctioned one. The judges on *RPDR* do criticize Ongina for her wigless aesthetic by noting that it comes at the cost of the illusion of femininity: RuPaul says in the very first judges' critique, "I was very impressed [with your performance], although when I see you, I still see a little boy; I would love to see more of a little lady,"[57] and celebrity photographer and guest judge for the episode Mike Ruiz notes during the judges' deliberation, "I have to say, I see a little boy. It's not an illusion to me."[58] In the subsequent episode, "Girl Group Challenge," Ongina does powerfully state in her talking head interview that "last week, the judges told me that I look like a boy in a dress, and I wanted to elevate that this week to not so much boy in a dress but drag queen in a dress."[59] At the close of the season, when looking back on it in review, the judges did have some kinder and more celebratory things to say of Ongina's wigless aesthetic: Merle Ginsberg ultimately says, "I really loved that she was giving us head, if you will. She worked the head piece and the hat and the little veils."[60] Almost a decade later, we see season 9's winner Sasha Velour take the wigless aesthetic not just to an iconic level but to an indexical level as well: upon entering the workroom in season 9's first episode, she tells us, "I am a bald, fashiony, artistic, weird queen" as she tells her fellow competitors, "I'm a visual artist. I love telling stories with art and with drag."[61] And it is not until the seventh episode of her season that we find out exactly which story she is telling with her artistic bald drag. When the workroom conversation prior to hitting the main stage turns to the queens' experiences with high school, high school traumas, and then to loved ones and battling terminal illnesses, Sasha shares, "Right after I graduated from college, my mom was diagnosed with cancer. Chemo made her lose all of her hair."[62] "That's why I'm a bald queen. When she lost her hair, she felt she couldn't be beautiful," Sasha says, and she continues, "I am a bald queen to represent for my mother. Taking all of that and turning that into drag in my own way was the most important thing I've ever done in my life."[63] So while certain queens like Ongina might take to baldness out of preference or for decidedly androgynous looks and forego the gender blurring aid of hair for other "blurring" technologies (such as hats, hoods, and veils) that metonymically stand in for hair to frame their genders in their drag identities, other queens like Sasha become their entire gendered identities without wigs at all.

RuPaul herself, however, embodies and lives this *hair/no hair* dictum by maintaining his brand of "hair today, gone tomorrow"[64] across gender as *bald with glasses* out of drag and two wigs and contact lens *in* drag.[65] Edgier iconic queens such as season 1 and *All Stars* season 1's Nina Flowers and season 8's Acid Betty strut a fine line between the wig/no wig, hair/no hair camps by showing scalp at the same time as gluing-down hair, but in very non-traditionally natural ways. Nina Flowers proudly states, "I don't consider myself as a female impersonator. I like to be more androgynous. It's an extravaganza," but she does voice that "I'm pretty sure that some people are not very comfortable about the kind of drag that I do, but that is exactly what makes me stand out: that I'm different."[66] On her fierce runway looks, judge Santino Rice comments, "It's got like that real aggression, and a real twisted beauty about it," and RuPaul, too, does critically note that "Your image is so strong, I'd love to see a softer side of Miss Flowers. I'd love to see the flower."[67] At the close of the season, however, when looking back on it in review, the judges had nothing but awed reverence for what Nina brings to drag: Rice boldly states, "Nina wasn't going for something that was natural and subtle. She wanted to just really exude this like punk energy,"[68] and RuPaul herself, says, "Each week was like a new episode of *It Came from Planet Nina*, and I love-love-loved it!"[69] With Acid Betty, similar to Nina Flowers, she knows she is different and that some people may not understand and/or be comfortable with the type of drag she does. Upon first walking into the workroom in season 8 (2016) and showing nearly full scalp with an outrageous blue acid-washed wave of hair glued to the top of it, Acid Betty declares in what sounds like her signature disclaimer, "No need to adjust your TV sets: this acid trip is all real."[70] "My drag style is completely over-the-top," Acid Betty says of herself: "Basically, a drug trip without the drugs."[71] If long hair might blur gender in drag/trans- performativity, *no hair* might actually do blurring one better: no hair might *erase* gender.[72] For queens such as Acid Betty, Nina Flowers, Sasha Velour, and Ongina, who have perhaps non-coherent drag queen identities within mainstream cultural understandings of drag, their drag might be more posthuman and postgender in not strictly being "female impersonation" but in being more of a neo- "gender fuck" drag aesthetic that can push drag past what it is (or was). RuPaul was first starting out in the early 1980s, and she notes that "[m]y drag look back then was 'gender f@&k'—more of a social statement than female impersonation. Smeared lipstick, tattered prom dress, and combat boots…. The look suited the anti–Reagan sensibility of the time and gave me satirical edginess."[73] With contemporary drag queens who push and challenge the boundaries of drag in their art, I see their drag as still drag and them as still drag queens, but their work is less "female impersonation" and more, as RuPaul says of his early work, "a non-conformist statement about the superficiality of our consumer society."[74]

Cosplay queens such as Phi Phi O'Hara (from season 4 and *All Stars* season 2) are another example of a non-coherent interpretation of drag that is not preoccupied with female Realness but with social commentary. For Sasha Velour specifically—who tells us, "My drag name is my actual name, Sasha. That was the name I was born with, and my whole life, I've had people tell me that it's a girl's name, so the logical conclusion is to just become a girl"[75]—drag is "the artform of the queer imagination" and is "all about beauty that *goes beyond gender*."[76] So when RuPaul asks Sasha, moments before crowning her "America's Next Drag Superstar" in the Grand Finale of season 9, "Now Sasha, I've heard you talk before about how your late mother inspired your drag, what do you think she'd say if she were here tonight?,"[77] Sasha's decidedly gendered response is important and telling: "I think she would be so proud of me," Sasha says, "for going from a little boy who wore dresses in the living room to a little boy who wore dresses on this grand platform."[78] Sasha Velour (MFA holder and Fulbright Scholar) is that little boy with a girl's name all grown up and embodying the queer imagination that is drag in a mainstream cultural moment when the seams of gender, and of drag as simply *female impersonation*, are coming undone.

While the drag identity may be non-coherent, for the looks to work (whether femme chic, acid trip, or anime), they must be polished and maintained. Just as with removing your shoes to "lip-sync for your life," queens snatching off their wigs on stage is a massive no-no.[79] Of course, there will always be *someone* to bend, blend, and circumvent the "rules," and for drag and wigs with wig-snatching, it is season 5 and *All Stars* season 2's queen Roxxxy Andrews. In her "Lip-Sync for Your Life" battle on the seventh episode of season 5 (titled "RuPaul Roast"), which aired March 11, 2013, Roxxxy removed her wig in an epic stunt—no doubt to shock the judges due to Shannel's wig accident that started a "Lip-Sync for Your Life" trend[80]—only to reveal another wig underneath! The morning of the day that the "RuPaul Roast" episode aired, RuPaul took to Twitter at 9:03 a.m. to instruct casually as drag mother to us all that "[w]hen 'performing' on stage, in the bedroom or in the backseat of a trick's car, never remove your wig or high heels." The morning *after* the "RuPaul Roast" episode, at 11:27 a.m. on March 12, 2013, she Tweeted, "AMENDED: Never remove your wig while performing, unless you're wearing another wig underneath." This moment has become a meme in the culture of *RPDR*, and we see it pop back onto the radar of the Twitterverse whenever we need a good reminding—either for fun and a throwback to brighten our day[81] or to shadily, and passive-aggressively, put queens in their places.[82] Roxxxy herself also revisited and revamped this drag/trans- trope that she largely seems to have authored in her talent show performance on the first episode of the second season of *RPDR All Stars* (2016) where she transformed it yet again in treating her top-most wig as a metaphorical item of clothing by definition (recall the *OED* here) as part of her burlesque strip tease: as Roxxxy tantalizingly sheds her articles of clothing to reveal (the sexy artifice of) her body, so she does with one wig to show forth another underneath.[83] And in canonizing this moment as a true meme in *Drag Race* culture, season 9 winner Sasha Velour, as part of her first Lip Sync for the Crown Battle Royale performance against fellow Top Four queen Shea Couleé, lifts and shakes her wig to the climactic beat of Whitney Houston's "So Emotional" to reveal a torrent of rose petals that cascade down over her—the Tweet, of course, at 8:28 a.m. on June 27, 2017, following the live airing, reads: "Never remove your wig while performing, unless you have a gaggle of rose petals underneath. #DragRace" with an accompanying .gif of the now iconic rose-petals-plus-wig-snatching moment.

## RuPrimer 3: Drag Bodies as Rhetorically Anatomical Bodies

All of this fashion history, drag/trans- visual culture, and embodiment discussions align with and come out of my idea that there necessarily is a naked drag body, that there is and must be drag in/of nakedness, and that RuPaul on and across *RPDR* teaches us that our human bodies are just as built, just as constructed, just as fashioned as are drag bodies. RuPaul, of course, even reminds us pedagogically, "You know, I've always said, drag doesn't change who you are; it actually reveals who you are."[84] Utterly ironically, then, after all this discussion and explication of clothes and of clothing being put on to construct a body that essentially has no clothes put on it, the naked drag body might just show up inferentially as our actual human bodies—rhetorically, physically, and yes, anatomically. And it does so, I want to posit as I move to conclude, through the physically embodied rhetoric of our anatomy as we have learned it from RuPaul and from *RPDR* and its paratextual cultures.

Jeanne Fahnestock, in her book *Rhetorical Figures in Science* (2002), explores "[t]he inverted bicolon, known in Greek rhetoric as the antimetabole" and notes that it "is a particularly easy structure to identify."[85] She continues, "The only distinguishing feature of the antimetabole is that at least two terms from the first colon change their relative places in the second, appearing now in one order, now in reversed order. In the process of changing their syntactic position in relation to each other, these terms change their grammatical and conceptual relation as well."[86] "The antimetabole," Fahnestock states, "can iconically express corrective inversions, identity claims[,] and claims of reciprocal causality."[87] The icon, from Charles Sanders Peirce's trichotomy of signs (that is, the icon, the index, and symbol), denotes likenesses as it resembles and imitates, and it is this iconicity of identity claim expressions (i.e., the quality of semblance shared between identity and claims of identity) that Fahnestock notes is within the power of the antimetabole that is most pertinent to my arguments in this essay, and we see that fabulous lexical example at work with drag/transbodies in that "double inversion" that Esther Newton pointed out in *Mother Camp* (1972) of what drag itself says: "My 'outside' appearance is feminine, but my essence 'inside' is masculine. ... My appearance 'outside' is masculine, but my essence 'inside' is feminine."[88]

Slavoj Žižek provides a similar example, too, from psychoanalysis. In his *The Ticklish Subject: The Absent Centre of Political Ontology* (1999), he writes that "paradoxes have a fundamental bearing on the way cyberspace affects the subject's symbolic identity,"[89] and while he does not use the word *drag* nor *trans-* once in the example he chooses to represent this idea, he most definitely employs antimetabolic logic to an identity claim of drag/trans- proportions very near that of Newton's. "[L]et us imagine," Žižek begins,

> a rather common case of a shy and inhibited man who, in cyberspace, participates in a virtual community in which he adopts the screen persona of a promiscuous woman; his stance, of course, is that of "I know very well I am really just a shy, modest guy, so why shouldn't I briefly indulge in posing as a promiscuous woman, doing things I could never do in real life?"—however, are things really so simple and straightforward? *What if this man's real-life persona (the Self he adopts, the way he behaves in his actual social interaction) is a kind of secondary "defence-formation," an identity he adopts as a mask in order to "repress" or keep at bay his true "inner Self," the hard core of his phantasmic identity, which lies in being a promiscuous woman, and for which he can find an outlet only in his private daydreaming or in anonymous virtual community sexual games?* In *Seminar XI*, Lacan mentions the old Chinese paradox of Tchuang-Tze, who awakens after dreaming that he is a butterfly, and then asks himself: "How do I know I am not a butterfly who is now dreaming that he is a man?" *Does not the same hold for our shy virtual community member: is he not in fact a promiscuous woman dreaming that she is an inhibited man?*[90]

The two chiastic instantiations[91] that Žižek uses here are Tchuang-Tze asleep and dreaming that he is a butterfly who awakes and consciously asks how does he know he is not now a butterfly dreaming he is man (where "asleep" and "awake," "man" and "butterfly," "dreaming" and "conscious[ness]" all switch grammatical and conceptual locations from one instance to the other), and the shy man online performing as a digital promiscuous woman who is a promiscuous woman offline living as an actual shy man (where "shy man" and "promiscuous woman," "online" and "offline," "performing" and "living," and "digital" and "actual" all switch grammatical and conceptual locations from one instance to the other). But drag/trans-, of course, realizes these antimetaboles in a very conscious manner *outside* of dreamscapes and *exterior to* cyberspace. Pushing Žižek's example further, if the "shy virtual community member" were to close the *SecondLife* window on their computer, dress up as their "promiscuous woman" avatar, and go lip-sync Lady Gaga's "Born This Way" at the nearest LGBTQ+ club—or if they were to seek out and begin gender confirmation surgeries and therapies—they would actualize their virtual experience in a very real and oxymoronic awake-and-dreaming kind of phenomenon.[92]

Fahnestock, however, does point out that "just as it is possible to arrange words in a diagrammatic way that suggests their conceptual relationship in a figure, so it is possible to arrange data and other visual units to express the same 'figural logic,'"[93] and applying this to the figure of the antimetabole, we would get, as she says, "a kind of visual antimetabole."[94] "It is only one step, then," Fahnestock notes, "from the verbal iconicity of some of the figures to visual iconicity, to a representation of the ideational patterns epitomized by verbal figures in purely visual codes. Hence it is possible for the figures to be presented in diagrams and illustrations as well as in the verbal arrangements defined as figures."[95] Fahnestock here does mean arranging images in relation to each other to form a visual antimetabole, so while the perfect visual antimetabole of drag/trans- might be, for example, a Photoshopped image of RuPaul out of drag looking in a mirror and seeing himself in drag, there is another physical/visual instantiation of the drag/trans- antimetabole—i.e., what drag/trans- individuals physically to do our bodies to transform and/or to transition … and what we do with "wigs, heels, and undergarments," as taught by RuPaul and *RPDR*. To "reverse their relative positions," to borrow Fahnestock's words here,[96] a drag queen, for example, tucks/hides their penis and stuffs a bra to create the bodily illusion that is coded as female, while a drag king, to complete the example, tapes/binds their breasts and stuffs briefs to create the bodily illusion that is male-coded. The tucking/taping/binding and the stuffing switch places physically as a body moves from one coded gender to the other, from one bodily colon to the other.

On the embodied or physical and social side of drag/trans- individuals, Judith Butler would seem like the natural, and even perhaps expected and anticipated, major voice to position myself in dialogue with—what with her canonical poststructuralist revelation that gender is performative[97]—but I want to dialogue instead with another and more contemporary major voice in cultural studies, literary theory, and gender and transgender studies, Jack

Halberstam, who says that "[g]ender always comes from elsewhere rather than forming the truth of the body."[98] This is a concept, Halberstam points out, "that was beautifully laid out back in 1978 by sociologists Wendy McKenna and Suzanne Kessler in their groundbreaking book *Gender: An Ethnomethodological Approach*" in which they "both describe and explain the centrality of gender attribution."[99] And by "gender attribution," Halberstam says, "[McKenna and Kessler] mean the ways in which we all ascribe genders to all the bodies we encounter by rapidly scanning bodies and making assumptions about their morphologies and orientations."[100] "[F]ar ahead of poststructuralist gender theory," Halberstam illuminates, "Kessler and McKenna also note ... that biology is not the key to gender attribution."[101] "Instead of [that split-second assessment of] gender attribution being based on genitalia,"[102] genitalia, Halberstam says McKenna and Kessler note, "are mostly assumed."[103] And it is, thus, "[w]ith these arguments [that McKenna and Kessler] laid the foundations for Judith Butler's famous formulation in *Gender Trouble*: that gender does not emerge as a cultural interpretation of sex, but rather, sex circulates as a cultural interpretation of gender."[104] The way that Halberstam crafts this paraphrase of Butler's "famous formulation" is, of course, with the rhetorical move of the antimetabole, which is, in my arguments, the iconic rhetorical figure for understanding drag/trans- bodies.

"Antimetaboles," Fahnestock states, "can express not only causal reversals but ... an even stronger causal interdependence, a sense that two entities *always require each other* and therefore *cannot be separated*."[105] This seems to be immediately true of drag/trans- bodies and identities. And with what RuPaul and *RPDR* shows us through their pedagogical framework of "wigs, heels, and undergarments" being the assumed attributes of gender in and across drag bodies, we can see how the binary of Male and Female, with the figure of the Greek letter χ (chi) joining and crossing them, becomes—just like nakedness—a continuum and not a line. Drag is not *cros*s-dressing in crossing the binary line; drag is *antimetabolic*-dressing in the infinity loop of the continuum. And this matches beautifully with Fahnestock's language on the rhetorical figure of the antimetabole: "The perfect antimetabole should, once again, consist of two balanced cola, each of which repeats the same two terms while reversing their relative positions. The result of this reversal with balance is that one colon, in effect, *mirrors the other*."[106]

## *Conclusion*

In contemporary culture, including cultures of teaching and learning and wider popular and public cultures, we might be close to a shared understanding and acceptance of gender as a social construct, but that has taken us three decades since Butler's writing in 1990. We might today be at the brink of acknowledging how we construct gender socially in our day-to-day lives, but we are only at the very onset of even considering that sex, too, is a social construct. The foundation of this paradigm shift is not in *RPDR*—we already are, in academic discourse, shifting from "biological sex" to "anatomical sex" discourse—but as I have argued and shown in this essay, both RuPaul and the enterprise of the show have lessons and scripts embedded in them from the start. And they come out through play and performance with what constitutes a body naked in drag/a naked drag body, what builds the drag body across itself ("wigs, heels, and undergarments"), and what the drag body argues rhetorically and in and of itself from this naked drag anatomy. But it is RuPaul and *RPDR* that are bringing them together and then pushing them further on the global stage of this global classroom with global learners. And this is happening popularly and publicly, as Giroux very importantly identified and explored pedagogically, instead of just inside the walls of the academy.

Hickey-Moody et al. also note that "[i]f we consider pedagogy in its simplest form, it requires the teaching of some new practice or knowledge to learners (or the learning of something 'out there' by some individual or group)."[107] The "out there"–ness evident in *RPDR* is this thrusting to the fore of the social constructedness and the social dimensions of anatomy and the bursting of the gender binary. As a pedagogical platform that functions first and foremost as a cultural platform, *RPDR* is primed, as Giroux says of culture, to "play[] a central role in producing narratives, metaphors, and images that exercise a powerful pedagogical force over how people think of themselves and their relationship to others."[108] But the platform itself with a passive viewership is not enough: as teachers, we have to embody what Zygmunt Bauman in his *Society under Siege* (2002) calls the "art of translating individual problems into public issues, and common interests into individual rights and duties."[109] We have to actively take up what RuPaul and *RPDR* are putting down. The paradigm shift won't happen without this, and we cannot afford to wait another thirty years for our academia to bleed into public and popular culture when, pedagogically, we are set to antimetabolically reverse this.

## Mini Challenge: Discussion Questions

- In this essay's discussion and theorization around undergarments shaping the culturally gendered body (of cis and trans bodies as informed by drag bodies), Mayberry notes that cismen/men-

assigned-male-at-birth are interestingly exempt from this. To what extent is this true? To what extent is it changing? And outside of undergarments, what other "technologies" (to borrow Salah's term here) do we see cismen/men-assigned-male-at-birth using to create and maintain their bodies?
- *RPDR* importantly and interestingly shows us the transformational process and "in between" moments of the competing queens getting ready in the workroom—how does this fit, and not fit, into Mayberry's arguments in this essay?
- What other examples of visual rhetoric do we see across *RPDR* beside the visual antimetabole? We hear a plethora of puns, but are there visual puns? Thinking of other rhetorical devices, when we add "visual" in front of them, what do they become and how/where do we see them in *Drag Race*?

## *Maxi Challenge: Activities and Assignments*

- This essay's title, "And where is the body?," comes from Salt-N-Pepa's 1995 song, "I Am the Body Beautiful" that was used in the opening montage of *To Wong Foo, Thanks for Everything! Julie Newmar* (1995) with Wesley Snipes and Patrick Swayze getting ready in drag from shower to out-the-door for their queenly characters. Compare and contrast this scene in *To Wong Foo* to other popular culture examples of getting-into-drag-montages-with-music (i.e., 1993's *Mrs. Doubtfire* with Robin Williams, Harvey Fierstein, and Scott Capurro set to Aerosmith's "Dude (Looks Like a Lady)," or 2006's *She's the Man* with Amanda Bynes, Jonathan Sadowski, Amanda Crew, and Jessica Lucas set to Joan Jett & The Blackhearts' "Love Is All Around"). Consider, too: What music, what mannerisms, what drag/transformation technologies … and why/how?

## Notes

1. This essay has a living history across many Indigenous nations from my researching, writing, and conferencing of it in various parts and pieces along the way to bring it to this publication. This essay itself was started at the University of Guelph (Ontario, Canada), which resides on the treaty lands and territory of the Mississaugas of the Credit and on the ancestral lands of the Attawandaron people, and it was first shared publicly as such while visiting the Gaylord National Resort and Convention Centre on the National Harbor in Maryland, adjacent to Washington, DC (United States) and situated on the area between

the Potomac and Anacostia Rivers that was and continues to be the ancestral lands of the Piscataway, along with the Anacostank, Pamunkey, Mattapanient, Nangemeick, and Tauxehent peoples. This essay came to its mature form here while working at St. Jerome's University at the University of Waterloo (Ontario, Canada), which is located on the Haldimand Tract, the land promised to the Six Nations of the Grand River that includes six miles on each side of the Grand River and is the traditional territory of the Attawandaron, Anishnaabeg, and Haudenosaunee peoples. This essay also involves pieces of research from my dissertation at the University of Waterloo that was shared at a conference while visiting the University of Cincinnati (Ohio, United States), which is on the land of the Osage, Shawnee, Myaamia, Adena, and Hopewell peoples. As a white settler-scholar, I am humbled by the opportunities to live on and to work across these stolen lands, and I deeply thank and recognize all the generations of people who have cared for them—for thousands of years. Their historical relationships with the land continue to this day, and I am committed to the hard, painful, and ongoing necessary work of truth and reconciliation.

2. "Face, Face, Face of Cakes." *RuPaul's Drag Race*, season 3, episode 7, Logo TV, 28 Feb. 2011. *Amazon*, https://www.amazon.com/gp/video/detail/B004JGWASG/ref=atv_dp_season_select_s3.

3. *Ibid.*

4. Hickey-Moody, Anna, et al. "Pedagogy Writ Large: Public, Popular and Cultural Pedagogies in Motion." *Critical Studies in Education*, vol. 51, no. 3, 2010, p. 227—italics original.

5. *Ibid.*, p. 228.

6. Sandlin, Jennifer A., et al. "Mapping the Complexity of Public Pedagogy Scholarship: 1894–2010." *Review of Educational Research*, vol. 81, no. 3, 2011, p. 336.

7. "Face, Face, Face of Cakes."

8. *Ibid.*

9. *Ibid.*

10. *Ibid.*

11. "The Queen Who Mopped X-Mas." *RuPaul's Drag Race*, season 3, episode 1, Logo TV, 24 Jan. 2011. *Amazon*, https://www.amazon.com/gp/video/detail/B004JGWASG/ref=atv_dp_season_select_s3.

12. "Face, Face, Face of Cakes."

13. *Ibid.*

14. *Ibid.*

15. *Ibid.*

16. "The Queen Who Mopped X-Mas."

17. *Ibid.*

18. *Ibid.*

19. *Ibid.*

20. "Born Naked." *RuPaul's Drag Race*, season 7, episode 1, Logo TV, 2 Mar. 2015. *Amazon*, https://www.amazon.com/gp/video/detail/B00TG0HXVE/ref=atv_dp_season_select_s7.

21. *Ibid.*

22. RuPaul. *Workin' it!: RuPaul's Guide to Life, Liberty, and the Pursuit of Style*. itbooks, 2010, p. ix.

23. *Ibid.*

24. Marlatt, Daphne. "Self-Representation and Fictionalysis." *Tessera*, vol. 8, 1990, p. 14.

25. *Ibid.*

26. "RuPaul Charles: We're All In Drag." *Oprah's SuperSoul Conversations* from iTunes, 17 Jan. 2018, itunes.apple.com/us/podcast/oprahs-supersoul-conversations/id1264843400?mt=2.

27. RuPaul. *Workin' it!*, p. ix.

28. *Ibid.*, pp. x–xi.

29. RuPaul. "Born Naked." *Born Naked*. RuCo Inc., 2014—emphasis added.

30. To a keen eye for fashion, pop culture, and satire (everything RuPaul loves and *RPDR* is about), this entire first episode of *RPDR* season 7 can actually be read as an unclocked homage to/recreation of Altman's film in its framing. The mini-challenge that RuPaul begins the season and episode with "isn't just a photoshoot," RuPaul tells them (as per six previous

seasons of *RPDR* tradition), "Oh, hell, no! It's a Fashion Week Extravaganza" where they "need to dig in [their] trunks and model two of [their] very best looks: one from [their] Spring Collection, and one from [their] Fall Collection" ("Born Naked"). The mini-challenge itself is set, styled, and edited in a play on Fashion Week televization: sitting along the left side of the catwalk, in true Fashion Week protocol, are the VIP guests, judges, and designers—for *RPDR*, that is sitting judge Michelle Visage, RuPaul himself, style superstar Carson Kressley, *RPDR* season 4 alumna Alaska (who in 2016 will become the winner of *RuPaul's Drag Race: All Stars* season 2 and the second queen inducted into RuPaul's Drag Race Hall of Fame), and RuPaul's hair and make-up artist Mathu Anderson—black-and-white footage of the models getting ready backstage is dropcut to tease and foreshadow the runway looks, and the categories (i.e., "Spring 2015") flash on the screen for each part of the runway. And the concluding runway of the episode, of course, is the naked runway. In this way, the episode functions intertextually as a contemporary reimagining of *Prêt-à-Porter*—with drag queens!

31. See "Born Naked."

32. In the premier episode of the entire series, the first runway challenge is for the queens to create their looks out of thrift store clothing and accessories from the dollar store ("Drag on a Dime"), and in the first episode of the fifth season of *RPDR*, the queens are challenged to create looks of "Hollywood glamor" from whatever thrown-away scraps they can salvage from a dumpster in Beverly Hills ("RuPaullywood or Bust").

33. "Drag on a Dime." *RuPaul's Drag Race*, season 1, episode 1, Logo TV, 29 Jan. 2009. *Amazon*, https://www.amazon.com/gp/video/detail/B001RGOIWW/ref=atv_dp_season_select_s1.

34. "Meet the Queens." *RuPaul's Drag Race*, season 9, episode 0, Logo TV, 2 Feb. 2017. *Amazon*, https://www.amazon.com/gp/video/detail/B06XK36FZS/ref=atv_dp_season_select_s9.

35. "Girl Group Challenge." *RuPaul's Drag Race*, season 1, episode 2, Logo TV, 9 Feb. 2009. *Amazon*, https://www.amazon.com/gp/video/detail/B001RGOIWW/ref=atv_dp_season_select_s1.

36. In a 2020 design challenge on the fifth season of *All Stars*, RuPaul does say that "you can use your own hair, heels, and underpants, plus materials from the F&S Fabrics wall" ("The Charles Family Backyard Ball"). The three categories are still the same, though worded differently, from the very first episode ever: hair/wigs; heels; and undergarments/underpants.

37. Salah, Trish. "transsexuality/gender dysphoria." *Encyclopedia of Feminist Theories*, Routledge, 2000, p. 476.

38. In her entry for *transgender*, Salah writes that "[t]he meanings of the term 'transgender' are various, rapidly evolving and highly contested. Commonly[,] transgender functions either as name employed by individuals at odds with their physical sex, and/or, as an umbrella term for all those whose gender does not follow directly from their apparent sex or the sex to which they were assigned at birth" (475). She further states, "In this second sense, transgender may include: intersexuals, female-to-male (FTM) transsexuals and male-to-female (MTF) transsexuals, butches, femmes, drag queens and kings, cross dressers, nellies, transgenderists" (475). On *transsexuality/gender dysphoria*, Salah writes that it "is an experience of strong conflict between one's sense of self as a gendered and sexed being, and one's anatomical sex" (476), and that "transsexuals desire to bring the body into congruity with the self through a variety of technologies" (476).

39. While Cox reveals her naked trans- body in *Orange Is the New Black* as a MTF transbody, Buck Angel, for another example, reveals his naked trans- body in his adult film work and documentaries as a FTM trans- body that exists through body-building, hair technologies such as a shaved head and facial hair, and/or top surgery. Top surgery for FTM trans- people is having the breasts removed surgically. For MTF trans- people, top surgery is breast augmentation, and bottom surgery is having the penis "removed and inverted," as Cox-as-Burset said in *Orange Is the New Black* ("Lesbian Request Denied"). As *Shameless*' Trevor says of his top surgery when Ian asks him if he "used to have like tits 'n' shit," "Yeah, I got 'em chopped the fuck off, it was the best day of my life" ("I Am the Storm"), and as Buck Angel's (now ex-) wife Elayne says of Buck's transition, "He was female at birth, and through taking testosterone and working out and having surgery to remove his breasts, he's a man. So that's not a small cock, it's a huge clit" (*Mr. Angel*). "My chest surgery was my sex change,"

Buck says, "That was the whole turning point of my life when I did that," and he also notes, on FTM bottom surgery, that "I chose not to have bottom surgery because I personally do not feel that that surgery is good enough for me. I don't want to say that it's a bad surgery… my own choice is that I don't think it's a good surgery, and I don't understand why somebody would want to have a penis that bad, a penis that doesn't really operate like a genetic man's penis operates: the amount of money you spend on it, the amount of recovery time" (*Mr. Angel*). And on his own surgery, and in academic language that we can apply to think through transmen's top surgeries as their process, Jack Halberstam writes, "The procedure was not about building maleness into my body; it was about editing some part of the femaleness that currently defined me" (*Trans\** 23).

40. These undergarment technologies for drag queens may overlap with those for transwomen depending on transition, access to funds for surgeries, personal desires and understandings of identity congruity, etc. For drag kings and transmen, undergarment technologies can be stuffed briefs or boxers, name-brand chest binders, or perhaps tensor bands or the always industrious roll of duct tape. It is important to point out that women assigned female at birth, in trying to reach the cultural idea(l) of the feminine body, also wear all of the items listed here and above that drag queens and transwomen wear, and it is interesting to highlight that the same cannot be said for men assigned male at birth and drag kings and transmen. The undergarment technologies that drag kings and transmen wear to align their bodies with the idea of the masculine body is just with that: the idea, *not* the ideal. The culturally masculine body is not, as the culturally feminine body is, one shaped/transformed/tortured by underwear.

41. "The Grand Finale." *RuPaul's Drag Race All Stars*, season 1, episode 6, Logo TV, 26 Nov. 2012. *Amazon*, https://www.amazon.com/gp/video/detail/B009VB83GW/ref=atv_dp_season_select_s1.

42. "Supermodel Snatch Game." *RuPaul's Drag Race*, season 8, episode 5, Logo TV, 4 Apr. 2016. *Amazon*, https://www.amazon.com/gp/video/detail/B01BZGNENC/ref=atv_dp_season_select_s8.

43. *Ibid.*

44. Recall that the "Born Naked" episode's goal was "nude illusion resort wear" *not* bare naked.

45. Halberstam, Jack. *Trans\*: A Quick and Quirky Account of Gender Variability*. University of California Press, 2018, p. 23.

46. In the climactic scene, the central antagonist Sheriff Dollard (portrayed by Chris Penn) storms into town holding the shoe that Vida (portrayed by Patrick Swayze) lost when fleeing from Sheriff Dollard's assault on her when he pulled her car over and made her get out so he could molest her. "Whoever belongs to this shoe," he screams in a terrifying inversion of the Cinderella fairy tale, "come forth now!" This sparks a *Spartacus* moment of loyal protection when the entire town exits their homes to confront Dollard and all take ownership over the shoe: "I believe that shoe is mine," one says; "Can I have my shoe, please?" says another.

47. Semmelhack, Elizabeth. *Heights of Fashion: A History of the Elevated Shoe*. Bata Shoe Museum, 2008, p. 49.

48. *Ibid.*, p. 52; It is interesting here that Semmelhack notes that it is the corset in tandem with the high heels that enhance Monroe's hourglass shape because corsets almost necessarily are undergarment elements of clothing (as previously discussed with naked drag/transbodies) that "could be hidden from view under one's clothes, [while] high heels could not" (61). As Semmelhack also points out, "Lingerie became a booming industry in the 1980s" (59), and "[t]he high heel's use as a boudoir accessory was a resounding success, so much so, that the high heel itself was transformed into a type of lingerie" (61).

49. "WTF!: Wrestling's Trashiest Fighters." *RuPaul's Drag Race*, season 4, episode 2, Logo TV, 6 Feb. 2012. *Amazon*, https://www.amazon.com/gp/video/detail/B007142CFE/ref=atv_dp_season_select_s4.

50. "Keeping it 100!" *RuPaul's Drag Race*, season 8, episode 1, Logo TV, 7 Mar. 2016. *Amazon*, https://www.amazon.com/gp/video/detail/B01BZGNENC/ref=atv_dp_season_select_s8.

51. *Ibid.*
52. RuPaul. *Workin' it!*, p. 130.
53. *Ibid.*, p. 125.
54. *Ibid.*
55. Original drag superstar Divine (1945–1988) famously says, "I won't wear any of my work clothes on a television talk show," and when asked in a CNN interview, "Where is the Divine we all know?" she laughs and importantly replies, "In the closet and a couple of suitcases right now" (qtd. in Schwarz).
56. RuPaul. *Workin' it!*, p. 130.
57. See "Drag on a Dime."
58. *Ibid.*
59. "Girl Group Challenge.."
60. "Extra Special Edition." *RuPaul's Drag Race*, season 1, episode 7, Logo TV, 16 Mar. 2009. *Amazon*, https://www.amazon.com/gp/video/detail/B001RGOIWW/ref=atv_dp_season_select_s1.
61. "Oh. My. Gaga!" *RuPaul's Drag Race*, season 9, episode 1, Logo TV, 24 Mar. 2017. *Amazon*, https://www.amazon.com/gp/video/detail/B06XK36FZS/ref=atv_dp_season_select_s9.
62. "9021-HO." *RuPaul's Drag Race*, season 9, episode 7, Logo TV, 5 May 2017. *Amazon*, https://www.amazon.com/gp/video/detail/B06XK36FZS/ref=atv_dp_season_select_s9.
63. *Ibid.*
64. RuPaul. *Workin' it!*, p. 42.
65. RuPaul's choice to be bald out of drag definitely makes it easier and less messy to glue down his wigs for getting into drag, and this is interesting in historical connections to men cutting their hair short for the express purpose of wearing wigs. And on his wigs, RuPaul notes that each "is actually two wigs" (*Workin' it!* 89), and that the full effect is comprised of "a full lace-front wig, plus a comparably sized matching piece to add volume on top" (88). "My whole career is based on an intricate system of pulleys and lifts, smoke and mirrors!" she says (63), and she importantly points out as well that "[p]eople assume I live my life in drag, but I don't. I think it's a lot easier for them to grasp full-time drag than part-time job" (61).
66. "Drag on a Dime."
67. *Ibid.*
68. "Extra Special Edition."
69. *Ibid.*
70. "Keeping it 100!"
71. *Ibid.*
72. To be clear, no hair in *drag performances* might erase gender. No hair on the ever-increasing number of straight men today in our contemporary is seemingly having the exact opposite effect—in fact, a January 2017 article in *Woman's Day* magazine titled, "Bald Men Are More Intelligent, Successful, and Masculine, Says Science" opens by telling its female readership, "If your husband is worried about losing his hair, you can now let him know that his life is only going to be better" (Beniaris).
73. RuPaul. *Workin' it!*, p. 84.
74. *Ibid.*
75. "Meet the Queens."
76. *Ibid.*—emphasis added.
77. "Grand Finale." *RuPaul's Drag Race*, season 9, episode 7, Logo TV, 23 June 2017. *Amazon*, https://www.amazon.com/gp/video/detail/B06XK36FZS/ref=atv_dp_season_select_s9.
78. *Ibid.*
79. True to my own gendered identity, I have always innately understood that my wig is tantamount to my female identity. It is always the last piece of my transformation to go on, and it is always the first piece of my transformation to come off; I am truly female just after and just before these respective polar moments. Anything else remains part of my gender oscillation. When I first started doing academic drag as a conscious and decided project of embodied cognition at the University of Windsor (Windsor, Ontario) during Master of Fine Arts studies, my peers and supervisors consistently criticized me for not exploring this

fissure in a performative way. They wanted, and they expressed so in these words, to see me "rip off my wig" to conclude each guest lecture and conference paper I performed in drag as part of my thesis body of work to showcase the dichotomy of my gendered selves. I was (and remain) vehemently opposed to this deliberate breakdown in a live and public setting, but it is most certainly a fetish in drag/trans- bodies and performance art: uncannily, people want to see the queen without her wig on, they want that peek behind the curtain, they want that confirmation of the illusion, but (as with Medusa) they do not want to/cannot look directly. Once they do, it is over: the wig reveal breaks the "poetic faith" (as Coleridge would call it) of the drag show and shatters the audience's "willing suspension of disbelief for the moment" (*Biographia Literaria* 478).

80. In the show's premiere season, Shannel did a jump move during her Lip Sync for Your Life performance in episode three ("Queens of All Media") that caused her Medusa-headpiece to shift, detach, and fall forward to expose her out-of-drag hair, hairline, and wigline underneath. She continued the performance, however, very proudly and in defiance of her wardrobe malfunction in a move that allowed her to show her "vulnerability" that the judges so wanted to see from her. Her intense energy in that moment of potential defeat has awkwardly inspired subsequent drag queens to tear off their wigs in an attempt to rechannel that moment of Shannel's and win their lip sync battle in an effort to show their vulnerability and willingness to go wigless. More often than not, though, it falls worse than flat.

81. For example, see the Tweet with accompanying .gif from October 25th, 2015.

82. For example, see the Tweet with accompanying .gif from April 26th, 2015.

83. "All Star Talent Show Extravaganza." *RuPaul's Drag Race All Stars*, season 2, episode 1, Logo TV, 25 Aug. 2016. *Amazon*, https://www.amazon.com/gp/video/detail/B01KGB99VI/ref=atv_dp_season_select_s2.

84. "RuPaul's Best Judy's Race." *RuPaul's Drag Race All Stars*, season 4, episode 8, Logo TV, 1 Feb. 2019. *Amazon*, https://www.amazon.com/gp/video/detail/B07KWPRZ5M/ref=atv_dp_season_select_s4.

85. Fahnestock, Jeanne. *Rhetorical Style: The Uses of Language in Persuasion*. Oxford University Press, 2011, p. 123.

86. *Ibid.*

87. *Ibid.*, p. 127.

88. Newton, Esther. *Mother Camp: Female Impersonators in America*, University of Chicago Press, 1972, p. 103.

89. Žižek, Slavoj. The Ticklish Subject: The Absent Centre of Political Ontology, Verso, 1999, p. 329.

90. *Ibid.*—emphases added. This, of course, is also a dualistic trope in much of superhero graphic novel and comic culture, ripe as it already is with so much queerness, transness, and dragginess. The two perhaps most iconic superheroes to wrestle with this antimetabolism in their selves vs. secret identities are Bruce Wayne/Batman (specifically in Frank Miller's mini-series *Batman: The Dark Knight Returns* (1986)) and Superman/Clark Kent, who, famously, has as his secret identity not a caped crusader but the (arguably *non-*)costumed *Daily Bugle* Reporter Clark Kent. And for a more contemporary sci-fi/fantasy literary example of Žižek's "rather common case" from the other end of the binary gender spectrum, see Ernest Cline's incredible character Aech/Helen Harris in *Ready Player One* (2011) and *Ready Player Two* (2020).

91. I write "chiastic instantiations" here because Žižek does not use the figural form of the antimetabole in his example but exemplifies through antimetabolic logic in a looser form for which the chiasmus allows but the antimetabole does not. As Fahnestock notes, "The perfect antimetabole should, once again, consist of two balanced cola, each of which repeats the same two terms while reversing their relative positions. The result of this reversal with balance is that one colon, in effect, mirrors the other" (124).

92. Žižek does, to be sure, counter his example very carefully as he unpacks it, for he notes that "[t]his level is not that of 'reality' as opposed to the play of my imagination—Lacan's point is not that, behind the multiplicity of phantasmic identities, there is a hard core of some 'real Self'; we are dealing with a symbolic fiction, but a fiction which, for contingent reasons that have nothing to do with its inherent nature, possess performative power—is socially

operative, structures the socio-symbolic reality in which I participate" (330). "The status of the same person," Žižek continues, "inclusive of his/her very 'real' features, can appear in an entirely different light the moment the modality of his/her relationship to the big Other changes" (330).

93. Fahnestock, p. 41.
94. *Ibid.*; a readily identifiable and perhaps obvious, though old, visual antimetabole is the *taijitu* from Chinese philosophy (more commonly known as the yin-yang or Yin and Yang).
95. *Ibid.*, p. 42.
96. *Ibid.*, p. 124.
97. While she does not say it explicitly in her *Gender Trouble: Feminism and the Subversion of Identity* (1990), instead she problematically and very unfortunately uses drag as a metaphor for her arguments, Butler is arguing for gender as performative along J. L. Austen's lines of language as constantive and as performative (i.e., performative language brings, as if alchemically, a change to the systemic order based solely on utterances—an umpire yells, "You're out!" and the batter *becomes out*.) For Butler, what she should have argued instead in *Gender Trouble* is that when a doctor or midwife looks between a newly-born human's legs and binarily calls out, "It's a boy!" or "It's a girl!," that this is a performative utterance that casts the newborn into this cultural role—essentially, the baby, like the batter, becomes not out but *becomes a boy or a girl*.
98. Halberstam, p. 58.
99. *Ibid.*
100. *Ibid.*
101. *Ibid.*
102. *Ibid.*
103. *Ibid.*, p. 59.
104. *Ibid.*
105. Fahnestock, p. 141—emphasis added. Again, think of Yin and Yang and the *taijitu* from Chinese philosophy—see footnote above.
106. *Ibid.*, p. 124—emphasis added.
107. Hickey-Moody, Anna, et al., p. 232.
108. Giroux, Henry A. "Cultural Studies, Public Pedagogy, and the Responsibility of Intellectuals." *Communications and Critical/Cultural Studies*, vol. 1, no. 1, March 2004, p. 62.
109. Bauman, Zygmunt. *Society under Siege*. Blackwell, 2002, p. 74.

# She Already Done Had Herses
## *When Drag Curates Culture*

"Katya, where'd you get your outfits, girl, American Apparently Not?"
—Trixie Mattel, season 7 contestant;
*All Stars* season 3 winner[1]

## *Learning Outcomes:*

By the end of this section, we should be able to…

- Describe the ways drag can be used to engage with age, nationality, race, and culture.
- Express the ways a drag family forms, identifies itself, and fosters a sense of community among its members.
- Examine how drag, reality television, and *RPDR* (as a point of intersection) have addressed, and in instances propagated, cultural appropriation, political division, and revisionist history/herstory.
- Deconstruct the artifices that mask for audiences the socio-economic impact of drag and the competitive aspects of the series on "RuGirls" and local artists/performers.
- Debate the ways that comedy, satire, and parody within the drag community can affirm and/or combat stereotypes of minority groups.
- Develop a methodology for identification, assessment, and response to cultural insensitivity and appropriation.

### Note

1. "Divine Intervention." *RuPaul's Drag Race,* season 7, episode 9, Logo TV, 27 April 2015, *Amazon,* https://smile.amazon.com/gp/video/detail/B00TG0HXVE/ref=atv_dp_season_select_s7.

# Pop the Corn and Teach the Children

*Drag Lessons in Gender, Race, and Class Beyond RuPaul's Televised Curriculum*

Russ Martin

As the matriarch of *RuPaul's Drag Race*, henceforth *RPDR*, RuPaul is one of the drag world's most visible educators. *RPDR* now dominates drag culture on a global level, but the traditional community-based knowledge exchange between drag artists remains alive and well in local drag scenes all over the globe. These lessons represent an alternative curriculum for fans and performers who seek to go beyond the drag education packaged up for television by RuPaul and the producers of *RPDR*. With *RPDR*, RuPaul has taught an entire generation about the history and politics of drag, but her supremacy as the headmistress of all drag culture begs the question: What—and whom—does her drag curriculum leave out?

Drawing from an ethnographic study of the Toronto drag scene, this essay explores how *RPDR* has influenced Toronto's drag community and what lessons the city's drag artists have taken from the show. It will demonstrate how the Toronto drag scene receives, reinterprets, and resists the curriculum presented by *RPDR* and detail the concurrent community-based teaching and learning that happens in the Toronto scene through mentorship, mic work, and the long-held tradition of drag families. This alternative curriculum of local learning represents a more inclusive drag classroom than the one RuPaul presides over on *RPDR*. As a grassroots knowledge exchange rooted in a scene with a more than 70-year history, this alternative curriculum is also less tied to the pursuit of capital than *RPDR*—a reality television show that exists within a format commonly associated with neoliberal values.[1] This critical ideological difference leads to a sharp contrast in lessons relating to gender, race, and economics presented via these two competing curricula.

Drawing from scholar Will Straw's work on scene theory, I argue *RPDR* now acts as global drag culture's dominant "system of articulation," a term Straw uses to describe the way culture is interpreted through an audience's understanding of a particular global art form or genre.[2] In the case of his seminal 1991 essay, "Systems of Articulation, Logics of Change," Straw argues the globalized cultures of alternative rock and dance music constitute "systems" that act as an "articulatory force" that influences how those forms of music are made and understood in local music scenes.[3] Following this line of thinking, I see *RPDR* as a system of articulation that not only dictates trends in drag, but also provides the contemporary drag fan a rubric for understanding drag's cultural meaning. I contend the show influences how drag is interpreted by fans and informs how gender, race, and class are negotiated and taught in the Toronto drag scene. *RPDR* has created a new, economically driven global drag scene, which looms large over the local scene in Toronto. This is not, however, a one-way dialog; I contend that there are what Straw calls "lines of influence"[4] between *RPDR*-led global drag culture and local drag culture in Toronto, meaning that what happens in local drag scenes such as Toronto's can also influence global drag culture. My participant interviews and field work demonstrate that *RPDR* has had a great impact on the Toronto drag scene, prompting neutral, positive, and negative effects. The results in this essay are drawn from a larger ethnographic study that included a year and a half in the field, concluding shortly before the launch of *Canada's Drag Race* in July 2020, and a series of semi-structured interviews with nine research participants who took part in the 2018 edition of a Toronto-based drag pageant, Crews and Tangos Drag Race, henceforth CTDR. The interviews occurred throughout 2019 and during a virtual presentation and drag show during the summer of 2020.

*RPDR* has immense pedagogical potential as a cultural text. As Henry A. Giroux posits, culture is "the social field where goods and social practices are not only produced, distributed, and consumed, but also invested with various meanings and ideologies implicated in the generation of political effects."[5] Such is certainly the case for *RPDR*; as Colin Whitworth asserts in "Sissy That Performance Script! The Queer Pedagogy of *RuPaul's Drag Race*," the show has proven to be a useful tool for teaching its non-queer audience about LGBTQ+ identities and cultures.[6] The educational value of *RPDR* has been taken up within the academy by educators like Joe E. Jeffreys, who teaches a semester-long course on *RPDR* and its impact at The New School in New York City. The paratextual universe surrounding the show itself even invites viewers to view it pedagogically via the spinoff *Drag U*, as David J. Fine and Emily Shreve point out in "The Prime of Miss RuPaul Charles: Allusion, Betrayal and Charismatic

Pedagogy."[7] Drag was, however, pedagogical long before *RPDR*. Judith Butler, for example, famously used drag in *Gender Trouble* to illustrate how gender is a social construct that is naturalized via a series of cultural inferences about masculinity and femininity.[8] Many other scholars have used drag in the classroom, including Ursirus College's Domenick Scudera, who writes that studying drag forces students to challenge the gender binary,[9] and the prolific drag scholar and ethnographer Steven P. Schacht, who took hundreds of students to drag shows over the years[10] and chronicled how it challenged straight male students' homophobia.[11] Scudera and Schacht draw similar conclusions about the usefulness of drag as a tool to teach gender, but neither contends with how *RPDR* now teaches some of the same lessons in the public sphere. (Schacht was writing prior to *RPDR*'s debut). As educators draw on drag as a pedagogical tool, they must now also consider what lessons students may have learned from *RPDR* outside of the classroom.

Beyond the classroom and the academy, drag is still inherently pedagogical. As Giroux contests, "Pedagogy, at its best, implies that learning takes places across a spectrum of social practices and settings"[12] The drag education that happens via *RPDR*, and at related events such as live tours and conventions featuring *RPDR* alumnae, is what Giroux calls public pedagogy. The same is true for drag shows at all types of venues, from nightclubs to restaurants and libraries, and related events such as the wildly popular phenomenon of *RPDR* viewing parties at bars and restaurants. Each such drag event is a cultural and political site where the work of public pedagogy takes place. Consider the task of hosting a drag show as an example; drag performers who act as the host of a show are skilled at what's known as mic work—entertaining and instructing the audience. As hosts, these performers teach audience members who may be new to drag culture about the norms and expectations of the space.

One Toronto performer, Allysin Chaynes, for example, begins one of her monthly shows with a call and response speech in which she explains consent, respect, and her drink order (her favorite shot is two shots, should you happen upon one of her shows). The politically-minded Toronto-based drag collective House of Kings, meanwhile, begins all of its shows with a land reading to acknowledge the original caretakers of the land they're performing on. The hosts of House of Kings also explain that they've created an anti-racist space and stand with Black Lives Matter—then they point out the exits for anyone who does not. Such moments of public pedagogy contribute to the local drag curriculum in Toronto. They also provide an opportunity to add to and correct *RPDR*'s curriculum; at *RPDR* viewing parties in particular, hosts often critique the show's politics, thus educating their audience on drag culture beyond *RPDR*. Below I will explore how this local curriculum interacts with, responds to, and resists the lessons of *RPDR*.

## *RPDR* as Drag 101: *RPDR* Has Taught an Entire Generation—the Drag Baby Boomers

The participants of the ethnographic study conducted are a group of young millennials and members of Gen Z, defined by Generation Z authors Corey Seemiller and Meghan Grace as those born after 1995.[13] Several of the participants were teenagers—or even pre-teens—when *RPDR* made its debut in 2009. On average, they list the show's fifth season in 2013 as the first they watched live as it aired, and none report having watched *RPDR* live during its first season. For more than half of this group, *RPDR* represents their very first introduction to drag culture, and all of the participants list *RPDR* as one of the reasons—if not *the* reason—they started doing drag. One of the older participants states they had seen several television shows and movies featuring drag performers prior to watching *RPDR*, but they list a film RuPaul appears in, *To Wong Foo, Thanks for Everything! Julie Newmar* (1995),[14] as their first exposure to drag, further underscoring RuPaul's impact on this group. Given the context of *RPDR*'s explosion into mainstream culture coinciding with their coming of age, this group is representative of a generation of *RPDR* fans who have now started practicing drag themselves and are often referred to as the drag baby boom.[15] As the first generation of drag performers to learn the art form at least partially from *RPDR* and its paratextual cultures, the drag baby boomers have honed their craft with unprecedented access to educational materials about drag. This influence has led many of them to become skilled practitioners, but their drag is often also informed by the commercialism of *RPDR* and the glossy, expensive drag showcased on the program.

At the most rudimentary level, *RPDR* functions as a "gateway drug" for drag culture at large. *RPDR* was a tool of discovery and education for the research participants on their fan journey from audience member to performer. Within fandom studies, there is a bounty of evidence that suggests taking part in fan activities can be a transformative experience that leads to personal and social gains. In "The Cultural Economy of Fans," John Fiske posits that fans are able to translate the cultural capital they acquire in the fan world into their daily lives.[16] The *RPDR* fandom offers such transformative experiences for fans, especially for fans who are young, queer, and looking for validation in the media they consume. As an educational text, *RPDR* not only teaches these young fans about drag, but also about queer life, queer history, and the multiplicities of queer identity. The fan culture surrounding the show is also pedagogical; superfans of *RPDR* discuss, debate, and learn more about the history and politics of drag on online platforms and in person at *RPDR*-related fan events. *RPDR* often introduces them to new books, podcasts, and YouTube videos that teach them more about both drag culture and queer life. For example, *RPDR* fans who discover Bob the Drag Queen and Monét X Change's podcast *Sibling Rivalry* will learn about the intersection of Blackness and queerness, toxic masculinity, and anti–Black racism within the *RPDR* fandom.

One research participant, Silencia, describes her progression from *RPDR* fan to drag artist like this: "[*RPDR*] opened my eyes, for someone with very little exposure to the drag scene or the drag community, or even drag performers. It opened my eyes: 'Oh this is a thing. Cool, I can do it too.'"[17] Another participant, Selena Vyle, worked for several years as an actor and comedian before she discovered *RPDR* and began experimenting with drag. Through watching the show, Vyle gained an understanding of the socioeconomic reality of drag as a career path:

> If you had told me before *Drag Race*, or if I had never watched *Drag Race*, that I should be a drag queen I wouldn't have known what it meant, really. I wasn't really going to drag shows…. I didn't really know how much work went into it. I didn't know how much money there was to be made. I didn't know what the club life was like. I wouldn't have gotten involved.[18]

Vyle's experience follows a typical pathway towards drag performance for the drag baby boomer, and it also shows just how fertile the Toronto drag scene is for fledgling performers. At the time of our interview, less than a year after Vyle competed in CTDR and two years into her drag career, Vyle works as a drag artist several times a week. She is the headline performer at two weekly shows, acts as the co-host of a weekly *RPDR* viewing party, and regularly books additional gigs. As a student of drag, Vyle discovered the realities of life as a drag artist via the lessons of *RPDR*, but the show's curriculum only represents a fraction of her education: Vyle is a member of the House of Lix and learned the drag ropes from her mother, the drag performer Vicki Lix. For Vyle, the combination of *RPDR*'s pedagogical content and community-based learning in the Toronto scene proved to be a powerful combination, providing her all the knowledge, skills, and abilities needed to succeed as a drag performer.

## *Ru Girls as Teachers: In* RPDR's *Classroom, the Show's Stars Are Its Teachers*

Many of the research participants cite one particular *RPDR* contestant as a drag teacher who had an acute impact on their craft. In many cases, seeing a particular style of performance receive adulation on *RPDR* validated their own aspirations. This causation illustrates a direct line of influence between *RPDR* and the Toronto drag scene. For example, research participant Harmony, who typically sings live rather than lip syncing, lists *RPDR* contestant Adore (season 6, *All Stars* season 2), a singer who has successfully branded herself as a drag musician, as a primary influence. Lucinda Miu, who trained as an actor and produces theatrical, narrative-driven drag shows as part of a troupe called The Diet Ghosts, says the theatrically-minded Jinkx Monsoon (season 5), whose drag draws from the traditions of vaudeville, showed her a drag artist can succeed by focusing on performance craft rather than of-the-moment references. Selena Vyle says she was inspired by how Bob The Drag Queen (season 8) spoke on *RPDR* about using drag as a form of protest, relating the *RPDR* star's involvement in social justice movements to the way she weaves politics into her own drag practice.[19] Viewing *RPDR* as an educational text, each of these *RPDR* stars can be seen as a key teacher for a member of the participant group.

Though *RPDR* contestants inspire, validate, and teach aspiring drag performers, the show's acceleration of drag's trend cycles also creates a pressure cooker for up-and-coming artists still honing their craft. The show's winners often excel at a particular style or aspect of drag—season 3 winner Raja is a runway model and fashion maven; season 6 winner Bianca Del Rio is an insult comedian; and season 7 winner Violet Chachki is an aerialist styled as a femme fatale. Each winner, in turn, ushers in a season of popularity for their particular style of drag, which spills over into local scenes as audiences crave seeing what they've just witnessed on television live in the clubs. In this way, *RPDR* cast members teach the audience about new styles of drag. According to Miu, drag audiences in Toronto became especially responsive to dance performance after hometown hero Brooke Lynn Hytes—a trained dancer who studied at the National Ballet School of Canada—appeared on season 11 of *RPDR*:

> I know that a lot of my friends are very insecure right now about the fact they've never taken a dance class in their life because of [Brooke]. When Violet won, I remember feeling very confident about my future. I was like: "Oh you know what? I make my own looks, I love to corset. My future's fine." Whereas now it's a very different tune of: "I don't know how to dance, oh yikes, what am I going to do?" It's interesting how the show informs what you should be good at.[20]

One of the easiest ways to see *RPDR*'s influence on drag is via a close look at the faces of the performers in the Toronto drag scene. If one has seen enough *RPDR*, they may recognize eyes, noses, or lips painted on the faces of Toronto performers. Several participants point to the proliferation of makeup trends shepherded into drag culture by particular *RPDR* contestants, from contouring the tip of one's nose in the shape of a heart (Shuga Cain, season 11) to 1960s-style false bottom eyelashes (Farrah Moan and Valentina, both season 9 and *All Stars* season 4) and rhinestones glued directly under one's eyelid (Naomi Smalls, season 8 and *All Stars* season 4). The popularity of drag-based makeup tutorials on YouTube has also increased since *RPDR*'s debut, and many of the most-viewed tutorials feature *RPDR* contestants showing fans how to achieve their makeup looks. One research participant, Miss Scotto, even refers to YouTube as her "first drag mom."[21] Miss Scotto cites one *RPDR* contestant in particular, Miss Fame (season 7), as a drag educator who taught her makeup. Recalling her early education in drag makeup, Miss Scotto says Miss Fame's detailed YouTube tutorials were how she learned foundational skills such as how to contour one's face. Speaking of the tutorials, she explains, "They're so in depth, that even if you follow it the worst way possible, because you're following it, it's still going to end up looking good."[22]

Beyond the steps of gluing down one's eyebrows or drawing on an exaggerated lip, *RPDR* stars also teach non-makeup lessons through their YouTube tutorials, such as self-confidence and perseverance. Lucinda Miu, for instance, cites a piece of advice from a Miz Cracker (season 10 and *All Stars* season 5) tutorial as a necessary drag lesson that inspired her to move past the self-doubt learners are bound to encounter on their educational journey:

> Miz Cracker once said in a makeup tutorial: "I paint, but if it's not going well, you just have to finish it. They're not going to see your makeup, they're coming to see you."[23]

This is the type of advice drag offspring often receive from their parents. In the post–*RPDR* drag baby boom, this parental role is often virtually filled by *RPDR* contestants, but for my research participants, these stars are a complement to local drag teachers rather than a replacement. Miss Scotto and Lucinda Miu, for instance, both belong to a drag family and partake in community-based drag education.

Like the route to drag itself for drag baby boomers, drag YouTube tutorials are a new phenomenon that runs counter to the community-based way drag makeup was taught prior to the *RPDR* era. Research participant Tash Riot explains that many Toronto artists now resemble *RPDR* stars rather than seasoned members of their own community:

> All the older queens in the community are like: "We didn't have YouTube tutorials. You used to hope that a girl would think you're pretty enough that she'd let you watch her paint once and you'd lock it in your memory."…I love talking to the legendary queens in the community that have stories like that. Because, with the *Drag Race* girls, it's like, yeah, I can go online and watch Aquaria do three

different make-up tutorials and it's, like, so you can learn how to do exactly her face. And you definitely see some queens who you're like: "Oh, you learned from this queen and you can see exactly [what they're doing]." It's a really easy way to learn. With local girls, you used to have the thing of, "Oh, you look like your drag mother," but now you can look like any "x" queen from the show.[24]

In addition to visual influence, direct lines of influence between *RPDR* and the Toronto drag scene can be observed audibly. Almost immediately after a song is featured in a lip sync battle, DJs at drag bars will add it to their playlists and drag artists will start to perform it. As Lucinda Miu attests:

I find that if a song appears on the show, you will hear it in clubs. If it's an older song, it gives you a little bit more allowance to do it … then you kind of have a reference, the audience has a reference. It's kind of introduced into the lexicon of drag fans.[25]

Tash Riot echoes Miu, listing Demi Lovato's 2017 pop hit "Sorry Not Sorry" as one recent example. The song was featured in a high-energy lip sync battle between Brooke Lynn Hytes and Yvie Oddly during season 11 of *RPDR*, two years after it was promoted as a single. After that much-discussed lip sync, Riot began performing the song in her act:

When the "Sorry Not Sorry" lip sync happened, everyone was like: "OMG THIS SONG!" So you start doing "Sorry Not Sorry" at your weekly shows because people want to hear it. It's smart to keep in the loop with stuff like that.[26]

This is a good example of why many research participants feel the need to pay attention to *RPDR*. By including a nod to the show in her act, Riot is acknowledging the shared cultural meaning the song "Sorry Not Sorry" has acquired within the fan world of *RPDR*. Doing so is an act of fan service; local drag shows are typically filled with many *RPDR* fans, and engaging with *RPDR* is an easy, clever way to engage with the audience. It can also be seen as a pedagogical nod to the *RPDR* curriculum; knowing that drag fans are often students of the show, Riot draws on their fan knowledge as a way to invite them in to learn more about her and her drag practice.

One research participant, Miss Fiercalicious, is known locally for her cosplay-style re-creations of *RPDR* star Naomi Smalls' looks. On stage, she often performs one of Smalls' songs, "Pose," as well as the RuPaul track "Adrenaline," the latter of which was the soundtrack to a much-discussed lip sync battle featuring Smalls on *RPDR*. In our interview, Miss Fiercalicious says Smalls is one of her primary influences and that audiences, the majority of whom are already familiar with Smalls, instantly recognize the reference and react very positively to the Smalls-inspired act. She additionally frames Smalls pedagogically as one of her key drag teachers:

When I first started drag, Naomi Smalls was definitely someone who I was inspired by and looked up to. Visually, we're very similar. We're both half–Black, we have similar body types. It was easy to look at her and learn how to do drag from her. I didn't have a lot of similar role models, so seeing her on TV helped me with my own drag.[27]

Miss Fiercalicious performs RuPaul's "Adrenaline" in a Naomi Smalls-inspired outfit on Zoom. Originally in color.

## Toronto's Local Drag Curriculum: Community-Based Learning in Toronto

While the research participants unanimously list *RPDR* as a primary influence, this is not to suggest *RPDR* has completely replaced the traditional pathway to drag: discovering drag at the local level, then apprenticing in one's local scene under the guidance of one or more seasoned performers. This is what is known as the apprenticeship teaching perspective; according to the *Teaching Perspectives Inventory*, teachers who hold the Apprenticeship perspective "know what their learners can do on their own and where they need guidance and direction; they engage learners within their 'zone of development.'"[28] This apprenticeship style of teaching is common in the Toronto drag scene. New performers will often receive guidance from a veteran performer on a particular zone of development ranging from how to properly style a wig to how to handle an unruly or drunk audience member. This learning takes many forms, from observing an established performer's mic work to trading tips in dressing rooms, critiques offered from judges during drag competitions, and mentorship via one's drag family.

In drag culture, the widespread practice of choosing one's own non-biological family as a queer person has been semi-formalized as the longstanding tradition of having a drag "family" of non-biological drag parents, siblings, aunts, etc., who help new drag artists learn the craft. As Cameron Crookston establishes in "Passing the Torch Song: Mothers, Daughters, and Chosen Families in the Canadian Drag Community," drag families have been an important part of drag culture for decades and are still vital to many contemporary drag artists.[29] Several participants in this study, for example, have a drag mother who assists them in their drag career. In addition to the Apprenticeship perspective, this style of education often falls under the category of the Nurturing teaching perspective, meaning that drag parents encourage their children's efforts "while challenging [them] to do their very best by promoting a climate of caring and trust, helping people set challenging but achievable goals, and supporting effort as well as achievement."[30] The nurturing teaching perspective understands that some learners "have histories of failures resulting in lowered self-confidence,"[31] which is particularly valuable for queer students of gender performance who may have received scorn for their gender expressions within their birth families, geographic or cultural communities, or workplaces.

Drag families are also part of the lexicon of *RPDR*; many contestants speak about their drag families on the show, which has featured multiple members from particular drag families, such as the Davenport family (Sahara, Kennedy, Honey, A'keria, Monét X Change, and Ra'Jah O'Hara) and the House of Edwards (Shangela, Alyssa Edwards, Laganja Estranja, and Plastique Tiara). Crookston argues that "in taking a drag daughter under her wing, a drag mother connects their daughter to cultural artifacts from the art form's history."[32] I add that in this current era of mainstream drag, drag families serve as connective tissue in drag scenes, passing down localisms and strengthening the local scene's cultural persistence in the face of the global, corporate influence of *RPDR*. Further, these grassroots, localized traditions are now interwoven with the cultural forces of *RPDR*, creating the two-way dialogue between related cultures that Straw calls lines of influence between the local and the global.[33]

One weekly theme during the 2019 edition of CTDR, in particular, demonstrates the Toronto drag scene's capacity to produce its own culture rather than simply borrowing from *RPDR*. During this week, contestants were challenged to impersonate an artist from the local drag scene for a challenge dubbed the "Night of 1,000 Toronto Performers." Rather than looking outwards at drag happening within the highly commercial parameters of *RPDR*, the event organizers asked the contestants to look to their own community for inspiration. One performance from that evening, which I will detail shortly, stands out as resisting the ideologies of queerness and gender presented on *RDPR*. *RPDR* has a gender-specific format, meaning that the show almost exclusively presents drag as the domain of cisgender gay men presenting femininity. Contestants are regularly criticized for any quality deemed masculine by the judges. By contrast to what is typically showcased on *RPDR*, there are many performers in the Toronto drag scene who revel in presenting both feminine and masculine signifiers—especially drag queens who feature masculine-coded body hair alongside classically feminine wigs, makeup, and dress. Allysin Chaynes, who participated in CTDR 2014 and is known for her hairy chest, told me her intention is to subvert the idea that hair on particular body parts should be associated with a specific gender.[34] This subversion was taken an additional step further by 2019 CTDR contestant Akira, who chose to impersonate Chaynes during the Night of 1,000 Toronto Drag Performers. Akira, who is an AFAB (assigned female at birth) performer, painted their chest to mimic Chaynes' rich thicket of dark, curly chest hair. Akira's performance that evening was exceptionally layered; an AFAB artist presenting a masculine signifier (chest hair) as part of their impersonation of an AMAB (assigned male at birth) artist's (mostly) feminine drag. In creating these layers of gender and meaning, Akira blurs together fandom and locality, masculinity and femininity, and cosplay and community, creating a performance that is distinctly of their own scene.

Beyond a commentary on gender, the performance also demonstrates that despite the availability of *RPDR* episodes, YouTube tutorials, and the like, the exchange of technique, knowledge, and support is alive and well in the Toronto drag scene. On Instagram, Akira later revealed that Chaynes not only lent them the wig they wore during the performance in order to perfect their look, Chaynes also taught them how to perform one of her signature numbers. Though *RPDR* may have inspired contestants in CTDR to start doing drag, it is the support and ingenuity of their community that allows them to succeed on the stage. However, when Chaynes competed in CTDR in 2014, Akira would have been barred from the competition—at that time, the competition was not open to AFAB performers. The mentorship Chaynes offered to Akira and the layered, nuanced gender performance it produced is a testament to the progression of the gender curriculum offered by CTDR, which I will explore at length below.

## Teaching Gender: How the Toronto Scene Provides More Nuanced and Inclusive Lessons

Each annual edition of CTDR is overseen by a different drag artist—typically, a seasoned and well-respected former contestant who is now part of Crews and Tangos' regular stable of performers. In 2017, the competition was overseen by Xtacy Love, who won CTDR in 2013 and is drag mother to *Canada's Drag Race* season 1 star Priyanka (her full drag name is Priyanka Love). CTDR's host makes a number of executive decisions about the competition, from choosing weekly themes to dictating guidelines about who can enter. When Xtacy took the reins, she made a controversial decision: opening the competition up to all types of drag performers and people of all genders. The move allowed AFAB queens to compete in CTDR for the first time. Prior to 2017, CTDR had turned AFAB performers away[35]—as *RPDR* still does. While many in the community praised Love's inclusivity, the performer also received considerable backlash for her effort to progress beyond so-called traditional drag. Reflecting on the decision in a 2019 Facebook post, Love writes:

> The amount of HATE messages I got when I opened up #CrewsAndTangosDragRace to all forms of drag with the support of #CrewsAndTangos was staggering and overwhelming and it continued the entire season that I ran it. I had many breakdowns over it to be entirely honest.[36]

The view that gay cis male drag queens originated drag in the absence of women is ahistorical. RuPaul herself has said, "Great women have inspired great drag queens,"[37] but beyond serving as muse, women have actively participated in cultivating drag culture from the inside for nearly 150 years. The burlesque troupe The British Blondes, formed in the 1860s, for example, performed in both masculine and feminine garb.[38] Beyond similarities in style and a symbiotic relationship of influence, some women burlesque performers even consider themselves "female drag queens."[39] Cisgender women have been part of drag culture in drag's contemporary era, too, both as drag queens and kings, but their contributions to drag culture have often been pushed to the sidelines. The space in drag culture they are most conspicuously absent from is *RPDR*; while newer drag shows like *Dragula*, *Camp Wannakiki*, and *House of Drag* have included AFAB drag artists, *RPDR* has yet to evolve past its gender-specific format. AFAB drag artistry is simply not on RuPaul's drag curriculum.

Each research participant for this study is well-versed in the arguments for and against the inclusion of AFAB queens in the local drag community; it is clearly a topic they have all previously discussed at length. Outside of the research group, I have additionally observed the topic be hotly debated within queer circles on social media, in person at drag shows, and in both the queer and mainstream popular press. The research participants uniformly agree no 2018 CTDR contestants expressed any concerns with AFAB queens participating in the competition. The one AFAB queen who participated in this study, Tash Riot, says she felt supported by her fellow contestants: "No one else in the competition that I was competing against had an issue with [my gender]. They've had my back."[40] Riot adds she was welcomed by Crews and Tangos' management and the performer in charge of the 2018 competition, Carlotta Carlisle. Riot has also been hired to perform at Crews and Tangos on a regular basis following the competition. While Riot identifies her CTDR experience as positive, the majority of participants state they believe AFAB contestants in CTDR face additional challenges cis male contestants do not face.

For example, while performers of all genders are embraced by CTDR, the audience is not always as welcoming. Several participants report having had to educate friends and audience members about AFAB drag artistry. This is what would be called "learner-to-learner" engagement in a traditional classroom; students learn with and from each other. Participant Selena Vyle explains: "We'd hear whispers, when we were standing in the audience, like, 'Why is she in the competition? She's a real woman. It's not fair.'"[41] Participant Barbra Bardot explains the issue in another way:

> I've heard people say: "Oh, it's easier for [AFAB queens]. They've been doing makeup their whole lives, their bodies are the shape of their bodies." But none of that is true. They haven't been doing drag makeup their whole lives.... I don't think that they're at an advantage and I think they're fighting more barriers than [cis gay male drag queens] to get places. I welcome them being in a competition because being on stage gives them the exposure and it helps open up a conversation.[42]

Both Vyle and Bardot report having used Riot's participation in the competition as a teachable moment for members of the audience. Bardot admitted several people she invited to the competition were unfamiliar with AFAB drag artistry and initially reacted poorly towards it: "I had the conversation so many times, how [AFAB artists] are also drag queens. We're all drag queens."[43] While this initial reaction is rooted in exclusion, this is a positive, progressive opportunity for education. Season 1 of *Canada's Drag Race*, meanwhile, showcases another such moment featuring Indigenous artist Ilona Verley, who is of the Nlaka'pamux Nation. In the premiere episode, Verley explains that they are two-spirit, which means they honor both their masculine and feminine energy:

> Growing up, I was so in this mindset of, "You are male, you have to be male." As I grew up and got more involved in my own culture, I learned about being queer and being two-spirit, which means finding yourself in between the male and the female energy, but acknowledging both of them.[44]

It is an excellent teachable moment, but for many drag fans, it also highlighted a missed opportunity—couldn't the show similarly welcome AFAB artists and teach the audience about their identity and place in drag culture? Perhaps that moment is on the horizon: in an interview for a magazine article, *Canada's Drag Race* producer Mike Bickerton told me casting was "open to all" and the show's casting team made decisions based only on "charisma, uniqueness, nerve and talent" (a line borrowed from RuPaul)—leaving the door potentially open to those who do not fit into *RPDR*'s gender-specific format. Representatives for the show did not, however, answer specific questions relating to the casting of drag kings or AFAB queens.

## *Teaching Economics:* RPDR *Has Taught Drag Should Look Expensive, and That's a Problem for Local Performers*

Drag labor is, in most cases, precarious work. Drag artists in Toronto typically do not work for a single employer; they are often booked for a single night of work at a time and are paid via a myriad of financial arrangements rather than being on an employer's payroll. Drag artists on the local level typically do not make high wages, and the social leverage they gain as popular or well-known performers often does not translate to social or cultural capital outside of niche queer social circles. Only two of my nine research participants work in drag full-time. Such is often the case; even RuPaul, arguably the world's most successful drag artist, has referred to drag as her "part-time job."[45] In spending time embedded in this community, I learned that working in drag full-time is an anomaly, but not impossible in Toronto. During our interviews, several research participants spoke about working in the service sector in addition to drag, or in other cash economies such as sewing garments for fellow artists. Many drag performers in Toronto make ends meet by performing a number of different jobs within the world of drag and queer nightlife, from styling wigs to teaching makeup classes, deejaying, and working the door at parties. Some also have established careers in professional fields and work as schoolteachers, media personalities, project managers, and veterinary technicians. When they are at their drag jobs, either at one-off gigs or working more regularly as part of a bar's house stable of performers, the majority of drag performers in Toronto are afforded very few of the protections provided to other workers such as job security, medical insurance, and other benefits like dental coverage. Drag artists typically work in a cash economy and are not part of any union, as are actors or other entertainment industry workers. This type of work is common for queer people according to Hollibaugh and Weiss, who posit that neoliberal economic restructuring has squeezed many queer workers out of the traditional economy altogether, pushing them into cash or other alternative economies.[46]

While conducting my ethnography, I interviewed a separate group of Toronto-based drag artists about their finances for a series of articles for *Flare* magazine.[47] These performers disclosed how much they are typically paid for drag and drag-adjacent jobs. On the lower end, they report earning about $50 for deejaying and working the door at drag events, jobs they typically dress in drag for. Most list $100 as a baseline fee for performing, though they also acknowledge the free labor they did while working to establish themselves in Toronto, such as performing at open stage events and taking part in competitions such as CTDR that do not pay contestants. According to the artists I interviewed, corporate clients pay the most for jobs such as performing at branded Pride events and appearing in advertisements, but those opportunities are few and far between. Every one of the artists I interviewed expresses that it is a struggle to make ends meet as a queer artist in Toronto—even for those who have full-time work in addition to working in drag.

Complicating matters, *RPDR* has heightened audience expectations for how glossy—and expensive—drag should be. It has taught the audience that drag is elaborate, extravagant, and pricey. Even from season 1, *RPDR* positioned drag as expensive: Shannel proudly announced she'd brought $25,000 worth of costuming and rhinestones on the show's very first episode.[48] Season 9 winner Sasha Velour disclosed she spent $4,000 (USD) on costumes to wear on *RPDR*,[49] and Miz Cracker (season 10, *All Stars* season 5) has spoken about taking out a bank loan to buy things for the show. These performers are splurging on outfits, wigs, and shoes with the understanding the exposure they will receive from *RPDR* will lead to future financial gains, but most artists in the Toronto scene have no such safety net. Given the relatively low fees drag performers in Toronto receive, they simply do not have the funds to compete with the luxe visuality of *RPDR*, but audiences are not necessarily attuned to this financial disparity—the cost of doing drag is rarely one of the lessons of the show (Monique Heart's frank commentary about money on season 10 is a notable exception). When *RPDR* fans attend a local show, Vyle says they expect to see expensive garments—and when they don't, they're quick to critique:

> People think that what they see on TV needs to translate to what you see in the club. They'll read you for your looks, they'll read you for your performances. And they'll compare you to a queen they saw on TV who's doing it with a lot more money behind them. That's the only negative drawback I would say. We now have to keep up with what's happening on TV.[50]

This is a point of contention for many of the research participants. *RPDR* fans who have found their way to local drag shows have a specific framing for drag; the drag they are familiar with is within the context of reality television. It is perfectly lit, shot in HD, color-corrected, and professionally edited. The contestants have been cast and edited to appear as appealing (or perfectly villainous) characters, and the expensive garments showcased are out of reach for most Toronto-based performers.

The corporate infrastructure *RPDR* has built is specifically designed to support the show and put money in the hands of its creators, not in the pockets of local performers. Many fan events such as live tours and fan conventions are produced by the same production company behind *RPDR*, World of Wonder. As a result of this, many of the financial opportunities of this new era of commercially viable drag are available almost exclusively to *RPDR* alumnae. There is without a doubt a commercial trickle-down effect for drag artists in local scenes such as Toronto's—gigs opening for performers featured on *RPDR* and hosting *RPDR* viewing parties are obvious examples—but several research participants expressed frustration with the disparity between the economics of *RPDR* and the global drag scene and the economics of local drag in Toronto. Lucinda Miu, who produces events with her drag family and is thus dependent on revenue from ticket sales, explains: "[P]ersonal friends of mine won't shell out a $5 or $10 cover fee [at a local event] but they will go see a Ru Girl for $100 to $250."[51]

The perceived value of a drag artist who has basked in the glow of television fame became particularly apparent when Toronto's own Brooke Lynn Hytes appeared on *RPDR*. For several years in the early 2010s, Hytes performed regularly at bars in Toronto's Gay Village, but never, to my knowledge, drew a crowd quite like the one that showed up at the popular drag venue Woody's in Toronto following her *RPDR* debut in February 2019. When Hytes hosted a viewing party for the first episode of *RPDR* she appeared in, the line curled out the bar doors and around the block; one Woody's staff member later claimed the bar welcomed more patrons that night than during the 2018 Pride festival. Research participant Porcelain Tylez expresses frustration that these *RPDR* fans hadn't supported Hytes in her pre–TV career:

> The lineup was down the street. That's the impact [*RPDR*] has on the culture. You'd never see that at a regular night. But she's famous…. That's disgusting. They're there for their hometown girl, but they never saw her before she was on the show.[52]

Tylez is using hyperbolic speech when they call the crowd "disgusting"; I understood this statement to be said partially in jest, but the disparity between the fanfare *RPDR* receives and the fan support for the local scene is a real frustration for Tylez. This sentiment is shared by several other research participants as well as other performers I have spoken to in Toronto. I have observed Toronto's drag scene to be vibrant, active, and even commercially viable, with at least a handful of small-scale shows every night, but the official fan activities for *RPDR* operate at a much larger scale.

There is also a great disparity between what drag performers in Toronto earn and the potential for income if a performer has appeared on *RPDR*. It has been reported that fees for *RPDR* alumnae are often in the thousands.[53] Season 6 performer Laganja Estranja told *Vulture* her booking fee is $1,500 (USD) per show, adding that performers showcased on the show since it moved from Logo to VH1 in 2017—thus reaching a much wider audience—charge as much as $5,000 (USD) per show.[54] By contrast, booking fees for Toronto performers are a small fraction of the fees *RPDR* stars command (as mentioned, $100 is the typical baseline booking fee).[55]

One night at Crews and Tangos, Allysin Chaynes offered a useful analogy: if *RPDR* is the massive chain store, they are the farmer's market of drag. While Chaynes was making a joke as part of her act, this is actually a useful way of thinking about global versus local drag; like any McDonald's, H&M or Walmart, *RPDR* is part of a stable of business endeavors owned by a large corporation with international reach. (*RPDR* is a VH1 property, under the NBCUniversal umbrella, which is part of ComCast). Using Straw's lines of influence, it can be understood that the trends in an independently owned clothing store may eventually end up in H&M, but what's available at H&M also influences the local boutique as it signifies what is currently happening in mainstream fashion and offers shoppers an easily accessible competing product.[56] The same is true for *RPDR*; as I have previously argued, what happens in local drag scenes influences what is later seen on *RPDR*, but what is seen on *RPDR* also influences—and often competes with—what happens in the local scene.

## *Teaching Race: RPDR's Refusal to Teach Anti-Racism Reflexively Makes Race Education Vital*

The race-related topic the participants are most eager to discuss is the rampant racism in *RPDR* fan culture. Participants unanimously agree the *RPDR* fandom has a major racism problem. Racism in the *RPDR* fan base has been a perennial topic on fan message boards and in the media. Season 8 winner Bob the Drag Queen, for instance, has pointed out that the most popular *RPDR* contestants on social media share two qualities: they are white and thin.[57] At the time she made this observation, six *RPDR* queens had garnered more than one million followers on Instagram and each of them was white. The only BIPOC queen to reach more than one million followers on Instagram at that point was RuPaul herself. Research participant Harmony links drag audiences' frequent preference for thin, white performers to wider Western ideals, which are reinforced by the beauty pageant-style format shared by *RPDR* and CTDR. Harmony argues that drag is multicultural on the grassroots level, which leads to diverse casting on *RPDR*, but once the contestants arrive, they are filtered through the lens of reality television and the Western tradition of the beauty pageant:

> It's one of those interesting things where the show is innately multicultural because drag is multicultural and also so much of drag comes from POC communities. Then it's also, like, when you're putting so much of the show into a beauty pageant format, obviously our Westernized ideals of beauty are going to come into play and they're going to favour [*sic*] the white girls. They're going to favour [*sic*] the skinny people.[58]

Many *RPDR* alumnae, such Bebe Zahara Benet and Asia O'Hara, have been vocal about the racist vitriol they have received from fans on social media. These calls have not been adequately addressed by RuPaul or *RPDR*; while the show is diverse, a self-reflexive lesson on anti-racism is not yet on its curriculum. O'Hara is one of several BIPOC *RPDR* contestants to receive death threats and Benet, the Black winner of *RPDR* season 1, has noted users flooded her social feeds with monkey emojis and racial slurs following her appearance on *RPDR All Stars* season 3.[59] Research participant Lucinda Miu asserts this is something she has frequently observed on social media:

> There are a lot of contestants, particularly Black queens, from *RuPaul's Drag Race*, who experience a lot of awful comments on their Instagrams [*sic*]. Their successes are lesser than their white counterparts and their failures are even worse. I think that we all know how bad racism is in our day and age, but I feel like sometimes we have a misconception that as part of the LGBT+ community that we understand what it feels like to be oppressed and what it feels like to be harmed and unsafe so you would think that we wouldn't contribute to that but sadly we really, really do.[60]

During a 2018 interview, *RPDR All Stars* season 4 contestant Monét X Change offered this to me as a starting point for any conversation about race and *RPDR*:

> It's important to recognize that *RuPaul's Drag Race* is one of the most ethnically diverse competition reality shows ever. In season 10, eight of us were of colour [*sic*]. You have the five Black girls, Kalorie Karbdashion, Vanessa Mateo and Yuhua [Hamasaki]. You don't see that on *The Real World: Battle of the Seasons*.[61]

X Change is certainly correct on this point. It is also critical to note that *RPDR* has made stars out of many BIPOC drag artists, X Change included, and that the fact they have not been as well received by fans as their white peers is, in part, a product of wider systemic racism. X Change frames the issue of racism as one of wider visibility, noting that *RPDR* fans are not used to seeing people of color on TV in general, positing the fan base for *RPDR* is different from, for example, shows like *The Real Housewives of Atlanta* that feature predominantly Black casts.[62] *RPDR* has also had its share of BIPOC winners, including, to name a few, Benet, Bob the Drag Queen, Bianca Del Rio, Raja, and Tyra Sanchez. Indeed, *RPDR* is more progressive than many of its counterparts in terms of celebrating BIPOC excellence on screen, but the show's treatment of race also raises some concerns.

*RPDR*'s depiction of race cannot be separated from the way race is represented on reality television at large. As Jay Clarkson argues, "[T]he reality TV apparatus bears great responsibility for re-essentializing [sic] race."[63] Elaborating on this point, Grace Wang explains that as a genre, reality television "adheres to and authenticates racialized narratives and stereotyping by embodying them in the characters of 'real' people."[64] In other words, the framing of reality television suggests to its viewers that characters are in fact not characters at all, but real people, and any racialized narratives or stereotypes are not television tropes but authentic parts of a cast member's personality. Many other reality shows, including *RPDR* predecessor *America's Next Top Model*, have also been accused of employing racialized stereotypes and re-essentializing race.[65]

In terms of *RPDR* specifically, a number of scholars[66] have demonstrated how the show plays up racial stereotypes. Eric Zhang attests that "Drag Race's contestants of color—Asian, Black, Latin[x] and Native American alike—are often rewarded for incorporating racial stereotypes into their performance."[67] Zhang cites season 3 contestant Manila Luzon, a Filipino-American drag artist whose name pays homage to her mother's heritage, in particular for "appropriating Asian stereotypes into her routine, underscoring her racialized [sic] body on stage."[68] Manila's presentation of race on the show, which includes switching *L*s and *R*s to create a stereotypical pan-Asian accent, is also called out by Hodes and Sandoval, who attest Manila "embodies a series of racist stereotypes that are presented as scenes of comedic relief."[69] McIntyre and Riggs likewise call out *RPDR*'s linguicism,[70] defined by Robert Phillipson as "ideologies and structures where language is the means for affecting or maintaining an unequal allocation of power and resources."[71] McIntyre and Riggs contend there is an over-emphasis on the English language capabilities of Puerto Rican contestants, writing that "the show's evocation of both linguistic imperialism and stereotypes based on assumptions about Puerto Rican culture perpetuate the exclusion of those from the global South."[72]

In Toronto, many of the most popular and respected drag performers are BIPOC, a point participant Harmony makes during our interview. Harmony underscores the impact racism within the *RPDR* fandom has had on drag audiences in Toronto, while also asserting that the influence is not strong enough to have kept Toronto's BIPOC performers from succeeding in the local scene. Here she cites a handful of examples of local BIPOC stars, including two future *Canada's Drag Race* season 1 contestants:

> It has a larger impact on the audience. In Toronto, the thought leaders in the drag community are 90% POC. When you name the top five people who work regularly that come to your mind in Toronto drag, it's Sofonda Cox, Jada Hudson, Priyanka, Tynomi Banks, and Baby bel-Bel. [Baby bel-Bel] is the only white queen out of all of them. I don't think that people who are doing drag are being negatively affected by the race issues on the show but I think the audiences are.[73]

There are parallels between *RPDR* as a diverse television show and Toronto as a city that prides itself on embracing multiculturalism. Participant Miss Fiercalicious articulates this experience as a BIPOC performer in the scene via this anecdote:

> One time I was at Woody's during Pride and this one person called me the n-word out of nowhere. The Woody's staff was amazing, they had them removed. [Racism] still exists. You might not think so in a city like Toronto that is so multicultural, you wouldn't expect racism to be alive, but it happens unfortunately.[74]

Miss Fiercalicious continues by explaining such overt racism is just one aspect of white supremacy in drag culture:

> It also exists in more subtle terms now in ways that you wouldn't expect, like having unfair expectations of Black artists, asking them to perform songs only by other Black artists, or comparing them to white queens and not having the same expectations for everyone that you do for Black artists.[75]

In one of our interviews, Fiercalicious also calls attention to a conversation started by her friend and drag colleague Luna DuBois in June 2020. DuBois posted about her experiences with the Toronto drag bar The Drink and started a petition calling for accountability from one of the managers, who, the petition alleges, has been both racist and transphobic.[76] Following DuBois' post and petition, many other BIPOC and otherwise marginalized community members started to speak out about their own experiences in queer spaces in Toronto. This call-to-action provided another educational moment: through DuBois' labor as a drag educator, local drag fans and performers—especially those who are white—began to learn more about the experiences of BIPOC artists and patrons at drag shows. This is not an easy nor pain-free process, but it is an essential part of the drag curriculum in Toronto—and in other cities, too. Around the same time, for example, a group of drag artists in Chicago started the Chicago Black Drag Council to address racism in the Chicago drag scene. This labor of critiquing one's own community and place in white supremacy is essential to teaching race in local scenes—even if anti-racism is not on RuPaul's curriculum.

## Conclusion

Over the course of the past decade, *RPDR* has drastically changed the way drag is taught. The show's public pedagogy represents an entire generation of drag baby boomers' first real lesson in drag. As drag culture's dominant system of articulation, *RPDR* has informed how drag is understood by its audience via its drag curriculum. This essay demonstrates, however, that the drag education offered by *RPDR* is not drag culture's only curriculum. For decades prior to the show's debut, drag was taught via a community-based exchange of ideas, skills, and knowledge. This style of learning is still active in drag scenes around the world. In Toronto, there is a drag curriculum beyond *RPDR* taught in bars, dressing rooms, and other types of venues all over the city. Operating outside the neoliberal realm of reality TV, this grassroots curriculum offers inclusivity to those left out of *RPDR*'s classroom, including, notably, AFAB drag artists. Attending drag shows in Toronto will also offer drag fans an education on what drag looks and feels like when practiced by artists with limited access to capital. Finally, the scene offers lessons in anti-racism not on *RPDR*'s lesson plan.

This ethnographic study was led by the contributions of its research participants and thus reflects their various identities. As such, I didn't focus on, for example, the vast contributions of transgender and non-binary artists to Toronto's drag culture, nor the burgeoning re-emergence of drag kinging that has taken place in Toronto in recent years. Both are topics worthy of unique scholarship outside the scope of the study. The sociocultural fabric of Toronto's scene, I should note, is unique, though there are likely lines of influence between Toronto and many other scenes—especially in this global era of drag.

The results of my ethnography do not suggest the Toronto drag scene is inherently progressive. It is, without a doubt, more inclusive than *RPDR* in respect to gender, but it has many of the same problems with racism, classism, and misogyny that *RPDR* does—though they manifest and become visible in different ways. Drag education beyond *RPDR* is ultimately student-led; this is true both for the drag artists who participated in interviews and for myself as an ethnographer. The lessons detailed in this essay on class, gender, and race, are available to any drag fan or artist in Toronto, but as the ethnography unfolded, I sought these specific lessons out as a scholar, a drag fan, and a student of drag culture. It is possible to avidly attend drag shows in Toronto and see mostly white performers, rarely see AFAB artists or hairy queens, and avoid drag kings almost altogether. However, for those looking, the city provides a deep and diverse drag curriculum within reach of any student.

## Mini Challenge: Discussion Questions

- What are some other examples of public pedagogy?
- How do other public figures (such as authors, artists, and politicians) act as educators in the public sphere?
- This essay explores the ways in which gender is explored and taught by drag performers. Who did you learn about gender from, and how?

## Maxi Challenge: Activities and Assignments

- As a written assignment, students are asked to view one episode of *RuPaul's Drag Race* and identify three moments of pedagogy, either from the judging panel to the contestants, contestant to contestant, or show to audience. Then they will be asked to explain (200 words per response) what is being taught and whether it is a successful education method.
- Using this essay as a starting point, students will gather in breakout groups and discuss public pedagogy that takes place in other pop culture texts such as sports, music, and fashion. They will be asked in particular to discuss the politics of what's being taught in the texts they identify.
- As either a written assignment or a classroom discussion, students will be asked to identify other community-based teaching and learning models from their own lives and communities, exploring the question: How does teaching and learning take place in my cultural, geographic, and/or interest-based community?

## Notes

1. Boyd, Jade. "'Hey, We're from Canada, but We're Diverse, Right?': Neoliberalism, Multiculturalism, and Identity on So You think You Can Dance Canada." *Critical Studies in Media Communication*, vol. 29, no. 4, 2012, pp. 259–274.

Patterson, Natasha. "Sabotaging Reality: Exploring Canadian Women's Participation on Neoliberal Reality TV." *Canadian Journal of Communication*, vol. 40, 2015, pp. 281–295.

2. Straw, Will. "Systems of Articulation, Logics of Change: Scenes and Communities in Popular Music." *Cultural Studies*, vol. 6, no. 3, 1991, p. 369.

3. *Ibid*.

4. *Ibid*.

5. Giroux, Henry A. "Cultural studies, public pedagogy, and the responsibility of intellectual." *Communication and Critical/Cultural Studies*, vol. 1, no. 1, p. 59.

6. Whitworth, Colin. "Sissy That Performance Script! The Queer Pedagogy of RuPaul's Drag Race." *RuPaul's Drag Race and the Shifting Visibility of Drag Culture*, edited by Niall Brennan and David Gudelunas, Palgrave Macmillan, 2017, p. 141.

7. Fine, David J., & Shreve, Emily. "The Prime of Miss RuPaul Charles: Allusion, Betrayal and Charismatic Pedagogy." *The Makeup of RuPaul's Drag Race: Essays on the Queen of Reality Shows*, edited by Jim Daems, McFarland & Company, 2016, p. 169.

8. Butler, Judith. *Gender Trouble*, 3rd ed., Routledge, 1999, p. 24.

9. Scudera, Domenick. "The Professor Is a Drag Queen," *Chronicle of Higher Education*, vol. 61, no. 16, 2015, p. 1.

10. Schacht, Steven P. "Beyond the Boundaries of the Classroom: Teaching About Gender and Sexuality at a Drag Show." *Journal of Homosexuality*, vol. 46, no. 3–4, p. 225.

11. *Ibid*., p. 233.

12. See Giroux, p. 61.

13. Grace, Meghan, & Seemiller, Corey. *Generation Z*, Routledge, 2019, p. 11.

14. Kidron, Beeban, director. *To Wong Foo, Thanks for Everything! Julie Newmar*. Universal Pictures, 1995.

15. Crookston, Cameron. "Passing the torch song: Mothers, daughters, and chosen families in the Canadian drag community." *Q2Q: Queer Canadian Theatre and Performance*, edited by Peter Dickinson, C.E. Gatchalian, and Kathleen Oliver, vol. 8, Playwrights Canada Press, 2018, p. 62.

16. Fiske, John. "The Cultural Economy of Fans." *The Adoring Audience: Fan Culture and Popular Media*, edited by Lisa A. Lewis, Routledge, 1992, p. 35.

17. Silencia. Personal interview. 2 Jul. 2019.

18. Vyle, Selena. Personal interview. 8 May 2019.

19. See Vyle.

20. Miu, Lucinda. Personal interview. 6 May 2019.

21. Scotto, Miss. Personal interview. 2 Sept. 2019.

22. *Ibid*.

23. See Miu.

24. Riot, Tash. Personal interview. 10 Jun. 2019.

25. See Miu.

26. See Riot.

27. Fiercalicious, Miss. Personal interview. 8 Jul. 2019.

28. "The Five Perspectives." *Teaching Perspectives Inventory*, Teachingperspectives.com/tpi/.

29. See Crookston, p. 55.

30. See "The Five Perspectives."

31. *Ibid*.

32. See Crookston, p. 58.

33. See Straw, p. 369.

34. Chaynes, Allysin. Personal interview, *Feel Your Fantasy*, Vol. 1, No.1, 2018. 16 Oct 2017.

35. Willard, Jeremy. "Toronto's faux queen phenomenon." *Xtra*, 15 Apr. 2016, www.Dailyxtra.com/torontos-faux-queen-phenomenon-70719.

36. Love, Xtacy. "All drag is valid…" *Facebook*, 28 Jun. 2019, www.facebook.com/missxtacylove/posts/2318980471520852.

37. "Queens of All Media." *RuPaul's Drag Race*, season 1, episode 3, Logo TV, 16 Feb. 2009. Amazon, https://www.amazon.com/gp/video/detail/B001RGOIWW/ref=atv_dp_season_select_s1.

38. Dodds, Sherril. "Embodied Transformations in Neo-Burlesque Striptease." *Dance Research Journal*, vol. 45, no. 3, 2013, p. 77.

39. Lynn, Sally. "'It is the Ugly That is so Beautiful': Performing the Monster/Beauty Continuum in American Neo-Burlesque." *The Journal of American Drama and Theatre*, vol. 21, no. 3., 2009, p. 16.

40. See Riot.

41. See Vyle.

42. Bardot, Barbra. Personal interview. 15 Jul. 2019.

43. See Bardot.

44. "Eh-Laganza Eh-Xtravaganza." *Canada's Drag Race*, directed by Shelagh O'Brien, Saloon Media, 2020.

45. RuPaul. *Workin' It!: RuPaul's Guide to Life, Liberty, and the Pursuit of Style*, It Books, 2010, p. 61.

46. Hollibaugh, Amber, & Weiss, Margot. "Queer Precarity and the Myth of Gay Affluence." *New Labor Forum*, vol. 22, no. 3, 2015, p. 22.

47. Martin, Russ. "Monét X Change, Miz Cracker and The Vixen Get Real about Racism and RuPaul's Drag Race." *Flare*, 26 Jun. 2018, www.Flare.com/tv-movies/rupauls-drag-race-racism/.

48. "Drag on a Dime." *RuPaul's Drag Race*, season 1, episode 1, Logo TV, 29 Jan. 2009. *Amazon*, https://www.amazon.com/gp/video/detail/B001RGOIWW/ref=atv_dp_season_select_s1.

49. Oltuski, Romy. "How Much it Costs to Be a Drag Queen, According to *RuPaul's Drag Race* Winner Sasha Velour." *InStyle*, 20 Dec. 2018, www.Instyle.com/celebrity/money-talks/sasha-velour-rupauls-drag-race.

50. See Vyle.

51. See Miu.

52. Tylez, Porcelain. Personal interview. 7 Aug. 2019.

53. Chapman, Sam. "Local Drag Performers Often Don't Get Paid Enough to Even Cover the Cost of Their Outfit." *The Stranger*, 21 Sept. 2018, www.Thestranger.com/slog/2018/09/21/32646576/tip-your-local-drag-queens-they-need-it.

54. "The Most Powerful Drag Queens in America." *Vulture*, 10 Jun. 2019, www.Vulture.com/2019/06/most-powerful-drag-queens-in-america-ranked.html.

55. See Martin.

56. See Straw, p. 369.

57. Henry, Phillip. "RuPaul Needs to Take Responsibility for the Racism on Drag Race." *them*, 28 Jun. 2018, www.Them.us/story/racism-rupauls-drag-race.

58. Harmony. Personal interview. 8 Aug. 2019, 14 Jul. 2020.

59. Martin, Russ. "Monét X Change, Miz Cracker and The Vixen Get Real about Racism and RuPaul's Drag Race." *Flare*, 26 Jun. 2018, www.Flare.com/tv-movies/rupauls-drag-race-racism/.

60. See Miu.

61. Martin, Russ. "What's In Your Drag Bag" *Flare*, 21 Jun. 2019, www.Flare.com/tag/whats-in-your-drag-bag.

62. *Ibid*.

63. Clarkson, Jay. "Contesting Masculinity's Makeover: Queer Eye, Consumer Masculinity, and 'Straight-Acting' Gays." *Journal of Communication Inquiry*, vol. 29, no. 3, 2005, p. 2005.

64. Wang, Grace. "A shot at half-exposure: Asian Americans in reality TV shows." *Television and New Media*, vol. 11, no. 5, 2010, p. 405.

65. Bui, Long T., & Strings, Sabrina. "She Is Not Acting, She Is." *Feminist Media Studies*, vol. 14, no. 5, 2014. p. 824.

66. See Bui and Strings; Hodes and Sandoval; McIntyre and Riggs; Zhang.

67. Zhang, Eric. "Memoirs of a GAY! Sha: Race and gender performance on RuPaul's Drag Race." *Studies in Costume & Performance*, vol. 1, no. 2, 2016, p. 65.

68. *Ibid*.

69. Hodes, Caroline, & Sandoval, Jorge. "RuPaul's Drag Race: A study in the

commodification of white rule-class femininity and the etiolation of drag." *Studies in Costume & Performance*, vol. 3, no. 2, p. 158.

70. McIntyre, Joanna, & Riggs, Damien W. "North American Universalism in RuPaul's Drag Race: Stereotypes, Linguicism, and the Construction of Puerto Rican Queens." *RuPaul's Drag Race and the Shifting Visibility of Drag Culture*, edited by Niall Brennan and David Gudelunas, Palgrave Macmillan, 2017, p 61.

71. Phillipson, Robert. "Linguistic imperialism." *The Sociological Quarterly*, vol. 39, no. 3, 1992, p. 514.

72. See McIntyre & Riggs, p. 61.

73. See Harmony.

74. See Fiercalicious.

75. *Ibid.*

76. Dubois, Luna. "Now that I have your attention…" *Facebook*, 3 Jun. 2020, www.facebook.com/misslunadubois/posts/283282076179622.

# "Cultural appropriation! That's what we never heard"
## *Performing Indigeneity on Reality Television and Beyond*

### Maggie Ward

"O honey! Pocahontas? Oh honey!
More like poke a hunty"[1]
"U can't appropriate ur own culture"[2]
"Oh honey, half breed honey?
More like ready to breed honey"[3]
"just bc she is native doesn't give that right…"[4]
"Come on casino queen"[5]
"I don't understand the problem, drag queens always dress
using other cultures, of course it's a costume it's drag!"[6]

Above are but a handful of the comments responding to drag queen, comedian, and recording artist Trixie Mattel's February 2019 Instagram post in which she[7] dons a pink headdress made of what appears to be plastic feathers and a long, glittering pink loincloth with matching top.[8] As is evident from these few examples, the image, as well as others that followed, have prompted a number of misogynistic and racist reactions pertaining to Indigenous womanhood and have also sparked a debate about an issue not unfamiliar to contemporary, mainstream drag: cultural appropriation. These social media discussions, largely focused on whether or not Trixie, who is Ojibwe on her mother's side, has the right to wear and perform in the costume, reveal at least two significant attitudes regarding performed Indigeneity both within and without the context of drag: that drag culture and drag performers are often considered exempt from "politically correct" modes of public discourse and are therefore permitted to engage in any kind of performance or representation, and that performances of racial or cultural stereotypes are acceptable when enacted by members of the group being "played." The "playfulness" of drag, while often perceived to challenge hegemonic notions of gender, thus also has the potential to reify hegemonic notions of race and culture. As such, the appropriative and misrepresentative drag performances analyzed here potentially teach audiences that racial and cultural identities are as open to parody as gender, despite the fact that, as artist Nine Yamamoto-Masson reminds us: "Black, Indigenous, and People of Colour [sic] often face ridicule, discrimination, social backlash, violence for features that are celebrated when worn by [non–Black, non–Indigenous, and/or white] people."[9]

This essay will work to trace the ways in which *RuPaul's Drag Race* (*RPDR*) informs these ideologies by examining how certain "Indian Princess" performances are accepted and celebrated on the show. Investigating two cases of Indigenous dress by two different contestants[10]—Monét X Change in season 10 and Raja in season 3—I will demonstrate how this celebration ultimately acts as cultural erasure and has the potential to reinforce those stereotypes that lead to sexual violence and the disappearance and murder of Indigenous women and girls. The essay will then return to Trixie Mattel and will compare her act of cultural misrepresentation to the appropriations of the *RPDR* contestants in order to nuance discussions of cultural appropriation and to explore the pedagogical implications of such performances. Central to these interrogations is the degree to which these performances are contextualized. We must question the extent to which these performances are located, or not, in specific contexts in order to best understand their impacts as either subversive and educational or as ignorant and damaging. Thus, my purpose here is not to police Trixie's identity nor to question her Indigeneity, but rather to explore how her *de*contextualized performances and images may elicit harmful audience responses that work to reproduce colonial violence and discrimination. Finally, I turn to the work of Two-Spirit Cree visual artist Kent Monkman, whose artistic persona, Miss Chief Eagle Testickle, figures in many of his paintings and performance art. With the insertion Miss Chief into his work, Monkman's art is often perceived as disrupting, reimagining, and *re*contextualizing representations of Indigenous peoples in colonial art. However, some of his more recent pieces commit some of the same harms as those perpetrated former *RPDR* contestants. Comparing Monkman's drag acts to those of Raja, Monét, and Trixie, I seek ultimately to identify the ways in which drag can succeed in its subversive and radical potential for educating audiences—not only on the harmful effects of cultural appropriation, but more broadly on colonial histories and Indigenous modes of resistance and refusal. I also seek to identify the ways it can, and does, fail.

## RuPaul's Drag Race: *Revolutionary or Regressive?*

Lauded for its entertainment value and for offering platforms for queer, trans, and non-binary performers, *RPDR* has received numerous accolades for its ostensible success in challenging hegemonic notions of gender and sexuality. Yet, as several scholars have pointed out, even as it highlights the constructed nature of gender through subversive appropriations—though most often with cis men impersonating women—the show also works to reproduce racial and cultural stereotypes by encouraging racially essentialist performances of gender, or else applauding racially or culturally appropriative performances. In an especially critical examination of this phenomenon, Sabrina Strings and Long T. Bui note that "amid gender play on *RuPaul's Drag Race* there is an adherence to racial 'authenticity,'" where, "for the [B]lack and [B]rown characters on the show, racial realness means staying 'true' to one's off-stage ethnic/racial identity, a requirement not enforced for the white and Asian characters [the "Heathers"] on the show."[11] Focusing specifically on the show's third season and the judges' evaluative distinctions between the Heathers and the "Boogers" (the Black and Brown contestants), Strings and Bui assert that, for white and Asian queens, "race, when in drag, is malleable. It is equally open to performance as gender."[12] Significantly, they point out the harm embedded in these performances:

> [R]acial play recalls all too readily the violent history of minstrelsy, and creates legitimate concerns for the [B]lack and [B]rown contestants about damning representations of Other social groups. Unfortunately, this racial rigidity remakes race into the biologically fixed category from which gender has just escaped. In other words, race is naturalized even as the gender is destabilized.[13]

While the degree to which gender is *actually* destabilized on *RPDR* is questionable,[14] the show's expectation of essentialist racialized performances by Black and Brown contestants and the celebration of racial play by white and Asian queens point to the ways in which, as Hodes and Sandoval note, "the embodiment of racialized gender stereotypes is central to the success of the show and the successful branding of the contestants."[15] This, in turn, leaves these performances "caught in a state of unresolvable tension or in fatally un-subversive appropriations," preserving the racist status quo.[16]

While Strings and Bui and Hodes and Sandoval point to the ways in which race is performed and essentialized on *RPDR*—including, for instance, Filipino-American contestant Manila Luzon's winning performance as a stereotypical pan-Asian woman in season 3—less attention has been paid to

Indigenous appropriation on the show and the kinds of ideologies these acts reinforce.[17] Indeed, while Nishant Upadhyay offers an excellent analysis of Raja's appropriative performances in season 3[18] and her complicity in settler colonialism, to which I will return, they also state that their aim is "not simply to make an argument against cultural appropriation. While those critiques are important, they are often taken up by decontextualizing the issue and effacing the larger structural processes of power, commodification, and consumption at play."[19] While this is certainly true, as analyses of appropriation tend to become individualized or else emphasize intentionality, Upadhyay appears to fail to recognize that, as Dionne Brand writes:

> Cultural appropriation is not an accusation, it is a critical category. [...] It proposes that imagery, images, the imagination and representation are deeply ideological in that they suggest ways of thinking about people and the world. This critique goes beyond the mere notion of "good" and "bad" representation; it is more concerned with how we see, enact and re-enact, make, define and redefine, vision how we lived and how we are going to live.[20]

In this sense, then, cultural appropriation critiques *are* deeply contextual and are inextricably linked to structural issues. They are not simply questions of artistic freedom or freedom of speech; rather, they locate "the production of the text and the production of the author [or performer] within the practices that give rise to gender, race, class subordination, and colonial subjugation."[21] Put differently, to interrogate cultural appropriation is to interrogate cultural imperialism, whereby the dominant (white) culture oppresses the cultural life of the dominated people. To discuss cultural appropriation in this context is to attend to the colonial thefts of Indigenous lands, languages, lifeways, and lives; to examine the "common-sense" racist assumptions and ideologies that promote Indigenous cultural and political erasure; and to explore the ways in which "the spoils of [...] conquests—the people and their culture—become artifacts of that conquest."[22] Ultimately, it is to make visible the links between cultural production and colonial violence.

Before turning to *RPDR*'s appropriative performances, it is important to understand how commercial drag culture in general also supports these racist displays. As Dejan Jotanovic reminds us in his column "What Do We Do with Bad Drag?": "We're constantly told that drag as art centers itself on principles of freedom, liberation, experiment. To be in drag is to defy and deny the shackles of the status quo. This 'anything goes' ideology then opens the trapdoor for performers [...] to espouse their bigotry."[23] Referring here specifically to derogatory jokes made by comedy queens, Jotanovic asks: "Do [drag performers] ever even consider that the empowerment they might feel—saying controversial and shocking statements on stage—will only serve to further disempower others? [...] These words grant legitimacy by easing [audience] tensions, by letting them laugh. Is it worth it?" According to RuPaul himself, the answer might worrisomely be, "yes." In an interview with *The Guardian* in 2015, RuPaul explains that "drag is dangerous. We are making fun of *everything*."[24] Discussing the U.S. network Logo TV's decision to drop the transphobic line "You've got she-mail!" from the show, he remarks: "I would not have changed it, but that's their choice. Our intention was always coming from a place of love. On paper, you cannot read intention, so it was actually hurtful. [...] when someone doesn't get the joke or feels offended by it, it's a lose-lose situation, because you can't explain a joke. It isn't funny if you explain it."[25] For whom, though, are these "jokes" funny in the first place? At whose expense are they being made? Are they transgressive, or are they violent? What do they teach audiences about their political implications and how seriously we ought to take systemic problems? Judith Butler posits that drag is not inherently subversive, but depends upon context, performer intent, and audience response. "Parody by itself is not subversive," she writes,

> and there must be a way to understand what makes certain kinds of parodic repetitions effectively disruptive, truly troubling, and which repetitions become domesticated and recirculated as instruments of cultural hegemony. A typology of actions would clearly not suffice, for parodic displacement, indeed, parodic laughter, depends on a context and reception in which subversive confusions can be fostered.[26]

While Butler is specifically attending to gender performance and the radical possibilities—or lack thereof—for rethinking gender and sexuality, her points allow us to consider the ways in which such mockery, whether comedic or artistic, potentially works to render racial and cultural stereotypes acceptable and to condone the material violence by which they are often accompanied, rather than to mobilize resistance. This is the true danger in drag: not its ability to "make fun of everything," but its power to legitimize violence against other marginalized groups.

## *Cases of Indigenous Appropriation on* RuPaul's Drag Race

I will begin this study by examining perhaps the only explicit mention of Indigenous cultural appropriation on *RPDR* in order to illustrate how this phenomenon itself has been deemed mockable by drag as it is presented on the show. In the eighth episode of season 10 (2018), entitled "Cher: The Unauthorized Rusical," the remaining seven competitors were challenged to sing in a tribute to pop culture icon Cher, portraying her in different eras of her career. As this challenge's roles, lyrics, and costumes were assigned by

RuPaul and the show's producers, and as the show itself does not offer space for defiance, the performer's choices are not at issue here, but rather the kinds of performances that are encouraged by the show.[27] Monét X Change, an Afro-Caribbean American cis-male contestant, who would go on to win the fan-voted Miss Congeniality crown for season 10 and later the fourth spot in the *All Stars*' Drag Race Hall of Fame, was assigned "70s Variety Show Cher." Monét was directed to perform a "tribute" to Cher's 1973 hit "Half-Breed," donning a feather headdress and singing a parodic version of the song's lyrics. In the original version, Cher claims a half–Cherokee identity and laments the inability to fit in with either white or "Indian" society, repeating the derogatory identifier "half-breed" in the chorus. Monét's rendition replaces "half-breed" with "cultural appropriation," ostensibly mocking Cher's appropriative performance:

> "Cultural appropriation!" That's what we never heard.
> "Cultural appropriation!" That wasn't even a word.
> "Cultural appropriation!" Come on, it was another time.
> We just called it fashion, bitch, we evolved with the times.[28]

While these lyrics may be read as ironic, calling attention to the ways in which accusations of appropriation are dismissed, I argue, instead, that they *allow* for this dismissal by rendering these belated accusations comic, thereby legitimizing appropriative performances. Indeed, as Monét performs, the camera cuts to the judges' table, showing RuPaul, Michelle Visage, and guest judges Andrew Rannells and Billy Eichner laughing in response to the lyrics, including the verse "I would dress up like an Indian / I wore a headdress, be a gypsy queen / A fortune-telling witch from New Orleans."[29] Furthermore, the performance is applauded, with Eichner deeming it "one of [his] favorites" and Rannells calling it "spot on and perfect."[30] While the purpose of the challenge was to offer the best Cher impersonation and is thus the criteria—voice, mannerisms, etc.—upon which Monét was judged, the assignment and celebration of her performance as *this* particular Cher speaks volumes. Not only did the producers deem "Half-Breed" worthy of reproduction, but the judges reinforced the acceptability of Indigenous appropriation despite its contribution to violent, racist depictions of Indigenous people. This position was reaffirmed on Twitter after the episode aired when the official *RuPaul's Drag Race* page posted a GIF of Monét's performance along with the "Cultural appropriation!" refrain.[31] Significantly, this post prompted several viewers to express their distaste for the performance, pointing out that naming appropriation by appropriating and calling out racism with racism only bolsters structural systems of oppression. As such, while the assignment had the potential to critique Cher's Indigenous appropriation, it instead reinforced power imbalances by catering to that white supremacist "common-sense racist ideology" to which Brand directs our attention.[32] Intention is irrelevant when the result is racism.

Monét's assigned performance as "Pretendian" Cher is not the first rendition of performed Indigenous femininity on *RPDR*; rather, it is only the most *recent*. Raja's appropriation occurred in the ninth episode of season 3 (2011), entitled "Life, Liberty, and the Pursuit of Style." The main challenge of the week was to film a patriotic message for American military troops and to serve "Yankee Doodle Drag" on the runway. Raja, who is Indonesian-American, presented herself to the judges in a feathered headdress, buckskin dress, and turquoise jewelry, prompting judge Santino Rice to immediately hypersexualize the look, exclaiming "Nava-HO!" and, later, asking Raja to "take [him] to her tipi." Further, during the judges' critiques, RuPaul rhetorically posed an imperialist question, "Can you get more American than Native American?" This leads Raja to raise her hand and utter a stereotypical "Indian" greeting, "How," at which the judges laughed.[33] From these reactions, it is clear that Raja's appropriation of Indigenous dress cannot be separated from broader racist and colonial ideologies.

In their analysis of this performance as evidence of *RPDR*'s "complicit[y…] in processes of white supremacy and settler colonialism,"[34] Upadhyay points out: "[F]or the show's judges to validate [Raja's] mimicry demonstrates how settler colonialism is normalized, invisibilized, and celebrated,"[35] enabling non–Indigenous people to "participate in and claim belonging to settler states."[36] Cherokee scholar Rayna Green notes that this is nothing new, as "playing Indian" is "one of the oldest and most pervasive forms of American cultural expression" and is central to the formation of an "American identity."[37] Tracing their history since contact, Green highlights the genocidal quality of these performances: "[T]he play Indian roles depend on dead Indians. In order for anyone to play Indian successfully, real Indians have to be dead. Americans have to believe them dead or kill them off."[38] In this sense, when non–Indigenous drag queens like Raja "play Indian," they reinforce what Patrick Wolfe calls the "logic of elimination."[39] The logic of elimination is the ideological foundation of settler states like Canada and the United States, whereby settlers seek to dispossess Indigenous peoples for capitalist gains, often by attempting to literally remove Indigenous peoples from the land. This is carried out through a combination of physical and cultural-political genocide, through a range of strategies that deliberately aim to suppress Indigenous knowledge systems and practices and to disrupt kinship networks. One key means through which this is attempted is the targeted sexualization of Indigenous women, exemplified through Santino's remarks on Raja's costume. Cree/Métis scholar Kim Anderson explains that, given the political power traditionally held by Indigenous women, colonizers worked to invent the "Indian princess" in order to render Indigenous women "more accessible, less powerful, and within the grasp of the white man."[40] "'Indian princess' imagery," Anderson elaborates, "constructed Indigenous women as the virgin frontier, the pure border waiting to be crossed. The enormous popularity of the princess lay within her erotic appeal to the covetous European male wishing to lay claim to the new territory. This equation of the Indigenous women with virgin land, open for consumption, created a Native female archetype"[41] that, in Green's words, "does what white men want for money or lust."[42] Herein lie the detrimental effects of performances like Raja's: by presenting herself to the judges as a "sexy Native woman," Raja reproduces and promotes colonial discourses that perceive Indigenous women as what Sherene Razack calls "inherently rapeable" and thus as conquerable as Indigenous lands.[43] These same ideologies underlie ongoing sexual violence toward and the murders and disappearances of Indigenous women, girls, and Two-Spirit/queer (2SQ) folks, intentional tools used to attack Indigenous sovereignty and to naturalize settler presence and entitlement. Raja's appropriative performance is critically tied to this ideological and material colonial violence, and its celebration must be understood within this context.

As is apparent in these cases, costuming alone does not fully account for the anti–Indigenous racism embedded in acts of cultural appropriation. From Santino Rice's hypersexualizing comments to the seemingly parodic lyrics assigned to Monét X Change, settler epistemologies play a crucial role in the reproduction of colonial practices and the erasure of Indigeneity elicited by cultural appropriation. With this is mind, I will now return to season 7 contestant and *All Stars* season 3 winner Trixie Mattel's Instagram feed in order to more closely examine how audience responses are often complicit in validating these performances and thus legitimizing anti–Indigenous racism.

## *Trixie Mattel and the Case of Cultural Misrepresentation*

Trixie Mattel, otherwise known as Brian Firkus, is a cis-male, half–Ojibwe drag performer who, unless pointedly asked, rarely draws attention to his Indigeneity. Indeed, in one interview he remarks:

> Yeah, I am half–Native American—but, I read this comment that I am "white presenting," and now I think that is kind of funny to say. I mean, let's be honest, I don't look Native American. I mean, my facial features are Native American, but my skin is paper white. I grew up off the reservation, so I don't have a lot of ownership of that part of my ethnicity.[44]

Instead, Firkus refers to himself as "debilitatingly Caucasian"[45] and identifies Trixie as "a character who is full-in white, Valley Girl and rich."[46] She is "Barbie, but with extremely unrealistic beauty standards."[47] I highlight this distinction here not to police Firkus's Indigenous identity, nor to claim that his personal association with whiteness makes Trixie's costume appropriative. I am not in a position to do so. Rather, my intention here is to critically consider the audience reactions to Trixie's photos in Indigenous-coded dress, as both Indigenous and non–Indigenous respondents make specific reference to her Indigeneity as a means through which to debate the "acceptability" of her performances.

Significantly, the cultural appropriation discussion sparked by these images does not emphasize Trixie's "right" as a drag queen to "wear whatever she wants"; rather, fans debate her "right" to engage culturally with her Indigeneity. Responding to her first post, captioned "Nude delusions," some fans credit Trixie for paying "homage to his own heritage AND icon and legend Cher! It's almost as if this is an artistic and fun take on traditional native American cultural and ceremonial apparel!" writes _bewltched.[48] Likewise, others such as austinj3500 note that it is Trixie's "choice to represent her culture the way she wants too [sic]."[49] On this side of the appropriation debate, fans like rickrichter argue: "Cultural appropriation is someone wearing costumes to make play at someone else's culture. Trixie is Native American. Yes, she plays a basic white girl, but she is representing her culture."[50] Similarly, cheokima writes:

> Cultural Appropriation comments to someone who is actually ½ Native American is by far the most disrespectful and ignorant comment you can make so damn early in the day. I'm happy that she's actually using her "white girl" character to embrace her actual roots. It's refreshing. It's *educational*. It's a moment. There is no disrespect. […] This is *education*. This isn't racism. This isn't Appropriation. Let her embrace her roots.[51]

Fans on this side of the debate thus suggest that intracultural appropriation is not possible, as Trixie's Indigenous ancestry is thought to render her exempt from these critiques, despite the fact that her headdress imitates those worn by various Plains peoples and are traditionally earned by men, not women.

On the other hand, respondents such as A_minus_ call Trixie/Firkus to task for "misrepresenting his Indigenous culture by donning a fake headdress for the sake of entertainment."[52] Oji-Cree poet jaye simpson (jaye_simpson) also points to "this gross misrepresentation," noting that Trixie "often only claims Indigeneity when it's convenient. The over sexualization of our women, girls, two spirit and trans folk have led to MMIW [Missing and Murdered Indigenous Women]. She's white coded and has a responsibility to use that perceived privilege to *educate* and use her platform to bring attention."[53] Echoing simpson in a comment on a later post captioned "Can people please stop HARPing on this costume,"[54] imj5000 writes: "No! People can't stop harping on this costume @trixiemattel! You claim to be part Native American but only when it serves a comedic purpose for you. A majority of the time you claim to be a 'white woman' or 'white girl' & that's your choice. But Do NOT pick & choose when to exploit your Native ancestry when it suits you & appropriate it in a negative way."[55] He adds:

> A Native headdress or piece of clothing inspired by that regalia has deep cultural significance and is a badge of honor by those who have earned the right to wear it. [...] Additionally the headdress itself is not worn by every tribe, there are specific tribes that wear them. By wearing this it only feeds into the stereotype that we as Native people are a "pan Indian" culture [...]. If in fact you honor & are proud of your Native heritage you wouldn't create a mockery or caricature of your ancestry & invest some time to *educate* yourself on the history of your tribe.[56]

By attending to Trixie's selective use of her Indigeneity, these respondents refrain from accusing her of cultural appropriation, but emphasize the harmful effects of such performances.

Worth noting here is the emphasis these critiques place on the pedagogical potential of Trixie's performances. As many commenters point out, Firkus could have used his platform to educate his audiences with regard to Indigenous cultural practices and histories and to draw greater awareness to ongoing colonial violence, particularly against Indigenous women and Two-Spirit/queer (2SQ) people. Indeed, while *RPDR* contestants have relatively little freedom to resist or refuse particular assignments, Trixie's performance was part of her own *Skinny Legends* show. As such, she had the liberty to radically subvert representations of Indigenous women and 2SQ folks generally and in response to those performed on *RPDR*. Instead, as these audience responses demonstrate, Trixie's performance not only perpetuates the sexualization of Indigenous women, but also encourages the ongoing erasure of Indigenous history and presence by failing to offer much beyond a stereotypical representation.

As Sarah Tucker Jenkins points out, "[T]he idea that racist stereotypes are acceptable when performed by members of that race is problematic at best. [...R]acist images are always racist, regardless of who is portraying them. In fact, images perpetuated by members of the marginalized group, may be more dangerous, because the public considers them acceptable."[57] With nearly 2000 comments, the first image of Trixie in this costume has received some of the highest traffic on her Instagram page. As noted at the beginning of this essay, the photos have elicited a number of responses that highlight both the degree to which these images perpetuate the hypersexualization and degradation of Indigenous women, as well as, more broadly, the ways Indigeneity is treated glibly by settlers. From thekylestrasser's comment "*begin beating Indian drums frantically* 'HALF-BREEEEED' *hair toss*"[58] to zachtheberge's comment "I have no reservations about this and it's a trail of white tears of people who don't like or appreciate it,"[59] these comments point to the harmful effects of performances that bastardize Indigenous cultures and belittle mass dispossession and colonialism. Significantly, the latter comment echoes a racist pun made by RuPaul on *Drag Race*. Critiquing Alexis Michelle in season 9, he remarked: "Your Native American couture left the judges with… reservations."[60] That such insensitive commentary should be repeated by fans illustrates the impact of *RPDR*'s anti–Indigenous racism and the ways in which the show has helped shape these violent ideologies.

What becomes especially clear in the case of Trixie's performance, as with those on *RPDR*, is the crucial necessity of contextual information in critiques of appropriation, though it is difficult to determine which context is authoritative. As mentioned, Trixie's costume is part of her *Skinny Legends* show, which she toured in the UK. According to Instagram user melushadodangoda,

> At her show, Trixie clearly says her costume isn't meant to be worn as a joke towards her culture. Someone asked her why she doesn't incorporate her culture into her drag. She said it's because being Native isn't a performative thing and she doesn't need to dress in a way that embraces whatever stereotype of a native person you have in mind. The costume is making fun of white girls appropriating native culture. That's why she wore it.[61]

Likewise, amyowst writes: "She literally performs a clarinet solo of 'Colors of the Wind' [from Disney's *Pocahontas*] after walking out in this. If you don't understand that it's a big 'fuck you' to the caricatured image of what being native looks like, then I'm sorry it's lost on you. It's not mocking traditions, it's mocking people who think wearing a costume like this is all being native means. It's satire."[62] This context returns us to the specificity of drag. As a performance art originally based on parody, drag has always held the power to radically subvert the status quo. However, as is evident in the reactions to Trixie's costume, this radical subversion cannot happen if the act is decontextualized from that which it is (potentially) intended to invalidate. Without context, these images and appropriations only work to further violence against Indigenous peoples and women/2SQ people in particular. As Cree-Métis Instagram user bezeren points out, these kinds of drag performances "must come with a detailed explanation […] otherwise it just feeds into the problem."[63]

## Miss Chief Eagle Testickle: Defiance in Drag?

In contrast to Trixie's decontextualized cultural misrepresentation, Cree visual and performance artist Kent Monkman deploys in his work his gender-fluid alter-ego Miss Chief Eagle Testickle—a play on the words "mischief" and "egotistical"—to explore colonial histories and to demonstrate the complexities of historical and contemporary Indigenous experience. Miss Chief is a glamorous "time-traveling, shape-shifting, supernatural being"[64] who could be mistaken for another drag queen impersonating Cher's "Half-Breed"; however, the critical quality of Monkman's work is evident, for Miss Chief often reverses the colonial gaze to challenge mythic representations of Indigenous peoples as they are depicted in nineteenth-century Euro-Canadian art. Counter-appropriating paintings by artists such as George Catlin and Albert Bierstadt and inserting Miss Chief in them, Monkman works to recontextualize national narratives and to reverse and disrupt popular images of Indigenous peoples appropriated and decontextualized by European men.[65]

Miss Chief's presence in these works is powerful: not only does she look back at European settlers, but she dominates them. In a 2020 painting entitled *Nation to Nation*, for instance, Miss Chief stands tall in her red thigh-high boots and black-and-white feathered headdress while a Mountie kneels before her and performs oral sex.[66] This piece reorders the imagined racial and gendered hierarchy upon which colonization is founded, for Miss Chief reclaims sexual power over a white man hired to control her and her fellow Indigenous peoples. While discussing another piece entitled *Heaven and Earth* (2001), Daniel Heath Justice (Cherokee), Bethany Schneider, and Mark Rifkin point to the commonality of this practice in Monkman's oeuvre, noting that his work often "offers important ironic commentary on the sexualized history of colonialism, but it also reverses power dynamics, repositioning the familiar status of Native Bodies (often those of women) as submissive victims of the colonial erotic to assertive and enthusiastic agents of unashamed sexual subjectivity while also intimating the penetrability of white male bodies."[67] Significantly, however, these works do not simply depict sexual violence with the roles reversed. Indeed, the facial expressions and body language of both parties suggest willing participation. The Mountie in *Nation to Nation* kneels with his mouth open, one hand on Miss Chief's abdomen and the other wrapped around her erect penis. His erection is also visible, yet barely noticeable, for it is shadowed by Miss Chief's stature. Miss Chief, too, appears to consent to the tryst: her hands rest atop the Mountie's behatted head, and she wears a victorious smirk on her face. In this way, Monkman uses drag to resist the dominant racist heteropatriarchal depictions of Indigenous women and

## 154   She Already Done Had Herses

2SQ people, refusing to reproduce stereotypes without radically satirizing them for decolonial purposes.

Not all of Monkman's work, however, engages in this kind of decolonial practice. His more recent painting, *Hanky Panky*, has received significant criticism from Indigenous women, trans, and 2SQ people for its portrayal of what many are calling "revenge rape." Released on May 16, 2020, the painting depicts Miss Chief surrounded by Indigenous women—said to be inspired by the *okihcitâwiskwêwak*, the traditional council of Cree law keepers—smiling and laughing in a lodge. With his pants around his knees, a Justin Trudeau lookalike is held down by women in front of Miss Chief, as the likenesses of former Canadian prime ministers look on. Miss Chief holds up a large red hand, which appears to be both a reference to a symbol meant to honor MMIWG and a sex toy Miss Chief is preparing to use on the man in front of her. An RCMP officer lies on the ground beyond, appearing to have just received the same treatment. While *Nation to Nation* offers symbols to indicate consent between Miss Chief and the Mountie, and while Monkman claims that in *Hanky Panky* it "is not a punishment, but rather a consensual act that Miss Chief willingly delivers,"[68] the painting presents no such evidence. Thus, rather than using drag to unsettle colonial ideas, in this piece Monkman simply reproduces them by disrespecting sacred protocol and encouraging violence. As simpson points out, "Having restitution portrayed as sexual violence in with Indigenous women cheering it on is perverse and not subverting the narrative at all."[69]

Monkman has also made questionable choices when employing Miss Chief in his performance art. In his 2017 short film, *Another Feather in Her Bonnet*, Monkman, as Miss Chief, "married" legendary French fashion designer and iconoclast Jean Paul Gaultier at the Montreal Museum of Fine Arts (MMFA) as part of Gaultier's *Love Is Love* exhibit. The exhibit contained several of Gaultier's bridal creations, an extension of his 2011 presentation of three wedding gowns at MMFA, one of which featured a floor-length white feathered headdress originally created in 2002. The "wedding" between Gaultier and Miss Chief—in which she wore the headdress—sought to address Gaultier's act of appropriation. The couple were pronounced "collaborators" as Gaultier "receiv[ed] Miss Chief Eagle Testickle as [his] muse, [his] inspiration and spiritual guide, til death do [them] part," while Miss Chief, "in wearing this headdress as a symbol of Jean Paul's love," took Gaultier "to have and to be clothed by, as long as [they] both shall live."[70] In an interview with *Fashion*, Monkman furthers explains the significance of this performance, particularly highlighting its pedagogical purpose: "Through the alliance of marriage, we learn to understand and forgive the mistakes of our partners and build true understanding. And better understanding is really at the core of all my work."[71] He goes on: "You can't police how artists draw influence from the world, but you can create awareness about what's cool and what's not and how to collaborate and engage each other in a respectful way. [It is possible to] educate and develop sensitivity around cultural appropriation versus mutual exchange."[72] Here, Monkman argues that collaboration between Indigenous and non–Indigenous artists has the potential to resolve issues of appropriation. However, this performance does not reverse Gaultier's theft, nor does it necessarily even challenge it, for Miss Chief accepts Gaultier's apology on behalf of all Indigenous peoples and claims the appropriative headdress for herself as though she has the ultimate authority to determine its acceptability. Further, much like Trixie, Miss Chief renders the headdress consumable and performs for, in Lindsay Nixon's (Cree-Métis-Saulteaux) words, "the gaze of the yt daddies" like Gautier,[73] who clearly find this act quite amusing—Gaultier simpers his way through his vows. Thus, Miss Chief's role in this performance serves not to confront Indigenous appropriation, but rather complies with the desires of white, gay, cis-male culture—much like *RPDR*. In doing so, rather than shifting Indigenous appropriation from a one-sided account to an opportunity for dialogue, Monkman's performance in *Another Feather in Her Bonnet* works to reaffirm those audience responses to Trixie's costume that deny the possibility of mishandling cultural representation. Thus, while Monkman claims his work is pedagogical, the "lessons" offered tend to appeal to the voyeuristic desires of white audiences. This, in turn, begs the question: Who does Monkman's work truly serve?

## Conclusion

In a Facebook post made in 2015, four years after her time on *RPDR*, Raja made a statement addressing accusations of cultural appropriation made against her:

> I need to say something. Those who accuse me of "cultural appropriation" are those who have never left their front lawns, mostly in their small American towns. That is, assuming you have a lawn, or a life. I travel, a lot more than you. No seriously, I travel a lot more than most. I come from a mixed background of European and Asian, and I grew up in the hood. Bite me, get a passport, and gag on my sick ass style. Don't be mad at the person who celebrates cultures that he has experienced and loved first hand. It's always the ones who sit around watching it thru a screen that have the biggest, worthless opinions. K bye!![74]

Here, Raja makes at least three claims about those who recognize the racism embedded in her performance: first, that they presumably live in poverty and/or are undereducated; second, that they are culturally deficient; and third, that they cannot engage in critical conversation that stems from popular media. By becoming defensive and arguing that her critical audiences are ignorant, rather than considering the problems with her costume choices, participating in a respectful conversation, or even apologizing for her performance, Raja highlights the elitism and entitlement that are ingrained in culturally appropriative performances, and especially those that involve "playing Indian" on a public format such as *RPDR*. In doing so, she demonstrates precisely what *RPDR* teaches us: that Indigenous appropriation merits celebration rather than criticism, particularly when the look is "gag-worthy," and that cultural and political sensitivity have no place in drag.

By reinforcing this idea, drag as it is presented on *RPDR* largely serves the white gaze, reproducing colonial concepts of Indigeneity that render Indigenous peoples and cultures as stereotypical, mockable, and ultimately imaginary and consumable. By decontextualizing their performances from both that which they seek to represent, each of the queens examined in this essay, including Trixie Mattel, promote ideologies that enable violence against Indigenous peoples and especially against women and 2SQ peoples. Kent Monkman, on the other hand, sometimes uses drag to mimic colonial structures and to deconstruct and subvert those very ideologies. However, he, too, increasingly engages in similar behavior, reproducing colonial practices and accommodating acts of appropriation "for all the capitalist daddies of the Beaux Arts."[75] While these instances reveal the complexities involved in critiquing an already marginalized medium like drag, it is nevertheless necessary to question not only how drag is being mobilized, but also how audiences are receiving and employing the information garnered from these performances. If the result, as with the comments on Trixie's Instagram feed, is anti–Indigenous racism, then we must continue to ask, as Jotanovic does, "[W]hat do we do with bad drag?"[76]

## *Mini Challenge: Discussion Questions*

- Citing specific challenges and/or performances, in what ways does *Drag Race* serve the white gaze?
- Examining the social media accounts of particular queens, how are audiences responding to particular performances? In what ways do these responses highlight the impact, for better and/or worse, of these performances?
- What strategies of resistance, such as reappropriation and refusal, are taken up by *Drag Race* contestants or drag performers more broadly?

## *Maxi Challenge: Activities and Assignments*

While drag is often a parodic, anything-goes artistic medium, it can nevertheless perpetuate harm. Thus, while it is important to understand drag's subversive potential, it is equally important to critically examine its limitations and the effects particular drag performances can have on racialized communities. **Teaching these performances alongside the specific histories with which they interact will allow instructors to better contextualize both the costumes worn by contestants and the comments made by the judges on *RPDR*.** The purpose is not to debate whether a performance is appropriative or not—those discussions tend to act as distractions—but rather to examine its impact and its ties to the settler colonial project.

### Notes

1. chaztrone. "O honey!" *Instagram*, 10 Feb. 2019, https://www.instagram.com/p/BtsWTFPgDZN/.
2. freyaviney. "U can't appropriate." *Instagram*, 10 Feb. 2019, https://www.instagram.com/p/BtsWTFPgDZN/.
3. jbrentstamper. "Oh honey, half breed honey?" *Instagram*, 10 Feb. 2019, https://www.instagram.com/p/BtsWTFPgDZN/.
4. tsistsistas. "just bc she is native." *Instagram*, 10 Feb. 2019, https://www.instagram.com/p/BtsWTFPgDZN/.
5. efxir. "Come on casino queen." *Instagram*, 10 Feb. 2019, https://www.instagram.com/p/BtsWTFPgDZN/.
6. arela_haro. "I don't understand the problem." 10 Feb. 2019. https://www.instagram.com/p/BtsWTFPgDZN/.
7. Throughout this essay, I use she/her pronouns when referring to the performers' drag personas. In cases where I refer to the performers out of drag, I use their lived pronouns.
8. Firkus, Brian (Trixie Mattel). "Nude delusions." *Instagram*, 10 Feb. 2019, https://www.instagram.com/p/BtsWTFPgDZN/.
9. Dam Bracia, Lillian. "Weighing in on Cultural Appropriation and Drag." *INDIE Magazine*, 30 August 2017, https://indie-mag.com/2017/08/cultural-appropriation-and-drag/.
10. These are not the only two moments of Indigenous appropriation on *RPDR*. In episode 10 of season 9 (2017), the "Gayest Ball Ever," the top five competitors were challenged to "create a look inspired by the legendary group, The Village People." The queens were given five options: "Cowboy, Cop, Native American, Construction Worker, and Leather Biker." Alexis Michelle, a white cis-male contestant, chose the Native American, wanting to, in her words, "give something that'll feel a little bit tribal, but also ready-to-wear." Designing her own costume, Alexis hit the stage wearing a turquoise-stoned corset, patterned skirt, and a wooden bow on her head. The judges critiqued her aesthetic choices, deeming the costume poor quality. This suggests that there are standards in drag against which these performances are measured. These standards, however, do not pertain to the racist nature of the performance, but rather to the caliber of the costume.
11. Strings, Sabrina, & Bui, Long T. "'She Is Not Acting, She Is': The Conflict Between Gender and Racial Realness on *RuPaul's Drag Race*." *Feminist Media Studies*, vol. 14, no. 5, 2014, pp. 822–836: p. 823.
12. *Ibid.*, p. 832.
13. *Ibid.*

14. Caroline Hodes and Jorge Sandoval note that "the show can be read as an important cultural text that polices the boundaries of gender through the reproduction of both the gender binary and the reification of what [bell] hooks refers to as white, ruling-class femininity" (152).

15. Hodes, Caroline, & Sandoval, Jorge. "*RuPaul's Drag Race*: A Study in the Commodification of White Ruling-Class Femininity and the Etiolation of Drag." *Studies in Costume & Performance*, vol. 3, no. 2, 2018, pp. 149–166: p. 156.

16. *Ibid.*, p. 155.

17. It is important to note that the racialization of Indigenous peoples is a colonial tactic. As Upadhyay reminds us, "Indigenous peoples are rendered as another ethnic minority within the settler states, akin to other racialized peoples, effacing the coloniality of Indigenous dispossession" (8–9). As such, I am not seeking to equate performed Indigeneity with other forms of racial essentialism portrayed on the show, but rather to demonstrate how Indigeneity is treated as another "racial Other" to be embodied by non-Indigenous contestants.

18. Only one of these performances is discussed here. The other occurred episode 6, "The Snatch Game," where contestants were asked to wear their favorite drag on the runway. Raja wore what she called a "global" look—"Apocalypto Amazon gal"—which prompted RuPaul to comment, "Girl, the natives are restless."

19. Upadhyay, Nishant. "'Can you get more American than Native American?': Drag and Settler Colonialism in *RuPaul's Drag Race*." *Cultural Studies*, 2019, pp. 1–22: p. 13.

20. Brand, Dionne. "Whose Gaze, and Who Speaks for Whom." *Bread Out of Stone*, Vintage Canada, 1994, pp. 145–168: pp. 163–64.

21. *Ibid.*, p. 164.

22. *Ibid.*, p. 162.

23. Jotanovic, Dejan. "What Do We Do With Bad Drag?" *Into*, 10 October 2018. https://www.intomore.com/culture /what-do-we-do-with-bad-drag.

24. Nicholson, Rebecca. "RuPaul: 'Drag is dangerous. We are making fun of everything.'" *The Guardian*, 3 June 2015, https://www.theguardian.com/tv-and-radio/2015/jun/03/rupaul-drag-is-dangerous-we-are-making-fun-of-everything.

25. *Ibid.*

26. Butler, Judith. *Gender Trouble: Feminism and the Subversion of Identity.* Routledge, 1990, p. 189.

27. This is not to divert from Monét X Change's responsibility for the performance, but acts as a clarification of the structures limiting her agency in such performances and the show's normalization of anti-Indigeneity as common and available to everyone.

28. "The Unauthorized Rusical." *RuPaul's Drag Race*, season 10, episode 8, VH1, 10 May 2018. *Amazon*, https://www.amazon.com/gp/video/detail/B07B68P55J/ref=atv_dp_season_select_s10.

29. *Ibid.*

30. *Ibid.*

31. @RuPaulsDragRace. "Cultural appropriation! @monetxchange #DragRace." *Twitter*, 10 May 2018, 8:55 PM, https://twitter.com/RuPaulsDragRace/status/994742819116871681.

32. See Brand, p. 159.

33. "Life, Liberty, and the Pursuit of Style." *RuPaul's Drag Race*, season 3, episode 9, Logo TV, 14 Mar. 2010. *Amazon*, https://www.amazon.com/gp/video/detail/B004JGWASG/ref=atv_dp_season_select_s3.

34. See Upadhyay, p. 6.

35. *Ibid.*, p 13.

36. *Ibid.*, p. 5.

37. Green, Rayna. "The Tribe Called Wannabee: Playing Indian in America and Europe." *Folklore* vol. 99, no. 1, 1988, pp. 30–55: p. 30.

38. *Ibid.*, p. 49.

39. Wolfe, Patrick. "Settler Colonialism and the Elimination of the Native." *Journal of Genocide Research*, vol. 8, no. 4, 2006, pp. 387–409: pp. 387, 388, 390, 393, 399, 401, 402.

40. Anderson, Kim. "The Construction of a Negative Identity." *A Recognition of Being: Reconstructing Native Womanhood*. Sumach, 2000, pp. 99–115: p. 101.

41. *Ibid.*, p. 101.
42. Green, Rayna. "The Pocahontas Perplex: The Image of Indian Women in American Culture." *The Massachusetts Review*, vol. 14, no. 2, 1975, pp. 698–714: p. 711.
43. Razack, Sherene H. *Looking White People in the Eye: Gender, Race, and Culture in Courtrooms and Classrooms*. University of Toronto Press, 2001, p. 69.
44. MacDonald, Baz. "A chat with Trixie Mattel—RuPaul's Drag Race star, Billboard charting musician and TV show host." *The Wireless*, 8 March 2018. https://www.radionz.co.nz/news/the-wireless/375162/a-chat-with-trixie...rupaul-s-drag-race-star-billboard-charting-musician-and-tv-show-host.
45. Weaver, Caity. "Trixie Mattel Is for Men (and Women and Kids)." *GQ*, 29 November 2017. https://www.gq.com/story/rixie-mattel-is-for-men-and-women-and-kids.
46. Brooke, Zach. "Q & A: Trixie Mattel." *Milwaukee Mag*, 8 September 2015. https://www.milwaukeemag.com/qa-trixie-mattel/.
47. Weaver.
48. _bew1tched. "homage to his own heritage." *Instagram*, Feb. 2019, https://www.instagram.com/p/BtsWTFPgDZN/.
49. austinj3500. "choice to represent her culture." Feb. 2019, *Instagram*, https://www.instagram.com/p/BtsWTFPgDZN/.
50. rickrichter. "Cultural approrpriation is someone wearing costumes." *Instagram*, Feb. 2019, https://www.instagram.com/p/BtsWTFPgDZN/.
51. cheokima. "Cultural Appropriation comments to someone." *Instagram*, Feb. 2019, https://www.instagram.com/p/BtsWTFPgDZN/.
52. A_minus_. "misrepresenting his Indigenous culture." *Instagram*, Feb. 2019, https://www.instagram.com/p/BtsWTFPgDZN/.
53. simpson, jaye (jaye_simpson). "this gross misrepresentation." *Instagram*, Feb. 2019, https://www.instagram.com/p/BtsWTFPgDZN/.
54. Firkus, Brian (Trixie Mattel). "Can people please stop HARPing on this costume?" *Instagram*, 12 Mar. 2019, https://www.instagram.com/p/Bu7UaiPg2sQ/.
55. imj5000. "No! People can't stop harping." *Instagram* Mar. 2019, https://www.instagram.com/p/Bu7UaiPg2sQ/.
56. *Ibid.*
57. Jenkins, Sarah Tucker. *Hegemonic "Realness": An Intersectional Feminist Analysis of RuPaul's Drag Race*. MA Thesis, Florida Atlantic University, 2013, p. 84.
58. thekylestrasser. "*begin beating Indian drums frantically." *Instagram*, Feb. 2019, https://www.instagram.com/p/BtsWTFPgDZN/.
59. zachtheberge. "I have no reservations about this and it's a trail of white tears." *Instagram*, Feb. 2019, https://www.instagram.com/p/BtsWTFPgDZN/.
60. "Gayest Ball Ever." *RuPaul's Drag Race*, season 9, episode 11, Logo TV, 2 June 2017, *Amazon*, https://www.amazon.com/gp/video/detail/B06XK36FZS/ref=atv_dp_season_select_s9.
61. melushadodangoda. "Can people please stop HARPing on this costume?" *Instagram*, 12 Mar. 2019, https://www.instagram.com/p/Bu7UaiPg2sQ/.
62. amyowst. "She literally performs a clarinet solo of 'Colors of the Wind' after walking out in this." *Instagram*. 10 Feb. 2019. https://www.instagram.com/p/BtsWTFPgDZN/.
63. bezeren. "Nude delusions." *Instagram*. 10 Feb. 2019. https://www.instagram.com/p/BtsWTFPgDZN/.
64. Monkman, Kent. "Biography." *Kent Monkman*. https://www.kentmonkman.com/biography.
65. It is crucial to note, however, that some of Monkman's work itself commits racist appropriation, as in his *Miss Africa* piece. For more, see shaneseanne, "Miss Anti-Blackness: Kent Monkman and Black Imagery." *Nutmeg and Sage*, 21 May 2020. https://nutmegandsage.blog/2020/05/21/miss-anti-blackness-kent-monkman-and-black-imagery/.
66. Monkman, Kent. *Nation to Nation*. 2020. https://www.kentmonkman.com/painting/nation-to-nation.
67. Justice, Daniel Heath, Schneider, Bethany, & Rifkin, Mark. "Heaven and Earth." *GLQ*, vol. 16, no. 1–2, 2010, pp. 1–3: p. 1.

68. Monkman, Kent. "Hanky Panky." *Instagram.* 16 May 2020. https://www.instagram.com/p/CARCAYogg7w/.

69. @fka_jayesimpson. "I'm just gonna publicly say it. I don't like the new Kent Monkman piece. I think it's inappropriate. Consent is first and foremost. Having restitution portrayed as sexual violence in with Indigenous women cheering it on is perverse and not subverting the narrative at all." *Twitter,* 15 May 2020, 8:46 PM, https://twitter.com/fka_jayesimpson/status/1261458086163648513.

70. Kent Monkman Studio. "Another Feather In Her Bonnet | Miss Chief Eagle Testickle & Jean Paul Gaultier." *YouTube,* 24 January 2019. https://www.youtube.com/watch?v=8gMwwf1xFpc.

71. Jay, Sarah. "Jean Paul Gaultier Married Kent Monkman to Apologize for Cultural Appropriation. Here's Why It Matters." *Fashion,* 13 November 2018. https://fashionmagazine.com/style/jean-paul-gaultier-cultural-appropriation/.

72. *Ibid.*

73. Nixon, Lindsay. *nîtisânak.* Metonymy, 2018, p. 168.

74. Gemini, Raja. "I need to say something." *Facebook,* 24 May 2015. https://www.facebook.com/RajaOfficial/ posts/i-need-to-say-something-those-who-accuse-me-of-cultural-appropriation-are-those-/1099553886727638/.

75. Nixon, p. 167.

76. Jotanovic.

# RuPaulogetics

*Assimilation, Backwash, and the Charisma of Queer Pedagogy*

DAVID J. FINE

"I may be the host of this show," RuPaul professes in season 10's reunion episode, "but you—all of you—are my teachers."[1] This comment not only signals education's importance in *RuPaul's Drag Race* (*RPDR*) but also endorses a particular pedagogy, one in which teachers learn with their students. Of course, this remark is far from remarkable. *RPDR* has, from its inception, drawn upon the language of education to describe the relationship between RuPaul and her girls. In this essay, I dilate on this didactic relation and distill its significance for queer pedagogy. As the quotation above indicates, RuPaul claims *RPDR* as a space in which she also learns. I will suggest, however, that RuPaul's unshakable faith in drag's subversion inhibits her ability to engage lovingly with critique. As *RPDR* inches closer and closer to the mainstream, RuPaul has increasingly adopted a stance that asserts drag's rebelliousness at the outset. This defensive position prevents RuPaul from facilitating the sort of dialogue—essential in the queer and feminist classroom—that invites disagreement and abides ambivalence. Ultimately, RuPaul's apologetic pedagogy refuses negativity, and I argue that this teaching practice, while appealing to mainstream sensibilities and progressivist politics, risks a doctrinaire dismissal of life's unhappy subjects.

With a close analysis of *RPDR*'s tenth season, I show how RuPaul's theory of drag interferes with her practice of education. Faith that good drag disrupts conventional identity and contests conservative politics usurps pedagogical practices that might, in real time, challenge racism, classism, and transphobia. To chart this dynamic, I first examine RuPaul's pedagogy in relation to *RPDR*'s success. I suggest that her response to drag's mainstreaming sharpens a longstanding tension, within the series, between queerness and assimilation. Significantly, she grounds this defense of drag's subversion in spirituality. The second section extends this inquiry and demonstrates how RuPaul's snowballing defensiveness blocks engagement with dark affect, including anger and shame. As the reunion makes clear, RuPaul entertains violence, melancholy, and loss only to the extent that drag has helped her girls transcend their suffering. This move is a dangerous one. I therefore call, in the third section, for teachers to attend to the messy emotions and failed desires of LGBTQ+ pasts and presents. Following Eve Kosofsky Sedgwick, my critique of *RPDR* takes a reparative turn and examines queer and feminist scholars whose work draws upon spiritual practice. I engage with this thinking in order to bear witness to a queer pedagogy that faces, rather than erases, shame and suffering.

After all, these issues do not concern RuPaul alone. On the contrary, I find her example illustrative of a changing LGBTQ+ classroom. Marriage Equality and the Trump Administration have spurred students' desire for actionable responses to injustice and affirmative representations of queerness. This desire, while sane and sensible, engenders a queer tolerance intolerant of the backward and the dejected.[2] In this milieu, instructors face a twofold temptation: they might, on the one hand, engage with LGBTQ+ history in a way that—sometimes forcefully—reinforces a progressivist narrative; on the other hand, they might demystify this emancipatory account in a way that—sometimes unthinkingly—reinforces an us-vs.-them binary. If the former approach employs LGBTQ+ content to bequeath a happy ending, then the latter responds cynically to that positivity by revealing oppression's continuity in the present. This critical response becomes a pedagogical problem, however, when it pins oppression's causes wholly onto (less enlightened) others.[3] In different ways, both approaches push bad feelings—sadness, uncertainty, guilt—away and neglect the resources that depressive affect offers. To connect with those assets, this essay makes the case for educators to stay the course with queer negativity, because its shame-facing pedagogy builds students' capacity to think beyond binaries.

## *Assimilation: It Gets Better*

To be clear, I do not intend to throw RuPaul under the school bus. She provides educators with an important—if imperfect—example of queer pedagogy. My analysis of season 10 aims, instead, to clarify a pressing pedagogical issue: the lure to impart progressivist narratives. In the twenty-first century, optimistic visions tempt all participants in the LGBTQ+ classroom; however, a rainbow-ready outlook risks repudiating the continued reality of oppression and discrimination. As such, this section clocks *RPDR*'s pedagogical instruction in light of the show's success. RuPaul's self-protective reaction to this achievement is, on my view, a mistake, but her response echoes a common sensibility, among educators, that discussions of sexuality and gender are *ipso facto* radical. In this context, season 10 proves a particularly rich case study. The diverse cast wrestles openly with race and class and cuttingly articulates—even against RuPaul's instruction—the political intricacies surrounding drag performance. I describe this tension before explaining how RuPaul's New-Age understanding of drag neutralizes it. Courting simony, RuPaul's spiritualized pedagogy sells a repackaged fantasy of bodily transcendence.

Educational discourse has permeated *RPDR* from the reality-television show's beginning. As early as the first season's third episode, RuPaul tells the contestants: "Hello, students, Professor Ru here."[4] *Drag U* (2010–2012)—an early spinoff in which queens teach cisgender women tricks of the trade—only makes the subtext explicit: drag is a university. The Werk Room serves, first and foremost, as a schoolroom. RuPaul gives her girls assignments, mentors them through the process, and assesses their learning outcomes. In other words, she instructs, coaches, and evaluates the contestants. And yet, it is notable how little RuPaul has adjusted her instruction over the years. Despite the move to VH1, six Emmy awards, and twelve seasons, her teaching methods remain surprisingly stable. Indeed, the series' shift from margin to center has affected neither RuPaul's syllabus nor her pedagogy in any discernable way. She teaches with the same tried-and-true techniques and proclaims, regardless of mass appeal, *RPDR*'s subversive impact.

This pedagogical continuity becomes strikingly visible in season 10. This season celebrates a decade of *RPDR* and marks the series' first go-round after newfound popularity and industry recognition. These fourteen episodes air in 2018, following RuPaul's first Emmy win in 2016 and the show's transfer to VH1 in season 9. The change from LogoTV to VH1 alone doubles viewership.[5] Given these accomplishments, one might expect an alteration in approach or tone, if for no other reason than to push new buttons; instead, the show sticks to the script and embraces its legacy. The premiere repurposes the first-ever challenge—"Drag on a Dime"—and features former queens in its mini-challenge. Season 10 marks its milestones, then, with a return to the show's roots, and RuPaul reasserts their radicalness. Even with unprecedented visibility, she holds her ground: "[D]rag becoming mainstream? Honey, please. That's not going to happen, mainly because the mainstream wants you to choose an identity so they can sell you beer and shampoo. That's just the way it is."[6] In this promotional interview for season 10, RuPaul distances drag from conventional consumption. She asserts drag's challenge to materialist values despite the obvious objection: how is she not profiting from a queer identity that *RPDR* has circulated and, in part, constructed?

Season 10 charges up these tensions. Eureka's return—after a cheerleading injury in season 9—ensures that her wardrobe has benefited from a fame-enhanced year of cash flow. Her material advantage silhouettes other queens' complaints. For instance, Monique Heart laments her lack of coin and its impact on her runway looks.[7] On a similar thread, Miz Cracker notes how the poverty of her youth taught her resourcefulness.[8] She later asks Aquaria if the rumors of a sugar daddy back in New York are true.[9] Of course, this financial preoccupation is not new. The drag-on-a-dime challenge foregrounds this concern at the series' outset. What has changed, though, is the risen bar on costuming and the barriers it creates. This change produces an unfair advantage for returning queens, on the one hand, and widens the gap, on the other, between urban contestants and backwoods contenders. Although RuPaul insists in the first-ever recap that drag is about "taking what you got, no money, but a big imagination, and turning it out,"[10] the competition clearly requires increasing amounts of capital. The idea that conspicuous consumption concerns the mainstream alone is, indeed, a hard sell.

Against this backdrop, RuPaul distinguishes between drag as popular culture and drag as counterculture. She places *RPDR* within the latter category but for a very specific reason. "In drag," she continues in the same interview, "we are shape-shifters. We don't hear the rules. We change every day."[11] She juxtaposes this mutability to dominant culture's petrification. "People need a box to understand how to navigate their lives. They need a grid to go 'Oh, I'm here and that's there.' They're not fluid in the way of saying 'I'm both male, female, [B]lack, white. I'm earth. I'm united.' Drag says, 'I'm fucking *everything*.'"[12] RuPaul distances drag performers from the ordinary world's boxes and grids. Queens, unlike pedestrian subjects, know they can alter selves. This fluidity—she notes in her second book, *Workin' It!* (2010)—bequeaths shamanistic insight. Consequently, RuPaul's explanation moves quickly from material markers of identity to cosmic unification. On her view, drag is not transgressive because it challenges systemic injustice; rather, drag disentangles people from their egos and offers access to a higher plane. Drag challenges the ordinary sense that one has an identity marked by gender, race, and class in the first place.

This spiritual take has amplified in recent years. In the 2019–2020 holiday issue of *Vanity Fair*, cover-girl RuPaul claims that merely a "superficial aspect of drag is mainstream. Like, 'Ooh, girl' or 'Hey girlfriend!' or 'Yaaas.' That's mainstream culture."[13] Corny catchphrases announce *RPDR*'s arrival to the mainstage, but that, according to RuPaul, is a superficial scratch on the surface of the real. True drag proves transgressive in its rejection of what normal people accept as reality. In this metaphysical sense, she asserts, yet again, that "true drag really will never be mainstream. Because true drag has to do with seeing that this world is an illusion, and that everything you say you are and everything it says that you are on your driver's license, it's all an illusion."[14] As these comments suggest, RuPaul understands drag as a force that liberates consciousness from ordinary reality. Her understanding evokes an oft-repeated refrain from *Drag U*: "the miracle of drag" occurs when an outer change (of clothes) effects an inner transformation (of spirit). Drag uses illusion to destabilize larger fabrications. It takes one behind the curtain, where one sees that "the emperor is wearing no clothes."[15] Through their elevated routines, queens reveal the illusions that cloak reality itself.

RuPaul's third book—*GuRu* (2018)—yokes this spiritualism. Marketed during season 10, *GuRu* advocates for pure awareness, which empowers the dedicatory "sweet, sensitive souls out there in the world" to find healing and love.[16] The text itself fuses coffee-table and self-help genres in order to fashion a spiritual guide. Its goal is nothing less than to "uncover ancient sacred realness."[17] In the beginning, RuPaul instructs that, truth be told, "you are not your clothes, you are not your profession, you are not your religion. You are an extension of the consciousness that guides the universe, for which there is no name because it cannot be defined."[18] This heady insight grounds her opening statement on drag. "That's why," she declares, "all the superficial things you list as your identity are in reality your 'drag.'"[19] If one takes RuPaul at her word, then she appears to reduce gender, race, and class to performances or mirages. And yet, this detachment from embodiment is, for RuPaul, essential. Drag facilitates the (often painful) disassociation of the authentic self from identities and relationships that tie the ego to this illusory world. As such, RuPaul teaches practices that effect detachment from one's everyday perception of self and other.

To this end, *GuRu* mixes spiritual teachings, including a call for prayer and meditation, with beauty tips. Compare, for instance, the keen observation—"There's a certain detachment sensitive people must maintain to endure the harsh realities of the world"—with the sensible advice: "Keep your neck and bosom area unobstructed to give the appearance of a longer neck."[20] At first, it might seem that sacred mantras about self-transcendence have little bearing on profane instructions about fake eyelashes; however, these two strands connect. According to RuPaul, an ability to detach from the ego and observe the self objectively enables the requisite perspective for contouring, posing, and padding. "You must be willing to see yourself from outside yourself," she instructs: "[P]roportions are everything. Most people don't realize just how much they react to proportions."[21] As spiritual practice, drag heightens awareness by, first, revealing the ego's illusions and, second, teaching practitioners how to manipulate others' (often reactionary) perceptions. This disciplined artform has a sublime payoff: it detaches one from the accrued negativity and identity markers that closet one's glamazon. "Drag is," therefore, "the highest form of being, of showing our best selves to the world."[22] Far from mainstream, true drag belongs to ascetics.

*GuRu* distills the queer piety behind RuPaul's defensive pedagogy. When questioned about *RPDR*'s alleged assimilation, RuPaul asserts the miracle of drag at the outset and then reads the signs in a way that confirms its preordained subversion. I have coined the term "RuPaulogetics" to describe this dynamic, which places RuPaul, pedagogically, in the position of the one who knows the truth that sets others free. Tellingly, she insists on drag's rebellion despite—or, perhaps, because of—salient changes in popular U.S. culture. To a newly inclusive audience, she markets subversion, hawking a destabilized identity—*vis-à-vis* drag transformation—available on iTunes. This fusion of queerness and consumption explains why viewers find RuPaul in the position of defending drag's transgression: edge sells.[23] And yet, I believe the stakes are higher. Although her apologetic stance speaks to issues of LGBTQ+ assimilation and pride-bedazzled commodification, the core tension exceeds whether drag has retained its offense. The religious resonance of "RuPaulogetics" intentionally signals RuPaul's rebranding of an old desire: namely, the wish to escape the body. She preaches consumerism's transformative power at the expense of embodiment's real cost.[24]

RuPaul may criticize mainstream culture for stabilizing identity for profit, but she equally markets fluidity. Take, for example, DragCon, "a convention that celebrates 'the art of drag, queer culture and self-expression for all.'"[25] This convention is not counterculture but, strictly speaking, a counter culture, where, in 2016, customers purchased $2.3 million worth of supplies and merchandise.[26] With DragCon, RuPaul sells the art of self-transcendence. Capitalist convention emboldens the convention. As Sara Ahmed explains, "*convention* comes from the verb 'to convene.' To convene is to gather, to assemble, or to meet up. A convention is a point around which we gather. To follow a convention is to gather in the right way, to be assembled."[27] Ahmed captures what I see as conventional in DragCon: the event gathers people around goods, which they consume. In exchange, it gives attendees a bonus of feeling, because they have gathered "in the right way." They have rightly assembled under the banner of LGBTQ+ politics. In a sense, they purchase a feeling of transgression. RuPaul's convention thus peddles the unconventional conventionally. In turn, season 10's DragCon challenge teaches contestants to internalize this "merch-first" outlook.[28] They learn, through education-oriented panels, how to brand themselves efficiently.

Always behind these capitalist conventions lies the spiritual guru. "I feel at my core that I am a teacher. I am here," RuPaul elucidates in *GuRu*, "to be a conduit. I know how to make magic. I have the ability to help people cross over to their greatness and realize their potential."[29] On the same page, the inset proclaims that teaching in a nutshell: "Ego loves identity. Drag mocks identity. Ego hates drag."[30] RuPaul links her pedagogical vocation to this transmission of truth. *GuRu* encourages deep seekers to practice what RuPaul preaches, in part, by setting aside the childish things that mark the ego. This teaching practice has, however, at least two problems. First, it pictures—in the bad-reading-of-Butler way—drag as a self-willed action that expunges identity markers, along with the powers and privileges adhered to them. In fact, it risks marking those who remain attached to those markers of gender, race, and class as unnecessarily bitter or, worse, simpleminded. Second, it characterizes—in a bad-reading-of-Buddhism way—spirituality as something that escapes bodies, along with the oppression and the shame stuck to them.[31] In fact, it risks othering the pain of others in a way that renounces, if not straight-up pathologizes, their personal experience. This twofold teaching for transcendence proves, in theory and in practice, positively fascist.

## *Backwash: It Gets Bitter*

Thus far, I have unpacked the whitewashing spirituality that animates RuPaul's defense of drag. In this section, I argue that this defensiveness warps her teaching practice, because she refuses evidence that mars drag's immaculate subversion. RuPaul has helped queens refine and market their craft; she has also created platforms for telling and selling LGBTQ+ stories. Her instruction rests, however, on a totalizing theory of drag that extirpates complications. With a careful study of her facilitation, I highlight moments when her apologetic stance refuses true engagement with negative affect. When confronted with anger and shame, RuPaul counters with a progressivist view, which recognizes pain so long as one has overcome it. She thereby forecloses accounts that fail to conform to the cheerfully privileged plotline. This insistence on a happy ending might sell, but it impedes her ability to accept critique, especially criticism that views drag as, in the words of Judith Butler, "implicated in the regimes of power by which one is constituted and, hence, of being implicated in the very regimes of power that one opposes."[32] To stress this implication, I draw on Brazilian educator Paulo Freire's work and show how RuPaul's investment in progressivist politics leads to an authoritarian pedagogy.

While *RPDR* criticizes the Trump administration for its reactionary politics, its own pedagogical subtext betrays a compromising complicity. Key here are RuPaul's recurrent allusions to *The Prime of Miss Jean Brodie*. In Muriel Spark's 1961 Catholic novel and its subsequent 1969 film adaptation, Miss Brodie teaches "the crème de la crème"; assiduously, she places "old heads" on her girls' "young shoulders."[33] RuPaul kneads these words into her empire. *Drag U*'s opening credits, for example, paraphrase the text—"we here at *Drag U* are in the business of putting drag-queen heads on women's shoulders"—and, as Emily Shreve and I have argued, RuPaul's "bring-back-my-girls" refrain evokes Maggie Smith's Oscar-winning performance.[34] These campy references not only solidify RuPaul's role as teacher, but also expose a political underbelly. Miss Brodie is dismissed, after all, "on the grounds that she had been teaching Fascism."[35] Miss Brodie's instruction silences critique in favor of group cohesion and preaches rebellion against the status quo. Each time RuPaul references Miss Brodie, she alludes to a teacher with fascist leanings.

Amidst nationalist resurgence, Miss Brodie's name provocatively resurfaces. In the same *Rolling Stone* interview that defends drag's subversion, RuPaul aligns herself openly with Edinburgh's finest pedagogue: "I feel like Jean Brodie. Every year we present a new set of queens through our show and they're launched into the world. I love that. It's like giving birth."[36] In advance of the season 10 premiere, she makes this statement, which hauntingly frames the season's pedagogical misfires. For she still puts drag-queen heads on young-girl shoulders: "I've watched these kids in their audition reels and I fall in love with them before I even meet them. To watch them blossom is like being a gardener who plants seeds and watches them flower."[37] As the figurative language implies, she plants seeds in fertile soil. She assumes a dominant position in this instruction and thus retains the power associated with the traditional teacher. She even refers to the contestants as "kids," which disempowers and distances them from her. The consistency of her references to Miss Brodie and the maintenance of a teacher-student power imbalance belie her pedagogy's progressiveness in spades.

In Brodie fashion, RuPaul conserves her role as expert knower. She sets predestined limits on learning and, while advising season 10 queens, comes terribly close to telling them exactly what to do. She practices what Freire describes as the banking method, where "the scope of action allowed to the students extends only so far as receiving, filing, and storing the deposits."[38] RuPaul's chat with Asia O'Hara, during the "Snatch Game" episode, reflects this educational approach. Asia has decided to portray Beyoncé. RuPaul expresses concern, since Beyoncé has proven a difficult sell in past seasons. She instead suggests that Asia, given her Texan roots, consider another member of Destiny's Child. The advice is not terrible. The pedagogical problem arises in the judging, where RuPaul criticizes Asia for not taking her advice. The implication is that Asia ought to have followed her lead, no questions asked. Not surprisingly, viewers witness other queens reading between the lines of RuPaul's walk-through comments in order to discern what she wants. They learn their lessons and, obediently, adjust their performances. Suffice it to say, this methodology does not accord with critical pedagogy's best practices. Quite the opposite, it retains the classical sense of the teacher as top who inserts knowledge into bottoms who lack it.

In *Pedagogy of the Oppressed* (1968/1970), Freire argues that the student-teacher polarity must dissolve because the world is not cleanly divided into bad oppressors and good victims. "In truth," he writes of the oppressed, "the boss was 'inside' them."[39] Freire's critical pedagogy heeds the power that incriminates all subjects. This incrimination makes pure oppressor-oppressed, bad-good dichotomies moot. For this reason, Freire insists that, in revolutionary education, "both are simultaneously teachers *and* students."[40] This comment sounds like RuPaul at the reunion; however, Freire stresses that the "pedagogy of the oppressed is an instrument for their critical discovery that both they and their oppressors are manifestations of dehumanization."[41] Students and teachers alike must recognize that they reinforce oppressive values and participate in violent structures. No one stands apart with hands clean. From this angle, RuPaul's reliance on the banking method signals a stubborn refusal of embroilment. Her teaching methods maintain the distance necessary to ossify her authority, which places her in the ecstatic position of liberating others. She possesses the knowledge and expertise that free minds. She deposits and makes bank.

The reunion episode of season 10 magnifies the failure of RuPaul's direct instruction. Many astute commentators have noted how the charged exchange among The Vixen, Asia, and RuPaul exposes racial tensions long present in the series.[42] I want to examine this altercation for what it reveals pedagogically. On my reading, the reunion demonstrates RuPaul's denial of drag's implication in systemic oppression, including misogyny, racism, and economic injustice. This refusal sets the stage for The Vixen, who, upon arrival to *RPDR*, announces: "I'm just here to fight."[43] The Vixen's aggression has ties to her anti-racist activism. For many years, she has organized Chicago's *BlackGirlMagic*, a drag concert that showcases queens of color. She thus brings an advocate's sensibility to the competition and consistently calls out white privilege. Astutely, she articulates how dominant narratives position her as an "angry Black woman."[44] This script replays at the reunion, where RuPaul pushes The Vixen to explain her antagonistic behavior. The Vixen does not take the bait; instead, she tries to redirect attention to Eureka's conduct. "Everybody's telling me how I should react," she states, "but nobody's telling her how to act."[45] When that statement produces no critical reflection, she leaves the stage.

The Vixen challenges racism, and she underscores how white privilege operates on *Drag Race*. As such, she sours the show's happy ending. Her anger's very presence upsets RuPaul's progressivist agenda because The Vixen signals the continuity of homophobia and racism. She remains angry. Indeed, The Vixen is negative, which is exactly what Eureka accuses her of being.[46] In their dispute, negativity emerges as a worse sin than racism. Many (white) queens have used drag to escape a dark past, and, consequently, they reject any reminder of it. Hence, The Vixen's menace: she neither sanitizes nor silences. She uses her fury. Her affect activism evokes Audre Lorde, for whom "anger expressed and translated into action in the service of our vision and our future is a liberating and strengthening act of clarification."[47] Rather than value this elucidation, the *Untucked* scuffles and subsequent reunion skirmish bespeak the tendency to call "unjust" the one who identifies injustice. In *The Promise of Happiness* (2010), Ahmed names the threat of these killjoys, whose "failure to be happy is read as sabotaging the happiness of others."[48] By calling into question white privilege, The Vixen derails other queens' happiness. By withholding a smile, she jeopardizes RuPaul's fantasy of drag freed from oppression.

It is within this precise context that viewers should place RuPaul's agitated exclamation at the reunion. When she yells at Asia—"Look at me, damn it, I come from the same goddamn place she comes from"—she resurrects the argument for transcendence.[49] Look at me, she says: I am Black, gay, and happy. The Vixen, by implication, has not properly detached from her background. RuPaul has achieved this detachment, which proffers enlightened contentment. This serenity contrasts with Asia, who is visibly upset. Asia's sadness, which prompts RuPaul to lose her temper, follows in The Vixen's glum footsteps. Asia believes they have failed a community member. "We're not just drag queens," she insists; "we're people, and now we've got one of our people outside."[50] According to Asia, they ought to have stepped up and helped The Vixen, who needs support. "We are the first people," she claims, "we are the first people to say that people aren't treating us right,"[51] but no one reaches out to The Vixen. Pointedly, RuPaul cuts from Asia's critique to Dusty Ray Bottoms, a white queen who shares a triumphant account of moving past religious-based shame. In this instant, RuPaul makes it perfectly clear that *RPDR* exists to share stories of triumph not tragedy. Shame belongs to the annals.

*RPDR*'s forward-looking thrust merits critical scrutiny, especially in a moment of increased LGBTQ+ visibility. Learning from this example, educators might resist advancing a progressivist, glamazon-primed agenda at the expense of negativity. Doom and gloom teach, and a happiness imperative must not silence critique. This reminder is even more essential under the Trump administration, because, as Ahmed notes, the "risk of promoting the happy queer is that the unhappiness of this world could disappear from view. *We must stay unhappy with this world.*"[52] RuPaul attempts to efface shame and anger, but there are many reasons why her girls might feel down. Moreover, drag does not need to lift people up. As The Vixen explains, "[A] lot of people say drag should only be an escape from reality, but drag can also help us to face reality and deal with it."[53] Drag can reveal the illusion of reality, as RuPaul believes, or, as The Vixen suggests, the reality of illusion. Illusions have, The Vixen insists, real-life consequence, but human beings can work to change them. This transformative struggle—one that good education supports—happens, though, alongside pain.

*RPDR*'s blithe pedagogy displays a problematic propensity, one that addresses queer injury only to transcend it. This dynamic easily transfers from green screen to blackboard. In the classroom, this buoyant flight from pain occurs in roughly two ways. Educators either, like RuPaul, leave hurt in the past or, in their critique-driven analyses, identify enduring injustice but then point toward others—outside the academy—who enable this harm to continue. In effect, the latter response creates a spiritualized transcendence of its own: students and teachers understand the discursive forces that enchain the unthinking masses, and they thereby rise above the melee. The best in queer pedagogy, however, challenges this distance. Its queered methods require all participants to encounter negative affect and messy inclinations. As Susanne Luhmann explains, "[W]hat is at stake in a queer pedagogy is not the application of queer theory (as a new knowledge) onto pedagogy"; rather, "at stake are the implications of queer theory and pedagogy for the messy processes of learning and teaching, reading and writing."[54] This mess dirties all minds. Nobody is immune from institutionalized disease. Everyone should feel—and accept their share of—shame.[55] That inclusion includes the instructor, who is, as Freire maintains, justly implicated.

RuPaul does not touch this emotional mess. Assumed radicality prevents her, like Miss Brodie, from learning with and from others. Indeed, RuPaul cannot even hear The Vixen's critique. That criticism would require her to process her own positionality's ambivalence. After all, she is someone who has suffered by the very system from which she now benefits, and that system persists in its harm. It takes resolve, of course, to acknowledge this implication, and, for this reason, bell hooks stresses self-actualization's vital place in higher education.[56] Professors do not stand apart or above. They must do the inner work necessary to face their demons, too. Queer pedagogy embroils everyone in learning's muddle and asks them to query how power shapes what and how one knows. "Instead of posing (the right) knowledge as answer or solution," Luhmann insists that educators of a queer slant must, time and again, "pose knowledge as an interminable question."[57] With drag as the answer, RuPaul rejects the reunion's pessimism. She lectures—to all those with ears to hear—on her solution to suffering. Nevertheless, RuPaul's desire to surpass negativity does not remove pain. On the contrary, it pains some in order to heal others.

## *Charisma: Pedagogy of the Depressed*

RuPaul's spirituality enables her to detach from darkness and henceforth to profit by an optimistic pedagogy. Her teaching for transcendence paradoxically depends, however, on the extant suffering that individuals, once on the show, just need to get past. Contestants' prior hurt fuels the inspirational narrative: they voice their suffering on camera and, through RuPaul's counsel, overcome it. These tales of *rudemption* offer drama and consolation, but they too often situate sadness in the past or reattach negativity to othered individuals or groups. With this tendency in mind, I pivot slightly from RuPollyanna and examine the critical classroom, one grounded in the hermeneutics of suspicion. RuPaul has many failures, but I want to stress how frequently teachers follow her affective lead. In analyzing *RPDR*, they might be quick to condemn RuPaul instead of sitting with the ways in which we, too, occupy compromised positions. I therefore suggest that educators learn to incorporate teaching's shame—a depressing register of our own implication in unjust systems—into the LGBTQ+ classroom. We must, in a reparative spirit, teach our unredeemed entanglements. We thereby model a tolerance for ambiguity and cultivate, with students, a capacity to think beyond binaries.

In "Teaching/Depression," Eve Sedgwick wrestles with negative affect and theorizes a queer pedagogy attuned to ambivalence. Drawing on the work of Melanie Klein and Silvan Tomkins, she recalls how often we eject complicated emotions: "[M]any of us are familiar," she argues, "with situations where our own or other people's preemptive need to disown feelings of racism, misogyny, anti–Semitism, and so forth—feelings that almost inevitably arise but are experienced as intolerable—is liable to propel circuits of interpersonal accusation that are explosive with the very forms of hatred that are under internal erasure."[58] An inner rejection displaces bad feelings, which reemerge elsewhere. This displacement results from an inability to withstand ambiguity. Sedgwick describes this incapacity by way of the paranoid/schizoid position, typified by "three rather violent things": "the ego's inability to tolerate anxiety or ambivalence; its consequent strategy of splitting both its objects and itself into fragments that can be seen as exclusively good or bad; and its aggressive expulsion of intolerable parts."[59] The paranoid knower identifies the bad bit and removes it. This "aggressive expulsion" creates a purely good object (to attach to) and offers correct, certifiable answers. The ego loves the sanitized result, but this way of knowing reinforces dualistic, either/or thinking.

Sedgwick links this paranoid dynamic to the hermeneutics of suspicion. With faith in detection and exposure, students in suspicious classrooms demystify texts and unveil their hidden meanings.[60] Educated in distrust, these learners inevitably trouble texts like *RPDR*, revealing their problematic politics and retrograde attachments. In fact, I have advanced a critique along these lines: the show's racial blindness and consumerist bent problematize its pedagogy. And yet, to remain at the level of critique is to oversimplify. *RPDR* brings pleasure to many viewers, and RuPaul is an important teacher. She has curated, however imperfectly, a queer herstory and has brought drag talent to my mother's television set. RuPaul has also championed LGBTQ+ rights for decades. I want our teaching to hold this good with its bad. A nonbinary view allows us to explore, in Sedgwick's words, "the many ways selves and communities succeed in extracting sustenance from the objects of a culture—even of a culture whose avowed desire has often been not to sustain them."[61] On the ground, this pedagogy necessitates sensibilities trained to endure life's unending ambiguity.

Humility and wonder help keep these tensions together. Sedgwick stresses that, unlike the paranoid/schizoid position, the "threshold to the depressive position is the foundational, authentically difficult understanding that good and bad tend to be inseparable at every level."[62] This sensibility, of course, grounds Sedgwick's influential call for reparative reading, and it is "the position from which it is possible to begin using one's own resources to assemble or 'repair' the part-objects into something like a whole, albeit a compromised one."[63] The depressive position accepts ambivalence and resists simplistic dichotomies. From there, it repairs. This reparation is depressing, because it requires everyone to register failure, to renegotiate interaction, and to disclose complicities. No one detaches purely, and that is a sad reckoning. "We feel these depressive pressures," Sedgwick explains, "in the forms of remorse, shame, confusion, depression itself, mourning for the lost ideal, and—most often relevant—a sad understanding of the inexorable laws of unintended consequences."[64] Notably, this stance, which is always provisional, values shame and sadness as embodied ways of (un-)knowing. It learns with them, demanding neither blissful progress nor perfect action.

A queer teaching attuned to negativity makes it possible to engage lovingly with critique, because we have acknowledged our failures and wrestled with our shames. It is, however, difficult to achieve the fragile, temporary recognition that the "good and bad tend to be inseparable at every level." We want them purely separate. Consider, from this perspective, season 10's

"Evil Twins" challenge. In this episode, the five remaining queens create two looks: one captures their outré glamazon, and the other their inner saboteur. Immediately, RuPaul divides the good from the bad. Queens then confront their bad side, which "oozes negativity," only to leave it behind them. "You can look," RuPaul cautions, "just don't stare."[65] Throughout the challenge, RuPaul equates the inner saboteur with the ego—"the saboteur, the ego, really wants to kill you"—and coaches her girls to move past the inner, negative voice: "I hear you, thanks for sharing."[66] On the surface, the episode acknowledges the good and the bad; however, in their isolation, the challenge refuses the reality of their inseparability. In effect, RuPaul uses the lesson to teach others how to pluck the lotus from the mud. She forces the redemptive storyline, fostering a consolatory fantasy of good's ultimate separation from bad. It is fitting, therefore, that Miz Cracker, who struggles openly with depression, goes home.

"Evil Twins" concretizes *GuRu*'s overall vibe. "I'm a living witness," RuPaul avers, "to the revelation that once you get rid of the negativity in your world, everything and everyone that might be blocking you, you will live in the light."[67] This harsh lighting encourages, though, a dualistic-leaning paranoia: it shines light on the dark to send it packing. Against this view, I propose a shame-embracing pedagogy, one that attends to teaching's flushed failures. These failures gesture in two directions at once: first, the everyday upset of a bad lesson or an awkward encounter and, second, the larger systemic injustices that taint higher education. As we teach, we unavoidably mess up; in addition, many of us participate in systems that sharpen, for instance, class division. Apologies are necessary: discussion of individual error and institutional wrong ought to distinguish feminist and queer spaces. With frank admission of our own participation in unjust systems and disclosure of how we benefit by them, we learn with and from our bad feelings. This dialogue testifies to shame as constitutive of queerness and ever-present, as Ellis Hanson has argued, in learning environments.[68] The LGBTQ+ classroom is, after all, not a world apart; rather, it is a part of this world. Teaching's good remains knotted up, irrevocably, in its bad.

What does this queer pedagogy look like in practice? Well, for one thing, teachers do not use the classroom as a space to reinforce easy binaries, especially the dualism of the good liberal and the bad conservative. We resist the temptation to vilify in service of the feel-good hit. Life is not that simple, and our teaching should not be either. We train—ourselves and others—for political nuance and moral complexity. We cultivate something like Gloria Anzaldúa's mestiza consciousness. As she maintains, "[I]t is not enough to stand on the opposite riverbank, shouting questions, challenging patriarchal, white conventions. A counter stance locks one into a duel of oppressor and oppressed; locked in mortal combat, like the cop and the criminal, both are reduced to a common denominator of violence."[69] This lockdown slowly kills progress, since "it's a step towards liberation from cultural domination. But it is not a way of life."[70] In contrast, queer pedagogy cultivates viable, both/and sensibilities as it encounters life's muddle. We collectively strengthen our capacity to muddy binaries by, in Anzaldúa's words, "developing a tolerance for contradictions, a tolerance for ambiguity."[71] This awareness, charitably queered, "operates in a pluralistic mode—nothing is thrust out, the good the bad and the ugly—nothing rejected, nothing abandoned."[72] This inner work is, for Anzaldúa, deeply spiritual.

While one might read a spiritual turn as apolitical tolerance—as adaptation to unjust worlds—it is, in fact, an argument for continued confrontation with injustice. Engaged pedagogy necessitates teaching practices and affective sensibilities that help educators face (and survive) depressing realities. Moreover, a tolerance for ambiguity strengthens resolve to address the oversights within our own field. For example, queer theory's anti-social strand has been, as Mari Ruti notes, "promoted mostly by white gay men interested in the subversive potential of radical negativity, particularly the connection between jouissance and self-undoing."[73] Paranoid knowing routinely rests on privilege: systemic injustices—racial, gendered, and classed—back the institutions that make alienating critique, in many cases, sustainable. While the anti-social strand draws important attention to the dangers of assimilationist politics, its theory embraces negativity at the expense of emotional repair. As a result, "the relational strand has been promoted by 'the rest of us,' by those who have been interested in the complex entanglements of sexuality with class, race, gender, nationality, and other collective identity markers."[74] Although I do not wish to reject the powerful insights gleaned from the anti-social strand, it seems to me vital that queer classrooms combine critique with care.

In this pursuit, spiritual practice has, perhaps, a place. Critics—such as Anzaldúa, hooks, and Sedgwick—turn to spirituality, because their activism requires self-discipline. They integrate spiritual teachings, though, without disavowing, like RuPaul, material realities of color, sex, and cash. Spiritual practice grounds them, instead, in the reality of constant struggle. As hooks explains,

> [F]eminists in general have come to rethink spirituality. Ten years ago if you talked about humility, people would say, I feel as a woman I've been humble enough, I don't want to try to erase the ego—I'm trying to get an ego. But now, the achievements that women have made in all areas of life have brought home the reality that we are as corruptible as anyone else.[75]

If the LGBTQ+ movement has achieved similar success today—and I believe it has—then we should remember spirituality's resources. These resources include not only ego-mitigation and honed mindfulness but also wherewithal for living on life's unhappy margins. It is exhausting to bear ambiguity and draining to confess culpability, but spirituality helps us to live with and within our skin's clammy fragilities and botchy failures.

Season 10 bears witness to the reality that vulnerable communities continue to turn to religion for sustenance. Monét X Change and Monique Heart emphasize their connection to the Black church. This bond is an uneasy one. Monique makes it painfully clear that "you can't be Black and gay … this is like heresy," but even her use of "heresy" signals a religious referent.[76] Whereas Dusty and Blair St. Clair break religious ties, Monét and Monique maintain contact. At the reunion, Monique testifies to her "love" for "this one we call God" and to the strain of repairing her relationship with her mother.[77] These comments contrast with Dusty, who has just discussed her conversion therapy and decision to snap familial bonds. Dusty promises viewers that, despite her horrific experience, "it will get better."[78] Still, this promise is, at least in part, one that racial privilege affords. RuPaul validates Dusty's choice and emphasizes the need to detach from (non-supportive) presences—*cf.* The Vixen—but a more robust account of queer survival requires consideration of the affective and financial resources that we have at our disposal. Cutting and running remain a queer luxury, and, for those who stay behind, religion offers backing that we should take seriously. To view religion as mere false consciousness is to devalue, often from a privileged position, its relational sustenance.

Sedgwick brings this support explicitly to academic work and, in her late writing, suggests that spiritual practice might help us nudge recognition to realization. "Where is the gap," she wonders, "between knowing something—even knowing it to be true—and realizing it, taking it as real?"[79] In a reflection on Buddhism, she shows how its teachings not only trouble everyday binaries but also realize those troubling truths in bodily practice. The question is, for Sedgwick like hooks, one of praxis. Sedgwick casts doubt on critical theory's privileging of epistemology, as if knowing about injustice were enough to undo it. Knowing is not living differently. This emphasis on knowledge enables, furthermore, paranoid projection: "[W]hat I'm wary of is the whole, anthropological rhetoric of ascribing 'beliefs'—ascribing them always, it seems, to someone who is not oneself. Somehow beliefs are never what *I* have, only what *they* have."[80] Sedgwick invites critics to step back—practicing non-attachment instead of detachment—and to appreciate the gap between our understanding and our doing. How does knowing truly lead to living differently? This shift, on my view, concerns relations of love and care at school. Indeed, what if we thought of the word "queer" primarily as a verb, one that requires perpetual practice to bring its teachings from transcendent theory to imminent realization?

*　*　*

RuPaul's primetime pedagogy walks a stiletto-fine line between facilitating and fortifying herstory. Educators toe the same line when they presume the progressiveness or transgression of queerness.[81] Within this context, RuPaul's apologetics offers a timely reminder of something that the best teachers already know: pedagogy's radical promise rests not in content but in practice. LGBTQ+ representation alone does not challenge homophobia and misogyny; however, educators might contest oppressive systems from inside the classroom. As a practice of freedom, queer pedagogy rests on curated engagement with emotional messiness, political ambivalence, and human frailty. It models continued interaction with broken, fallible people in fallen worlds. In its candid vulnerability, its teaching methods queer relations among students and teachers by disaggregating power from routinized roles. "Teacher/student relationships are," hooks claims, "arenas for disrupting our addiction to dualism, and we are called upon to really strip ourselves down, to where we don't have guides anymore."[82] Teachers might learn from the student body in a way that queers even queenly authorities.

Educators, though, must listen. It is perilous to enter the classroom with the correct answer and right politics. We can straightforwardly teach, like RuPaul, toward the solution that we ourselves have found. We, too, easily adopt apologetic postures that impede criticism. This silencing happens. It happens, often, unintentionally. I take this happening to be one motive behind Ahmed's request to put the hap back in happiness. "Caring for happiness," Ahmed warns, "can so often translate into caring for others on the condition that they reflect back an idea you have of how a life should be lived."[83] We should not teach others how to be happy; instead, Ahmed reclaims the chance—the hap—of caring. A queer pedagogy of care would acknowledge unpredictability and remain open to unforeseen possibilities. "Maybe," she wonders, "we can reorient caring from caring for someone's happiness to caring what happens to someone or something: caring about what happens, caring whatever happens. We might call this a hap care rather than a happiness care."[84] Applying Ahmed's argument to queer pedagogy, this methodology would separate learning outcomes from happy endings. It would minister to the needs of individuals necessarily distinct from us. This schooling would allow students to grow independent of our orthodoxy.

This practice is incredibly difficult, but it is a work of love. The spiritual dimension to this care emerges in the discipline required, for this "hap care would not be about letting an object go, but holding on to an object by letting oneself go, giving oneself over to something that is not one's own."[85] In Ahmed's account, we do not detach from others. We really love them. Simone Weil conceptualizes this *caritas* in terms of the distance between devouring and looking. "When a human being is in any degree necessary to us," she writes, "we cannot desire his good unless we cease to desire our own."[86] It requires an enormous effort to disentangle ourselves from our own need for happiness, but this unlearning is necessary. This love will not reaffirm the regnant model of the teacher as top with truth to implant; instead, it will imagine new encounters with and across differences of knowledge, experience, and ability. Such loving disorientation is queer pedagogy's gift, one that unmoors the affective and relational dynamics of our studies. As a matter of fact, LGBTQ+ courses explore desire, attachment, and love: they should take the lead in this reeducation, because—as I've learned from RuPaul—if you can't love somebody else, how in the hell are you going to love yourself?

## *Mini Challenge: Discussion Questions*

- How has consumer culture both aided and impeded LGBTQ+ social movements? Identify moments on *RPDR* where commodification has impacted the show's representation of gender and sexuality.
- How have recent seasons of *RPDR*, including *All Stars*, engaged with the social-justice issues addressed in season 10? Is this engagement, in your opinion, effective?
- Beyond season 10, where have spirituality and queerness intersected in *RPDR*? How do you explain—in the words of a character from Radclyffe Hall's *The Well of Loneliness* (1928)—"this curious craving for religion" within the LGBTQ+ community?

## *Maxi Challenge: Activities and Assignments*

- Introduce students to Critical University Studies. In "RuPaulogetics," I argue that teachers should acknowledge their position with higher education and address their implication within systems of injustice. One way to approach this discussion is through Critical University Studies. To this end, I recommend that instructors integrate at least one reading from the emerging field. Jeffrey J. Williams has a short but important piece—"Deconstructing Academe"—in *The Chronicle of Higher Education* that should work well. For a queer take, consider Adrienne Rich's "Toward a Woman-Centered University."

- Trouble progressivist narratives intentionally. Heather Love has argued for the importance of LGBTQ+ histories, even when tragic. I suggest, therefore, that instructors actively engage learners with narratives that resist consumption-oriented feel-goodery. This study can take many forms. Instructors might choose to integrate texts or topics that shed light on continued oppression or persistent discrimination. Alternatively, they might craft assignments that require students to research past communities or historical figures.
- Encourage students to hold *both-and* positions. I have found it fruitful to create assignments that require students to reflect on the position from which they interpret texts. The goal is not only to increase metacognition, but also to reinforce the point that two people can look at the same evidence and reach different conclusions. To this end, I have created a "bifocal" essay assignment that requires students to make two claims about the same passage of a text; they then run the two mini-essays parallel to one another. In this case, I might ask students to examine a scene or conversation from one episode of *RPDR* from two different perspectives. Of course, it is important to use this assignment to reinforce the multiplicity of possible perspectives. The goal, after all, is to trouble rather than to reinforce binaries!

## Notes

1. "Queens Reunited." *RuPaul's Drag Race*, season 10, episode 13, VH1, 21 June 2018, Amazon, https://www.amazon.com/gp/video/detail/B07B68P55J/ref=atv_dp_season_select_s10.
2. For an overview of this tendency, look to Heather Love, *Feeling Backward: Loss and the Politics of Queer History* (Harvard University Press, 2009: pp 1–30).
3. Felski, Rita. *The Limits of Critique*, University of Chicago Press, 2015, p. 41.
4. "Queens of All Media." *RuPaul's Drag Race*, season 1, episode 3, Logo TV, 16 Feb. 2009. Amazon, https://www.amazon.com/gp/video/detail/B001RGOIWW/ref=atv_dp_season_select_s1.
5. Spanos, Brittany. "RuPaul on 'Drag Race' Success, Being and Introvert, Survival Playlist." *Rolling Stone*, 19 Dec. 2017, par. 9
6. *Ibid.*
7. "Snatch Game." *RuPaul's Drag Race*, season 10, episode 7, VH1, 3 May 2018, Amazon, https://www.amazon.com/gp/video/detail/B07B68P55J/ref=atv_dp_season_select_s10.
8. "10s Across the Board." *RuPaul's Drag Race*, season 10, episode 1, VH1, 22 Mar. 2018, Amazon, https://www.amazon.com/gp/video/detail/B07B68P55J/ref=atv_dp_season_select_s10.
9. "The Last Ball on Earth." *RuPaul's Drag Race*, season 10, episode 4, VH1, 12 April 2018, Amazon, https://www.amazon.com/gp/video/detail/B07B68P55J/ref=atv_dp_season_select_s10.
10. "Extra Special Edition." *RuPaul's Drag Race*, season 1, episode 7, VH1, 16 Mar. 2009, Amazon, https://www.amazon.com/gp/video/detail/B001RGOIWW/ref=atv_dp_season_select_s1.

11. Spanos, par. 9.
12. *Ibid.*, par. 3.
13. Lawson, Richard. "The Philosopher Queen." *Vanity Fair*, no. 713, Holiday 2019/2020, p. 80.
14. *Ibid.*
15. *Ibid.*
16. RuPaul. *GuRu*. HaperCollins, 2018, p. xi.
17. *Ibid.*
18. *Ibid.*, pp. xi–xii.
19. *Ibid.*, p. xii.
20. *Ibid.*, pp. 25, 72.
21. *Ibid.*, p. 10.
22. *Ibid.*, p. xii.
23. On the interrelation between LGBTQ+ politics and markets, consult Alexandra Chasin, *Selling Out: The Gay & Lesbian Movement Goes to Market* (St. Martin's Press, 2000: pp. 1–27).
24. For this critique's feminist grounding, see Susan Bordo, *Unbearable Weight* (University of California Press, 2003, p. 275).
25. "RuPaul's DragCon LA." *Wikipedia*, Wikipedia Foundation, 30 Jan. 2020, https://en.wikipedia.org/wiki/RuPaul%27s_DragCon_LA. Accessed 20 March 2020.
26. Abraham, Amelia. "Pink Runways & Strip Lighting: My First Time at Drag Con." *Refinery 29*, 30 May 2019, par. 10.
27. Ahmed, Sara. *The Promise of Happiness*. Duke University Press, 2010, p. 64.
28. "DragCon Panel Extravaganza." *RuPaul's Drag Race*, season 10, episode 6, VH1, 26 April 2018, *Amazon*, https://www.amazon.com/gp/video/detail/B07B68P55J/ref=atv_dp_season_select_s10.
29. RuPaul, p. 170.
30. *Ibid.*
31. See "Agent of Change: An Interview with bell hooks," by Helen Tworkov, *Tricycle*, 1992, par. 2 for what bell hooks characterizes as "Tina Turner Buddhism."
32. Butler, Judith. *Bodies that Matter*. Routledge, 1993, p. 125.
33. Spark, Muriel. *The Prime of Miss Jean Brodie*. HarperCollins, 2009, p. 5.
34. Fine, David, & Shreve, Emily. "The Prime of Miss RuPaul Charles: Allusion, Betrayal, and Charismatic Pedagogy." *The Makeup of RuPaul's Drag Race*, edited by Jim Daems, McFarland, 2014, p. 171.
35. Spark, p. 134.
36. Spanos, par. 13.
37. *Ibid.*
38. Freire, Paulo. *Pedagogy of the Oppressed*. Continuum, 2003, p. 72.
39. *Ibid.*, p. 64.
40. *Ibid.*, p. 72.
41. *Ibid.*, p. 48.
42. For an insightful response, refer to John Paul Brammer, "How the Vixen Exposed the Racism of RuPaul's Drag Race" (*them*, 22 June 2018).
43. "10s Across the Board."
44. To hear her explanation, view "Tap that App." *Untucked: RuPaul's Drag Race*, season 10, episode 3, VH1, 5 April 2018, *Amazon*, https://www.amazon.com/gp/video/detail/B07BN7Q5ZM/ref=atv_dp_season_select_s10.
45. "Queens Reunited."
46. "The Last Ball on Earth."
47. Lorde, Audre. "The Uses of Anger: Women Responding to Racism." *Sister Outsider*, Crossing Press, 2007, p. 127.
48. Ahmed, p. 66.
49. "Queens Reunited."
50. *Ibid.*

51. *Ibid.*
52. Ahmed, p. 105—emphasis original.
53. "Snatch Game."
54. Luhmann, Susanne. "Queering/Querying Pedagogy? Or, Pedagogy Is a Pretty Queer Thing." *Queer Theory in Education*, edited by William F. Pinar, Lawrence Erlbaum Associates, 1998, p. 151.
55. For more on the queer ethics I reference, see Michael Warner, *The Trouble with Normal* (Harvard University Press, 1999: p. 36).
56. hooks, bell. *Teaching to Transgress*. Routledge, 1994, p. 15.
57. Luhmann, p. 151.
58. Sedgewick, Eve. "Teaching/Depression." *The Scholar and Feminist Online*, vol. 4, no. 2, Spring 2006, par. 6.
59. *Ibid.*
60. To flesh out this picture, consult Rita Felski, *The Limits of Critique* (University of Chicago Press, 2015: p. 86).
61. Sedgewick, Eve. *Touching Feeling*, Duke University Press, 2003, pp. 150–151.
62. Sedgewick, "Teaching/Depression," par. 7.
63. *Ibid.*, par. 8.
64. *Ibid.*
65. "Evil Twins" *RuPaul's Drag Race*, season 10, episode 11, VH1, 7 June 2018, *Amazon*, https://www.amazon.com/gp/video/detail/B07B68P55J/ref=atv_dp_season_select_s10.
66. *Ibid.*
67. RuPaul, p. xii.
68. For a controversial account, see Hanson "Teaching Shame." *Gay Shame*, edited by David M. Halperin and Valerie Traub (University of Chicago Press, 2009: pp. 132–164, p. 132).
69. Anzaldúa, Gloria. *Borderlands/La Frontera*. Aunt Lute Books, 2007, p. 100.
70. *Ibid.*
71. *Ibid.*, p. 101.
72. *Ibid.*
73. Ruti, Mari. *The Ethics of Opting Out*. Columbia University Press, 2017, p. 6.
74. *Ibid.*
75. hooks, "Agent of Change," par. 8.
76. "Queens Reunited."
77. *Ibid.*
78. *Ibid.*
79. Sedgewick, Eve. "Reality and Realization." *The Weather in Proust*, edited by Jonathan Goldberg, Duke University Press, 2011, pp. 206–215, p. 208.
80. *Ibid.*, p. 212.
81. Bersani, Leo. "Is the Rectum a Grave?" *October*, vol. 43, Oct. 1987, p. 205.
82. hooks, "Agent of Change," par. 7.
83. Ahmed, Sara. *Living a Feminist Life*, Duke University Press, 2017, p. 266.
84. *Ibid.*
85. *Ibid.*
86. Weil, Simone. *Waiting for God*. HarperCollins, 2009, p. 132.

# May the Best Drag Queen Win
## *The Competitive Nature of Drag*

> "I wanted to genuinely thank her for giving me the inspiration to be the kind of person who realizes that I can do whatever I want. If that means becoming an internationally famous drag queen, great! If that means stepping away from a competition because the rules don't feel like they're for me? That's in the spirit of what I've learned from Ru. I felt, in that moment, like she was hearing me."[1]
> —BenDeLaCreme, season 6 contestant,
> *All Stars* season 3 contestant

## *Learning Outcomes:*

By the end of this section, we should be able to…

- Identify the mediums of mass media that contain content featuring *RPDR* and its queens.
- Interpret the narratives, storylines, and edits being depicted in a range of spaces (the competition, the confessional, and *Untucked*).
- Articulate the influence and messaging of current and former contestants beyond their depiction on the series.
- Question *RPDR*'s effectiveness in depicting the LGBTQ+ community fairly, accurately, and/or ethically.
- Assess the subtext of the show's cultural references, plays on gender norms, and brand of humor.
- Develop a framework for assessing drag, pedagogy, media, and *RPDR*—i.e., RuPedagogies.

### Note

1. Nolfi, Joey. "*RuPaul's Drag Race All Stars 3*: BenDeLaCreme on how Thorgy, aliens, and Wite-Out made a martyr." *Entertainment Weekly*, 2 Mar. 2018, https://ew.com/tv/2018/03/02/rupauls-drag-race-bendelacreme-on-how-thorgy-thor-aliens-and-wite-out-made-a-martyr/.

# Gay Super Bowl

## *Homonormative Authorization, Instruction, and Discipline Through Sports Media Borrowings*

### Nathan Workman

RuPaul introduced *RuPaul's Drag Race's* (*RPDR*) season 12, episode 4's "The Ball Ball" (2020) by saying, "Did you know, *Drag Race* and sports have a lot in common? They both involve competitions, colorful outfits, and balls!"[1] Puns made throughout the fashion extravaganza satirize sport with campy references to athletic prowess and hidden testicles. Another example from season 9 (2017) features show judge Ross Matthews introducing the new lip-sync-for-the-crown format by parodying sport's television graphics, commentary, and the logo of sports cable giant *ESPN*.[2] Connections to drag and sport are not limited to *RPDR*. The 1990 documentary *Paris Is Burning* begins by comparing the ballroom scene to sports.[3] And throughout Hollywood, drag characters have engaged in sports to juxtapose an unexpected athleticism with their outward gender presentation. The *Mrs. Doubtfire* (1993) scene starring Robin Williams as a middle-aged father playing an elderly nanny who excels in soccer exemplifies this.[4] However parodic, sports have always influenced *RPDR* and follow a tradition of drag representation in media exploring competitive gender performances. To these ends, I argue *RPDR*'s references to sport act to satirize traditional masculinity while reinstituting a homonormative masculine hierarchy within gender performance communities.

Overt connections run throughout the series, such as the physical fitness mini challenges in season 1 (2009)[5] and season 5 (2013),[6] and *All Stars* season 1's (2012) basketball mini challenge.[7] Also, maxi challenges such as season 4's (2012) professional wrestling challenge,[8] season 9's (2017) cheerleading challenge,[9] and season 11's (2019) "Draglympics" challenge[10] embody athletic performance. In addition to ableist concerns when testing for the physical conditioning of contestants to codify their productive potentials as franchise investments, these challenges relate athleticism to behavior, character, and bodily discipline to visualize intangible qualities like contestant motivations, drives, and passion for drag through physicality. Resembling drag and sport in film, these comparisons seek to prove individual, communal, and economic value within heteronormative power structures, such as the family, workforce, and state. To these ends, *RPDR* perpetuates the privilege of homonormative cisgender gay men in drag performance cultures to meet concerns regarding industry, economy, and representation.

Subtler nods to sports' masculine privilege exist within the series, such as on season 3, episode 2 (2011), when contestants Mimi Imfurst and Venus D-Lite discuss cosmetic surgery. Mimi says Venus's cheek implants are similar to "baseball players taking steroids, you're sort of cheating" at female impersonation.[11] Through Mimi's statement, producers position Venus's femininity as unnaturally enhanced to make normative the cisgender gay male performance of drag within the competition. Here, the cheating corollary implies feminizing body modifications provide an unfair advantage in comparison to male-coded bodies without such procedures. Together, these gestures to drag and sport begin to exemplify *RPDR*'s self-conception as the "gay Super Bowl,"[12] which reproduces patriarchal oppression by creating hierarchies of value among drag artists.

*RPDR*'s brand of drag media, like nationalized sports, is a popular cultural practice that reifies dominant ideological projects with diverse participants, but under hegemonic control.[13] RuPaul, as "mother," coach, and disciplinarian molds his "girls" into performers modeled after his career within heteronormative entertainment industries. Subsequently, alternative ways of performing gender are excluded or marginalized to frame the cisgender gay male performance of femininity as the epitome of success within drag culture. Like modern sports, *RPDR* has commercialized and globalized its ideology within media systems from regional, cultural, and folk forms. Sports media scholar Rod Brookes identifies similar homogenizing practices in the formation of modern sports as "an attempt to *discipline* and *commodify* adult play."[14] He notes sport formations standardized "space, time, and conduct" while channeling "physical and emotional expression [...] within societal limits."[15] Though *RPDR* has diversity, this standard articulates success and market value through bodily standards, gender presentation, class, and racialized taste cultures that often perpetuate normative cultural ideals. Essentially, *RPDR* presents itself as the instructor, distributor, and arbiter of a professional drag league by teaching regimes of practice that maintain and perpetuate its authority.[16]

Queering *RPDR* would imagine a less disciplined definition of drag that allows for more variation within the franchise. Ultimately, I critically relate the franchise's investments in homonormative masculinity to sport's construction of masculine privilege within administrative, media, and economic spheres.[17] *RPDR* reifies masculine privilege by resembling a sports-like property, exemplified through its use of professionalism, narrative practice, and evaluative metrics. Reading *RPDR*'s pedagogical project as a homonormative drag sports league examines how certain practices become dominant. Masculinity as a knowledge construct adapts to shifting cultural challenges, including the incorporation of the previously marginalized (such as cisgender gay masculinities) to maintain hierarchal authority. In centering *RPDR*'s masculine pedagogy, I examine the process of knowledge cultivation and show how a queer franchise thought to subvert authority can ultimately reproduce normative compliance.

## *Neoliberalism: Masculinities, Homonormativity, Marketized Equality, Reality Television, and Knowledge Production*

*RPDR* teaches how marginalized groups can monetize difference to access normative power within, as neoliberal scholar Julie A. Wilson posits, a *marketized equality* framework.[18] Citing Lisa Duggan's examination of neoliberalism's influence within LGBTQ+ activism, Wilson asserts the movement moved away from advocating for the "downward redistribution of resources and power" for "inclusion in the burgeoning enterprise culture."[19] Wilson, again citing Duggan, contends that the bodies that mattered within this privatized culture were *homonormative* or "those that conformed to dominant cultural ideals of the nuclear family, bodily modesty, [...] control, self-care, and enterprise in the market."[20]

Further defining homonormativity, Lisa Duggan says it is "a politics that does not contest dominate heteronormative assumptions and institutions, but upholds and sustains them, while promising the possibility of a demobilized gay constituency and a privatized, depoliticized gay culture anchored in domesticity and consumption."[21] Basically, those closest to normative societal privileges, like whiteness, binary gender presentation, and affluence, have more opportunity and visibility within marketized equality frameworks. Wilson posits "marketized equality privatizes collective struggle [...] only merit[ing] [societal recognition] through self-enterprise and competition."[22] Therefore, homonormativity reifies existing privileges because one must already possess the necessary capitals to compete. For example, to do well on *RPDR*, one must cultivate a network of drag artisans, digital media competencies, and the self-promotion to make the most of one's show opportunities.

To these ends, how masculinity is performed within *RPDR*, or a queer sport's influenced reality-competition program, offers a window into homonormativity as a pedagogy. Masculinity scholar Raewyn Connell discusses masculinity and femininity as "gender projects," which are simply "a way [...] social practice is ordered."[23] Masculinity is just one "place" within gender which produces "a series of 'effects' in bodily experience, personality, and culture."[24] *Hegemonic masculinity*, then, defined as the gender practice which currently embodies the problem of patriarchal legitimacy—or the pedagogical instruction of male dominance and female subordination—is not the only type of masculinity in practice, but does represent the most widely instructed form.[25]

Practitioners of masculinity come to learn it from different historical trajectories that intersect—or interact—with race, class, and sexuality, among others.[26] Importantly these *multiple masculinities* simultaneously challenge and reify hegemonic masculinity's current hierarchy,[27] which works to control "cultural ideals, institutional power, and capital production."[28] Noting *hegemony* is a system of societal control, which Wilson cites through the Gramscian definition of hegemonic power in class relations as "maintained through [the] ongoing, ever-shifting cultural processes of winning *the consent* of the governed,"[29] the marginalization of queer drag performers on *RPDR* can be understood through the pedagogical positioning of homonormative masculinity as expert, instructor, and valuable. This positioning is maintained by devaluing and feminizing performances deemed common, underdeveloped, or too reminiscent of so-called pedestrian femininities. This constructs queer knowledge and drag expertise under gay male understandings of hyper-femininity, individuality, and masculine notions of professionalism. *RPDR* presents this pedagogy—or competition—as fair and open to all; however, this homonormative institution is still more accessible for certain classed, racialized, and gendered bodies.

Further, reality TV scholars Skeggs and Wood's concept of an "economy of personhood" helps frame *RPDR*'s homonormative masculine privileging. They define this concept as a scrutiny of "bodies, parts, and practices for corporate interest" and their commodification along existing constructions of classed, gendered, and racialized norms.[30] When subjectively assessing market viability, centering how *RPDR* frames the history of drag to mainstream audiences necessitates examining the contradictory burden *RPDR* has to validate drag economically within heteronormative industries and represent diversity within the practice. Conversely, while monetizing queer subversion within normative industries, *RPDR* must suppress or discipline challenges to its capitalist validity from marginalized performers that prove the inequalities of its value system.

Failure to realize the franchise's homonormative ideals are framed to prove the pedagogy of the program correct rather than reveal the limitations of a biased institution. *RPDR* teaches that contestants must divest from interdependent mindsets, such as class consciousness, racialized identity, and queer solidarity, to realize normative success through individual self-work. This follows bourgeoise ideologies of hard work, self-care, and bodily discipline to prove the individual worthy of reward and merit for their contributions to capitalist markets.[31] This exists in stark juxtaposition to drag's historic legacy within collective-based rights movements. Ultimately, RuPaul's post-racial and post-feminine celebrity is modeled as an exemplar for marginalized groups to realize their own normative success. Proving this instruction hollow, many transgender contestants and contestants of color have described industry prejudices despite individual merit or worthiness.[32] If RuPaul can succeed in America as a "too Black, too gay, and too feminine" person, anyone can, right?[33]

## *Instituting Difference: Masculine Bias in Bodily Identity, Behavior, and Skill*

*RPDR* perpetuates its masculine privilege through favoring assigned-male-at-birth drag queen performances of femininity as more physically strenuous, professional, and expert in relation to assigned-female-at-birth drag performers.[34] Regarding the creation and curation of knowledge expertise, Ann Hartman breaks down the definition of "profession" to center a key part of its meaning as the possession and ownership of specific areas of knowledge.[35] In this case, cisgender gay men have positioned themselves as expert female performers over people more closely identified to femininity in their gender presentation through the instruction and control of drag knowledges. It's akin to male athletes being paid more to perform the same sport as female athletes.[36] Patriarchy and homonormativity as pedagogical projects have conditioned the social order to value the masculine performance of a cultural practice over the feminine or non-gendered.[37]

Also, to protect the value of cisgender gay male drag as expert, discourse contradictorily depicts transgender and female-identified performers as more naturally equipped to perform feminine drag and simultaneously as less impactful gender satirists because of this so-called natural dividend. Essentially, *RPDR* frames female performances as less deserving of compensation, recognition, and social capital in attempts to maintain knowledge that reifies male economic, cultural, and authorial control. To validate this, RuPaul has said drag is "punk rock" when men reject masculinity to perform femininity.[38] Under this logic, women paradoxically are essentialized as not subversive enough to satirize patriarchy when they are more apt to understand its domineering effects.

Primarily, *RPDR* judges how well contestants transform along the traditional gender binary to value and visualize one's drag skill. RuPaul emulates this every episode by appearing first as masculine (as instructor and coach) and then finishes in drag to judge relationally to his own example. This marginalizes contestants outside of the gender binary unable to present such duality.[39] Similar to nationalized sports leagues, the franchise imagines itself as *the* professional league of drag in entertainment as evident in this tweet by RuPaul claiming, "You can take performance enhancing drugs and still be an athlete, just not in the Olympics."[40] Referring to transgender inclusion, this implies there should be an equalizing criterion in which all contestants face fair evaluation. However, it also casts suspicion on trans performers who take hormones and/or have gender affirmation surgeries as having an unfair advantage compared to cisgender gay males.[41] Also, by mentioning the Olympics, this constructs *RPDR* as an international drag expert in comparison to marginalized drag performance cultures, implied to be amateurish and symbolically feminized by the relationship.

The show has had some transgender representation and contestants with feminizing body modifications. For example, Chad Michaels, Detox, Cynthia Lee Fontaine, and Trinity the Tuck have all had feminizing surgeries that the show frames as a serious commitment and masculine sacrifice to enhance their drag careers. The ability to present masculine seems to be the deciding factor between reading these body modifications as an enhancement rather than as a transitional step. This further proves the arbitrariness and construction of gender more broadly. RuPaul has flatly said he would not accept a contestant who has transitioned,[42] drawing the line at breast augmentation and/or gender confirmation surgery.[43] So far, no trans queens have competed having undergone top surgery. Viewing the show with a sports lens reveals this excessive oversight privileging male contestants.[44] In essence, barring cisgender women and transgender women from competing with cisgender men is framed as enforcing all contestants play with the same anatomical equipment.[45] This standardization seeks to regulate the amount of time and tasks all have to engage with while getting into drag. However, this conception perpetuates drag as being male dominated.[46]

In addition to bodily scrutinization, RuPaul is positioned as an unbiased umpire and referee with neutral allegiance to all; however, he acts as the show's behavioral, taste, and process disciplinarian.[47] In addition to performances, RuPaul also judges contestant attitudes and strategies. This function coaches contestants into homonormative commodities that prove the merit of the franchise's pedagogy. RuPaul's positionality as "mother" to her "girls" resembles a parental relationship of which the child is supposed to learn behavioral, social, and life lessons from the parent. In addition, "good" pupils are encouraged and rewarded for their perseverance and willingness to implement judge's criticism. Season 12's (2020) Heidi N Closet exemplifies this relationship when she implemented RuPaul's advice within many challenges. While compliance is encouraged, unwanted behavior is quickly disciplined to expected regimes of positivity, decorum, and productivity beneficial for the franchise's pedagogical project. Most notably, season 7's (2015) Pearl conflicted with the show's expected behavioral regimes when criticized for seeming lackluster and low energy during filming. This resembles sport's organizational control of athletes' behavior on and off the field. Ultimately, this scrutiny exists because of the franchise's reciprocal relationship with the player, in which both are seen to reflect the values of the other.[48]

Furthermore, both sport and *RPDR* cultivate pathways to attain "professional" designations. Sport does this through institutions, standards, and behaviors emphasizing training through childhood, college, and finally to professional play. *RPDR* scouts for performers also embedded within institutionalized networks. Viable performers usually have years of experience in pageant systems, queer clubs, or other venues largely controlled by homonormative ownership within LGBTQ+ communities. Many successful contestants are positioned as professional drag experts hailing from an institutionalized drag culture or space. This codes their performance as a learned masculine practice rather than naturally embodying femininity. Providing a few examples: Chad Michaels is framed as an expert celebrity impersonator; Alaska is framed as a knowledgeable *RPDR* superfan; and Raja is framed as an expert makeup artist and fashion model, legitimated intertextuality from working on *America's Next Top Model*.

Comparatively, outsiders to institutionalized drag spaces are cast to compete with in members. Narratively, they are cast to reify the constructed expertise of queens from privileged drag circuits. This tension is exemplified between season 12's "bedroom queen" Aiden Zhane (from Georgia) and Brita (from New York City). Though performing similarly, Brita struggled with her placement in relation to Aiden who she imagined should be fairing worse than herself simply based on her drag pedigree and regional knowledges privileging urbanity over rural areas.[49] Substantiating this privileging, many of Brita's fellow season 12 New York City drag sisters validated her perceptions simply based on pre-existing social capitals and geographic location.

Reading *RPDR*'s narrative framings for sports parallels shows how the franchise teaches homonormativity similarly to how sports commentators construct narrative biases within athletic bouts. Sports narratives, such as regional vs. national, amateur vs. professional, and innate ability vs. technological/artificial enhancement, permeate between the two. Often these relational dichotomies code gender biases, such as how amateurism is coded feminine and professionalism masculine. Influenced by these dichotomies, *RPDR* employs discourses of physicality, competition, and conflict that pit diverse performers together, but on unequal footing.[50] Thusly, homonormative masculine privilege circumscribes the spaces and optics of physical engagement.[51]

## *Eureka vs. The Vixen: Homonormative Discipline, Narrative, and Instruction*

Eureka and The Vixen's season 10 (2018) feud regarding professionality further exemplifies how masculine gender bias favors homonormative contestants. Conversely, unprofessionalism is also employed when RuPaul disciplines contestants to substantiate show pedagogy. These focuses ultimately inform the limitations of homonormativity and claims to the possession of legitimate knowledges during The Vixen and RuPaul's season 10 confrontation. Framing debates regarding professionalism, behavior, and teachability, I argue Eureka's return from injury framed their season 10 rivalry and informed The Vixen's resistance to *RPDR*'s homonormative pedagogical project.

Eureka, a season 9 and 10 (2017; 2018) contestant, is a white, plus-size pageant queen from rural Tennessee who injured her knee during the season 9, episode 2 cheerleading challenge.[52] Endeavoring with the injury, Eureka was informed mid-season that doctors wouldn't let her continue. Eureka subsequently received an invitation to return next season. Injury stories in both reality television and sports teach audiences that through hard work, discipline, and perseverance, one's self-sacrifice should be rewarded. Thusly, it matters that Eureka was brought back on season 10 to continue this storyline because it informs her feud with The Vixen.

A self-described unapologetically Black queen from Chicago, The Vixen's series narrative used her Black Lives Matter activism to teach audiences about racial discrimination within LGBTQ+ communities.[53] With both Eureka and The Vixen edited with narratives of perseverance, hardship, and excellence in drag, per their respective cultures, the two were framed in contention quite often. The Vixen insinuated Eureka was over-reliant on personality, unprofessional, and attention seeking.[54] Eureka claimed she was being nice and didn't understand The Vixen's criticisms, despite instigating The Vixen into confrontation.

During the season 10 reunion, The Vixen abruptly left when RuPaul insinuated that The Vixen was unprofessional and not disciplined enough to separate individual opportunity from intersecting oppressions. The Vixen continued to declare the necessity of challenging discrimination, claiming her call out behavior necessary to create more opportunity for herself as a Black drag queen.[55] This double framing paints Eureka as overcoming individual hardship while depicting The Vixen as allowing societal pressures to control and limit her success. Personal injury and systemic racism are not comparable, though I contend they were falsely conflated here to comment on their relations to homonormativity, professionality, and teachability. Both were framed as unprofessionalism; however, Eureka was deemed teachable and The Vixen's unreachable.[56] The Vixen's self-removal contrasts with Eureka's struggles to remain within the competition (from season 9), framing their conflict within homonormative ideologies of professionalism while sidestepping the classed and racial dimensions influencing the conflict.

Their feud encapsulates how reading *RPDR* through sporting narratives reveals their reproduction of homonormativity. Binary oppositions between white/Black, poor/rich, and masculinity/femininity drive the show's confrontations. Eureka's story was seen as a "positive" overcoming of individual hardship while The Vixen's was seen as a "negative" dwelling on Black communal oppression. Aiming for larger systemic critiques, The Vixen's message deconstructed how the show universalizes LGBTQ+ communities into homonormative individuals. Her negative reactions to these systems conflicted with the franchise's regime of positivity required to maintain its capitalistic relations and pedagogical project. Excessive discipline and scrutiny for issues The Vixen believed worth fighting for lead to her exit and proved the limits of *RPDR*'s pedagogical mission.[57]

*RPDR* depicted The Vixen's racial activism as limiting individual opportunity. A reason why Eureka was privileged can also be viewed from economic concerns, resembling those of Colin Kaepernick's Black Lives Matter protest.[58] Within a sports media framework, Eureka's season narrative is historically imagined to be more universal, market friendly, and familiar within rugged individualist, white, masculine ideology. The Vixen's is shaped by racial, gender, and class understandings of systemic oppression and liminality for Black and Brown bodies within white society.[59] Proving the pedagogical limits of homonormativity as a universalizing ideology, Eureka's embodiment of white homonormativity won out within the narrative. The show simply does not give the ideological space to discuss these complex positions and is threatening to its white gay cultural center.⁶⁰ By creating standards of judgment that either parody or reproduce sports-like influence, *RPDR* nationalizes various drag performances while circumscribing others. When examined this way, we can question how hierarchies are created and homonormativity is privileged within ongoing LGBTQ+ neoliberal policies and market realities, especially when diverse value systems are framed in contention.⁶¹

## *Drag and Sports Media Paratextual Parallels: Teach to Authorize/Perpetuate Hierarchy*

*RPDR*'s homonormative instruction is also apparent within their paratextual content. Their production company, World of Wonder (WOW), is an international authority, broadcaster, and curator of drag media.⁶² In maintaining this control lies a specific cisgender gay white U.S. centric way of representing other drag cultures, honed by a group of privileged homonormative storytellers.⁶³ Their digital distribution further resembles sports media, with the *RPDR* brand resembling an authoritative *ESPN*-like hub of drag coverage. Relating *RPDR* to *ESPN*: both frame themselves as authoritative leaders within drag and sport (respectively) and overwhelmingly construct U.S. masculinity as their normative center. Utilizing media scholar Jonathan Gray's definition of paratext, to read a text beyond "the thing itself, […] frame expectations," and offer ways to "structure a sense of what the text is actually about,"⁶⁴ I draw parallels between *RPDR* paratexts and sports media formats.⁶⁵ I then analyze *RPDR*'s fantasy league to discern the show's evaluative metrics and underlying instruction.

Regarding sport paratexts, sports media scholar Lindsey J. Meân contends *ESPN.com* helps reproduce "predominately white male heterosexual[ity]" as the central membership and primary consumers of sport and sport's media, despite a diverse array of sport they could feature.⁶⁶ This reproduces male sports as dominant, valuable, and worth media attention while also constructing the *ESPN* brand—and its male center—as authorities regarding all sports coverage.⁶⁷ Also, this positions audiences as an imagined community of sport's consumers around the centrality of masculinity, whiteness, and heteronormativity.

Similarly to *ESPN*'s masculine framings, *RPDR* produces a substantial amount of paratextual content to cultivate dominant homonormative readings. *RPDR* paratexts, hosted by show authorities and past winners, position audiences to critically evaluate drag through show values, often teaching why particular judgments were made. Also, these paratexts continue audience engagement with *RPDR* when seasons are not airing by producing commentary, interviews, and news similarly to *ESPN*'s continual (re)presentation of privileged masculine sports during their off-season.

*RPDR*'s paratexts then relate to sports media by presenting the cis-gender gay male performance of drag as the privileged cultural form. This is partially due to WOW's early success substantiating drag media. That *RPDR*'s executive producers are mostly white gay males also reifies the position of the franchise as gay male oriented,[68] positioning other drag performance cultures are marginalized, if at all represented. While possibly parodic, *RPDR*'s paratexts, most notably *The Pit Stop*, *Whatcha Packin*,' and *Fashion Photo RuView*, echo the sports-like structure of the main text to ultimately teach audiences and contestants to conform to homonormative values in exchange for professional success.

First, *The Pit Stop*, an official episode review show in which a season winner interviews former contestants to discuss strategies, plays, and stats, acts as a *SportsCenter*-like review providing expert opinions and past player perspectives. Next, *Whatcha Packin*' with show judge Michelle Visage offers a locker room reporter's lens regarding the previous episode featuring exit interviews with eliminated players. As the only permanent female show judge, Michelle Visage's position echoes female sideline reporters who enter masculine spaces to discuss player choices, feelings, and strategies regarding past plays. And finally, *Fashion Photo RuView* with Raja and Raven discuss the outfits worn on each episode and throughout off-season appearances. Raja and Raven are framed as experts in makeup, styling, and fashion who judge contestants based on Westernized notions of hyper-femininity and economic value. Opinions are framed through taste level, fit, and uniqueness to center what the franchise expects in terms of the "glamazon" style RuPaul and *RPDR* champion. In essence, these paratexts teach homonormative values through contestant failures and successes. By highlighting past players, behaviors, and tactics (similarly to sports media), *RPDR* produces preferred values and identities for contestant and audience consumption.

## *Evaluations and Rubrics:* The RPDR *Fantasy League*

Another example of *RPDR*'s sporting influence comes from their online fantasy league.[69] This promotional tool invites viewers to draft a team of contestants before a season begins and continually manage that team throughout a season's airing.[70] Each week, players select three contestants to play with the rest of one's team safe on the bench. Active players must accumulate enough points to ultimately win two tickets to the season finale.[71] In essence, players are playing to how they imagine production will frame storylines and contestants will perform. By influencing audience perceptions before a season begins, fans are encouraged to choose contestants reifying the franchise's homonormative investments in bodily performance and professionality to maximize scores. Here, franchise pedagogy is made numerical by cultivating expectations, training behavior, and disciplining undesired traits.[72]

For example, reading, shade, and contestant fights are rewarded in accordance with reality TV tropes and in recognition of *RPDR*'s cultural influences.[73] Also, self-sufficiency, discipline, and compliance with *RPDR* reify its overarching pedagogical project. Within *All Stars* season 4's (2018–2019) metrics, contestants receive positive evaluations for winning challenges, unexpected mainstage reveals, and expressing emotion within authorized spaces, like "crying in [the] confessional or workroom" (which is positively rewarded) in juxtaposition with "crying on the mainstage" (which is negatively scored).[74] Furthermore, points are deducted for general unprofessionalism. For example, "storms off set during main challenge rehearsal," "argues with Ru," and "quits/self eliminates."[75] These evaluations encourage fans to play into the brand's homonormative system, relying on individuality, self-branding, and company loyalty for greater legibility within the franchise.

*RPDR*'s evaluative metrics reveal and conceal important lessons. For instance, it shows how those in authority have the power to cultivate knowledge, reifying their position as instructor. For being a queer artform, the metrics presented do not reflect definitions of queer that question authority or one's place within institutional systems (such as "arguing with Ru" and self-removal). This is negative because it takes power away from authorities to perpetuate knowledge based on their value systems. A learner declaring autonomy from the teacher reveals ruptures within the pedagogical process cultivated by the knowledge producer. When the pupil asserts their decision to remove themselves because they've somehow failed the pedagogy or the pedagogy has failed them, the authors of that knowledge must reflect on the utility, cultures, and values their knowledge constructs.

To reach more audiences with a rigorous and informed pedagogical process, *RPDR* should allow for challenges to its pedagogy by diversifying and highlighting the potential of subjugated knowledges through mixed competition with other gender and drag performance cultures. Rather, when presented with this opportunity (as with The Vixen), they choose to reify their own authority rather than work to institute a stronger regime of knowledge informed by such challenges. An alternative to *RPDR*, *Dragula*, has done this, particularly on their third season which produced interesting dialogue between diverse gender performance artists.

## Conclusions

*RPDR* is popularly imagined as "*Monday Night Football* for the LGBTQ[+] crowd"[76]; however, I argue for the serious consideration of this relationship. However parodic comparisons began, there is a lot to learn about homonormativity and LGBTQ+ intra-community politics by delving into its posturing as "the gay Super Bowl."[77] Knowledges become substantiated when authorities can validate their ways of knowing and subjugate alternative knowledges from institutions they've created. To incorporate diverse knowledges, *RPDR* could decolonize its understanding of LGBTQ+ history,[78] diversify its production and on-screen representation, and divest from industry partnerships perpetuating or complicit in the privileging of homonormative systems.

Often reality TV and sport do engage with diverse representation within media; however, its dependence on normative systems for distribution and funding limit the potential of subjugated knowledges within these venues, as exemplified by the NFL when Colin Kaepernick received mainstream condemnation in 2017 for kneeling during the national anthem.[79] This is similar to other knowledge systems and their dependence on maintaining their educational processes, such as favoring certain demographics and disciplines over others (generally promoting the most economically valuable).

*RPDR* has a burden of representation problem despite its truly historic impact for diverse LGBTQ+ visibility on television. Their present patterns of representation still privilege and reproduce homonormative varieties of drag within their organization, narrative framings, and paratextual content. *RPDR* positions the cisgender gay men who own, produce, and judge the franchise with expert knowledge and authority through a lens of homonormative capital gains and industry investments. *RPDR* is similar to sports in that sports help teach and construct identity, relationality, and value within existing social structures while disciplining various cultural practices into productive standards.

Disbanding conceptions of *RPDR* as a drag sports league could lead to more equitable relations and representation, particularly regarding race and sex. Scholars studying trans athlete experiences and sex segregation in sports, Adrienne N. Milner and Jomills Henry Braddock II, argue the elimination of sex categories in sport would benefit not only transgender athletes but all individuals as athletic integration would lessen stigmas around "certain sports, body types, and behaviors [regarding] masculinity and femininity" and "promote freedom of identity, interest, and behavior for all."[80] Brookes also comments on masculine privilege within sports, saying, "[T]he overexposure of sportsmen and the underexposure of sportswomen is likely to reinforce the idea that women in sport are unusual."[81] Currently, *RPDR*'s homonormative pedagogy imagines cisgender gay male drag queens as the most lucrative gender performance culture to cultivate within mainstream industry systems.

*RPDR* has brought various queer influences together from different regional, cultural, and historical spaces, but with this they have also reproduced histories of LGBTQ+ oppression, conflict, and erasure. Through the mainstreaming of drag, marginalized LGBTQ+ history and groups are either erased from representation or asked to perform to higher standards and greater scrutiny for similar recognition. Marginalized LGBTQ+ contestants face biases within online and community spaces and face limited opportunity post-show. This reflects on authority makers within knowledge systems. As educators and scholars working in institutions among canons of knowledge, we must question the practices, spaces, and literal business of knowledge construction.[82] Importantly, realizing a knowledge system's investments, or one's place within it, comes from diverse engagements with knowledges outside of its imagined framework.

At its best, drag as an artform fosters inclusion, integration, and knowledge sharing.[83] Drag has a vital history of activism, community organizing, and fundraising which continues even within *RPDR*.[84] In viewing *RPDR*'s sporting influences through a homonormative instructional lens, I seek to resituate the potential of subjugated knowledges within mainstream distribution channels, of which *RPDR* could be if it diversifies, decolonizes, and desegregates its authoritative position. As a large LGBTQ+ transmedia franchise, *RPDR* cannot be everything for everybody; however, the LGBTQ+ story is best told honestly and inclusively by recognizing all cultural practices, spaces, and people who continue to contribute to the dream of queer and trans futurity.

## *Mini Challenge: Discussion Questions*

- How does *RPDR*'s narrative and production practices teach lessons about hierarchy, homosociality, and/or patriarchy?
- How has *RPDR*'s investment in homomasculinity further adapted to shifting cultural views of transgender and gender non-binary representation? How has the franchise balanced its pedagogical authority to teach a privileged version of drag and queer culture to mainstream audiences while navigating challenges to its instructional ideals? What qualities does the franchise seek to embody, and what omissions remain present within their production practices?

## Maxi Challenge: Activities and Assignments

- Compare how *RPDR* frames transgender and gender non-binary experiences in context with past and present ways trans and gender non-binary individuals are scapegoated in politics, sports, and other institutions. Is *RPDR* a sufficient venue to express trans and gender non-binary narratives within our current gender discourse? How is the franchise limiting and/or how is the franchise advancing gender inclusivity?
- How can paratextual media analysis be explored in context with the main textual artifact to instruct, advertise, and/or market its brand (or pedagogy) at large? How is paratext—especially of greater importance within our digital and multifaceted media environment—used here to further solicit and signal specific audience engagement and desired franchise strategies?

### Notes

1. "The Ball Ball." *RuPaul's Drag Race*, season 12, episode 4, VH1, 20 Mar. 2020, *Amazon*, https://smile.amazon.com/gp/video/detail/B08528GRKX/ref=atv_dp_season_select_s12.
2. "Grand Finale." *RuPaul's Drag Race*, season 9, episode 14, VH1, 23 June 2017, *Amazon*, https://smile.amazon.com/gp/video/detail/B06XK36FZS/ref=atv_dp_season_select_s9.
3. The full quotation is: "This society—going to a football game, basketball—that's their entertainment, you know. A ball is ours. We prepare for a ball. We may spend more time preparing for a ball than anybody would spend preparing for anything else. You know, a ball is like our world" (Jennie Livingston, dir. *Paris Is Burning*. Off White Productions, Inc. 1991).
4. For more movies featuring drag and sport performances, see Miguel A. Núñez Jr., playing a male basketball star donning female impersonation to play in a women's basketball league in *Juwanna Mann* (2002), Martin Lawrence as an undercover FBI agent impersonating a plus-sized grandmother who is an exceptional basketball player in *Big Momma's House* (2000), and Wesley Snipes as Noxeema Jackson playing in a lady's basketball league in *To Wong Foo, Thanks For Everything! Julie Newmar* (1995).
5. "Drag School of Charm." *RuPaul's Drag Race*, season 1, episode 5, Logo TV, 2 Mar. 2009, *Amazon*, https://smile.amazon.com/gp/video/detail/B001RGOIWW/ref=atv_dp_season_select_s1.
6. "Super Troopers," *RuPaul's Drag Race*, season 5, episode 10, Logo TV, 8 Apr.2013, *Amazon*, https://smile.amazon.com/gp/video/detail/B00B45B4X2/ref=atv_dp_season_select_s5.
7. "Dynamic Drag Duos." *RuPaul's Drag Race: All Stars*, season 1, episode 5, Logo TV, 19 Nov. 2012, *Amazon*, https://smile.amazon.com/gp/video/detail/B009VB83GW/ref=atv_dp_season_select_s1.
8. "WTF! Wrestling's Trashiest Fighters." *RuPaul's Drag Race*, season 4, episode 2, Logo TV, 6 Feb. 2011, *Amazon*, https://smile.amazon.com/gp/video/detail/B007142CFE/ref=atv_dp_season_select_s4.
9. "She Done Already Done Brought It On." *RuPaul's Drag Race*, season 9, episode 2, VH1, 31 Mar. 2017, *Amazon*, https://smile.amazon.com/gp/video/detail/B06XK36FZS/ref=atv_dp_season_select_s9.
10. "The Draglympics." *RuPaul's Drag Race*, season 11, episode 6, VH1, 4 Apr. 2019, *Amazon*, https://smile.amazon.com/gp/video/detail/B07P5GN25J/ref=atv_dp_season_select_s11.

11. "The Queen Who Mopped Xmas." *RuPaul's Drag Race*, season 3, episode 2, Logo TV, 24 Jan. 2011, *Amazon*, https://smile.amazon.com/gp/video/detail/B004JGWASG/ref=atv_dp_season_select_s3.

12. The franchise has invoked this comparison at least three separate times within the following episodes: "Social Media Kings into Queens." *RuPaul's Drag Race: Untucked*, season 10, episode 10, VH1, 24 May 2018, *Amazon*, https://smile.amazon.com/gp/video/detail/B07BN7Q5ZM/ref=atv_dp_season_select_s10; "LaLaPaRUza." *RuPaul's Drag Race: All Stars*, season 4, episode 6, VH1, 18 Jan. 2019, *Amazon*, https://smile.amazon.com/gp/video/detail/B07KWPRZ5M/ref=atv_dp_season_select_s4; and "Secret Celebrity Episode #101." *RuPaul's Secret Celebrity Drag Race*, season 1, episode 1, VH1, 24 Apr. 2020, https://www.amazon.com/RuPauls-Secret-Celebrity-Drag-Season/dp/B087MW4ZY7.

13. For more on sports media's hegemonic privileging, see Ava Rose & James Friedman, "Television Sports as Masculine Cult of Distraction." *Out of Bounds: Sports, Media, and the Politics of Identity*, edited by Aaron Baker and Todd Boyd (Indiana University Press, 1997: pp. 8–11).

14. Brookes, Rod. "Introduction." *Representing Sports*, Oxford University Press, 2002, p. 8.

15. *Ibid.*

16. RPDR is quickly franchising out within various international markets, primarily English speaking (*RuPaul's Drag Race UK*; *RuPaul's Drag Race Down Under*; *Canada's Drag Race*) but also adapting their formula for drag reality-competition programming within other cultural markets, most notably *Drag Race Thailand*; *Drag Race Holland*; and *Drag Race España*.

17. Also, I acknowledge the semi-scripted nature of reality-television. In this regard, *RPDR* resembles sports-entertainment more so than sports outright, like professional wrestling. Specifically, parallels between World Wrestling Entertainment (*WWE*) owner Vince McMahon and RuPaul (as figure head of *RPDR*) inform many of the scripted sports-like elements of competition that the folk cultural practices of professional wrestling and gender performance cultures share. Both are large media conglomerates dedicated to specific hegemonic versions of their respective cultural forms. Other professional wrestling cultures exist, like other drag cultures exist; however, they do not have the market share and visibility of *WWE* or *RPDR*. Therefore, as industry leaders, they expose and instruct audiences to accept the cultural representation of their respective artforms in their image. Sports enacts this on an even larger scale by teaching gender ideologies and instructing audiences to privilege cismale athletes as the most valued form of their respective sports despite alternative ways sports could be structured, like how leagues could integrate anatomical sexes or favor binary women's performances in economic media representation over binary men's competition, for examples.

18. Wilson, Julie A. "Enterprising Democracy: Neoliberal Citizenship and the Privatization of Politics," *neoliberalism*. Routledge, 2018, pp. 199–202.

19. *Ibid.*, p. 200.

20. *Ibid.*

21. Duggan, Lisa. "Equality Inc." *The Twilight of Equality: Neoliberal Cultural Politics, and the Attack on Democracy*. Beacon Press, 2003, p. 50.

22. Wilson, pp. 200–201.

23. Connell, Raewyn. "The Social Organization of Masculinity," *Exploring Masculinities: Identity, Inequality, Continuity, and Change*, edited by C.J. Pascoe and Tristan Bridges, Oxford University Press, 2016, pp. 136–144.

24. *Ibid.*, p. 138.

25. *Ibid.*, pp. 138–139.

26. *Ibid.*, pp. 136–139.

27. See media scholar Amanda D. Lotz, "Understanding Men on Television," *Cable Guys: Television and Masculinities in the 21st century* (NYU Press, 2014: pp. 19–51) for a more in-depth analysis of masculinities, media, and cable television. *RPDR*'s place within cable television as a reality-competition program with many genders, identities, and specific ways of performing many different varieties of masculinity, all in competition with each other, extends her work within this sphere.

28. Connell, pp. 138–139.
29. Wilson, Julie A. "A New Hegemony," *neoliberalism*, Routledge, 2018, p. 22.
30. Skeggs, Beverley, & Wood, Helen. "Introduction: Reacting to Reality Television," *Reacting to Reality Television: Performance, Audience and Value*. Routledge, 2012, p. 12.
31. Which sport also resembles through similar body and attitudinal self-work.
32. Henry, Ben. "Black "RuPaul's Drag Race" Queens Discuss the Racism They've Experienced from Fans of the Show and How It Affects Their Success," *Buzzfeed News*, November 22, 2019, https://www.buzzfeed.com/benhenry/rupauls-drag-race-fandom-racism.
33. RuPaul quoted saying his marginality as "too Black" for whites, "too gay" for Blacks, and "too feminine" for gays. See "Queens Reunited." RuPaul's Drag Race, season 10, episode 13, VH1, 21 June 2018, Amazon, https://smile.amazon.com/gp/video/detail/B07B68P55J/ref=atv_dp_season_select_s10.
34. The show could be evolving to validate gender fluidity and non-conformity more directly, as evidenced by Gigi Goode's season 12 storyline. Even if so, I still perceive the show as privileging masculine aspects of gender non-binary contestants and circumscribing transgender and assigned female at birth (AFAB) drag performers from the show. For more, see https://www.them.us/story/gigi-goode-opens-up-fluid-gender-identity-rupauls-drag-race.
35. Hartman, Ann. "In Search of Subjugated Knowledge," *Feminism, Community, and Communication*, edited by Mary E. Olson, The Haworth Press, Inc. p. 200, par. 22.
36. For a recent example, see Franklyn Carter, "Federal Judge Dismisses U.S. Women's Soccer Team's Equal Pay Claim." *NPR.org*, 2 May 2020, https://www.npr.org/2020/05/02/849492863/federal-judge-dismisses-u-s-womens-soccer-team-s-equal-pay-claim.
37. Of course, many drag queens cite strong female figures in their lives or media they want to emulate and find a safe social space to do so within drag cultures. It is also a space of gender exploration for men who want to identify more with their femininity. However, the mainstream valuation of male drag queens over other gender performers perpetuates masculine privilege within gender performance cultures.
38. Aitkenhead, Decca. "RuPaul: 'Drag is a big f-you to male-dominated culture,'" *The Guardian*. 3 Mar. 2018, https://www.theguardian.com/tv-and-radio/2018/mar/03/rupaul-drag-race-big-f-you-to-male-dominated-culture.
39. While other judges usually do not see the contestants out of drag, RuPaul obviously does and potentially keeps this in mind when making judgements on the show. Recently on season 12 (2020), a large part of Crystal Methyd's storyline centered around her mullet while not in drag. Having little to nothing to do with her drag character, this was brought up by RuPaul while she was in drag on the mainstage very frequently as a key interest to supporting her in the competition. Also, RuPaul mentioned season 7's (2015) Pearl received preferential treatment on the season because of their masculine presentation out of drag. See "Reacting to RuPaul and Michelle talking about me." *YouTube*, uploaded by pearlbizarre, 24 May 2020, 1:09–1:27, in which RuPaul on his podcast claims he knew Pearl would be a popular character because of his physical appearance out of drag. Also, *RPDR* has judged mini challenges featuring women performing as amateur drag kings ("Secret Celebrity Edition #102." *Secret Celebrity Drag Race*, season 1, episode 2, VH1, 2 May 2020, *Amazon*, https://www.amazon.com/RuPauls-Secret-Celebrity-Drag-Season/dp/B087MW4ZY7); however, drag king artists have not been cast on an official season yet.
40. Charles, RuPaul (@RuPaul). "You can take performance enhancing drugs and still be an athlete." *Twitter*, 5 Mar.2018, https://twitter.com/RuPaul/status/970709820364881920.
41. *RPDR* has also had trans contestants compete but did not make their transness a part of their show narrative. Most notably, season 3's (2011) Stacey Layne Matthews and season 4's (2012) Kenya Michaels. Many contestants also publicize their identity after their season. I mention this to further prove the arbitrariness and constructed nature of gender that claims to bar transgender women from competing on the show.
42. RuPaul's use of media to further his circumscription of transgender drag queens within the franchise resembles actors in sports media who question the fairness of transgender athletes competing within traditionally sex segregated sports leagues. Though as of 2021, this might be changing. For more, see sports media scholar Adam Love, "Media Framing of

Transgender Athletes: Contradictions and Paradoxes in Coverage of MMA Fighter Fallon Fox." *LGBT Athletes in the Sports Media* (Palgrave Macmillan, 2019: pp. 207–225).

43. See Aitkenhead.

44. For more, see Kim, Michelle. "Drag Race Alumni Criticize RuPaul's 'Conscious Exclusion' of Trans Queen." *them.us*, 24 Jan. 2020, https://www.them.us/story/rupaul-drag-race-season-12-trans-queens-detox-carmen-carrera.

45. The excessive disciplining of bodies on *RPDR* relates to modern struggles transgender athletes experience in sport. For more, see, Jeré Longman and Juliet Macur, "Caster Semenya Loses Case to Compete as a Woman in All Races," *The New York Times*. 1 May 2019, https://www.nytimes.com/2019/05/01/sports/caster-semenya-loses.html.

46. I recognize other drag reality-competition programs, like the Boulet Brothers' *Dragula*, the Sugar Baker Twins' *Camp Wannakiki*, and even *Drag Race Thailand* have cast transgender queens, assigned female at birth (AFAB) queens, and drag kings on their respective programs. However, this makes it all the more peculiar why *RPDR* has yet to more visibly and vocally integrate its competition and allows for greater scrutiny of mainstream gay assimilationist politics in media.

47. Decisions are of course made in consultation with other producers, executives, and stakeholders in the show's franchise. However, RuPaul is positioned as the example to emulate and authority of this evaluative process.

48. Further, the hierarchal relationship between institution and member brings greater discipline and scrutiny upon the lower-level member than the authorities controlling the institution receive, especially when money is part of the institutional relationship.

49. Season 12's Heidi N Closet is also from a rural area of North Carolina; however, Heidi was framed with experience as a pageant queen. Aiden was framed as outside of the club scene, and therefore her drag was interpreted as less valued in comparison to Brita's, who had social networks and capitals to fall back on when receiving critique.

50. For instance, Venus D-Lite's moments of physical altercation with Shangela during their season 3, episode 2 (2011) lip-sync. However fair production wanted to be after these incidents occurred, there were no interventions to curtail physical assault during early season lip-syncs. Also, the expanding of the mainstage space from a small runway strip, which caused more contestant interaction, into an almost four-by-four square in later seasons potentially sought to address these earlier oversights.

51. I will also mention the infamous season 3, episode 4 incident in which Mimi Imfurst picks up India Ferrah during their lip-sync. While fair to curtail this type of physical encroachment into other performers' space, *RPDR* potentially cast Mimi for this very incident and reframed it as objectionable after India's reaction to it. In the Gay.com *Queens of Drag* web series at 1:19, Mimi is shown picking up an audience member in similar fashion to how she picked up India Ferrah. See "Mimi Imfurst, Queens of Drag: NYC Ep8" *YouTube*, uploaded by Gay DotCom, 26 Oct. 2010, https://www.youtube.com/watch?v=nLS6q4Rnbns.

52. Eureka uses they/them pronouns. This analysis in no way minimizes this aspect of their gender expression. However, the inclusion of non-binary and transgender contestants has still been framed within homosocial gay male inclusivity.

53. "The Last Ball on Earth." *RuPaul's Drag Race*, season 10, episode 4, VH1, 12 Apr. 12, 2018, *Amazon*, https://smile.amazon.com/gp/video/detail/B07B68P55J/ref=atv_dp_season_select_s10.

54. "Snatch Game." *RuPaul's Drag Race*, season 10, episode 7, VH1, 3 May 2018, *Amazon*, https://smile.amazon.com/gp/video/detail/B07B68P55J/ref=atv_dp_season_select_s10.

55. See "Queens Reunited,"16:11–27:50. This confrontation reinforces RuPaul's neoliberal self-help public persona, which underpins individual responsibility and homonormativity tactics according to Lisa Duggan's definition. See his latest book *GuRu* (2018), the recently cancelled RuPaul talk show (Telepictures and Warner Bros. TV, 2019), and RuPaul's *Masterclass* in "Self-Expression and Authenticity" (2020) https://www.masterclass.com/classes/rupaul-teaches-self-expression-and-authenticity.

56. Asia O'Hara, a season 10 friend to The Vixen and also another Black contestant, criticized the show and RuPaul for letting The Vixen believe herself outside the pedagogical structure of the franchise. In fairness to the show, they immediately played this segment of

Asia criticizing the cast and production for letting The Vixen leave. However, the clip reinforces RuPaul's judgement and discipline style while perpetuating ideals of professionality the show's homonormativity relies on.

57. For more on this confrontation and racism within *RPDR*, see Phillip Henry, "RuPaul Needs to Take Responsibility for the Racism on Drag Race," *them.us*, 28 June 2018, https://www.them.us/story/racism-rupauls-drag-race.

58. As of May 2020, the NFL and *RPDR* have both made organizational statements in support of international Black Lives Matter movements in the aftermath of George Floyd's murder by Minneapolis police. Both have said they aim to do better regarding issues of racial justice and equity within their organizations, with specifically *RPDR*'s Instagram page saying they will block and censure racist comments Black contestants receive on their page, a long-time problem and allowance from the franchise. See @rupaulsdragrace, "RuPaul's Drag Race and drag as an art form would be nothing without…" *Instagram*, 12 June 2020. https://www.instagram.com/p/CBWj74rDMt5/. This is franchise growth from RuPaul's early season advice, being "don't look at the comments." However, like with the NFL, it remains to be seen how seriously (and how long) these organizations will actively practice anti-racism. See also the NFL tweet, "We, the NFL, condemn racism and the systemic oppression of Black People. We, the NFL, admit we were wrong for not listening to NFL players earlier and encourage all to speak out and peacefully protest. We, the NFL, believe Black Lives Matter. #InspireChange," *Twitter*, 5 June 2020, 6:31 p.m. https://twitter.com/NFL/status/1269034074552721408.

59. Again, in light of recent racial discourses and movements, it remains to be seen if previously normative realities like this will persevere within the culture. However, power in any form always has a way of re-inscribing their authority and influence.

60. For instance, the show's tellings of the Stonewall Riots glosses over intersectional nuances to depict a universal LGBTQ+ struggle for equality, unified around drag queen grit and visibility. In a Drag Herstory 101 segment, Marsha P. Johnson is collapsed into drag history rather than explaining the intersections of transgender communities and drag performance cultures ("Reunited!" *RuPaul's Drag Race*, season 6, episode 14, Logo TV, 19 May 2014, *Amazon*, https://smile.amazon.com/gp/video/detail/B00ICGYECE/ref=atv_dp_season_select_s6).

61. For more on this in *RPDR* scholarship, see Alyxandra Vesey, "'A Way to Sell Your Records': Pop Stardom and the Politics of Drag Professionalization on RuPaul's Drag Race." *Television & New Media*, vol. 18, no. 7, 2017, pp. 589–604. See also, Carl Schottmiller, "Excuse My Beauty!": Camp Referencing and Memory Activation on RuPaul's Drag Race," *Sontag and the Camp Aesthetic: Advancing New Perspectives*, edited by Bruce E. Drushel and Brian M. Peters, Lexington Books, 2017, pp. 111–130.

62. Their streaming platform, WOW Presents Plus, maintains broadcast control of *RPDR* in certain international markets and produces additional drag media content utilizing contestants from *RPDR*.

63. Vary, Adam. B. "Inside the Wondrous Expansion of—and Biggest Threat to—the 'RuPaul's Drag Race' Brand (EXCLUSIVE)." *Variety.com*, 29 May 2020, https://variety.com/2020/tv/news/rupauls-drag-race-international-all-stars-celebrity-sherry-pie-1234619728/.

64. Gray, Jonathan. "Texts." *Keywords for Media Studies*, edited by Laurie Ouellette and Jonathan Gray, New York University Press, 2016, pp. 199–200.

65. Along with context and intertextual readings, paratexts constantly make and remake a text and its meanings across different audiences. A few examples of paratexts include production notes, budgets, media promotions, merchandising, and fan interpretations. These multiple sites of meaning often contradict and complicate any one reading of a text; however, dominant readings can be made when assessing the cultural context, intertextuality, and the paratexts of a main text.

66. Meân, Lindsey. "Sport, Identities, and Consumption: The Construction of Sport at ESPN.com." *Sports Media: Transformation, Integration, Consumption*, edited by Andrew C. Billings, Routledge, 2011, pp. 162–180.

67. *Ibid.*, p. 166.

68. Young, Danielle. "RuPaul Attempts to Answer Diversity Question." *Essence.com*, 23 Sept. 2019, https://www.essence.com/videos/rupaul-drag-race-diversity-emmys/.
69. "*RuPaul's Drag Race: All Stars Four* official fantasy league," VH1/Viacom, Dec. 2018– Feb. 2019, www.Vh1dragracefantasyleague.com.
70. This has not been continued in 2020 for season 12 nor *All Stars* season 5.
71. Many of the previous fantasy league seasons are scrubbed from the Internet once the promotion ends; however, here is a video on VH1's YouTube channel featuring season 11 queens discussing the rules and platform. ("S11 Queens on How to Play RuPaul's Drag Race Fantasy League | VH1," *YouTube*, uploaded by VH1, 22 Feb. 2019, https://youtu.be/-ahdfzs2xdA).
72. While out of the purview of this essay, see Victoria E Johnson, "Everything New is Old Again: Sport Television, Innovation, and Tradition for a Multi-Platform Era." *Beyond Prime Time: Television Programming in the Post-Network Era*, edited. by Amanda D. Lotz (Routledge, 2009: pp. 114–137) for an in-depth analysis of how sports media employs digital paratexts and their affects within sports media viewership and imagined community.
73. i.e., Livingston's 1990 film *Paris Is Burning*.
74. See "*RuPaul's Drag Race: All Stars Four* official fantasy league scoring categories."
75. Ibid.
76. Gudelunas, David. "Digital Extensions, Experiential Extensions and Hair Extensions: RuPaul's Drag Race and the New Media Environment," *RuPaul's Drag Race and the Shifting Visibility of Drag Culture*, edited by Niall Brennan and David Gudelunas, Palgrave Macmillan, 2017, p. 240.
77. "LaLaPaRUza," *RuPaul's Drag Race: All Stars*, season 4, episode 6, VH1, 18 Jan. 2019, *Amazon*, https://smile.amazon.com/gp/video/detail/B07KWPRZ5M/ref=atv_dp_season_select_s4.
78. For more on knowledge circulation and history, see Linda Tuhiwai Smith, "Imperialism, History, Writing and Theory," *Decolonizing Methodologies: Research and Indigenous Peoples* (Zed Books Ltd., 2013: pp. 33–35).
79. Subsequent changes since May 2020, season 12 saw a lot of disqualified contestant Sherry Pie's episode winnings either matched or moved entirely to LGBTQ+ charities. The brand has become a lot more vocal about social issues online, as many corporate brands have, and in advocating for LGBTQ+ voting efforts, among other initiatives.
80. Milner Adrienne N. & Braddock II, Jomills Henry. "The Elimination of Sex Categories in Sport." *Sex Segregation in Sport: Why Separate is Not Equal*, Praeger, 2016, p. 112.
81. Brookes, p. 126.
82. For more on the study of institutionalized knowledges, see Grace Kyungwon Hong, "The Future of Our Worlds": Black Feminism and the Politics of Knowledge in the University under Globalization." *Meridians: Feminism, Race, Transnationalism*, vol 8, no. 2, 2008, pp. 95–115.
83. For knowledge sharing, I'll mention *RPDR*'s DragCon as a unique moment of drag knowledges, commerce, and fandom all interacting. There's lots to unpack with DragCon, however, and Carl Schottmiller has done extensive research in this area. See his upcoming book, *Camp Capitalism, Queer Memory, and RuPaul's Drag Empire: Excuse My Beauty!* (http://carlschottmiller.com/upcoming/) for more.
84. *RuPaul's Secret Celebrity Drag Race* (2020) donated to celebrities' charities of choice.

# Where Are the Jokes?
## *Comedy as Pedagogy*
### Peter Piatkowski

"I would gladly do my comedy without drag"
—Bianca Del Rio, season 6 winner[1]

During her hosting gig on *Saturday Night Live*'s 45th season,[2] RuPaul played herself in a sketch that focused on reading. For drag enthusiasts, reading is an important hallmark of drag culture. "Reading is the real art form of insults," the late/great drag queen Dorian Corey explains in Jennie Livingston's documentary *Paris Is Burning*.[3] Instead of leaving it to the confines of gay nightclub or a ballroom, RuPaul brought reading to the mainstream masses through one of the most mainstream television institutions there is: *Saturday Night Live*.

In the sketch, RuPaul appears out of drag and is volunteering at a library—wonderful play on the "Library is open" line that proceeds the reading challenges on *RuPaul's Drag Race*. To regular audiences of *Saturday Night Live*, this sketch is a peek into queer, specifically drag, culture—the disconnect dramatized by the confused looks of the other characters, all of whom are nonplussed as RuPaul's understanding of reading differs greatly from everyone else's. When in the sketch RuPaul announces the line, "Reading is what? Fundamental!"[4] an audience member spontaneously joins in on the "Fundamental!" knowing where the line was going. And instead of simply reading books as one would assume, RuPaul entertains her audience of school children and librarians with some well-thought slurs and insults.

The appearance of RuPaul on *Saturday Night Live* and introducing drag culture staples like reading cannot be underestimated when it comes to the mainstreaming of drag culture. In particular, reading—an arch, clever way of throwing shade, or insults to one's opponents—is an aspect of drag comedy that has reached mainstream (read: straight) audiences.

Corey helpfully defines shade as a refined form of reading in which "reading became a developed form where it became shade. Shade is, 'I don't tell you you're ugly, but I don't have to tell you because you know you're ugly.'"[5] She then concludes coolly, "and that's *shade*."[6] The sketch becomes a metafiction as Ru patiently is explaining reading to the other characters; her show *RuPaul's Drag Race* (*RPDR*) has been sharing parts of queer culture that have been niche and hidden. Before the mainstream success of *RPDR*, outsiders who weren't involved in drag ball culture would not have been privy to concepts like throwing shade or reading—these were practices that stayed insulated within the subculture. But RuPaul and her show has successfully opened up the space to learn these tropes (as well as other drag mainstays) and has essentially made the television show a living textbook.

Reading relies on quick wit, clever wordplay, cattiness, and the ability to use puns with an expert skill as "[d]rag performance is replete with layers of humor and antagonism."[7] That is why comedy queens do well with reading (though comedy queens aren't the only reading masters). But reading is just one aspect of a comedy queen's repertoire, and thanks to *RPDR*, mainstream audiences have been exposed to the comedy queen: a drag queen who uses drag as a vehicle for her comedy. *RPDR* has become a platform for many queens to find success outside the show's confines, and comedy queens have been able to find great success. Winners Bianca Del Rio, Jinkx Monsoon, and Bob the Drag Queen have seen their triumphs on *RPDR* translate to opportunities in film, television, radio, and live theater. Other queens who have not won, like Tammie Brown, Miz Cracker, Ginger Minj, BenDeLaCreme, Katya, Nina West, Trinity "The Tuck" Taylor, Trixie Mattel (who won the third season of the *All Stars* competition, despite her middling performance on her mothership season), Shangela, Pandora Boxx, and Willam, have also parlayed their time on the show into mainstream, multi-media success. The show and the queens' successes have opened up drag and ball culture to a wider audience, and specifically, the comedy that has come out of *RPDR* has become a vehicle for audiences to obtain different markers of drag, queer, and trans culture. The queens have become teachers, of sorts, using humor to not only educate their audiences on drag tropes, but more importantly, the humor has also been used as a means of educating audiences about queer cultural history. So much of what the comedy queens do with their act is about mining queer culture and making it available to their mainstream audiences, now grown exponentially because of the show's success (as well as the advent of social media).

Never before has there been a moment in popular culture as there has been in these past twelve years, in which niche and previously-obscure figures and moments in queer history have been so widely shared to bigger audiences. At a roundtable hosted by *Billboard*,[8] pop star/reality TV celebrity Tamar Braxton (a popular figure on *RPDR* both as a judge and a Snatch Game subject) moderated a discussion on a variety of subjects and prompted Willam to give the correct account of the Stonewall Rebellion, starting with the apocryphal story that the riots were inspired, in part, by Judy Garland's death. She also made the important point that though the Stonewall Riots in 1969 were the turning point, there were earlier instances of rebellion, in particular, the uprising at the Black Cat Tavern in Los Angeles, two years before the rioting at the Stonewall Inn in New York City. Though her participation in the roundtable was usually devoted to her dry, icy comedy, when necessary, she provided the largely light discussion with some important historical context, including name-checking Marsha P. Johnson as well as referencing Stormé DeLarverie, a Black lesbian who is thought to have been the instigator of the Stonewall Riots. So much of Pride and Stonewall has been flattened by the commercialization of the parades that having openly queer people control the narrative from a place that isn't necessarily propped up by a multi-billion dollar conglomerate chasing after the pink dollar, makes their output more than just entertainment—it's an education.

This essay will look at the way in which *RPDR* relayed an important aspect of queer, drag, and trans culture, as well as the intersection of race, ethnicity, and identity, through comedy to mainstream audiences, thereby exposing audiences to formerly arcane references, figures, and works of art. The show has given comedy queens platforms to perform in front of audiences that have been largely unheard of for drag performers, outside of a lucky few. The show has become a primer for audiences of drag/queer comedy in many ways, particularly in the challenges, but also in providing the queens with airtime to perform their shtick. When the queens participate in Snatch Game—the drag parody of the '70s game show, *Match Game*—they also use the television show to pay homage and to educate on queer, drag, and trans culture.

The organization of the essay will briefly address the intersection of drag and comedy. Drag and comedy have a long history, though too often, mainstream comedy has treated drag as a mean or homophobic joke. Popular straight comedians Milton Berle and Flip Wilson used drag in their comedy, and Billy Wilder's classic comedy *Some Like It Hot* (1959) employed drag as a major plot device. Some drag artists have been able to find a measure of success outside of strictly queer audiences: Jim Bailey, Charles Busch, Danny LaRue, Lily Savage, Charles Pierce, Lori Shannon, Coco Peru, and Lypsinka all created work that has been consumed by mainstream audiences, though nothing they have done approaches the multi-media empire that was created by *RPDR*.

Drag is an art form that seeks to disrupt gender roles and to subvert notions of masculinity and femininity—important aims for queer people whose existence is seen as an opposition to traditional gender roles. So, the comedy that comes forth from drag is a comedy that seeks to address these issues. Some of the comedy is biting and stinging, which can be attributed as necessary to survive in a homophobic culture[9] but much of it is subversive.

## What's So Funny About Drag?

The sight of a man in a dress was used as a sight gag in popular culture for many years.[10] From the silent pictures of Laurel and Hardy and Fatty Arbuckle to Billy Wilder's *Some Like It Hot*, to television sitcoms and films in the 1970s to the 1990s, drag has been used as a punchline for many years. The "funny" or "comedy" drag of Milton Berle, Flip Wilson, Jack Lemmon, et al., was a kind of "safe" drag that escaped the subversive quality of the act. When Berle and company performed in drag, it was not an homage, nor was it a nod to drag and queer culture, but a way of lampooning femininity as well as assuaging masculine anxiety. In Wilder's *Some Like It Hot*, the drag was so unconvincing and the premise so telegraphed—the men were in drag because they were "forced" into it—that audiences were safe to revel and enjoy the spectacle without worrying about co-signing to queer culture. More contemporary films like Sydney Pollack's *Tootsie* (1982) or Chris Columbus' *Mrs. Doubtfire* (1993) also used drag as a way of furthering the comedy narrative without spilling into queerness because the drag is "explained"—the men *have* to don drag, and they don't enjoy it, nor are they seeking to upend gender roles. Their respective plots explain that the men are forced into drag through the circumstances: in *Tootsie*, it's because a temperamental actor has damaged his reputation to such an extent that he turns to drag to find work; in *Mrs. Doubtfire*, an estranged father wants to be near his children, so he pretends to be an old woman and is hired as the nanny. They don't look to drag as an art form but as a way of attaining their goals, and both are written as reassuringly heterosexual.

So, drag isn't exactly something that has been hidden from mainstream viewers, so no one can claim that *RPDR* brought drag into the mainstream because there has been a steady presence of drag throughout the last century or so. The main difference once *RPDR* premiered is that it brought drag to the mainstream in a steady stream. Before the show's premier in 2009, RuPaul had forged a successful career as a singer, television personality, and sometimes-actor for over 20 years (though the show revived her career that had entered a period of relative slump) but she was not on television screens weekly. *RPDR* was able to feed a steady diet of queer and drag culture, and it became appointment television (gay bars throughout the U.S. host viewing parties, sometimes headlined by a *RPDR* alumnae). And during those weekly episodes, audiences were exposed to queer culture, particularly queer comedy. But the important distinction was that the queens were in on the joke and the sight of a man in a woman's dress wasn't the sole source of laughter, and the laughter was *inclusive*, meaning queer folks were in on the joke and laughing at themselves (whereas when Milton Berle staggered onto a TV set dressed in drag, that joke was *at* drag).

Because of the show's frequency, audiences were then given a primer lesson every week on the history of drag and comedy through its contestants. For audiences, it's a chance "to see further examples of a type of queer legitimacy in the show through references to historically situated drag icons and practices."[11] In season 2, we watched the first Snatch Game, in which comedy queen Pandora Boxx impressed the judges and RuPaul with her sendup of Broadway actress/singer Carol Channing. Her impression—a comedic take off on the performer more than an accurate impersonation—would start a "tradition" of sorts in the game, in which a queen (or two) would either bring out a niche figure of queer culture or perhaps a queer figure that would be relevant to older viewers, thereby introducing younger viewers to important queer pop culture figures (more on that later). It's here that the queens are the teachers, namely explaining and elaborating their lessons to their audiences. It isn't enough for Pandora to do a funny impression of Carol Channing, but there is an engagement in her history that takes place as Channing is introduced to the show's audiences—the queens who take on a historical subject take time to explain who the celebrity is and why she's important to queer pop culture. But the lesson doesn't end after the show airs, because once it does air, some of the queens will return to their Snatch Game impression in their shows, elaborating further on these lessons by bringing in more details and shading to their characters

What *RPDR* affords is twofold: a chance for viewers to be exposed to drag comedy as well as a strong platform from which the queens can spin off into successful careers as comedic performers. Their television audiences—largely middle-class and straight—will be taken along with the queens to learn about the different aspects of queer comedy, like reading and camp, through the various multi-media platforms that the queens find success in, in particular, stage and YouTube. Queens like Trixie Mattel, Katya, and Bob the Drag Queen would work their shtick into television, hosting a comedic chat show; Miz Cracker would use YouTube to become a vlogging comic, as does Willam with her "Daily beatdown"; and Bianca Del Rio, arguably the most successful comedian of *RPDR*, would become a headlining, stadium-touring act, selling out large venues like Wembley.

The show's success in launching the career of these comedy queens highlights the transformative and instructional power that these comedic performers possess.

## The Drag Comedy Boom: Bianca Del Rio

In the late 1980s to the early 1990s, network television went through what was commonly referred to as a comic boom, in which networks were hoping to duplicate the success of *Seinfeld*, *The Cosby Show*, or *Roseanne* by mining comedy clubs throughout the country for comedians to place in sitcoms. *RPDR* has created a similar comedic boom, elevating some of its stars to mainstream success.

The best way to look at the mainstream potential of *RPDR* is to look at the career of Bianca Del Rio, season 6 winner of the show. It was clear from the moment she entered the work room crowing, "Well, well, well. I hope you bitches are ready!" that she was a comedy queen who was operating on a level far more expansive than just drag.[12] Bianca (born Roy Haylock) was an accomplished drag performer, stand-up comic, and costumer before being cast on the show. She exhibited a polish that few of the other queens had, and she quickly became a fan favorite, especially as she dominated the show's challenges and was responsible for some of the most memorable moments and quotations of the show.

Predictably, she overshadowed the other queens in the stand-up comedy challenge and did very well in the Snatch Game, impersonating Judge Judy (though she lost the challenge to fellow comedy queen, BenDeLaCreme). Throughout her season, Bianca was reliable for memorable one-liners that aligned with her drag and comedic persona—that of an irascible, irritated cutup: when asked by Ru about her quickness, Bianca describes it as "instinctive," likening it to a "rolodex of hate," which she explains serves her well, when she's "faced with a situation, you just roll through [gesturing with her hands] and go, 'What do I have? What do I have? What do I have?'"[13] The coined term, "Rolodex of Hate" would become part of Bianca's public persona, even becoming the name of a comedy special. Looking deeper, one could also make the connection between Bianca and Joan Rivers, an obvious influence. Whilst Bianca sported a "rolodex of hate," Rivers famously catalogued her quips in a massive card catalogue. Though Bianca's filing system is metaphorical, it lends itself to a methodical system of organizing insults and slurs, and both Rivers and Bianca are celebrated for their ability to roast their subjects.

Throughout her season, Bianca showed off a bright wit that leaned heavily into her comedic persona that recalled Don Rickles (though in a dress). When put out by another drag queen's perceived whining, she spat out, "We are drag queens in a drag queen competition! The only thing worse is fucking prison!"[14] Or a typical Bianca read would be, "She's overthinking and she…. she's thinking about a sandwich"[15] referring to a heavier queen. Because *RPDR* is packaged and heavily produced, Bianca gets the winner's edit, which is aided, in part, by her never having to lip sync for her life. Though reality TV sets out to create archetypes—the Villain, the Ditz, the Good Guy—and *RPDR* isn't above that—Bianca manages to transcend reductive stereotypes because even though she has a sharp and mean wit, she's also shown to be caring and attentive to the needs of the other queens: being older than many of her competitors, she showed sensitivity to Trinity K. Bonet, who shared her HIV positive status, praising the younger queen's candor; though she was frustrated at times with Trinity's self-defeated attitude, she coached and coaxed a solid performance from her when the two were paired in a challenge.

Her natural sense of comedy plus her years of experience as a costume designer makes her a very strong competitor, which makes the winner's edit she gets all the easier. Bianca Del Rio, more than any other comedy queen on the program, has a comic persona that had been fully-formed before her debut on the show—she more than any other performer on the show built an alter-ego that has incorporated bits of her personality as well as her distinct point of view to craft a heightened version of herself.[16]

But aside from her dominant position on her season, she also works as a mentor of sorts to audiences about queer comedy and queer humor—specifically, the acid-tongued, sharp cattiness that is a hallmark of drag and queer comedy. Though *RPDR* isn't the first mainstream exposure of queer comedy, it's arguably the rawest, especially when compared to some of the other large-scale success that queer comedy has seen—namely *Will & Grace* or *Ellen*, both of which present a queer comedy that is far safer and more palpable to mainstream audiences (as well as being more inclusive so as not to alienate straight audiences who may not be as clued into gay parlance or lingo). For many straight audiences, when the characters of *Will & Grace* were mildly bitchy, there is a sense of a prurient thrill, akin to using a forbidden curse word. *Will & Grace* is an aggressively mainstream situation comedy on network television that boasted at one point more than 20 million viewers, so the comedy could not have been too subversive or queer. But *RPDR* was still outside the norm enough that it didn't have as much to lose as an NBC sitcom, which meant that there was far more freedom to represent a more authentic take on queer comedy, and one that harkened back to the kind of biting, cutting wit that Dorian Corey talked about in *Paris Is Burning*.

## *Intersectionality in Drag Comedy: Bob the Drag Queen and Miz Cracker*

Ethnicity and nationality have been major themes in comedy—particularly among Black, Latinx, Asian, and/or Jewish comedians. Queer identity has also been important among LGBTQ+ comedians, and with *RPDR*, audiences were privy to see the intersection of queer identities and racial/ethnic identities and how they played out in drag comedy. We can look at the work of Bob the Drag Queen and Miz Cracker, both of whom are part of a long continuum of Black and Jewish comedy, respectively. Both Cracker and Bob look to ethnic humor when constructing their comedic personae, given that there seems to be an unspoken rule that comedians of marginalized groups "find it necessary to make their ethnic affiliation a large part of their humor."[17] As outsiders commenting on the status quo (read: straight, white, Christian male), Cracker's and Bob's comedy is seemingly othered.

After his win on *RPDR*, Bob the Drag Queen enjoyed mainstream success, similarly to that of Bianca Del Rio. Along with higher profile gigs as a drag entertainer, Bob also found herself making music, hosting TV shows with Trixie Mattel, and even scoring a comedy special, *Bob the Drag Queen: Suspiciously Large Woman* that bore the influences of Richard Pryor, Whoopi Goldberg, and Eddie Murphy, in how Bob talked about her upbringing, being a young Black queer kid in Georgia. In the canon of Black comedians, Eddie Murphy's concert film, *Delirious* (B. Gowers, 1983), is a seminal text, one that would influence nearly every concert film since its release. Much of the contemporary criticism about *Delirious* centers on Murphy's anti-gay material—a particularly noxious blend of AIDS-era homophobia and gay panic that has made the film wholly problematic. Gay comic Guy Branum writes, "*Delirious* was the special that made me fall in love with stand-up, that taught me the language of the art form, and stood as the paragon of what confidence in comedy can and should be."[18] Branum defines *Delirious* as the work of art that inspired his love of comedy, but it also "taught me the building blocks of the homophobia that would keep me closeted and self-hating into my twenties. I was forced to accept that as deeply as my love of stand-up comedy was baked into me, Murphy's disgusted view of gay men was as deeply in my bones."[19]

bell hooks saw Murphy's anti-gay act as a reaction to the systematic oppression and resultant emasculation of Black men, which in turn, led to heightened homophobia and misogyny amongst Black male comics. hooks writes that "[m]any heterosexual [B]lack men in white supremacist patriarchal culture have acted as though the primary 'evil' of racism has been the refusal of the dominant culture to allow them full access to patriarchal power, so that in sexist terms they are compelled to inhabit a sphere of powerlessness deemed 'feminine' and have thus perceived themselves emasculated."[20] She goes on to say that "Murphy 'proves' his phallic power by daring to publicly ridicule women and gays."[21]

Performing in front of an ornate throne, Bob the Drag Queen picks up the mantle by taking on taboos as her predecessors did. Just as Murphy took on taboos of sexuality and race, Bob the Drag Queen does, as well; though in the context of her concert film, there's a telling difference. When Murphy does his bit about gay men, whom he repeatedly refers to as *faggots*, he is taking shots *at* them and *about* them. When Bob zeroes in on one of the few straight men in the audiences, she upends the expected power dynamic—though the audience member is a straight, cis white male, he's in Bob's house, and she—a Black queer drag queen—is in charge. Her exchange with him is biting, but funny. When confirmed that the man was straight, Bob nodded and said, "I knew I smelled something funny."[22] She then continues, "Is that Axe Body Spray?" referencing the cologne popular among straight men (with a social connotation of its users as lacking in taste or class).[23] She then picks up on any tension that a lone gay man may have in a room full of queers by roaring, "Your fear makes me feel strong!"[24]

The work that Bob does in *Suspiciously Large Woman* is educate her audiences on the intersection of two subcultures: Black and queer identities, particularly Black and queer identities in the South. Filmed at Center Stage Theater in Atlanta, Georgia, Bob is speaking at once to a choir of peers as well as novices. The audience members—all of whom cheer in approval when she name-checks various counties and towns in Atlanta—are insiders to her work. But she is also speaking to audiences at home who may not understand Black queer Southern culture. Bob the Drag Queen is a New York City comedy queen, and she illustrates the disconnect of the two cultures by saying, "[Atlanta] is like New York, except everyone who's Brown is Black, everyone who's Asian is Black, and everyone who's white is scared."[25] The work of the concert also looks at issues of colorism when she jokes about the darkness of her skin (even mentioning the term "high yellow" in reference to light-skinned Black people).[26] These questions of race, gender, and region would have remained insular had it not been for Bob's fame and popularity, which led to the concert being released. And due to the film being released, Bob's work operates as a crash course through her point of view of being a Black queer person in a post–Obama America. It's important to note that little of the comedy in *Suspiciously Large Woman* is watered down to be appealing to white audiences. There are white members of the audience—many of whom know her from *RPDR*, but the engagement between her and the Black audiences is far more visceral and immediate, particularly when she dips into cultural trivia.

But also key is Bob's guise as a mentor and teacher. Bob is Miz

Cracker's drag mother, and during her time on the show, she also mentored Derrick Barry after their initial mutual hostility. Once they were paired in a challenge and Bob saw Derrick's commitment to hard work, her enmity thawed, and she helped her former opponent work through an acting challenge. In her concert, Bob again uses the identity of teacher to simultaneously teach as well as to commiserate. When she decries mocking Black people's names, she plunges into a crash course of cultural appropriation, highlighting how ethnic cultural tropes may have initially been met with resistance and cultural chauvinism, but eventually they become the norm. Bob's examples include Rock-and-Roll and Ragtime, two Black forms of art that have been mainstreamed after their early practitioners were seen as primitive or unsophisticated. She adds context to Black art and culture by pinpointing the relative youth of Black American identity and Black American history. She does this through comedy—astutely winding her way through cultural tropes—and stereotypes—whilst maintaining control of the narrative. When she picks up on cultural differences between white and Black America, it is far more substantial than the facile "White people act like *this*, and Black people act like *that*!" When attacking a seemingly low-hanging topic like Black names versus white names, one could assume that she would simply make light of Black people's names, but she does more than that: she pulls out the historical context to give some insight as to the reason behind the cultural phenomena of Black names.

Miz Cracker, on the other hand, comes from a tradition of the Jewish comic. Though her delivery and comic voice isn't Borscht Belt, there are elements of her comedy that hark back to Jackie Mason, Henny Youngman, Woody Allen, Carl Reiner, Fran Drescher, et al. Interestingly enough, I chose to group Bob and Cracker together because Bob is Cracker's drag mother—a concept that yet again feels alien and unknown to those who are not familiar with drag and its culture. When looking at Cracker, we also must have an idea of what "Jewish humor" means. While we cannot define it exactly, as every comic has their stamp on the concept, and there are other factors that shape a Jewish comic's voice, it's understood that much of Jewish humor can be defined as a commentary on the "tension of a social situation where he is explicitly excluded from full participation in a dominant society whose ways he regards both with suspicion and with a degree of condescension"[27]

Cracker incorporates her Jewish background into her comedy. Though she didn't win in her season, she amassed a large following that continued to support her as she competed on the most recent *All Stars* season (season 5, 2020). Miz Cracker, like Bob, uses comedy to "educate" her audiences, particularly when it comes to the intersection of queer and Jewish identities. Just as Bob goes to great lengths to use her platform to further causes that include racial justice (this is especially true after the renewed public interest in the Black Lives Matter movement after the murder of George Floyd and the subsequent protests), Cracker uses her work and her persona to talk about her Jewish identity. Though the majority of her YouTube series, *Jewtorials*, are about drag, make-up, and wig care, she also takes time to highlight important Jewish cultural tropes, though she does so in her distinct comedic methodology. For example, for the eight nights of Chanukah, she hosted a series of videos that take an irreverent look at the holiday and why it's important. So much of the narrative around Chanukah (because it usually falls in December) is defined by Christmas—particularly in how it's *not* Christmas, Cracker's take is far more interesting and engaging because she talks about Chanukah and Jewish culture on its own terms and not in relation to the dominant Christian holiday.

The format of the *Jewtorials* are very straightforward—she announces the show as "tutorials from a Jew!"[28] It's a clear example of Cracker taking on pedagogical approaches to educate her fanbase on Jewish culture. She names, engages, explains, and elaborates as she dresses her lessons in purposely-hacky comedy. When she introduces her lesson in Chanukah, she brings over a guest—and she starts off the lesson by intentionally blundering on what the holiday is about. She says, "From what I remember, from my childhood, Chanukah is a big Jewish Christmas. It's all about getting together as a family and giving gifts. And the menorah is basically like a Jewy Christmas tree."[29] She is then corrected by her guest, who gives a simple and succinct history of Chanukah. She then continues to act as the uninitiated by suggesting to her guest that Chanukah is the most important holiday in the Jewish calendar, which again is corrected. The point of the series is to not only entertain, but to engage and educate her fans on an important—though oft-misunderstood—part of Jewish culture. Her other *Jewtorials* are also educational, in which either she or a guest go over key elements of drag construction. This series affirms Miz Cracker as an educator, in much the same way that a skilled technician is an educator—she uses her platform, gained by her appearances on the show, to further the art of drag by doling out lessons to subscribers.

## *Show Girls and Entertainers: Jinkx Monsoon, BenDeLaCreme, Trixie Mattel, Katya*

The best example of the postmodern showgirl is Bette Midler, so it is no surprise that many of the more successful *RPDR* performers modeled their careers after a performer so important to the queer community. Midler was essentially at the Ground Zero of the AIDS crisis and the queer rights movement, being artistically reared in the Continental Baths in New York City, performing for towel-clad gay men. For the purpose of the essay I define showgirl as an all-round entertainer—a performer who successfully blends comedy, music, theater, and performance art into her show. Because none of these categories have strict boundaries, there is always some overlap. For example, Bob the Drag Queen could be considered a showgirl—her act is largely comedy and drag, but she does incorporate music as well. The other aspect of being a showgirl—and again, this goes back to the Midler reference—is that there needs to be a strong emphasis on camp and an excavation of camp and queer culture.

BenDeLaCreme is a season 6 contestant who had similar comic chops to Bianca Del Rio, though her comedic and drag persona was far lighter than Bianca's. BenDeLa did well in the seasons, even winning the Snatch Game with an inspired take on Maggie Smith from *Downton Abbey* (the genius of the impression was that it was a spirited take on Smith's character and not an impersonation of the actress herself), despite Bianca's popular Judge Judy gag. In the acting challenges, BenDeLa impressed the judges—when the queens had to do spoofs on horror slasher pics, Bianca was in a far stronger group and therefore glided to a win; one of the judges, fashion designer/reality TV vet, Santino Rice remarked that BenDeLa's performance was so strong, "if [BenDeLaCreme] had been on the winning team, she probably would've been the winner of this week's challenge,"[30] to the nodding consensus of the other judges, including RuPaul herself.

I mention BenDeLaCreme as well as the acting challenge because this is again a moment when *RPDR* and a contestant are a conduit for viewers to learn about queer culture via a certain brand of queer comedy. In the same way that John Waters' comedies are important to queer culture (more on that in a bit), slasher horror pics—particularly the campy, amateurish ones—are important in queer culture because so much of queer comedy is based on simultaneously lampooning and paying homage to art that misses the mainstream standards of good taste and high quality. Also, queer film theorists have embraced the horror genre. As Kenneth Figueroa writes, "While the surface goal of the horror genre is to instill fear and suspense, one will be surprised to find there are many underlying political themes, especially when it comes to its vivid congruence with queer culture."[31] Films like Jennifer Kent's 2014 *Babadook* and especially Jack Sholder's 1985 schlock-fest *A Nightmare on Elm Street 2: Freddy's Revenge* have found themselves canonized by queer film critics as important entries in the queer canon.

If tourists walk through any major gayborhood in a major city, they will probably see fliers for local theater shows that are takes off Hollywood schlock. In Chicago, I have attended shows that spoofed campy films like

*The Poseidon Adventure* (1972) or *The Birds* (1963). Gay comedy troupes put together shows that mine the inherent humor of films like *What Ever Happened to Baby Jane?* (1962) or television shows like *The Facts of Life* (1979– 1988). The more obscure and niche, the better.

BenDelaCreme and Jinkx Monsoon have become stewards of sort to this part of queer art, in much the same way that Charles Pierce is. Pierce wrote a series of popular and successful films and plays that spoof underestimated genres such as slasher films, surfer films, women's melodramas, or b-level sci-fi flicks. BenDeLa and Jinkx have joined forces and toured the world with shows that bring this queeny camp comedy to the masses due to their celebrity. They have done shows that spoof films like *Death Becomes Her* (1992); *To Wong Foo, Thanks for Everything! Julie Newmar* (1995); and *Hocus Pocus* (1993). These films are important in queer lore not because they are artistically accomplished or particularly important in the film canon. Of course, queer culture venerates canonical film culture, but there is also the almost-perverse pleasure in consuming culture that misses the mark.

I mention this because in London, *RPDR* is a phenomenon, and like in the States, the audience in the UK is largely queer youth as well as their young, straight, female allies. When Jinkx and BenDeLa performed in London's o2 Forum Kentish Town, I saw the audience lined up, and most would be assumed too young to capture all of the references that Jinkx and BenDeLa would throw at them thereby maintaining important aspects of queer culture alive and thriving. Thanks to streaming service and social media, though, these references do not escape younger audiences. Thanks to YouTube and Twitter, as soon as a cultural artifact is unearthed, it quickly does the rounds on these sites. For example, when Susan Sarandon played Bette Davis in the campy Ryan Murphy *Feud: Bette and Joan* (2017), and sang "Whatever Happened to Baby Jane?" as Davis, sly Internet watchers immediately scoured YouTube to judge the accuracy of Sarandon's impersonation—and quickly videos were edited to show both Sarandon and Davis, side-by-side, singing. Films like *Death Becomes Her* or *Hocus Pocus* become evergreen regardless of their quality or merit because they live on in these performances that are attended by younger audiences who may not have even been born when these films were released.

When speaking of finding success as a postmodern showgirl, one cannot underestimate the success of Trixie Mattel. Born Brian Michael Firkus, Trixie is an alter-ego that is an oversized, exaggerated, nearly grotesque cartoon of the Barbie doll. Her drag name was originally an insulting slur her abusive stepfather gave her. As she explains,

> I had a really hard time with my stepdad. Like if I was being too sensitive or acting too feminine, especially, he'd call me a trixie. You know for years, that was

like one of the worst words I could think of. So I took that name, Trixie, and it used to have all this hurt to it, and I made it my drag name, now it's something I celebrate. Something I'm so proud of.[32]

Trixie is an interesting example because unlike many of the other successful comedy queens, she did not do particularly well in her season. In season 7, she was a popular front runner because of her following on social media and because she was one of the queens to have a fully formed character. Like Bianca or BenDeLa, she had a quick wit and provided entertaining one-liners during the confessionals, but she failed to make a strong impression in her season, eliminated in the fourth episode before being invited to return only to leave in the tenth episode. With Trixie, this was a case of a drag queen with a significant following who proved to be very talented, but who is one who didn't thrive in the reality show genre. (Trixie would win the truncated *All Stars* season 4, mind you, though many felt her victor came due to BenDeLa's controversial self-elimination.)

Yet, Trixie found some of the biggest success outside of *RPDR*. Along with a thriving career in country music (she's one of the few *RPDR* alumnae who has exhibited genuine musical skill), Trixie has developed a comedic career, starring on a talk show with fellow *RPDR* contestant, Katya (born Brian Joseph McCook). What started off as a popular YouTube web series, *UNHhhh* (pronounced as an overheated moan) was spun off into a TV show on Viceland, *The Trixie & Katya Show*. Similarly to Miz Cracker's *Jewtorials*, Trixie and Katya's show was a vehicle for the two queens to discuss certain topics, some of them taboo and insular to the queer community. Topics such as death, money dating, and health are discussed between the two queens, who simply riff, doing expert improv, as they use humor to discuss various issues. The topics are mostly light, but they do reveal aspects of queer culture, particularly regional queer culture, as Trixie is from the Midwest and will talk about local gay minutia like Chicago's Market Days (a weekend summer festival in Chicago's Boystown neighborhood). The two also discuss drag and its history as well as their relationship to the art form—in one episode, for example, Trixie shares how as a child growing up in rural Wisconsin, her inspiration for drag came from Barbie dolls—specifically, the McDonald's Happy Meal Barbie dolls: "This is where my whole life comes from," Trixie says, holding up a selection of miniature Barbies.[33]

Aside from her show with Katya, Trixie also forged a successful career as a modern-day showgirl, performing as a country and western singer, stand-up comedian. Like BenDeLaCreme, cabaret shows have become an important part of her drag persona—her onstage patter an extension of her message. Like the aforementioned Bette Midler, the queens from *RPDR* have been able to become an integral part of queer culture through their onstage work, engaging with existing tropes of queer culture and history.

## Queer Comedy History 101: Snatch Game

Whenever Ru announces to the queens that the episode's challenge will be the Snatch Game, we hear the requisite screams of excitement and joy before the room plunges into a tense atmosphere as the queens start to work out their acts. Snatch Game is a great way for the show's contestants to distinguish themselves and to show off their ability to improvise, play, and make an impact. The format of the challenge mimics the 1970s game show *Match Game*. The premise is simple: a panel of celebrities are given silly questions, and they must each write down an answer. Two contestants are then given the question, and they have to come up with an answer and earn points for each celebrity that matches the answer. The 1970s *Match Game* was a camp classic and one that *RPDR* rightly parodies because it was merely an excuse to have b- and c-list celebrities, many of whom were essentially professional game show contestants, cut up and give vaguely naughty answers.

On "Snatch Game"—a crude parody of the original title—the queens are told to choose a celebrity, and then they must either do a humorous job in impersonating that performer or at least spin off a funny character from that celebrity. Celebrity judges act as the contestants who must try to match their answers with the queens. The reason why the game is so important is that the queens are competing in what is essentially a dog pile, and it's every queen for herself—when Ru throws an answer to a queen to simulate banter, another queen earns extra points for being able to muscle her way in and run with the gag if the first queen stalls.

The other reason why the Snatch Game is important from a pedagogical level is that it is here that the queens have the freest reign to indulge in their queer culture knowledge. Though most of the queens choose to impersonate pop stars or reality TV stars (including *RPDR* alumnae as well as twice Ru herself), it has also become a tradition for a season to have a handful of queens choose more obscure names. It is when that happens that the audience is then forced to do some quick research—Wikipedia or Google—to understand why the queen is dressed a certain way or why she is speaking with a funny accent. It is through this category that we also see our audience gain a richer understanding of queer pop comedy.

As mentioned earlier, in season 2, in the inaugural Snatch Game, we saw Pandora Boxx essay Carol Channing. Whilst many of the younger viewers may have initially been ignorant of Channing, because of the exposure on *RPDR*, Channing's work has reached a larger, younger audience. Channing's films—*Hello, Dolly!* (1964) and *Gentlemen Prefer Blondes* (1949) in particular—are considered staples of the American theater, and though she's no longer alive, her work deserves to live on. And because of

Pandora Boxx, Channing's work continues to survive. Subsequent seasons saw queens like Manila Luzon perform as Barbra Streisand for an *All Stars* season as well as Imelda Marcos for her competitive season. Manila's choice of Marcos is interesting because it's a dated choice—something that never worries drag comedy, which revels in the mustiness of an allusion or reference—but she pinpoints the broad strokes of what made Marcos so compelling: the single-minded greed and the obsessive collection of shoes.

Manila's choice of Streisand is important to note because Streisand is, of course, a key figure in pop camp culture, but again, one of "a certain age" and who may not be necessarily relevant to the target demographic of the show. And younger drag queens aren't necessarily impersonating Streisand anymore—though she was a popular figure for queens, going as far back as the early 1970s, when Jim Bailey would float onto a variety TV show set in '60s Streisand drag to sing a duet with Carol Burnett or Lucie Arnaz, and to tell a few jokes in Streisand's Brooklyn drawl. Other seemingly old-fashioned subjects include Ivy Winters doing Marilyn Monroe, Alexis Michelle winning her season's Snatch Game with her Liza Minnelli, both Mariah Paris Balenciaga and Alyssa Edwards tried their hand at Joan Crawford, Sasha Velour did Marlene Dietrich, and Alaska would do Mae West. Though the quality of the performances varied wildly, it cannot be overstated how impactful it was to have these figures resurrected, so to speak, by having popular drag queens—who thrive in the social media age in which our monoculture has been obliterated—perform as them. And we see this impact first-hand when looking at the twelfth season of *RPDR* and Aiden Zhane's essaying of Mae West, which borrows heavily from Alaska's shrugging interpretation. This tradition of celebrity impersonation—and specifically of these divas—lends itself to an important, if slowly disintegrating, aspect of queer culture that gets superficially revived when it is time for the queens to do the Snatch Game.

The other significant resultant of Snatch Game is when a queen chooses an obscure niche figure to play in the Snatch Game. The most notable example of this was when Jinkx Monsoon chose to do Edie "Little Edie" Bouvier, the socialite who became a shut-in with her mother, "Big Edie," in a crumbling, dilapidated mansion in New England. Big Edie and Little Edie became queer icons because of the 1975 documentary *Grey Gardens* by Albert and David Maysles. The film became a cult classic, especially amongst queer male audiences who took a shining to Little Edie, a frustrated performer who managed to maintain a white-knuckled grip on her fading beauty, despite diminishing mental health, living in desperately unhygienic conditions, and suffering from hair loss. Throughout the film, Little Edie engendered herself to queer audiences with her wit and her eccentric fashion sense—she would improvise clothing from material found around the house, turning a pair of sweatpants into a stylish headscarf.

Whilst the other queens were choosing their subjects, when Jinkx announced she was doing Little Edie, she was met with stony silence and a gallery of dropped faces, as each queen registered ignorance on who Little Edie was. Most people under the age of 30 also were probably confused as to who Jinkx was planning to impersonate. Jinkx's sure-footed performance did so well that social media platforms like YouTube and Twitter started to pop up with select scenes from *Grey Gardens* so that audiences could see who the real Little Edie was and to verify Jinkx's accuracy. In this instance the show—and Jinkx—both act as a conduit for information and history: in this particular case, it's a multi-layered lesson of film history, queer culture, and contemporary American history. *Grey Gardens* is introduced to a wider, newer audience not through a screening at an art house cinema nor a Film Studies college course, but through the art of drag and *RPDR*. In this instance, we are removed from the traditional classroom to attain knowledge of an important cultural product.

The aforementioned BenDeLaCreme did excellent on two Snatch Games—one in her competitive season, in which she beat the frontrunner, Bianca, with her riotous interpretation of Maggie Smith; but more importantly was her performance in her *All Stars* season as she, like Jinkx, chose to essay a more obscure figure in queer pop culture: gay comedian Paul Lynde. The choice of Lynde is perfect and creeps into meta-territory as not only is Lynde an influential comedian for queer comics, but he was exactly the kind of celebrity who thrived on game shows like *Match Game* or *Hollywood Squares*, in which he was called upon to lob puns and double entendres in his idiosyncratic pinched delivery. Though it didn't have the same impact that Jinkx's Edie impersonation did, BenDeLa's choice of Lynde can be argued to be the more impactful one because it speaks directly to the history of queer comedy and in particular highlighting a queer comic who was in a distinct position in that he was obviously queer, yet also simultaneously closeted. When approaching Lynde's comedy, one must contend with a severe cognitive disassociation in his mainstream success—his audiences delighted in his ability to turn the most mundane, silly line into something titillating and saucy simply with his panting style, yet he remains strangely sexless. I mentioned earlier that there was a drag that was deemed as "safe" when its queerness was put into an acceptable context—one that is not queer. And it is a similar fate that befall on Lynde's comedy—he was a cartoon figure, de-sexed, and made two-dimensional (with his participation).

So having a man like Lynde celebrated on a television show that does not shy away from sexuality or sexual identity is important because it affirms his queerness (even if it's decades after his death). What

BenDeLaCreme did with her impersonation is help Paul Lynde "come out," and audiences were clued into a charismatic and brilliant performer who was ahead of his time.

Other queens who also chose to pick interesting subjects include Robbie Turner who did Diane Vreeland and Miz Cracker who would try Dorothy Parker. Though both queens didn't impress judges with their choices, it represented an ambition in the show's tone—Cracker choosing Parker seems an apt fit, for Parker was renowned for her savage and hilarious wit and Cracker has positioned herself as a comedy queen. Kennedy Davenport, like BenDeLa chose to do a male queer figure, Little Richard, another person who is a towering figure not only in queer culture, but in Rock-and-Roll (many credit Little Richard for being an early architect of Rock music); that Little Richard also has a very complicated relationship with his queerness brings an unintended layer of subversion into the performance.

That Little Richard is a cis man who presents as quite feminine means that Kennedy's performance also schools audiences on the complexity of drag performance. Despite the show's purported narrow view of drag, having a cis man as a Snatch Game character is significant because Kennedy is also presenting a different kind of drag—it isn't drag king (the act of assigned-female-at-birth drag performers wearing traditionally masculine clothing), but a unique type of drag that doesn't seem to reject either masculine or feminine tropes, but instead embraces both. (Both Prince and Michael Jackson were also practitioners of this type of drag—essentially presenting themselves as very pretty, heavily-made up cis men.) Throughout the seasons, queens have done "boy" drag to the consternation of fellow contestants and the judges (especially Michelle Visage): Alaska flirts with Pee-Wee Herman-esque in "Draggle Rock,"[34] whilst Milk draws a controversial and mixed reception from the judges' panel when she chooses to emulate workroom RuPaul in a Klein, Epstein & Parker suit and a bald cap when the queens are tasked to choose a Ru look for the runway.[35] These moments in *RPDR* history are significant because the queens are side-stepping the show's thesis of drag to open up the conversation with the audiences. It's important to note that the men who are depicted in the Snatch Game—Paul Lynde, Little Richard, or Thorgy Thor's giggly work as Michael Jackson—are men who have themselves played with the performative nature of gender. In this instance, we see the queens are outpacing the show itself as relevant story tellers of drag.

There are other significant performances in Snatch Game that pay homage to the rich history of queer and trans pop culture and queer and trans history—Lineysha Sparks did Celia Cruz; Courtney Act did Fran Drescher; Milk tried Julia Child; Trinity Taylor did Amanda Lepore (on her competitive season) and Caitlyn Jenner (on her *All Stars* season); Ginger Minj did Tammy Faye Bakker; BeBe Zahara Benet would perform as Grace Jones; and Nina West would choose two queer comedy icons in one single Snatch Game: Jo Anne Worley, and Harvey Fierstein.

## Conclusion

Near the end of the fifth season, there were three queens left: Roxxxy Andrews, Alaska, and Jinkx Monsoon (who would eventually be crowned the season's winner). The challenge had the queens film a music video of RuPaul's song "The Beginning." The premise of the video was that the three queens were trading the roles of three courtroom characters: the Prosecutor; the Defense Attorney; and the Defendant. Both Alaska and Jinkx defined their drag persona on their comedic and acting skills, so they excelled. Roxxxy, who did well in earlier acting challenges, was not as strong and took her frustrations out on her castmates, accusing them of ridiculing drag. Jinkx took umbrage with that characterization and insisted that she takes both drag and comedy very seriously. The exchange between the three queens erupted after Roxxxy haughtily insisted that she takes drag seriously:

> I take what I do extremely professional and real and I don't make a joke out of everything. And [the judges] are gonna read me 'cause I'm lost because there's so much bullshit going on. [She gestures to Alaska] So, trying to sell comedy, [she gestures to Jinkx] trying to sell comedy, trying to outdo each other. I know what I've done ... and I'm ready to plead my case on this runway. This isn't a joke to me.... This competition is extremely serious and it's the rest of my life. Girl, I'm over it. Why do I have to make up a name to who I'm doing? I'm acting like an attorney. A bitch. Why do I have to have some kind of fucking character? [In a mocking voice, she continues:] "Well, I'm so-and-so. And I do this and I'm 80 years old." [In her normal voice and directly to Jinkx, she continues:] No, you're not 80 years old. You're Jinkx Monsoon playing a character.[36]

There's an unintended irony in Roxxxy's rant because as she complains about having to create a character and perform, she ignores the fact that she's in a drag competition and that everything the queens do is performance and crafting characters. As a pageant queen, Roxxxy found comedy queens inferior because Jinkx and Alaska (Alaska being a former ally) embraced untraditional drag instead of the beautiful, hyper-feminine drag that she prefers. Her rage against comedy continued the following day, when she tried to play off her rant with sarcasm, yet she still maintained that comedy should not have been key to the music video challenge. "All of our characters are not supposed to be funny," Roxxxy sniffed contemptuously.[37]

When challenged by her competitors, she dug in her heels, insisting that the challenge did not call for comedy: Alaska zeroed in on Roxxxy's issue, saying, "I love how you say 'comedy' like it's a bad thing."[38] "Well honey," Roxxxy retorted, "not all drag is comedy."[39]

It's here that Jinkx puts in her view, saying that she takes comedy very seriously. "Comedy is not poking fun at drag," she points out.[40] Roxxxy tersely interrupts her, implying that the focus on comedy in *RPDR* is an insult to drag. But Jinkx's studious and hard-working approach to comedy makes sense when looking at her comedic influences, particularly Lucille Ball, who is a major figure in Jinkx's comedy. "Through Lucille Ball," Jinkx writes, "I saw how a woman can bring you to tears with laughter with nothing more than a look."[41] Ball, a legendary comedienne, was also noted for her serious attitude towards comedy (she would rehearse stunts until she could land them perfectly). To Jinkx, the suggestion that comedy somehow besmirches drag is offensive because comedy is an important vehicle for her to get her message across—it is more than just something to do for a challenge on a game show. Comedy is as integral to her work as is the drag.

And that is an important take away that one must get when looking at *RPDR* and comedy. The comedy queens on the show are true pros—not merely clever queens who can think quickly on their feet and pull off a challenge. These are artists who approach their comedy with reverence. And even if they have not been given opportunities that *RPDR* afforded them, they would still be crafting their comedy. What *RPDR* has done is allowed for these queens to transcend telling their jokes for dollar bills at gay bars and night clubs, and instead has allowed for them to take their acts to large venues as well as TV and film—and they've also influenced and changed the comedy landscape as a result. And that's important because even though gay bars and nightclubs are queer safe spaces, if drag comedy is to make a significant change in our culture, it needs to do so outside of these safe or queer spaces. An important aspect of public pedagogy is for it to take place outside confined and established spaces. As E. Patrick Johnson writes, "[T]he places in which our work as performance artists/scholars is most needed is not in locations where transgressive work and radical discourse is the norm (if not passé), but in locales where those radical voices are muzzled by institutional racism, sexism, classism, and homophobia."[42]

## *Mini Challenge: Discussion Questions*

- Why is the use of comedy specifically significant when looking at the impact that drag culture can have on mainstream culture?
- How much of an oral history tradition can we see in *RPDR*, particularly with the Snatch Game?

- To what extent is there a connection between wit/comedy and marginalized communities?

## Maxi Challenge: Activities and Assignments

- This essay offers opportunities for crossover learning, particularly if we're looking at university-age students, but actively engaging with the essay by going to a drag show is an excellent way for the instructor to not only illustrate what I'm writing about, but also highlight the intersectionality of drag, comedy, race, and gender—and most importantly—as this is something especially true post-COVID, it would be an excellent way to highlight the precarious nature of queer performance art and the importance of supporting local creatives. Another way to support the essay would be to engage with other forms of political humor, not necessarily drag (although certainly could be, *à la* Melissa McCarthy as Sean Spicer on *SNL*), but looking at satire and how humorists such as Jonathan Swift, Mark Twain, Dorothy Parker, or Jane Austen used their wit to critique notions of class, gender, nationality and identity.
- My essay also engages with intersectionality of queerness and race; therefore, engaging with texts that explore those two issues when interlocking—looking at James Baldwin, Audre Lorde, or Marlon Riggs, for examples to see how Black queer thinkers used their art to speak to their various identities—allows for *RPDR* and its performers to be viewed in a larger context of marginalized communities using art to assert their identities as well as to criticize social conditions. Finally, I think viewing of Jennie Livingston's documentary *Paris Is Burning* is a great way to introduce the students not only to drag culture, but to ball culture as well as "reading," an important aspect of drag comedy. I think my essay would fit into a larger discussion of popular culture and film and television and how drag comedy is used to engage with mainstream culture.

## Notes

1. Smith, Nigel M. "Bianca Del Rio: 'I would gladly do my comedy without drag'" *The Guardian*, 17, Dec. 2016, https://www.theguardian.com/culture/tvandradioblog/2015/dec/17/bianca-del-rio-comedy-drag-queen-rupaul-rolodex-hate.
2. "RuPaul/Justin Bieber," *Saturday Night Live*, created by Lorne Michaels, performance by RuPaul, season 45, episode 13, Broadway Video, 2020.

3. *Paris Is Burning*. Directed by Jennie Livingston, Off-White Productions, 1990.
4. See "RuPaul/Justin Bieber."
5. See *Paris Is Burning*.
6. *Ibid*.
7. McNeal, Keith E. "Behind the Make-Up: Gender Ambivalence and the Double-Bind of Gay Selfhood in Drag Performance." *Ethos*, vol. 27, no. 3, Body, Self, and Technology, Sep. 1999, pp. 344–378, p. 345.
8. "'Spilling The Tea': The Queens Kiki on Gay Dating Apps & Lady Gaga's 'Born This Way.'" *YouTube*, uploaded by *Billboard*, 27 June 2017, https://www.youtube.com/watch?v=yBtji0rAFC8.
9. Oleksiak, Timothy. "When Queens Listen." *Reinventing (with) Theory in Rhetoric and Writing: Essays in Honor of Sharon Crowley*, edited by Andrea Alden, Kendall Gerdes, Judy Holiday, Ryan Skinnell, University of Press of Colorado, Utah State University Press, 2019, pp. 257–267.
10. *The Celluloid Closet*. Rob Epstein and Jeffrey Friedman, directors. HBO Pictures, 1996.
11. Edgar, Eir-Anne. "Xtravaganza!: Drag Representation and Articulation in *RuPaul's Drag Race*." *Studies in Popular Culture*, vol. 34, no. 1, Fall 2001, pp. 133–146.
12. "RuPaul's Big Opening: Part 2." RuPaul's Drag Race, season 6, episode 2, Logo TV, 3 Mar. 2014. Amazon, https://www.amazon.com/gp/video/detail/B00ICGYECE/ref=atv_dp_season_select_s6.
13. *Ibid*.
14. "Bianca Del Rio." RuPaul's Drag Race Wiki, 2020, https://rupaulsdragrace.fandom.com/wiki/Bianca_Del_Rio.
15. "Oh No She Betta Don't." *RuPaul's Drag Race*, season 6, episode 6, Logo TV, 31 Mar. 2014, Amazon, https://www.amazon.com/RuPauls-Drag-Race-Season-6/dp/B00ICGYECE. Betta Don't
16. Smith, Daniel R. "Persona." *Comedy and Critique: Stand-Up Comedy and the Professional Ethos of Laughter*, Bristol University Press, 2018, JStor, https://www.jstor.org/stable/j.ctv56fgq1.9.
17. Gillota, David. "'Cracker, Please!': Toward a White Ethnic Humor." *Ethnic Humor in Multiethnic America*, Rutgers University Press, 2013, pp. 76–103, JStor, https://www.jstor.org/stable/j.ctt5hjctg.7.
18. Branum, Guy. "The Rules of Enchantment." *My Life As a Goddess: A Memoir Through (Un)Popular Culture*. Atria Books, 2018, pp. 207–231.
19. *Ibid*.
20. hooks, bell. "Is Paris Burning?" *Reel to Real: Race, Sex and Class at the Movies* [e-book]. Routledge, 2008.
21. *Ibid*.
22. *Suspiciously Large Woman*. Directed by Cheyenne Picardo, performance by Bob the Drag Queen, Producer Entertainment Group, 2017.
23. *Ibid*.
24. *Ibid*.
25. *Ibid*.
26. *Ibid*.
27. Katz, Naomi and Eli Katz. "Tradition and Adaptation in American Jewish Humor." *The Journal of American Folklore*, vol. 84, no. 332, Apr—Jun., 1967, pp. 215–220.
28. "Night 1: What Is Chanukah?—Jewtorials Chanukah Special." *YouTube*, uploaded by World of Wonder,
22 December 2019, https://www.youtube.com/watch?v=5nDxKgUnwDk.
29. *Ibid*.
30. "Scream Queens," *RuPaul's Drag Race*, season 6, episode 3, World of Wonder, 10 Mar. 2014, Amazon, https://www.amazon.com/gp/video/detail/B00ICGYECE/ref=atv_dp_season_select_s6.
31. Figueroa, Kenneth. "Haunted: The Intersections of Queer Culture and Horror Movies," *Wussy*, https://www.wussymag.com/all/2017/10/6/haunted-the-intersections-of-queer-culture-and-horror-movies. Accessed 28 June 2020.

32. "Conjoined Queens," *RuPaul's Drag Race*, season 7, episode 7, 20 Apr. 2015, Amazon, https://www.amazon.com/gp/video/detail/B00TG0HXVE/ref=atv_dp_season_select_s7.

33. "UNHhhh Ep 57: 'The 90s' w/ Trixie Mattel & Katya Zamolodchikova," *YouTube*, uploaded by World of Wonder, 14 Aug. 2017, https://www.youtube.com/watch?v=z3OnRH5YXu8&list=PLhgFEi9aNUb2BNrIEecCGXApgeX7Yjwz8&index=76.

34. "Draggle Rock." *RuPaul's Drag Race*, season 5, episode 3, Logo TV, 11 Feb. 2013. Amazon, https://www.amazon.com/gp/video/detail/B00B45B4X2/ref=atv_dp_season_select_s5.

35. "Snatch Game." *RuPaul's Drag Race*, season 6, episode 5, Logo TV, 24 Mar. 2014. Amazon, https://www.amazon.com/gp/video/detail/B00ICGYECE/ref=atv_dp_season_select_s6.

36. "The Final Three, Hunty." *RuPaul's Drag Race*, season 5, episode 12, Logo TV, 22 Apr. 2013, Amazon, https://www.amazon.com/gp/video/detail/B00B45B4X2/ref=atv_dp_season_select_s5.

37. *Ibid.*

38. *Ibid.*

39. *Ibid.*

40. *Ibid.*

41. Monsoon, Jinkx, "Bio: The Making of Jinkx Monsoon," *Jinkx Monsoon,* https://jinkxmonsoon.com/bio/. Accessed 25 April 2020.

42. Johnson, E. Patrick. "Strange Fruit: A Performance about Identity Politics." *TDR* (1988-), vol. 47, no. 2, Summer 2003, pp. 88–116.

# Digital Drag and YouTube as Queer Space

## Queens as Influencers from Performance to Pedagogy

Florian Zitzelsberger

"When those who have the power to name and to socially construct reality choose not to see you or hear you ... when someone with the authority of a teacher, say, describes the world and you are not in it, there is a moment of psychic disequilibrium, as if you looked in the mirror and saw nothing. It takes some strength of soul—and not just individual strength, but collective understanding—to resist this void, this non-being, into which you are thrust, and to stand up, demanding to be seen and heard."
—Adrienne Rich, Author of *Blood, Bread, and Poetry*[1]

"Divine ran so Ru could walk. And Ru ran so I could walk."
—Violet Chachki, season 7 winner[2]

## Digital Drag on YouTube

*RuPaul's Drag Race* (*RPDR*) has become immensely popular on YouTube, not least because of the ever-growing online make-up community. For example, numerous influencers and make-up lovers have attempted to copy *RPDR* contestant Trixie Mattel's Barbie-like look with her signature contouring, extensively overdrawn lips, and heavy eyeliner, and shared their results on YouTube and Instagram. Lucy Garland, winner of the second season of *American Beauty Star*, has an entire series on her channel dedicated to creating spot-on replicas of some of the most beloved *RPDR* alumnae's looks on herself, including Trixie, Aquaria, Sasha Velour, Kim Chi, and Valentina. Patrick Starr likewise demonstrates make-up techniques on his channel, as well as other steps of drag transformation like gluing down a wig, thus enabling the viewers of his tutorials to (re)create drag looks. Other notable male and openly queer influencers like Jeffree Star or James Charles have collaborated with former contestants of *RPDR* such as Alyssa Edwards and Adore Delano in the former case, Farrah Moan and Plastique Tiara in the latter, or celebrate the art of drag through their own gender-bending make-up transformations. Lucy's make-up recreations, Patrick's "Drag 101" series, and Jeffree's and James's collaborations thereby combine a love for make-up (and their profession) with an interest in a very specific, "mainstreamed" drag culture, apparent in the adoption of drag slang or catchphrases from *RPDR* within these and other videos.[3] While their investment in drag make-up can be appreciated without any knowledge of *RPDR*, an at least vague familiarity with the show is required to understand the references made during these videos.

In times of social media, a substantial part of drag culture is taking place on the Internet, and it is therefore not surprising that a lot of former *RPDR* contestants now also operate their own YouTube channels. I want to call the performances on these self-governed channels *digital drag* in distinction to the queens' offline performances and their presence on other YouTubers' channels.[4] Digital drag, as I will argue in the following, possesses a pedagogical impetus precisely because of its relation to *RPDR*. I begin by mapping, in Foucauldian fashion, the "other space" of YouTube. As a transmedial, paratextual extension of *RPDR* on YouTube, digital drag can offer alternative perspectives on drag, queer identity, and community without being implicated in the aesthetic regime of the show or of hegemonic straight culture *a priori*. The heterotopic characteristics of this paratext, as a phenomenon that exists in relation to but separate from the show, supports the way in which Elizabeth McNeil et al. conceive of queer pedagogy, namely a "transformation of pedagogy as (tacitly heteronormative) reproductive tool."[5] The lens of phenomenology will assist me in illustrating how digital drag performatively produces queer spaces on YouTube, and how it prompts (re)positionings and (re)orientations within discourses of queer identities in the online realm. My theoretical discussion of digital drag is then followed by several case studies that focus on the queer ways of being in the (online) world as exemplified by queens on their own YouTube channels. I contend that queens' roles as influencers bridge the gap between performance and pedagogy by making them educators and advocates of queer communities and subjectivities. At the core of this essay, therefore, lies the question of how drag queens make use of the paratextual positioning and heterotopic structures of YouTube to facilitate such community building as a form of queer pedagogy. I will argue that digital drag is pedagogical in its advocacy of alternative epistemologies that transcend hegemonic understandings of embodiment and that affect the identification *with* one another, emphasizing the importance of togetherness.

## *Queer Positionings I: On the Paratextuality of YouTube*

The YouTube trends I outlined above, together with the examples I will consider more closely in the subsequent sections (namely, drag queens' *own* channels), can be regarded as paratexts of *RPDR*. A conceptualization of YouTube as paratext relies on a transmedial understanding of the latter and is dependent on what Henry Jenkins describes as convergence, which signifies "a cultural shift as consumers are encouraged to seek out new information and make connections among dispersed media content."[6] However, it is important to note that the extensions of *RPDR* I am referring to in this essay might not be official ones that are systematically dispersed, which originally serves as a requirement of transmedia storytelling according to Jenkins, but rather constitute unofficial extensions, or at least extensions with a varying degree of authorized relatedness to the show. As Matt Hills notes, "[T]ransmediality has frequently become paratextual in character instead of acting as a form of distributed textuality,"[7] highlighting the fact that, while such cases extend or add to its textual core (what Jason Mittell would call "mothership"[8]), they are not necessary elements of *RPDR* in the sense of additive comprehension, but find themselves in a hierarchical relationship to its core text. In other words, where *RPDR* can be viewed or properly understood on its own, its paratexts depend on a familiarity with the show if one is to fully understand them. By saying that transmedia paratexts move away from the notion of distributed textuality, Hills acknowledges that such paratexts do not have to be created, controlled, or disseminated by the producer(s) of the core text. This resonates with Jenkins's work on convergence culture, for it includes the perspective of unauthorized extensions, which he illustrates most prominently with fan practices. Despite varying degrees of "realness"—ranging from official content provided by VH1 and WOW Presents to affiliated content by former contestants, including appearances on other YouTubers' channels, to content inspired by or dedicated to *RPDR* (what we could perceive in terms similar to fan activity)—all of the aforementioned examples constitute paratexts to *RPDR* because their sheer existence is facilitated by, and

*Digital Drag and YouTube as Queer Space* (Zitzelsberger) 231

in turn expands, the universe of the show. For Hills, transmedia paratexts therefore respond to an economic argument in that they "can work collectively to reinforce brand value and omniscience."[9] Drag culture, in its rather mainstreamed variant, is not primarily engendered by *RPDR* itself. Rather, I want to suggest that the seemingly exponential number of *RPDR* paratexts, including the drag fringes of YouTube, performs brand identity and contributes to a heightened engagement with *RPDR*, allowing *RPDR* to enter realms previously not linked to drag culture.[10] The perhaps most widely received example for this is the show "UNHhhh," hosted by Trixie Mattel and Katya Zamolodchikova, which boosted both the popularity of the queens as well as the recognition of *RPDR* online. The fast-paced editing style was imitated by several other YouTubers, including James Charles, who paid homage to the series with his brother in a segment on his channel called "Brother and Sister."

Interaction and participation make social media paratexts communal in character. I am particularly interested in the potentialities of YouTube as a site of *queer* community building. While Michael Strangelove argues that "YouTube is home to all forms of sexual fetishes and marginal or underground sexual practices,"[11] I want to emphasize that, in our case, it is YouTube's position as paratextual to *RPDR* that makes it queer. The YouTube videos we will encounter in the subsequent sections are placed within the margins of the *RPDR* cosmos. Instead of viewing digital drag on YouTube as queer on the basis of *RPDR*'s relation to cultural hegemony, I want to stress that its relation to *RPDR* itself substantiates its queer potentialities. Being located in the margin should not be mistaken for *being* marginal in the sense addressed by Strangelove. Rather, reading digital drag on YouTube as paratextual articulates the perception of queer sensibilities not negatively through othered categories, and thus as limited, but positively and as limitless. Reverting to Gérard Genette and his original definition of the paratext as "a zone between text and off-text,"[12] we see how the in-betweenness of digital drag on YouTube, somehow belonging to *RPDR* while not being part of the official text, carves out discursive queer spaces that can exist outside of, yet always in relation to, *RPDR*. In this sense, then, I want to argue that the phenomenon of digital drag on YouTube, as proposed in this essay, "simultaneously represent[s], contest[s], and invert[s]"[13] the discourses to which it is other. I am employing the term "other" here deliberately and in the way the *para*-text is "other" to the text around which it is situated—i.e., in the sense of an alternative positioning. Digital drag on YouTube occupies a position within queer or drag culture rather than cultural hegemony, and it is located in the online spaces of YouTube rather than *RPDR*.

## Queer Positionings II: YouTube as Digital Heterotopia

Before turning to digital drag in more detail, I briefly want to contemplate on this queer positioning of digital drag as paratextual to *RPDR* by connecting drag on YouTube to Michel Foucault's concept of heterotopia. In his seminal "Of Other Spaces" ("*Des Espaces Autres*"), Foucault conceives of heterotopias as spaces that appear as "other to" the lived spaces of society. Heterotopias lie outside of the ordinary, of the accessible, and function in ways that differ from the actual spaces we inhabit. As such, these other spaces are in principle connected to all spaces (i.e., by representing or inverting the space to which they are other) and to the individuals inhabiting them. According to Foucault, heterotopias inevitably emerge in any society because of a need to create or inhabit an alternative space, one in which the governing rules of the society's lived space do not apply and which allows for different modes of embodiment and experience. As such, heterotopias are intricately connected to the shared beliefs and convictions (or knowledge in general) of a society. Heterotopias thus approximate a state usually associated with utopias in reality because of the alternative orientations these sites enable.[14] While the phenomenon of digital drag is not necessarily utopian, I suggest that its heterotopic characteristics tie in with its pedagogical impetus. Digital drag not only creates spaces that possess a potential for inclusivity and diversity, it first and foremost shows that there *is* room for diversity. If institutionalized education—with a clear emphasis on curricula whose processes of selection inevitably lead to an exclusionist politics—has taught us anything, it is that social space is always already occupied.[15] Digital drag makes a point about the way in which digital space reconfigures social space in ways that make it inhabitable for those who otherwise do not fit in.

The online realm of YouTube facilitates the establishment of numerous heterotopias in the sense that it creates spaces that are other to "real," lived spaces of society. In their investigation of new spatial media, Catherine Nash and Andrew Gorman-Murray focus on queer mobilities, showing "how queer subjects, through their use of new technologies, are being themselves remade within newly mobile, unstable and fragmented relational geographies."[16] While the relation of such (digital) heterotopias to the space that remains allows for the emergence of queer subjectivities, heterotopias should not be viewed as completely anti-hierarchical because power relations, marked by "the hierarchical social categories of race, gender, class and age, for example," also determine and shape the "constitution of new queer places."[17]

However, heterotopias hold the *opportunity* to bring together those who are likeminded or, more generally speaking, those who are oriented within or toward similar epistemologies. Akin to how Benedict Anderson views communities as always only imagined,[18] and therefore as reliant on (the assumption of) shared beliefs, online communities emerge as a product of sharing knowledge within the boundaries of a specific online space, on a specific platform, or across multiple outlets.[19] The kind of knowledge produced and disseminated online can differ significantly from hegemonic beliefs. As such, these online spaces and the communities that inhabit them (even if only digitally) establish heterotopias as they allow for alternative modes of being, embodiment, and experience that would not be possible, intelligible, or viable in real spaces. Kay Siebler, in *Learning Queer Identity in the Digital Age* (2016), succinctly summarizes that "YouTube channels offer a wild range of people a public forum, and a highly interactive one, for sharing information and defying status quo identities (or supporting them)."[20] In this sense, then, digital drag on YouTube holds queer potentialities because it is paratextual and heterotopic; digital drag is queer, for it constitutes a heterotopic paratext of *RPDR*. However, as a phenomenological perspective will show in the following, the relationship between digital drag and these other spaces is rather reciprocal and defies linear (unilateral) processes of signification, which substantiates its relation to queer pedagogy.

## *Approaching a Queer Pedagogy of Togetherness: The Phenomenology of Digital Drag*

In saying that digital drag on YouTube occupies a rather queer position because of its inhabitancy of spaces that are alternative or other to lived experience (in the sense that digital drag is heterotopic) and to *RPDR* (in the sense that digital drag is paratextual), I am invested in questions of spatiality in line with Sara Ahmed's assertion in *Queer Phenomenology* (2006) that queer "becomes a matter of how things appear, how they gather, how they perform, to create the edges of spaces and worlds."[21] Following this idea, then, I approach digital drag from a phenomenological position that highlights perception and experientiality. This also enables me to connect digital drag to queer pedagogy as outlined by Ava Laure Parsemain in *The Pedagogy of Queer TV* (2019):

> [C]ontemporary popular television teaches about queerness through entertainment. As a reception phenomenon, entertainment is an experiential response that involves enjoyment and manifests itself through pleasurable feelings such as exhilaration, laughter, curiosity, excitement, thrill, relief, enjoyable sadness, tenderness, melancholy and/or sensory delight.[22]

The pedagogical impulse of digital drag, in applying this argument, is thus contingent on familiarity and affect. Familiarity is an effect of repetition and, indeed, my approach to digital drag also follows the reiterative qualities of this phenomenon, be it intertextual references to *RPDR* and other texts, self-reference, or the citation of cultural norms. In all of these cases, digital drag, coming back to the quotation by Ahmed, is highly performative. The kind of performativity I am interested in grounds my work in phenomenology: by taking to YouTube, the queens as influencers *create spaces* that allow them to become pedagogues of realness through performance, which allows their audience to inhabit said spaces in return. My analysis will foreground the importance of affective alignment; the digital spaces I am referring to here are similarly *affected by* the bond forged between queen and audience. If, therefore, the digital spaces of YouTube are to be of pedagogical significance, then the pedagogy advocated by the queens is one of togetherness and community.

Stuart Grant contends that, for "Heidegger, we bring essence, as an interpretive condition, to the things we encounter in our daily lives to render them intelligible as what they are," and outlines the goal of phenomenological inquiry as establishing "what something is, to what it belongs, and on what grounds it emerges."[23] Essence, in this context, is not to be confused with essentialist assumptions about static core identities. Rather, essence can be related to the cognitive frames activated in the processes of perception. When viewing an object, the object does not appear individualized *a priori*. Instead, phenomenology advocates that the object is eventually perceived as individualized because of its assumed essence, which precedes the object.

While we may understand this as a kind of type-token relation (with the type describing the essence), I suggest turning to Judith Butler's work on performativity and its connection to phenomenology in order to come to a different conclusion. In *Bodies That Matter* (1996), Butler argues that performativity is "the reiterative and citational practice by which discourse produces the effects that it names" and, as such, it "delimits and contours the body that it then claims to find prior to any and all signification."[24] Following this reasoning, bodies are made coherent and intelligible because they adhere to and thus reproduce norms that precede the formation of the subject. These norms, which we can relate to Heidegger's notion of essence, possess a naturalized status and appear as familiar *because of* repetition. We subsequently need not see essence as what objects or subjects *are*, but as what they *do*. In other words, and I am adopting Butler's and Ahmed's terminology here, they are made legible and intelligible through a clear positioning or orientation. This is where the phenomenological approach I am establishing here and the previously outlined spatiality of YouTube (as a heterotopic paratext to *RPDR*) coalesce: "The concept of 'orientation' allows us then to rethink the phenomenality of space—that is, how space is dependent on bodily inhabitance."[25] As such, digital drag's inhabitancy of other spaces is of particular interest when thinking of its queer potentialities in that it performatively produces the (digital) space which it simultaneously inhabits. The other spaces of YouTube are queer because of their queer positioning as paratextual, and the examples I am turning toward in the following make YouTube paratextual and queer in return. It is the experience of this in-betweenness by both queen and audience member that allows digital drag to become a pedagogical tool that does not rely on hierarchically organized epistemologies.

Approaching the queer potentialities of digital drag on YouTube requires certain re-orientations. Grant argues with Maurice Merleau-Ponty that phenomenology is a matter of rethinking one's own position[26]; a "phenomenological investigation seeks the way in which the object of study gives itself, taking the terms of the study from the object itself."[27] In line with Ahmed, who understands orientation as a relation or entanglement between "the bodily, the spatial, and the social,"[28] I acknowledge that the queens' relation to the medium, the audience, and (drag) culture at large results in different orientations. As such, I will begin my case study of digital drag on YouTube by looking at drag queens as performers, before turning to their position as influencers and, ultimately, as educators. I want to emphasize that I conceive of these as overlapping categories and that all of my examples feature aspects of all three. Nonetheless, this distinction is made to provide a more nuanced picture of how the queens' orientations simultaneously figure as orientations of their audiences. At the core of each segment thus lies my initial question: How does digital drag make use of the other spaces of YouTube to advocate or facilitate queer community as a form of queer pedagogy?

## *Category Is ... Performer: Learning Through Experientiality and Affect*

YouTube complicates the concept of performance for several interrelated reasons, the most prominent one being the mediated nature of YouTube videos. As a consequence, digital drag contradicts performance scholars Philip Auslander's and Peggy Phelan's notions of performance as live and immediate,[29] because it is (pre)recorded, and dismisses Erika Fischer-Lichte's criterion of bodily co-presence,[30] because audiences and performers are separated spatially by a screen and also temporally if it isn't a live stream. However, as Sean Redmond suggests:

when there is a carnal alignment between these three actants [i.e., screen, performer, viewer], an incredibly powerful and transformative encounter happens—one that enlivens the flesh of the actor, ignites the senses of the viewer, and transforms the reception of the performance into an asemiotic or experiential one where feeling dominates and an affecting response is elicited.[31]

Looking at digital drag through the lens of phenomenology allows us to see the performative qualities of these videos because of the orientations and bodily/spatial/affective relations they imply. Additionally, I argue that because digital drag is paratextual, and therefore always already part of the mediatized world of *RPDR*, it self-consciously positions itself as a representation of the second degree, allowing it to break with the semiosis of its core text and enter into the realm of performance.[32] This effect is amplified by the hierarchical relationship between core text and transmedia paratext: while in principle logically dependent on *RPDR*, digital drag queers linear processes of signification by simultaneously referring to self and other (within and beyond the *RPDR* cosmos). The in-betweenness of digital drag and its resulting ambiguous positioning evoke a queer effect that cannot be captured by semiotic means. In this sense, digital drag resonates more deeply with Butler's assertion that drag "reflects on the imitative structure by which hegemonic gender is itself produced and disputes heterosexuality's claim on naturalness and originality"[33] than *RPDR* itself. Put poignantly, while the queer potentialities of drag have been naturalized and semiotically coded within *RPDR* (and thus arguably lost their subversiveness), the other spaces of YouTube can reinvigorate their disruptive asemioticity through performance.

Let us have a look at an example: Alaska Thunderfuck 5000. The runner-up of season 5 (2013) and winner of *All Stars* season 2 (2016) regularly produces content on YouTube and has a strong focus on performance, especially in terms of music. Her videos are strongly associated with performance and at times include recordings of live events, such as Alaska's rendition of Lady Gaga and Bradley Cooper's "Shallow" from the 2018 *A Star Is Born* at the Empire Music Hall in Belfast in early 2019.[34] This performance is particularly interesting for three reasons: (1) While Alaska is made up as Alaska on stage (in drag, additionally wearing a hat), she sings the part of the male lead, Cooper's character Jackson, and is joined shortly after by a man singing Gaga's (Ally's) part. In the sense that drag already queers gender through exaggerated, or even hyperbolic, performances of gender and thus denaturalizes it, this performance adds another layer and shows that gender, in addition, is unstable. Alaska's drag aesthetic, in combination with gendered vocal roles, foregrounds the link between body and voice while simultaneously divorcing it from gender, which can no longer be upheld as an identificatory core. (2) The performance is highly referential, not only in the sense that it plays with *A Star Is Born*, but also in the way it interweaves the lyrics with allusions to *RPDR*. For example, the line "I'm falling" is supplemented with "like Farrah Moan" by Alaska, which is a direct reference to the Variety Show from the first episode of *All Stars* season 4 (2018—aired shortly before the performance), during which Farrah Moan slips on her costume and falls on the runway. (3) Even more so, the performance is self-referential. Alaska is not only aware of her position within the framework of the *RPDR* cosmos, the performance in its entirety is also aware of its mediatization. This results in a break of the semiotic constitution of the medium which is contingent on heteroreference. By substituting the referent of this representation with the signifier itself, the hierarchical organization of signs collapses and gives way to the distinct feeling of being included in a live performance. This further manifests in the perspective of the video: the segment is filmed from the audience's point of view, and its frame is wide enough for us to see the audience that attended the live event. Some audience members can also be seen filming Alaska with their smartphones. While this, on the one hand, breaks with the illusion of liveness because the video reflects on its own mediatedness, the fact that it is not a live performance, the inclusion of the audience, whose applause, cheering, and singing we hear throughout the video, on the other hand, creates an illusion of bodily presence. Sharing this performance on Alaska's official channel therefore also results in inclusion because it allows those unable to attend the live event to access it—and to feel as though they were part of it.

In contrast to recordings of live performances, Alaska's channel also features several professionally produced music videos. The example I want to focus on in more detail is her single "Valentina,"[35] released after the end of season 9 of *RPDR* (2017), in which Valentina was shockingly eliminated during a lip sync to Ariana Grande's "Greedy." Similar to Alaska's "Shallow" performance, "Valentina," which constitutes a parody of the 2017 hit single "Despacito," is extremely referential. While the song choice itself and the Spanish chorus draw on Valentina's image as a Latinx queen, the lyrics more specifically recount iconic moments involving Valentina on the show, some of them more overtly (the use of a mask and references to Valentina's lip sync performance and elimination) than others ("We're sorry. You have reached a number that has been disconnected or is no longer in service" is a reference to Farrah Moan's statement during the reunion that Valentina no longer returns her calls). Other references include the question why Nina Bo'Nina Brown was not allowed to play Blac Chyna in the Kardashian musical maxi challenge, Aja's dissatisfaction with the judges' critiques during *Untucked*, or a rose petal reveal reminiscent of Sasha Velour's "So Emotional" lip sync from the grand finale of season 9. Alaska's performance is thereby also characterized by self-reference—she is wearing a snake bra in allusion to her being called the queen of snakes after her tantrum on *All Stars* season 2—and, as such, she connects her own storyline from the show with that of Valentina. This video performs this conflation through Alaska's drag aesthetic that merges both queens' looks, either with Alaska as Alaska wearing Valentina's mask or with Alaska dressed as confessional-look Valentina, queering drag altogether: Justin Honard a.k.a. Alaska Thunderfuck plays Valentina a.k.a. James Leyva, which playfully bends reductive (read: straightened) notions of drag as "men dressing up as women."[36]

In contrast to the "Shallow" performance, "Valentina" cannot uphold an illusion of bodily presence. Still, the video exemplifies how performance can establish community through affective alignment. Alaska echoes fan reactions to Valentina's unexpected elimination and gives voice to her own disappointment, contemplating "how many challenges [she] could have slayed / But they made [her] turn and walk away." Of course, Alaska's repeated use of the Spanish "favorito" holds a certain double entendre, for it simultaneously shows her appreciation for Valentina and alludes to the title of Fan Favorite the other queens of the season gave her (as opposed to being crowned Miss Congeniality). However, the underlying irony of this statement does not dissociate viewers from Alaska's performance. On the contrary, while a potentially positive response to Valentina affectively aligns Alaska with her viewers (who are presumably also fans of *RPDR*), they would need to be familiar with the show to comprehend this double meaning. As such, even an ironic or parodic reading of the video supports the notion of community because it presupposes a shared knowledge. This shared knowledge, in turn, contributes to a sense of intimacy between performer and audience,[37] which becomes a central point in how digital drag produces spaces for queer pedagogy: coming together as communicating at eye level; *sharing as teaching*.[38]

Since music videos have come to be a very conspicuous trend in queens' post–*RPDR* career paths, it is noteworthy that their performances follow different trajectories, a small selection of which I want to touch upon here: (1) As we have seen with Alaska's "Valentina," a lot of drag queens' music is based on parody, which is unsurprising in the sense that drag itself is parodic in its engagement with gender, an aspect explicitly referenced by Alaska. (2) Some queens use music to market themselves and to shape their brand identity. In "The Big Girl,"[39] season 9 and 10's Eureka O'Hara builds her brand as the self-proclaimed Elephant Queen on the basis of her being a plus-sized queen, the eponymous big girl. (3) In other cases, the (re)shaping of the individual brand happens in accordance with a reinforcement of *RPDR*'s brand value. One of the most common practices in this regard is the release of songs in the week the songs were featured on the show, such as Naomi Smalls's "Pose,"[40] which she first performed during the *All Stars* season 4 variety show. (4) Queens like Jinkx Monsoon consider themselves drag musicians and release music that, on the surface, has no connection to *RPDR* at all. "Cartoons and Vodka,"[41] for example, is a playful palimpsest of cartoons, which surely has the potential of evoking a feeling of nostalgia that signals a shared affective response by Jinkx and her audience.

To recapitulate, because digital drag is paratextual, it inherently holds a potential of breaking through the stasis and semiotic constitution of its core text in asemiotic, performative moments that unfold because of the perception of the queen, the performer, as a phenomenal body through the screen. Based on shared knowledge, cognitive and affective alignment (both evoked by means of referentialization) as well as the illusion or experience of bodily presence, digital drag creates a sense of community through performance. This potential for community building is rooted in YouTube's heterotopic structures: as a space that is *para* to, situated besides, *RPDR*, YouTube provides queens with agency over their own performances as opposed to streamlined and regulated (i.e., semioticized and coded) performances on the show. In this sense, digital drag is characterized by alternative orientations of performers toward audiences, themselves and their brands, the show—which, as we have seen, can also happen in a critical or parodic manner—or other queens and (drag) culture in general. Alaska's music video "The T"[42] illustrates how the last point, in particular, leads us to the next dimension, queens as influencers. Besides featuring beloved *RPDR* alumnae such as Adore Delano, Ginger Minj, Katya, Willam, and Trixie Mattel, Alaska comments on the 2016 presidential election: "Let's pay women an equal wage / No seriously, what the fuck."[43] Such statements emphasize digital drag's position as heterotopic paratext even more in that they unveil what we might consider the queens' personal (political) opinions, views that cannot be shared on the show unfiltered, contributing to a sense of authenticity that may eventually enhance a feeling of collectiveness.

## *Category Is…Influencer: Learning Through Intimacy, Authenticity, and Familiarity*

While performances are pedagogical in the sense that they represent moments where content and form (the "what" and "how") coincide, which possesses an impetus that can reach the audience via cognition or affect, queens' orientation toward their viewers as influencers more overtly foregrounds a link to pedagogy. The word itself, *influencer* or *to influence*, approximates pedagogy because influence aims at a change in perception—and at a reorientation. As McNeil et al. state, "queer pedagogy can destabilize hegemonic conceptions of the *status quo* or the normal."[44] At the same time, influence aligns with performance because, while it is initiated by the influencer (similar to how pedagogy hinges on an educator, for example) and is thus characterized by asymmetry, it eventually becomes meaningful in bilateral exchange. If performance emerges in the (perceived) co-presence of performer and audience, then influence emerges in the (assumed) co-presence of or exchange between influencer and audience. As such, I conceive of digital drag as an emergent phenomenon that endows the relationship between queens and audiences with new meaning, which reverberates with McNeil et al.'s imagination of queer pedagogy as one that pushes "both learners and teachers to think about the grounds on which their own identities are constructed," thus placing emphasis on "potential and possibility"[45] rather than stability and normativity. Indeed, and as the following will show, digital drag reflects on the construction of identity through the performance of an authentic and relatable online identity. Additionally, digital drag makes use of its status as a heterotopic paratext to engage with the constructedness of *RPDR*, which, in turn, enhances the approachability of and potentials for identifying with queens as influencers.

The first example I want to focus on is season 9's Kimora Blac. Similar to Alaska's "The T" video, Kimora shares her political views online. However, in contrast to Alaska, Kimora engages in a face-to-face conversation with her viewers in the sense that she sits down right in front of the camera and talks about politics while doing her make-up with a partisan blue-themed eyeshadow look.[46] In the video, she urges her viewers to register to vote during the 2020 presidential election, stating that "it's important we move this country forward into the future."[47] Advocating social and political change through a rhetoric of collection,[48] Kimora emphasizes that she has been keeping up with politics and suggests that her viewers also educate themselves. In line with this, she gives a shout out to season 5 and *All Stars* season 2's Coco Montrese who, as Kimora argues, is very opinionated and engaged in politics: "She definitely is someone that you guys can follow and really school yourself."[49] While Kimora's openness adds to her authenticity because of her affective response to the subject matter, it also stresses her relatability as a person. In addition, her rhetoric situates her at eye level with her viewers, which I regard as central to a queer pedagogy that works around hierarchies that are institutionally erected, and it connects her role as influencer to the context of education.

Queens communicating with their audience at eye level is only possible because they appear as approachable online. The title of Strangelove's book, *Watching YouTube: Extraordinary Videos by Ordinary People*, speaks directly to the importance of projecting a relatable personality on YouTube.

Drag queens, in contrast, are usually perceived as extraordinary. However, drag queens' online appearances on YouTube show their more personal and approachable side, which allows them to contribute to queer pedagogy from within the community. Kimora's position as an ordinary person becomes most apparent in her love for make-up. Excited about becoming an affiliate of Morphe, Kimora shares her enthusiasm for the make-up brand: "As a consumer, as a buyer, as a lover, I am a true Morphe babe."[50] Similarly, in her review of the Shane Dawson × Jeffree Star Conspiracy collection,[51] Kimora highlights the shared habits and attitudes between her viewers and herself. Just like her viewers, Kimora is a fan of the products she reviews in the video and, by extension, of Shane and Jeffree. The video also features a give-away, illustrating the aforementioned reciprocity of influencers and consumers—Kimora gives back to the people who helped her become an influencer; she and her viewers constitute a community.

I want to elaborate on the notion of authenticity and connect it to the concept of intimacy, the intersection of which can be found in YouTube's position as a heterotopic paratext to *RPDR*. For Parsemain, the show itself features techniques that evoke a feeling of authenticity because of the inclusion of a view behind the scenes, a "backstage" perspective, if you will:

> The workroom and the interview commentaries are coded as spaces of authenticity. Transformation processes that occur in the workroom (applying and removing make-up, putting on and taking off wigs and costumes) highlight performativity and draw attention to the continuities between masculine and feminine, reality and performance. This backstage aesthetic is pedagogical because it invites viewers to learn by empathising with the drag queens. [...] The backstage is a pedagogical space where the contestants open up about their gender and sexual identity and social issues like homophobia, transphobia, bullying, eating disorders, illness and death.[52]

The link between intimacy and pedagogy resonates with my previous remarks that queer pedagogy emphasizes togetherness and community through affective alignment. While it is certainly true that the workroom scenes or the queens' confessionals pose as means of creating an effect of authenticity, Parsemain's argument does not acknowledge that all of these segments are still part of the show and thus of a staged event and edited transmission. Digital drag, in contrast, is situated in the peripheries of the *RPDR* cosmos and, as a paratext, constitutes a realm that is connected to, yet separate from, the show. I suggest viewing this paratextuality as a form of being backstage. Following this reading, then, it shows that YouTube draws on the pedagogical potential of what Parsemain asserts in relation to the show and amplifies it *because of* the even closer proximity between audience and queen on YouTube.

In their videos, we get to know the queens outside of the televised format of *RPDR* and thus seemingly in the privacy of their own homes. At the same time, the online spaces of YouTube allow viewers and queens to interact *across* the privacy of their homes, which they cannot do during their time on the show. The ways in which queens share their opinions and make-up tricks online thus establish a sense of intimacy. This impression is sustained through their role as influencers, their status as ordinary people, through which they invite their fans to participate in their lives. In the Digital Age, we seem to be able to be best friends with our favorite influencers. As a heterotopic space, the governing rules of the show do not necessarily apply to YouTube and, as such, digital drag holds the potential of spotlighting authenticity because of its affiliation to the core text.

While Kimora's videos also fulfill this function as backstage to *RPDR*, other videos more overtly foreground their connection to the show. At this point, reviews of the show by former contestants have become a rather popular genre on YouTube. The review genre also serves as a prime example of how digital drag in the sense I am addressing it here differs from authorized content disseminated by VH1 or WOW Presents. The Snatch Game episode of season 12, for instance, was reviewed by Miz Cracker in "Review with a Jew,"[53] by Soju in an episode of "Shot with Soju,"[54] and by Nina Bo'Nina Brown in her "RAWVIEW,"[55] among others. All three videos add something unique to their reviews: Cracker interviews the eliminated queen; Soju's review is broadcast live on YouTube; and Nina's video includes skits, lip syncing, and other performances. In contrast, season 2 runner-up Raven and season 3 winner Raja give their opinions on the season 12 queens' runway looks on "Fashion Photo Ruview,"[56] a weekly series on WOW Presents that is also uploaded to their YouTube channel. The name of this series itself (*Ru*view) aligns it with *RPDR*, and personal opinions do not feature regularly in this format. Instead, their commentary is limited to tooting or booting the looks the queens present on the runway, most of the time in accordance with the judges' decisions and sometimes relativizing them. Another emerging trend associated with digital drag that foregrounds its connection to *RPDR* is queens uploading their audition tapes for the show after they finish their run on their respective seasons. While the review videos provide a glimpse backstage because queens can share their own experiences and comment on the production conditions of the show, the audition tapes take viewers even further backstage by unveiling some of the otherwise invisible or inaccessible aspects of the show. And in a way, these backstage accounts are truly educational. Audition tapes can function as guides to getting cast for the show; opinion pieces or (fashion) reviews can educate about successful or unsuccessful performances and often connect their content to the history of drag, even if in some cases this merely entails the tradition of the show. The influence queens as influencers exert, in other words, holds a pedagogical potential.

By seemingly taking its viewers backstage, digital drag on YouTube promotes proximity between performers and audiences. The technological affordances of social media additionally reinforce this bond. Content posted by queens is consumable independently from time and space, and queens speak to their audiences via their own screens. As a result, digital drag fosters community through familiarity and viewers' emotional investments; according to Crystal Abidin, the "allure of influencers is premised on the ways they engage with their followers to give the impression of exclusive, intimate exchange."[57] While intimacy online ultimately remains an illusion, from a phenomenological perspective, the *experience* or *perception* of intimacy through a feeling of being addressed individually and of knowing the queen is not any less real or relevant when it comes to questions of community building. On the contrary, as Alexandra Hauke and I argue in an article on Jeffree Star, being an influencer is "not only dependent on one's ordinariness but also on the validity of one's unique, sincere, and consistent identity."[58] Digital drag more overtly features consistent online identities than other influencers do. Because drag queens already come with a specific persona when leaving the show, their viewers know what to expect of them. The impression that we know these queens personally arises from our familiarity with them garnered from *RPDR*.

At this point, the queens' roles as performers and influencers somewhat paradoxically lead to rather conflicting interpretations of the phenomenon of digital drag: (1) Viewing digital drag in terms of performance highlights the imitative nature of gender constitution. Therein lies the subversive potential of drag, which, as we have seen, is limited in *RPDR* due to the assimilation to the show's normative demands and extricated through digital self-representations on YouTube. Consequently, digital drag teaches about the constructedness of identity (as well as the unoriginality of gender) and rejects reductive and essentialist notions of stable identities. (2) From the perspective of queens as influencers, digital drag does not necessarily follow this trajectory. Instead, drag queens on YouTube are seen as originals, as authentic people. The fact that the queens' drag personae are, similar to Chris Rojek's concept of the celeactor,[59] stable (because they are consciously performed and intentionally constructed), rather than resulting in distanciation, substantiates the authenticity of their performance. They appear as coherent whereas, on the show, the breakdown between staged performances and backstage storylines denaturalizes the performances of both drag and what is framed as personal, private identities. In this sense, digital drag does not educate as much *about* identity as it does *through* identity. The promise of familiarity and intimate exchange, of seemingly experiencing the private queen as opposed to their public image on *RPDR*, makes digital drag genuinely pedagogical because viewers can relate to the queens on an intimate, affective, and experiential level. I do not think that these two potentially conflicting interpretations are mutually exclusive. They merely arise out of different orientations, meaning that the relationship between queen, medium, and audience varies in both cases. As I indicated earlier, these orientations—and with them the queens' positions—are overlapping and exist simultaneously; they both contribute to community building in similar ways, namely via the establishment of connections and relations across the ontological border of the screen.

## *Category Is ... Educator: Learning Through Sharing, Representation, and Participation*

At the same time as the (felt/experienced) connection between queens and audiences offers fruitful ground for the previously discussed nexus of performance and influence, it also creates spaces for queer pedagogy. Digital drag's emphasis on affective alignment, proximity and intimacy, as well as the practice of sharing, whether it be stories or knowledge in general, enables viewers to "understand queer experiences and issues through empathy."[60] As such, queens' roles as both performers and influencers are always intrinsically connected to their position as educators. Looked at through the notion of orientation, queens as educators signify a conglomeration of the other two in that they are not primarily oriented toward either medium, self, or audience. Instead, I want to suggest that queens as educators make use of the other spaces of YouTube (as medium) to promote community among their audiences, in the sense of both community building online and belonging in the LGBTQ+ community, through their self-representations. Their ability to perform and their perception as influencers thus allow queens as educators to foreground queer ways of being in the world and, additionally, to show what it "mean[s] to be 'queer' in this age of digital technology."[61] The queer pedagogy of digital drag advocates alternative positionings and epistemologies that counter hegemonic convictions of, for example, gender, sexuality, or identity. This pedagogical impetus is thereby contingent on relationality, not only in the sense that it establishes queer contact between queens and audiences, but also because, as heterotopic paratext, digital drag exists outside of, albeit always in relation to, *RPDR* and, by extension, all remaining space, including hegemonic heteronormative culture. While all previously discussed examples can thus be viewed in terms of pedagogy,[62] in the following I want to look at videos that explicitly address questions of queerness or queer identities.

Violet Chachki introduces her channel as a place for "all things entertaining and glamorous but also a bit historical and educational."[63] Indeed, the videos featured on her channel celebrate fashion, beauty, and the art of drag by paying homage to the artists who came before Violet and, as such, foreground both an emphasis on educating about LGBTQ+ histories and communities as she acknowledges the lasting impact of queer icons and trailblazers. The example I want to single out here is a make-up tutorial inspired by cult figure Divine as part of her Digital Drag series, which lends its name to the title of this essay.[64] Violet begins her video by referencing Pride Month, claiming that she does not know what *pride month* means because, for her, pride happens all year long: "All the content I make is pride content. […] I thought it'd be cool, this month in particular, to celebrate people and queer icons that have inspired me, have inspired my drag, have inspired the gay rights movement, and have like a signature style, a signature look."[65] In the video, in addition to showing her viewers how to create one of these signature looks, similar to regular make-up tutorials, she explains where her choices come from and familiarizes her audience with the work of Divine, including her beginnings in pageantry and the transformation of her drag aesthetic after meeting director John Waters. To Violet, Divine was the first drag superstar in the realm of television and film, with classics such as *Pink Flamingos* (1972), *Female Trouble* (1974), or *Hairspray* (1988), even though she mentions Barbette, female impersonator and aerialist (like Chachki herself) in the 1930s, in passing as another precursor.

The season 7 (2015) winner connects this lesson on Divine with queer community building by establishing a connection between pasts, presents, and potential futures of drag and queer expression in general: "Divine ran so Ru[Paul] could walk. And Ru ran so I could walk."[66] The work done by Violet and the other queens who share their work on YouTube in turn paves the way for future queer endeavors in the online realm. Representation and participation thereby constitute key components in how queer communities are formed. We see their effects online all the time, with more and more people, especially of a younger demographic, turning toward social media to share their opinions, experiences, and love for make-up and the art of drag. Much of the queer representation we see online would not be possible if it were not for the immense popularity of *RPDR* and its paratextual spread into other realms like YouTube. As such, and in contrast to *RPDR*, digital drag does not only open up spaces for negotiating queerness, but *creates* new spaces where queer expression is possible, detached from the normative regulations of a TV show. I thus want to return to one of my opening arguments: digital drag is in itself performative because it produces and (re) configures queer-positive spaces that emerge as other to hegemonic spaces. These spaces can be seen as educational or pedagogical because of the communal work they render viable and the (social) change at which they aim.[67]

Having a public platform like a YouTube channel and the visibility of a former *RPDR* contestant certainly comes with a lot of expectations and, as Gia Gunn stated in her video "Transgender Queens on RuPaul's Drag Race,"[68] responsibilities. In the video, Gia responded to the infamous RuPaul interview where he argued that transgender women and so-called "bio queens" should not be allowed to compete on *RPDR*, which led to numerous allegations of transphobia or a generally cis-centrist bias of the show. RuPaul argued, "You can identify as a woman and say you're transitioning, but it changes once you start changing your body."[69] Rather diplomatic in her tone, Gia (who eventually returned for an *All Stars* season in 2018 as an out-and-proud transgender woman) speaks out for people of the LGBTQ+ community who are hurt or do not feel heard or seen by such a statement. While she acknowledges the success of the show in opening doors and prompting discussions in mainstream media about queer issues, she urges RuPaul, the show, and the viewing public to not stop there but continue with this practice.[70] I argue that one way of sparking or continuing these conversations lies in the paratexts of *RPDR*: social media in particular, through their interactive features, allow for a broader engagement with conflicted topics such as transness and drag. Gia uses the video to share her personal story, emphasizing that "the art form [of drag] is sacred as it represents [her] evolvement and self-discovery," shedding light on the transformative power of drag that goes beyond make-up and outfit, for which she is praised in the comment section.[71] What Gia teaches her viewers is ultimately not only how trans identities are excluded from or marginalized within dominant discourses within hegemonic and even queer cultures. She is also concerned with the potentialities of drag in terms of queer expression and queer subjectivity and reminds her viewers to "be confident in who [they] are."[72]

According to Gia, a reason for negative reactions toward RuPaul's interview lies in the different definitions of or approaches to drag. While Gia claims that, to her, drag is "universal," she argues that RuPaul bases his arguments on what she refers to as "traditional" notions of drag that highlight transformation and whose inherent irony is compromised if the drag artist is a woman assigned female at birth or a post-operative transgender woman.[73] As a heterotopic paratext to *RPDR*, such statements can be made because digital drag is only peripherally affiliated to the show. However, they always also refer back to the show. Therein lies the pedagogical potential of Gia's video: her perspective as a transgender woman who has competed on the show before complements the discourse of transness and drag with alternative forms of knowledge that the show cannot provide. Gia teaches her viewers about the multitude of possibilities drag possesses and that there is not one singular—or right—way to do drag. In this sense, Gia's videos contribute to the visibility of transgender queens in the context of the show by following in the footsteps of trans people of color who fought for and contributed significantly to the visibility of queer people in the Gay Liberation Movement. Gia suggests that drag and transness have a shared history and, as such, educates those for whom RuPaul's interview perhaps was the only point of reference regarding this discourse.

## *The Pedagogy of Digital Drag*

The queer pedagogy of digital drag, as has been shown, is one of connectedness and mutual understanding. Questions of community building, identity, and subjectivity lie at the heart of digital drag and (or, as a form of) queer pedagogy. Taken together, the three dimensions I touched upon—queens as performers; queens as influencers; and queens as educators—suggest that queer community building on YouTube is facilitated through processes of sharing (in the sense of producing and disseminating knowledge through narrative), affective and cognitive alignment, (the illusion of) bodily co-presence and proximity, the promise of intimate exchange as well as familiarity, emotional investment, representation, and participation. The pedagogy of digital drag is thereby contingent on its alternative and, as we have seen, rather queer positioning: as a heterotopic paratext to *RPDR*, digital drag creates spaces that are other to the more restrictive environments of the show or hegemonic culture in which such community building is impeded by a normative straightening of discourse. Digital drag thereby constitutes an emergent phenomenon that performatively (re)produces and queers space. On YouTube, drag queens are not just performers, influencers, or educators. Their embodiment of several overlapping roles highlights the immense potential of digital drag as a communal and pedagogical form that expresses alternative epistemologies, orientations, and relationalities between content, its contexts and creators, the medium, and consumers. While *RPDR* has taught us the importance of reading, digital drag decidedly takes a different route. It teaches us the importance of community. And so if reading is *what? Fundamental!*, then watching digital drag on YouTube is *what? Pedagogical*.

## *Mini Challenge: Discussion Questions*

- On their own YouTube channels, drag queens, who are most often perceived as extraordinary beings, assume the role of the ordinary, relatable social media influencer. How does this ambivalent

characterization of queens as simultaneously approachable and unapproachable contribute to the formation of community? How might this (online) community be connected to intercultural and digital pedagogies?
- In a YouTube video of your choice, identify overlaps between drag queens' roles as performers, influencers, and educators. What does their occupation of these different categories teach us about drag as well as (queer) identity?
- Where do you see pedagogical potential in the ways digital drag plays with proximity and distance (1) in terms of its relation to *RPDR* and (2) in the creation of community, especially during the COVID-19 pandemic?

## *Maxi Challenge: Activities and Assignments*

Since the essay is concerned with the phenomenality of digital drag and its queer positioning within the *RPDR* cosmos—and in order to discuss the influence of digital drag's ambivalent affiliation to the show on questions of subversion, community, and pedagogy—it is useful to **compare (para)textual elements with varying degrees of officiality.** For example, *RPDR* itself features with its confessionals and werk-room sequences an alleged glimpse backstage, providing a platform for queens to share their ideas. This function is more strongly pronounced in *RPDR*'s paratexts like *Untucked* or even the online presences of WOW Presents on YouTube and other social media. **Juxtaposing these different formats, students will be able to see how the (institutional and medial) frame of each allows queens to articulate themselves more or less freely.** Moving on to queens' own YouTube channels, students will perceive (dis)continuities among the examples that speak to the unique position of digital drag. These observations will help students approach digital drag as outlined in the essay which, in turn, will allow students to engage with any of the aforementioned examples critically by attending to the **potential of each to effectively queer discourses created and perpetuated by the show and how this potential facilitates the emergence of queens as (queer) pedagogues of realness.**

## Notes

1. Rich, Adrienne. *Blood, Bread, and Poetry: Selected Prose 1979–1985: Selected Prose 1979-1985*, W. W. Norton & Company, 17 July 1994.

2. "Divine | Violet Chachki's Digital Drag." Youtube, uploaded by Violet Chachki, 27 Jun. 2019, https://youtu.be/xkT6jtpCjtE.

3. See also David Gudelunas, "Digital Extensions, Experiential Extensions and Hair Extensions: *RuPaul's Drag Race* and the New Media Environment." *RuPaul's Drag Race and the Shifting Visibility of Drag Culture*, edited by Niall Brennan and David Gudelunas, Palgrave Macmillan, 2017, p. 231.
 4. While my discussion here is limited to former *RPDR* contestants and YouTube, I am sure that digital drag provides fruitful ground for further investigations into the significance of digital drag cultures and the digitization of entertainment and performance. I am polishing this essay during the COVID-19 pandemic, and it is interesting to see how the phenomenon I am describing here (and initially drafted for this edited collection pre-pandemic) is gradually becoming one of the main ways in which drag performance is made possible in times of physical distancing. The show also had to adopt digital means of performing, most significantly in season 12, where the reunion episode as well as the Grand Finale were hosted via video chat.
 5. McNeil, Elizabeth, James E. Wermers, and Joshua O. Lunn. "Introduction: Mapping Queer Space(s)." *Mapping Queer Space(s) of Praxis and Pedagogy*, edited by Elizabeth McNeil, James E. Wermers, and Joshua O. Lunn, Palgrave Macmillan, 2018, pp. 1–17, p. 4.
 6. Jenkins, Henry. *Convergence Culture: Where Old and New Media Collide*. New York University Press, 2006, p. 3.
 7. Hills, Matt. "Transmedia Paratexts: Informational, Commercial, Diegetic, and Auratic Circulation." *The Routledge Companion to Transmedia Studies*, edited by Matthew Freeman and Renira Rampazzo Gambarato, Routledge, 2019, p. 290.
 8. See Mittell, Jason. *Complex TV: The Poetics of Contemporary Television Storytelling*. New York University Press, 2015.
 9. Hills, p. 294.
 10. See also Henry Jenkins's notion of transmedia storytelling, especially the concepts of drillability and spreadability: Henry Jenkins, "The Revenge of the Origami Unicorn: Seven Principles of Transmedia Storytelling (Well, Two Actually. Five More on Friday)." *Confessions of an Aca-Fan*, December 12, 2009, henryjenkins.org/blog/2009/12/the_revenge_of_the_origami_uni.html.
 11. Strangelove, Michael. *Watching YouTube: Extraordinary Videos By Ordinary People*. University of Toronto Press, 2010, p. 87.
 12. Genette, Gérard. *Paratexts: Thresholds of Interpretation*, translated by Jane E. Lewin. Cambridge University Press, 1997, p. 2.
 13. Foucault, Michel. "Of Other Spaces." *Diacritics*, translated by Jay Miskowiec, vol. 16, no. 1, 1986, p. 24.
 14. Foucault thereby rests his notion of heterotopia upon six core principles: (1) the ability of every culture to constitute heterotopias; (2) the function of heterotopias is not ahistorical; (3) heterotopias' ability to combine several sites that are incompatible in reality; (4) heterotopias are linked to slices in time; (5) heterotopias are not freely accessible; and (6) heterotopias have a function in relation to all remaining spaces (pp. 24–27).
 15. See also Sara Ahmed's deliberations on space and affect. Sara Ahmed, "Queer Feelings." *The Routledge Queer Studies Reader*, edited by Donald E. Hall and Annamarie Jagose, Routledge, 2013, pp. 422–41.
 16. Nash, Catherine, and Andrew Gorman-Murray. "Queer Mobilities and New Spatial Media." *The Geographies of Digital Sexuality*, edited by Catherine Nash and Andrew Goman-Murray, Palgrave Macmillan, 2019, p. 30.
 17. *Ibid.*, pp. 32–33.
 18. Anderson, Benedict. *Imagined Communities: Reflections on the Origin and Spread of Nationalism*. Verso, 2006, p. 6.
 19. See also Page, Ruth. *Narratives Online: Shared Stories in Social Media*. Cambridge University Press, 2018.
 20. Siebler, Kay. *Learning Queer Identity in the Digital Age*. Palgrave Macmillan, 2016, p. 16.
 21. Ahmed, Sara. *Queer Phenomenology: Orientations, Objects, Others*. Duke University Press, 2006, p. 167.
 22. Parsemain, Ava Laure. *The Pedagogy of Queer TV*. Palgrave Macmillan, 2019, p. 4.
 23. Grant, Stuart. "The Essential Question: So What's Phenomenological About

Performance Phenomenology?" *Performance Phenomenology: To the Thing Itself*, edited by Stuart Grant, Jodie McNeilly-Renaudie, and Matthew Wagner, Palgrave Macmillan, 2019, p. 23.

24. Butler, Judith. *Bodies That Matter: On the Discursive Limits of Sex*, 1996, Routledge, 2011, p. xii; p. 6.

25. Ahmed, p. 6.

26. Grant, p. 25.

27. *Ibid.*, p. 26. See also Sondra Fraleigh, "A Phenomenology of Being Seen." *Performance Phenomenology: To the Thing Itself*, edited by Stuart Grant, Jodie McNeilly-Renaudie, and Matthew Wagner, Palgrave Macmillan, 2019, p. 90.

28. Ahmed, p. 181, n.1.

29. See Auslander, Philip. *Liveness: Performance in a Mediatized Culture*. Routledge, 2011; Phelan, Peggy. *Unmarked: The Politics of Performance*. Routledge, 1996.

30. Fischer-Lichte, Erika. *The Transformative Power of Performance: A New Aesthetics*, translated by Saskya Iris Jain, Routledge, 2008, p. 32.

31. Redmond, Sean. "Sensing Film Performance." *Performance Phenomenology: To the Thing Itself*, edited by Stuart Grant, Jodie McNeilly-Renaudie, and Matthew Wagner, Palgrave Macmillan, 2019, p. 167.

32. I hereby counter Henn et al.'s argument that "semiotic power of performances of self and of culture intensify" (290) via this form of mediatization over social media. See Ronaldo Henn, Felipe Viero Kolinski Machade, and Christian Gonzatti, "'We're All Born Naked and the Rest is Drag': The Performativity of Bodies Constructed in Digital Networks." *RuPaul's Drag Race and the Shifting Visibility of Drag Culture*, edited by Niall Brennan and David Gudelunas, Palgrave Macmillan, 2017, pp. 287–303.

33. Butler, p. 85.

34. "Shallow—Belfast—2.23.19." YouTube, uploaded by Alaska Thunderfuck, 24 Feb. 2019, https://youtu.be/99uByxN-ts4.

35. "Valentina—[Official]." YouTube, uploaded by Alaska Thunderfuck, 13 Oct. 2017, https://youtu.be/7SKkkfn2zLc.

36. On her Instagram, Valentina calls herself a "Non-binary Goddess," adding yet another layer to this discussion and exposing the cisnormative bias of such discussions of drag ("Valentina @Allaboutvalentina." *Instagram*, 2020, www.instagram.com/allaboutvalentina/?hl=en).

37. I will elaborate on the concept of intimacy or, rather, the illusion and perception of intimate exchange, in the section on queens as influencers.

38. I am building on Ruth Page's concept of shared stories here. Her distinction between sharing as a form of telling and distribution (18) can be used to approximate the ways in which social media can function as a medium of education—in the sense that they provide platforms for the production (telling) and dissemination (distribution) of knowledge and values.

39. "Eureka O'Hara—The Big Girl (Official Music Video)." YouTube, uploaded by Eureka O'Hara, 28 June 2018, https://youtu.be/QUhEl-LSw5Q.

40. "Pose—Naomi Smalls (Official Video)." YouTube, uploaded by Naomi Smalls, 16 Dec. 2018, https://youtu.be/-LnqdiACjdw.

41. "Cartoons and Vodka—Official Music Video—Jinkx Monsoon." YouTube, uploaded by Jinkx Monsoon, 12 Jan. 2018, https://youtu.be/ejWnwVWuoCo.

42. "Alaska Thunderfuck—The T (feat. Adore Delano) [Official]." YouTube, uploaded by Alaska Thunderfuck, 13. Oct. 2016, https://youtu.be/9Xw5VkCpxRg.

43. *Ibid.*

44. McNeil et al., p. 3.

45. *Ibid.*, par. 1.

46. "#SUPERTUESDAY—MAKE YOUR VOTE COUNT, ELECTION MAKEUP TUTORIAL & DRAG RACE REVIEW | Kimora Blac." YouTube, uploaded by Kimora Blac, 3 Mar. 2020, https://youtu.be/-QIdPnDGPAY.

47. *Ibid.*

48. For a discussion of the term "rhetoric of collection," see Paolo Gerbaudo, "Cahiers de doleance 2.0: Crowd-Sourced Social Justice Blogs and the Emergence of a Rhetoric of

Collection in Social Media Activism." *Media Activism: Charting an Evolving Field of Research*, edited by Victor Pickard and Guobin Yang, Routledge, pp. 139–150.

49. See "#SUPERTUESDAY—MAKE YOUR VOTE COUNT, ELECTION MAKEUP TUTORIAL & DRAG RACE REVIEW | Kimora Blac.."

50. *Ibid.*

51. "GIVEAWAY!! JEFFREE STAR X SHANE DAWSON CONSPIRACY PALETTE & FIRST IMPRESSION | Kimora Blac." YouTube, uploaded by Kimora Blac, 5 Nov. 2019, https://youtu.be/mDQbgBKI3GM.

52. Parsemain, p. 110.

53. "Miz Cracker's Review with a Jew—S12 E06 Feat. Aiden Zhane." YouTube, uploaded by Miz Cracker, 5 Apr. 2020, https://youtu.be/u8n2NR_yS-k.

54. "RuPaul's DRAG RACE Season 12 Episode 6 Review w/ Chester Lockhart | Shot With Soju LIVE!." YouTube, uploaded by Soju, 5 Apr. 2020, https://youtu.be/9yHpS3MLCZo.

55. "NINA'S RPDR SEASON 12 SNATCH GAME RAWVIEW." YouTube, uploaded by Nina Bo'Nina Brown, 5 Apr. 2020, https://www.youtube.com/watch?v=VJtXXcFUmXE.

56. "FASHION PHOTO RUVIEW: Frozen Eleganza." YouTube, uploaded by WOW Presents, 8 Apr. 2020, https://www.youtube.com/watch?v=HlK6DKeFvsA.

57. Abidin, Crystal. "Communicative Intimacies: Influencers and Perceived Interconnectedness." *Ada: A Journal of Gender, New Media & Technology*, vol. 8, 2015, http://adanewmedia.org/2015/11/issue8-abidin/.

58. Hauke, Alexandra, & Zitzelsberger, Florian. "Subscribe to My Empire: Jeffree Star and Self-Branding on YouTube." *The Power of Makeup: Evolving Commerce, Community, and Identity in the Modern Makeup Tutorial*, edited by Clare Douglass Little, Lexington Books, 2020, p. 88.

59. See Rojek, Chris. *Celebrity*. Reaktion Books, 2001. Rojek defines the cele-actor as "a fictional character who is either momentarily ubiquitous or becomes an institutionalized feature of popular culture. [...] They cater to the public appetite for a character type that sums up the times" (23). This concept can be used as an avenue into the question why the queens' personae are so stable: Once they appeared on the show, the queens are likely to be identified by or branded with certain traits and behavior. Their popularity from the show relies on these features so that, in order to keep their fan base, their drag persona will stabilize even more to satisfy the demands of the *RPDR* audience (an example for this would be Alaska playing into the queen of snakes image after her run on *All Stars* season 2). This also explains why queens who were portrayed in an unfavorable light on the show engage in a re-branding after their elimination.

60. Parsemain, p. 111.

61. Siebler, p. 13.

62. I have touched upon several examples of queer pedagogy in relation to community. Among the examples I did not address in detail are the clear educational function of tutorials as well as videos that promote and educate about specific content.

63. Chachki, Violet. "Violet Chachki." YouTube, www.youtube.com/user/VioletChachki/about.

64. See "Divine | Violet Chachki's Digital Drag."

65. *Ibid.*

66. *Ibid.*

67. See also Siebler, p. 24 and Donna Hancox, "Transmedia for Social Change: Evolving Approaches to Activism and Representation." *The Routledge Companion to Transmedia Studies*, Routledge, 2019, pp. 332–339.

68. "Transgender Queens on Rupaul's Drag Race | GIA GUNN." YouTube, uploaded by Gia Gunn Entertainment, March 6, 2018, https://youtu.be/la9QHkzID4M.

69. Levin, Sam. "Who Can Be a Drag Queen? RuPaul's Trans Comments Fuel Calls For Inclusion." *The Guardian*, March 8, 2018, https://www.theguardian.com/tv-and-radio/2018/mar/08/rupaul-drag-race-transgender-performers-diversity.

70. "Transgender Queens on Rupaul's Drag Race | GIA GUNN."

71. *Ibid.*

72. *Ibid.*

73. *Ibid.*

# Pedagogies, Praxis, and Privilege

*RuPaulean Communities of Care*

MANDY PENNEY

"It do take nerve to flatten the curve."
—RuPaul Charles, reunion episode, season 12

In the first few minutes of the reunion episode for the twelfth season of *RuPaul's Drag Race* (*RPDR*), Ru and "his girls" do not shy away from directly confronting the traumatic effects of the lethal COVID-19 pandemic. Noting that "for the first time in *Drag Race* herstory, 'safe' is a good word," RuPaul lets viewers know that all of the drag queen contestants are safe and healthy.[1] Following on the heels of the opening group number, the queens sing, "like Macaulay at Christmas / We're home alone, too."[2] The production choice to not pretend the final two episodes of the show were a reflection of "business as usual" represents an important pedagogical choice that educators working in formal academic spaces would do well to emulate; the show emphasizes shared experiences and solidarity during a troubling time. Watching the final two episodes of the twelfth season as a cis, white, and queer settler, anxious woman, and academic writing center administrator, as well as a fan of the *RPDR* franchise, prompted me to reflect on the intersections of my own identities and the ways that I can draw on *RPDR*'s public pedagogy as I work to support students, faculty, and staff at my institution.[3] To do so, I consider the ways in which the show enacts a public pedagogy that deftly pivots its strategies for audience engagement during a time of global crisis.

Overall, the reunion and finale episodes of season 12 offer a useful site of analysis on the intersection of place-making, transmediation, and the new COVID-19-prompted media landscape. In so doing, they have prompted me to reflect on my relationship with the show and how that relationship is mediated through the various identities and roles I inhabit and embody. On May 29, 2020, I curled up in my armchair on Treaty 6 Territory (London, Ontario) to watch the finale of *RPDR*, season 12. Joining me through a Discord audio channel was my friend, Jen, herself watching the finale from her home on Treaty 13 land (Toronto, Ontario). I was interested, as a fan, writing center administrator, and academic, to see how the show would—or would not—succeed in building community and audience engagement without the now-familiar glitzy spectacle of the live, audience-packed finale viewers have become used to in the pandemic pre-times.[4]

In this essay I suggest that the reunion and finale episodes of *RPDR* season 12 offer a useful consideration of the possibilities of flexible, online learning in keeping with Jenkins' claim in *Convergence Culture* (2006) that media practices are migratory—an "audience … will go almost anywhere in search of the kinds of entertainment experiences they want."[5] The production and scripting choices in these final two episodes of the season have implications for public pedagogy in their demonstration that place-making and world-making continue even when it feels as though the world is ending. And what we might discern from these episodes about public pedagogy are also of import for those of us working and learning in academic institutions, struggling to make sense of a changed world while supporting our colleagues and students. The presence of the current pandemic-inflected media landscape makes clear that transmediation is about more than the flow of media *across* different contexts and mediums; rather, it is the flow of media *beyond* and *on the other side* of everything we thought we knew about the capacity of technology to create human connection alongside meaningful opportunities for education and critique.

As educators, we can and should observe the ways in which *RPDR* and the classroom (physical or virtual) are paratexts to each other; at the same time, we must look to the show's pedagogical choices and strategies for their failures as much as their successes. One important takeaway for academics when considering the public pedagogy enacted in *RPDR* is that our institutions remain constrained by and implicated in the same neoliberal framework as the show; thus, while we work to enact an ethics of care—with our students, our colleagues, and ourselves—in a moment of global trauma, we must also acknowledge and confront the reality that the same capitalist and colonizing structures that we can, do, and should critique in *RPDR* are mirrored in our academic spaces.[6] If we want to truly enact an ethics of care as we move into upcoming academic years, we need to think both locally and systemically about our pedagogy and our praxis. On stage and in the classroom, these spaces are paratextual mirrors of each other, each informing and mimicking the other. Ultimately, approaching the 2020 move to online requires attention to both the individual and systemic elements of care, community-building, and equity. The final two episodes of *RPDR* season 12, "Reunited: Alone Together" and "Grand Finale," considered together with the seasons and episodes that precede them, gesture toward the possibilities of digital technology for engagement, wellness, and learning. What RuPaulean pedagogy ultimately makes clear, however, is that the show's attempts to educate viewers must always be recognized as operating within the constraints of its profitable position within the reality show television industry.

## *Reflection[7]: My "Problematic Fave"[8]*

I have been a fan of the *RPDR* series since watching my first season 8 episode on Netflix Canada in the summer of 2017. As a recently-out queer woman, I was deeply invested in absorbing every drop of queer culture and history that I could get my hands, eyes, and ears on. That summer was not just the summer of *RPDR*; it was also the summer of Leslie Feinberg's *Stone Butch Blues*, Julie Maroh's comic book *Blue Is the Warmest Color*, Patricia Highsmith's *The Price of Salt*, and Ann Weldy's pulp lesbian series *Beebo Brinker*. I lost myself in Andrew Scott's performance in *Pride*, and I rewatched the 1993 HBO docudrama about the origins of the HIV/AIDS pandemic, *And the Band Played On*. I wanted to digest queer art and culture as an out-and-proud member of the community. What drew me to *RPDR* was not one thing in particular; I loved the fashion, the diversity of drag aesthetics, and the spectacle of it all. More than that, though, I appreciated the moments of queer learning offered to me by RuPaul and her girls.[9] Kim Chi's performance of her song "Fat, Femme, and Asian" in the finale as part of the Top Three spoke to me as a fat, cis, femme, rhythm-deprived lesbian. Overall, *RPDR* was a part of my newly-discovered queer community and supplemented my learning through its engaging characters, narratives, and performances.

Even while I became a fan, however, I was very aware of the ways in which the show was problematic, particularly when it comes to race. There is no dearth of criticism on this topic in both scholarly and popular sources, from the appropriation of African American Vernacular English by cisgender white queens, to the challenges that are designed to emphasize whiteness—it is, after all, "Night of 1000 Madonnas," not "Night of 1000 Toni Braxtons." Many BIPOC former contestants, viewers, and scholars have taken the time to criticize the show[10]; criticism that is warranted because of the show's lack of attention to microaggressions and the various ways in which queens of color are at a disadvantage, whether it is because of economic reasons, challenges that are white in nature, or because of the ways in which whiteness is privileged more broadly in our culture and established as the norm against which all people—drag queens included—are measured, so that white queens are generally seen as more polished, more graceful, and more relatable.

In addition to my position in society as a queer, middle-class, white woman committed to doing the work of anti-racism, decolonization, and community care, I am also an educator with a dual background in STEM and the humanities, working as the coordinator of a moderately-sized writing center on a small, liberal arts college. As I have shifted my attention throughout my career from seeking faculty positions to staff ones, I have also become increasingly invested in reading and generating scholarship on teaching and learning (SoTL), especially where it intersects with decolonization, anti-racism, public pedagogy, wellness, and justice. I am still learning what this means for me and how to be a good ally and accomplice as a white educator and an administrator in a system that is still stacked against BIPOC students, faculty, and staff. I am increasingly aware of and frustrated by the ways that marketplace capitalism shapes our decision-making practices and ongoing marginalization of Black scholars and students, Indigenous scholars and students, and other scholars and students of color. In my current academic role, I am working to develop a framework for anti-racism, decolonization, and diversity in writing center contexts at all levels of administration, teaching, and community interaction, from interviews and hiring processes to training, mentorship, and teaching practices. It is not, of course, enough to be committed to these things in my workplace; it is my responsibility as someone who has benefited from my position as a white, middle-class citizen living on Treaty land to bring an intersectional and anti-racist lens to bear on how I move through the world more generally; the renewed media coverage of the Black Lives Matter movement in the wake of the murder of George Floyd and the additional state-sanctioned police violence in the United States during protests have underscored the importance of white people taking responsibility for racist violence and systemic marginalization. Thus, I try to bring this work to my interactions with *RPDR* as a white academic, a queer person, and an activist, watching the show critically and carefully.

My experiences watching the two final episodes of season 12 felt vastly different to my experiences watching other finales. The specter of SARS-CoV2, the novel coronavirus, had dis-regulated my emotions due to my normally well-controlled anxiety disorder, and I felt unfocused and frightened most of the time. Watching *RPDR* was, for me at that moment, an opportunity to escape—to enjoy something I enjoyed prior to the beginning of quarantine on March 13, 2020. Of course, the show rightly acknowledges the collective moment of trauma and illness at the beginning of the reunion episode and indeed throughout the two-episode run. RuPaul's upbeat and engaging dialogue with the queens and towards the viewers served to remind me that "Miss Coronavirus won't stop us."[11] In the face of this evolving and ongoing public health threat, RuPaul encouraged us all to take it on the chin and keep moving forward, even if, like contestant Nicky Doll, we were all "eating [our] feelings and performing online."[12]

References to the pandemic were ever-present throughout the episodes, and while I was initially concerned that these would trigger my diagnosed anxiety disorder, the show seemed to have the opposite effect: I felt more engaged and connected to the queens and the final challenges than I had in any of the previous, pre–COVID-19 seasons. Part of this sense of relationship and community came from Brita's early admission that she had left New York City to stay with her parents—something I myself had considered as someone with high-risk chronic conditions living near several virus hotspots—and the lightly-delivered line, "She's an asthmatic queen!"[13] The reminders that this is a collective problem (even if it is not equitably dispersed in its effects, with mounting evidence that low-income and racialized communities are disproportionately affected by both the virus itself and the economic ramifications of the pandemic) served to make me feel less alone, as RuPaul reminded me, several months into isolation, that "it do take nerve to flatten the curve!" The platform for the final two episodes of season 12 evokes the popular video chat platform, Zoom, that any number of institutions use to hold meetings and classes while we are working and studying from home. The theme and design of the reunion episode references the look and feel of a slumber party, with all of the queens wearing pajama drag and RuPaul dressed in comfortable leisurewear and a facekini; the reunion felt consciously designed to give the audience the sense of being on the live video chat *with* the queens. The reminder, after the familiar reading challenge, that "the library is officially closed until the governor says we can reopen,"[14] reminded me that the illness, death, uncertainty, and fear that the world is experiencing is transitory—that someday, inevitably, the pandemic will end.

The lip sync performances in the finale episode, too, felt enriched by virtue of the living room setup. Like the queens, most of the viewers would also have been in our homes while viewing these episodes, whereas in earlier seasons, fans would often congregate in clubs and bars, as well as at house parties, to share the excitement of the finale in a social setting. The intimacy of being invited into the queens' private spaces echoed meetings and mentoring sessions I have had with colleagues and students, and it invoked thoughts about consent and privacy and who gets to see into a student's interior and home life. One of the season 12 Top Three, Jaida Essence Hall, made creative and memorable use of her tiny living room space in her second lip sync number (to "Get Up" by Ciara featuring Chamillionaire). One of the show's regular judges, Ross Matthews, was so impressed by the professionalism and engagement in her performance that he pointed out that it was as though she were "performing in Madison Square Garden."[15] Ultimately, I was thrilled with Jaida's performance and success on the show, and my conversation with my friend Jen afterwards focused on our excitement that Jaida was recognized so powerfully, as well as some of the ways that the last two episodes felt timely and relatable.

## Drag Race as (Troublesome) Pedagogy/RuPaul as (Troublesome) Educator

Whether we determine him to be successful in his teaching or not, there can be little argument that RuPaul is a public pedagogue. He occupies a space that in a Venn diagram would represent the convergence of teachers, ministers, and celebrities.[16] If the drag professors on *RPDR* spinoff series *Drag U* are its faculty, RuPaul is the teaching Dean, overseeing both the curriculum and administration of the programs he has built. In part because of the reach and audience of his show and teachings, it is our responsibility as educators to engage with RuPaul's pop-cultural paratext, among others, because of what it can teach us about the learning that is taking place both inside and outside the classroom and beyond the academy. Henry Giroux's work on public pedagogy and learning consistently argues that teachers need to keep up with and be informed by our students through an awareness of the varied spaces other than the classroom in which they learn. I propose that we push this further and recognize that teachers can and should also participate in moments of public-facing education in order to get ahead of teaching practices; in engaging with both the *content* and *strategies* of public pedagogy in practice, we can transform our practice to create more engaging and accessible opportunities for teaching and learning in academic spaces.

Fans of *RPDR* can engage with the show and its contestants across a broad range of digital and live contexts. In addition to the show itself, its companion and spin-off series (e.g., *Untucked* and *Drag U* on television, and on streaming apps, *What's the Tee* podcast hosted by RuPaul and Michelle Visage, and *RuPaul Fashion Photo Ruview* on YouTube) offer the opportunity to learn more about the queens competing in the hallmark series, listen in on the drama and infighting behind-the-scenes while the *RPDR* hosts are deliberating, and enjoy more of the fashion analysis and discussion hosted by seasoned queens, including past winners and show frontrunners. More than this, as Florian Zitzelsberger maintains in the previous essay, the presence of digital drag prior to the emergence of the COVID-19 pandemic represents a pedagogical and paratextual relationship to *RPDR*, in that it exists both alongside and at a certain remove from the hit show. In the ways that digital drag on YouTube and elsewhere supplement, complement, and diverge from *RPDR*, these para-texts "bridge the gap between performance and pedagogy" in a way that allows for "alternative epistemologies that transcend hegemonic understandings of embodiment and that...[emphasize] the importance of togetherness." Even pre-pandemic, therefore, there existed a range of digital spaces for audience engagement. Each of these spaces differ in their aesthetic, their logistics, and their strategies for audience engagement (where, here, the "audience" is constituted by those who follow the *RPDR* franchise), but each in their own way represent spaces where the audience is educated in the art, history, and culture of drag. For Zitzelsberger, digital engagement with drag embodies a depth that is characterized by "affective alignment," through which audiences inhabit and engage with/in the spaces created by the queens-as-performers, queens-as-influencers, and queens-as-educators.[17] Indeed, as Sean Michael Morris asserts, "digital learning (and by necessity, digital pedagogy) takes place all over the web."[18]

What the COVID-19 pandemic changed about the pre-existing drag multiverse is the necessary elimination of live, *in-person* interactions between the show(s) and its audience(s). In a world where masking, physical distancing, hand hygiene, and a preference towards outdoor interactions have increasingly become the evidence-based mitigation measures to avoid becoming infected by the novel coronavirus, events like the traditional *RPDR* reunion and finale episodes—and indeed, all live drag performances—become potential super-spreader events. In response to this health and safety risk, the franchise and its queens moved even more fully online, in a move that was, perhaps, gratifying to queens such as Aja of season 9 and *All Stars* season 3 and Kyne of the premiere season of *Canada's Drag Race* who have had the term "social media queen" thrown at them in an effort to diminish their ability to turn out looks without filters and to perform live and on the runway. In season 12, contestant Aiden Zhane was also looked down on by the other queens—especially by Brita—because *RPDR* was the first time she performed outside of her home; in the reunion episode, she pointed out that the pandemic had forced a return to her roots: "I started a bedroom queen, and I'm still a bedroom queen."[19]

What the final episodes of *RPDR*'s twelfth season do so well is to bring together the intimacy that Zitzelsberger suggests is pervasive in digital drag with the spectacle of a reality television season finale. Where the top three queens of the season—Crystal Methyd, Gigi Goode, and Jaida Essence Hall—offer engaging lip sync performances and intricate costuming, the reunion episode is designed and delivered to, as Zitzelsberger says, "show [the queens'] more personal and approachable side[s]." The development of this intimacy has become prevalent since the beginning of the pandemic, as commercials, sports broadcasts, and even primetime dramas borrow from the web to develop what Glen Creeber, in *Small Screen Aesthetics: From TV to the Internet* (2013), calls "aesthetic 'authenticity.'"[20] However, this kind of authenticity and intimacy is not unique to digital spaces; it predates the creation of the modern Internet.[21] Indeed, long before we had the "Zoom view" shot so prevalent online and in television shows since the pandemic began, we might also see the echoes of the opening sequence for *The Brady Bunch,* which aired from 1969 to 1974. Indeed, this hybridity between the aesthetics of digital, DIY spaces such as YouTube and the polished, high-budget reality television show reflects the degree to which we cannot speak of "a set of universal and ahistorical characteristics for TV and in the internet."[22] Instead, we can embrace the "historically specific characteristics that involve a complex mixture of styles and techniques that reflect the hybridity of the past, the converging worlds of the present and the mosaic 'mash ups' that are likely to define much of the future."[23]

While the two final episodes of season 12—especially "Queens Reunited"—are ostensibly framed through the language of care and community, the degree of care can be called into question when supplemented with information beyond the boundaries of what viewers saw on their screens during those episodes. There are ways in which the final two episodes of the twelfth season of *RPDR* enact, at least to some degree, an ethos of care and community at a time of widespread societal upheaval. From checking in with each of the queens at the beginning of the reunion episode (asking them where they are in the United States and how they were doing) to applauding their efforts to help livestream the show from their varied locations across the country, RuPaul expressed her gratitude for their work during "extraordinary times": "I want to applaud all the queens for pitching in like never before to ensure that this show must go on."[24] She goes on to thank her crew, noting that "out of caution for everyone's safety, we are all working from home tonight."[25] A large number of campuses across North America are requiring faculty, staff, and students to return to face-to-face learning despite the ongoing increase in COVID-19 cases, though some have begun to backtrack those plans, citing the dire case counts, especially in the United States.[26] *RPDR* in this particular moment at the close of season 12 exemplifies a focus on health and safety that many institutions have neglected to show to their communities.

The final episodes of season 12 also lampoon some of the by-now common experiences that educators have likely experienced while participating in live video chats. From RuPaul's cheesy '80s style geometric background to Carson's frozen screen (and series of still photos with hilarious expressions) to contestant Heidi N Closet's disappearance from her camera, leaving only an empty chair followed by the sound of a toilet flushing, the show succeeds in finding the ridiculous-yet-shared moments in our current reliance on technology and holding them up as examples of our collective experiences.[27]

At the same time that the two post–COVID-19 episodes of season 12 manage to capture the shared and sometimes hilarious moments of navigating technology in order to connect with others, it also succeeds only in offering a cursory practice of care. In his blog post "Designing for Care: Inclusive Pedagogies for Online Learning," Jesse Stommel carefully unpacks the importance of ensuring that our online learning spaces are set up not just for continuity of learning, but for the explicit and careful practice of care and community. Key among the practices that he asserts are necessary is the recognition that not all students will experience the effects of the pandemic equally: "We need to write policies," he argues, "and imagine new ways forward, for these students, the ones already struggling, already facing exclusion."[28] While RuPaul takes the time to check in with each queen at the beginning of "Reunited: Alone Together," the queens have no opportunity to offer a response any more nuanced than that they are fine, along with an identification of where they are geographically. On the show or in the classroom, if educators are going to engage with those around them, and ask questions about well-being, taking the time for honest answers and careful listening are equally or more important than the asking of the question in the first place. Two of Stommel's recommendations for creating a sense of belonging in students are to ask questions that are "genuine and open-ended" *and* to "wait for answers."[29] RuPaul asks the questions, but there is little reflection or follow-up on the answers that he receives.[30]

RuPaul's inability or unwillingness to truly hear what the queens are saying, or to make space for commentary that may be uncomfortable or critical, is not solely a season 12 phenomenon, and while RuPaul is a successful Black drag queen, he has a history of being dismissive of queens who challenge him, even if what they are sharing are their own experiences of racism. Drag has to some degree gone mainstream, in large part due to RuPaul's long-standing influence, but only in particular ways and contexts. Certain drag bodies remain privileged above others, and, in *RPDR* particularly, deeply-fraught social justice issues remain largely unaddressed. Perhaps nowhere in *RPDR* is this gap made more apparent than in the "villain edit" received by The Vixen in season 10.[31] From her entrance catchphrase, "I'm just here to fight," to her exit commentary, "Evil triumphs when good queens do nothing," The Vixen made use of her time on *RPDR* to establish her place as a Black, activist queen, making herself few friends in the process.³² The conflicts she experienced during her time on the show (most notably with the season's winner, Aquaria, but also with fellow contestant Eureka O'Hara) magnify the work the show still tries and/or fails to do from an anti-racism lens. In her argument with Aquaria during *RPDR Untucked*, The Vixen reproaches Aquaria for referring to her as "negative," and the ensuing argument leads to Aquaria weaponizing her tears. As Phillip Henry puts it in his article for *them*, "Not only did Aquaria's actions create an 'angry Black woman' narrative for The Vixen, but it created that narrative for every Black person in the room who didn't come to Aquaria's defense."³³ The Vixen then points out the ways that the cameras mediate the viewers' experiences and affirm their racist stereotypes about the supposed angry Black woman tearing down the innocent white woman—a powerful but unacknowledged racism. In *RuPaul's Drag Race and Philosophy: Sissy That Thought* (2019), Guilel Treiber writes in their chapter, "Lip Sync for Your Life," that the show promotes two separate sets of values. The first are the "four cardinal virtues of the show, Charisma, Uniqueness, Nerve, and Talent (or the 'C.U.N.T. values'); the second are the 'A.S.S.E. values'—acceptance, solidarity, support, and empowerment."³⁴ The first set of virtues are individual, while the second represent a shared responsibility that individuals share towards one another and speak to the systemic violence and marginalization experienced throughout the LGBTQ+ community. Unfortunately, RuPaul, when forced to *choose* which set of virtues to extol, will generally lean into the former rather than the latter, and this focus on the individual's responsibility to and for themselves will almost always trump any deeper introspection into the root causes of the queens' behaviors, career trajectories, or relationships with one another.

In the reunion episode for season 10, The Vixen and Asia O'Hara are made to push back against RuPaul's "teachings" and educate the audience to mitigate RuPaul's commentary when The Vixen is called out for her heated exchanges with other contestants. After she responded to accusations that she "stirred the pot" with a number of the contestants, including Miz Cracker, Aquaria, and Eureka, RuPaul then asks her whether she should take responsibility for the inflammatory exchanges by behaving and speaking more calmly. After her pointed response about Eureka's attempts to manufacture how their arguments would be produced for public consumption, Asia O'Hara speaks up for The Vixen to point out that other contestants are piling up on her unfairly. The Vixen then famously observes that "everybody's telling me how I should react, but nobody's telling her [Eureka] how to act."³⁵ Not long after this moment, she thanks her fans, leaves the stage, and does not return. In a recent interview with Patrick Lenton, The Vixen connects her experiences throughout the season and in the reunion episode to the broader inequities and racism experienced by Black queens throughout the franchise's history:

> It happens every season. It takes a long time for the Black queens to get equal recognition, if they ever do. And so then once you're into the season, every altercation, every lip sync battle, everything you get, you see the bias, you see people distrust the Queens of Color. You see them make a million excuses for a white queen's misbehavior.[36]

Ultimately, The Vixen poignantly demonstrates and explains the microaggressions inherent in *RPDR*: "I was always judged more harshly for my reaction, than the initial action."[37] Former contestant Jaremi Carey also chimed in with his support for The Vixen on Twitter, calling out what he sees as the hypocrisy of RuPaul and the show for its supposed family values [*sic* throughout]: "Rupaul is going exactly what she is calling Vixen out for.... not listening and cutting off Asia. Look [I'm] done with the preachy drag bullshit, it is a family but it isn't either ... it is a produced TV family, SOMETIMES you are lucky to have people who will stop and listen..."[38] What The Vixen's experiences on the show highlight are the degree to which the show purports to be a platform for a message of equity and justice—through its sharing of individual stories, through its encouragement to viewers to register to vote, and through its sharing of queer history and culture—while failing to do the deep systemic work at best, and itself enacting the very marginalization that drag queens seek to eradicate in their work.

As a prominent and successful Black member of the drag queen community, RuPaul had an opportunity in the season 10 reunion episode to push back against depictions of Black drag queens—and, indeed, of Black women as well—as angry and combative; his role as a public voice and body educating the audience on drag and queerness offered the ideal platform to advocate for and demonstrate anti-racist care for a fellow Black queen. Asia calls out the injustice inherent in allowing The Vixen to walk away alone when they should have gone after her: "Here we are filming during Pride season," she admonishes, "and we let one of our sisters walk out the fucking room because nobody wants to fucking help her."[39] RuPaul's response is that he can only teach The Vixen through his own example and that while they are a community, they are also adults; likening his experiences to hers, he shouts at Asia, "I come from the same goddamn place she comes from. And here I am, and you see me walking out?...I have been discriminated against by white people for being Black, by Black people for being gay, by gay people for being too femme. Did I let that stop me from getting to this chair?"[40] With an opportunity to demonstrate Treiber's A.S.S.E. values, he instead focuses on C.U.N.T. values—that The Vixen is the victim of a problem of her own making. RuPaul's perception of his own success is that he achieved it by not allowing roadblocks to prevent him from achieving his goals—by demonstrating charisma, uniqueness, nerve, and talent. And even so, his final words on the moment are a supposed message of solidarity: "You know, the world is hard. It's hard to live on this planet. But we all have to learn how to deal with it … at the end of the day, we are a drag family, and as you can see, it doesn't always come easy."[41] This message of teaching ourselves to survive hardships—apparently unassisted—is used, ultimately, to segue to a gentle, kind treatment of the experiences of Dusty Ray Bottoms, a white queen whose religious parents forced him to attend conversion therapy, a deeply traumatic and homophobic experience that is not intricately linked with issues of race.

That RuPaul's experiential and narrative frame is one of hard work and determination is in keeping with Giroux's observation that under neo-liberalism,

> issues regarding schooling and social justice, persistent poverty, inadequate health care, racial apartheid in the inner cities, and the growing inequalities between the rich and the poor have been either removed from the inventory of public discourse and public policy or factored into talk show spectacles that highlight private woes bearing little relationship either to public life or to potential remedies that demand collective action.[42]

The discourse on *RPDR* is one that avoids nuanced discussion of complex systemic violence and marginalization. And though *RPDR* is not a talk show *per se*, it borrows from and is an offspring of that tradition in its marketing as reality television, positioning itself as a spectacle—an "extravaganza"—that adds elements of the talk show throughout the competition via confessionals, reunion episodes, and moments when RuPaul briefly chats with contestants in the Werk Room as they prepare for challenges. While topics such as racism, poverty, and violence are addressed on the show, they are presented largely as *individual* pain and trauma with little to no reference to the systemic ways that violence is exerted on Black bodies every day. Under such a framework, the show and its titular host become the exemplars of corporate culture, which "becomes both the model for the good life and the paradigmatic sphere for defining individual success and fulfillment…[and] whose aim is to produce *competitive* self-interested individuals vying for their own material and ideological gain."[43]

More than simply being shallow, *RPDR*'s moments of audience education also veer into explicit misinformation and violence through the erasure, policing, and further marginalization of trans bodies. RuPaul is famously on the record as stating that he would "probably not" allow a trans woman who has already undergone surgery to compete on the show.[44] While *RPDR* has had some trans contestants, including Gia Gunn, Carmen Carrera, and Monica Beverly Hillz, only Peppermint, a runner-up in the show's ninth season, Gia Gunn (in her stint on *RPDR All Stars* season

5), and Sonique on *RuPaul's Drag Race Holi-Slay Spectacular*, joined the show as out trans contestants. Meanwhile, season 12 was comprised entirely of cisgender men. In addition to this discrimination against trans people, RuPaul erases the work and bodies of the two trans women, activists, women of color, and, yes, drag queens, who were formative in the Stonewall Riots: Marsha P. Johnson and Sylvia Rivera. These two trans women were a part of the collective uprising against police brutality on the night of the Riots, and they continued to engage in important activism throughout their lives, including the founding of Street Transvestite Action Revolutionaries (STAR), an activist organization that opened the first LGBTQ+ shelter in North America.[45] However, RuPaul's framing of what precipitated the riots and who was responsible for them, in handing credit to a white Hollywood star, undermines the true LGBTQ+/BIPOC people responsible for the gay liberation movement. Even more, it also represents a failed opportunity to enact a pedagogy that makes public space for and gives credit to the BIPOC and queer and trans groups and individuals who must shoulder the burden of resisting their own marginalization in the face of their continued oppression and erasure.

In *RPDR All Stars* season 4, episode 8, the queens are given the task of making over their friends and partners (or "Best Judys") in drag. In introducing the challenge, RuPaul notes Judy Garland's status as a gay icon and identifies two common queer phrases that are influenced by her name and work ("Best Judy" and "Friend of Dorothy"). He then makes what constitutes at best a tenuous link between Judy Garland's funeral and the Stonewall Uprising, which occurred on June 27 and the early hours of June 28, respectively: "On the night of her funeral in June 1969," he claims, "the Stonewall Riots occurred. Fed up with police harassment, the patrons of the Stonewall used their grief over Judy's death to rise up and fight back, and the gay liberation movement was born."[46] In fact, Sylvia Rivera does attribute some of the high emotions of that historic night to the death of Judy Garland, musing in a 2009 interview with *Democracy Now* that "[y]ou could actually feel it in the air. You really could. I guess Judy Garland's death just really helped us really hit the fan."[47] However, to suggest that Judy Garland's death was the impetus for a collective uprising against police brutality that was *initiated by trans women and drag queens of color*, and to further suggest that her death represented the birth of the entire modern history of queer resistance to oppression is irresponsible, racist, and transphobic. RuPaul's long-standing refusal to reckon with these moments undermines his role as public pedagogue and confuses his status as a Black drag queen icon.

As is the habit of the *RPDR* franchise and its host, when larger controversies occur, they are rarely confronted on-screen or in other public venues.[48] While the two final episodes of the twelfth season—especially "Queens Reunited"—are ostensibly framed through the language of care and community, the degree of care can be called into question when supplemented with information beyond the boundaries of what viewers saw on their screens during those episodes. Most notably, the Top Three queens of the season—Crystal Methyd, Gigi Goode, and Jaida Essence Hall—were required to perform their final lip syncs at home. According to several fan discussion boards, however, Gigi, already benefiting throughout the season from her mother's expertise as a costume designer and her own whiteness, rented a studio space, nearly leading to her disqualification from the competition for breaking the rules.[49] Gigi's progress in the competition was tied, at least in part, to her ability to access her mother's expertise, the ability to learn to sew herself, and her access to enough disposable income to rent a studio space in Los Angeles. While this ultimately backfired, and Jaida Essence Hall, a frontrunner throughout the entire season, beat her out of the competition, that the discrepancy existed at all is further evidence of the ways in which white queens are often able to avail of resources and supports that queens of color cannot—a gap that is not addressed in any meaningful way on the show.

## *"Life Is Art's Best, Art's Only Pupil": Drag Queens and Teaching Praxis*

In his 1889 piece, "The Decay of Lying," Oscar Wilde offers an imaginative and engaging argument for romanticism over realism. The characters in the text, Cyril and Vivian, engage in socratic dialogue, and Vivian—clearly in the position of teacher—ends the dialogue with a series of doctrines. The third doctrine is particularly noteworthy in the way that it disrupts previous theories about the relationship between art and life: "Life imitates Art far more than Art imitates Life. This results not merely from Life's imitative instinct, but from the fact that the self-conscious aim of Life is to find expression, and that Art offers it certain beautiful forms through which it may realize that energy."[50] Of course, Wilde remains an important figure in queer history for his artistic work, his public defense of homosexuality during his trial for "gross indecency," and his dandy aesthetic. While his association with aestheticism might suggest a leaning away from using art as a vehicle for political discourse and activism, his prison letter to Lord Alfred Douglas makes clear that one's lived experiences must be taken into account: "To regret one's own experiences is to arrest one's own development. To deny one's own experiences is to put a lie into the lips of one's own life. It is no less than a denial of the soul."[51]

Wilde's aestheticism may well appeal to RuPaul, with his focus on beauty, poise, and pageantry. However, Wilde's lived experiences, and willingness to give them voice in the public sphere—"the love that dare not speak its name"—speak to the new cohorts of drag queens.[52] For drag performers like The Vixen, Asia O'Hara, Bob the Drag Queen, Jaremi Carey, Carmen Carrera, and others, their drag is informed by and makes explicit statements about what occurs beyond the confines of the runway and the Werk Room: their drag is a part of the curriculum. And it is what they do after *RPDR* that even more clearly marks them as pedagogues in their careful attention to intersectionality, systemic injustice, and public discourse: The Vixen with her *Black Girl Magic* show, Bob the Drag Queen, Shangela, and Eureka with *We're Here* (HBO, 2020– ), Peppermint and Bob's collaboration on *Black Queer Town Hall*, and Jaremi Carey with his public social media commentary about conditions on set. In taking on the role of educator, RuPaul assumes the same ethical responsibility that is incumbent on all teachers: to share accurate information, to make space for the symbiotic exchange of teaching and learning, to flatten hierarchies where possible, to enact radical care and anti-racism in learning spaces, and to keep everyone safe mentally, emotionally, and physically. But where RuPaul often fails, "his girls" succeed.

What the final two episodes of season 12 put into sharp focus are the very best and very worst of what the *RPDR* franchise has offered us through its eleven-year run to date. RuPaul dazzles his audience with a performance of pedagogy and care that does not truly represent an ethical praxis. The show's gestures towards learning and community are insufficient in confronting the existing white supremacist, neoliberal, and colonizing structures and systems that limit both the potential and safety of drag queens, especially racialized queens. Then again, if RuPaul is a pedagogue, so too are the queens who have also helped to catapult the show to success and educate audiences; these queens and their art are themselves a part of our cultural fabric. As a queer, academic, white fan of the show, I ultimately learn more about the history and culture of diverse drag traditions, about what it means to be systemically disadvantaged, and about the inequitable distribution of power between teacher and students from The Vixen, Jaremi Carey,[53] Monique Heart, Carmen Carrera, and Asia O'Hara than I do from RuPaul himself.[54]

At the end of his 2002 article, "Neoliberalism, Corporate Culture, and the Promise of Higher Education: The University as a Democratic Public Sphere," Giroux argues that as the neoliberal project progresses largely unabated, "[n]ew places and spaces of resistance have to be developed, and this demands new forms of pedagogy and new sites in which to conduct it while not abandoning traditional spheres of learning."[55] It would be arrogant of educators working in post-secondary institutions to assume that we are the only learning spaces that matter, and we should be looking to these other spaces to learn and to analyze other methodologies and frameworks for teaching and learning. Giroux emphatically suggests looking to student movements as an example of how to mediate the public work of the university against the corporate interests and values that continue to hold sway in its funding, policies, and curriculum. Educators have a role to play in these forms of resistance, he maintains, and good pedagogy—that is "moral and political"[56] pedagogy—"bears witness to the ethical and political dilemmas that animate the broader social landscape and are important because they provide spaces that are both comforting and unsettling, spaces that both disturb and enlighten."[57] If this is indeed the goal of a learning space and pedagogical practice—and I agree with Giroux that it is—then the true pedagogues we should be learning from are, perhaps, the contestants themselves.

## *Mini Challenge: Discussion Questions*

- How might your own social location—the intersection of, for example, your gender, race, class, and ability—influence the way you watch and think about *RPDR*?
- Has the current global pandemic influenced what you value most in education? What are the benefits and drawbacks of remote/virtual classes, and when the pandemic ends, what lessons should faculty, staff, students, and administrators take with us when we return to the classroom?
- What responsibility do educators have to be aware of popular culture and to incorporate it into their teaching? How does this translate to responsibilities in updating their pedagogy over time?

## *Maxi Challenge: Activities and Assignments*

- Think-Pair-Share: Have students brainstorm what their entrance line would be if they were to appear on *RPDR*. If they are comfortable, have them share with a classmate and discuss what they considered when writing their line.
- Individual Reflection: Using a resource like the University of Michigan's Social Identity Wheel (https://sites.lsa.umich.edu/inclusive-teaching/social-identity-wheel/), have students reflect in writing on their own social location and how it impacts their

viewership of a show about drag queens, many of whom are racialized and/or outside of the cis-gender binary. It is important that students not be required to divulge information about their social location, though some may choose to share.

## Notes

1. "Reunited: Alone Together." *RuPaul's Drag Race*, season 12, episode 13, VH1, 22 May 2020, Amazon https://www.amazon.com/RuPauls-Drag-Race-Season-12/dp/B08528GRKX. Typically, on *RPDR*, RuPaul makes it clear to the contestants that landing "safe" in a challenge is not good enough; while the top and bottom queens of the week generally remain on stage for their critiques and decisions around who wins that week's maxi challenge and who will lip sync for their lives, to be safe is to be unmemorable.

2. *Ibid.*

3. In making my identities and social locations explicit, I am indebted to those who have written about the importance of ensuring that academics transparently confront the dynamics of power and privilege in an attempt to challenge our (presumed) "authority." As Sean Michael Morris writes in *An Urgency of Teachers* (2018), "The instructor's own social location must be included in the narrative of the classroom so that there is a chance to decenter it. If we do not speak up about our own power…we have done too little to undo that power…. A silent authority silences without ever saying a word" (118).

4. As the *RPDR* franchise's audience grew, it expanded its venue for the grand finale episode of each season (though *All Stars* grand finales do not take place in large venues and are instead situated on the regular set of the show). In season 4, the finale was filmed at El Portal in Los Angeles (capacity 1346). In later seasons, the finale episodes took place at The Theater at Ace Hotel (capacity 2214) and the Orpheum Theater (capacity 1976), both in Los Angeles.

5. Jenkins, Henry. *Convergence Culture: Where Old and New Media Collide.* E-book, New York: New York University Press, 2006, https://hdl-handle-net.proxy1.lib.uwo.ca/2027/heb.05936. Accessed 20 July 2020.

6. Consider, as an example, the explosion of private proctoring services during the COVID-19 pandemic. Intended to discourage and discover instances of academic dishonesty during online exams, these services have been critiqued for the ways in which they violate student privacy, are inaccurate and ableist in the conclusions that they draw between bodily movements and student behavior, and discriminate against students of color.

7. In this essay, and in my writing more generally, I aim to enact and embody a writing praxis that explicitly acknowledges writing's Althusserian (always-already) dependence on individual positionality, social and economic contexts, and lived experience, in addition to cognitive processes. My approach borrows from principles of auto-ethnography, including consistent reflection and a focus on the role of subjectivity in the construction of knowledge and relationships.

8. Here, I am indebted to the defunct-but-archived Tumblr blog, *Your Favorite is Problematic*; its most recent post is dated for some time in 2016. The phrase "problematic fave" has come to indicate those pop culture texts and moments that a person will consume and enjoy despite an awareness of the ways in which their "fave" is implicated in systemic issues such as racism, xenophobia, homophobia, and misogyny. Originally, the term was used to indicate real people (usually celebrities), though its use has become broader to indicate texts and characters, as well.

9. Early in my fandom, I watched the episodes and absorbed the learning offered to me on *RPDR* with a fairly uncritical eye; however, I would come to recognize the constraints and contradictions in that learning, especially during the Best Judy challenge in *RPDR All Stars* season 4, episode 8 and the "Queens Reunited" episode of *RPDR* season 10.

10. Notable *RPDR* alumni who have since critiqued the show for its microaggressions,

poor labor conditions, and unethical editing and production practices include The Vixen, Carmen Carrera, Jaremi Carey (who performed with the drag name of Phi Phi O'Hara), and Gia Gunn. It is Carey's preference that he not be addressed by his former drag name, and he no longer identifies as a drag queen. BIPOC is an acronym generally used to indicate a broad range of racialized and marginalized groups, including Black people, Indigenous people, and other people of color.

11. "Reunited: Alone Together."
12. *Ibid.*
13. *Ibid.*
14. *Ibid.*
15. "Grand Finale." *RuPaul's Drag Race*, season 12, episode 14, VH1, 29 May 2020, Amazon https://www.amazon.com/RuPauls-Drag-Race-Season-12/dp/B08528GRKX.
16. In "Why RuPaul *Worked*: Queer Cross-Identifying the Mythic Black (Drag Queen) Mother," Seth Clark Silberman observes that RuPaul "repeats [New Age clichés] with the demeanor of a preacher so that the next time the audience sees her in a television interview they know how to chime in" (175). While Silberman's article predates the *RPDR* franchise, he identifies what we now know to be RuPaul's most identifiable *RPDR* lines ("everybody say love" and "if you can't love yourself, how the hell you gonna love somebody else? Can I get an amen in here?") as coming from her "most common sermon on *Video Soul*. That she recycles her sermon for different shows in different contexts demonstrates the continuity of her call-and-response" (175).
17. In their work on digital drag, Zitzelsberger observes that as compared to *RPDR*, through which the "queer potentialities of drag" lose their subversiveness, digital drag, particularly on YouTube, offers an opportunity for "disruptive asemioticity." I agree with this claim, but I would also suggest that the subversive opportunities of YouTube-based drag remain, to a certain degree, constrained by YouTube's position as a Google-owned platform that is inextricably enmeshed in private capital and neoliberal capitalism, as well as the contracts that queens sign with World of Wonder, which gives the production company some ownership over content released by contestants on *RPDR* for the duration of the contract.
18. Morris, Sean Michael, & Stommel, Jesse. *An Urgency of Teachers: The Work of Critical Digital Pedagogy*, Hybrid Pedagogy, 2018, p. 16.
19. "Reunited: Alone Together."
20. Greeber, Glen. *Small Screen Aesthetics: From TV to the Internet*, London: Palgrave Macmillan, 2013, p. 126.
21. My distinction between the Internet and the *modern* Internet is deliberate; here, I make space for the recognition that the origins of the modern Internet stem back to the 1970s when the Advanced Research Projects Agency Network (ARPANET), under the auspices of the U.S. Defense Department, developed the ability to allow communication between multiple computers within a network. In contrast, the World Wide Web was developed by Tim Berners-Lee, a computer scientist working at the European Organization for Nuclear Research (CERN), the Swiss nuclear research facility.
22. Greeber, p. 143.
23. *Ibid.*
24. "Grand Finale."
25. *Ibid.*
26. Whitford, Emma. "Hundreds of Colleges Walk Back Fall Reopening Plans and Opt for Online-Only Instruction," *Inside Higher Ed*, https://www.insidehighered.com/news/2020/08/12/hundreds-colleges-walk-back-fall-reopening-plans-and-opt-online-only-instruction. Accessed 15 Aug. 2020.
27. One night, while working on a draft of this essay, my Internet connection dropped, and when I reloaded my cloud-connected document, it briefly appeared as though I had lost about 1000 words of my writing. I was able to recover them, but I was reminded of the moment when Carson's screen appears to freeze and RuPaul asks "I think your screen is frozen, darling...is your connection okay?"
28. Stommel, Jesse. "Designing for Care: Inclusive Pedagogies for Online Learning." *Jesse Stommel*, 19 June 2020, https://www.jessestommel.com/designing-for-care/.

29. *Ibid.*

30. As RuPaul checked in with the queens during the reunion episode to ensure their safety and health, it occurred to me that we were not hearing about whether the disqualified drag queen, Sherry Pie, was safe and healthy. Sherry Pie, whose non-drag name is Joey Gugliemelli, was rightly disqualified from the competition when it came out after filming that he had assumed the identity of a casting director in order to solicit suggestive photos and video from at least five men. Gugliemelli apologized publicly through his Facebook page for the sexual harassment, and the show did its best to edit him out of the show from the second episode onwards. Had Gugliemelli not been referenced at all during the reunion, it may not have felt notable that the audience received no word about his health and safety; however, Brita reads Dahlia's elimination in the first episode as remarkable because Dahlia "[talks] a big game for someone who came in thirteenth place on a twelve-person season."

31. Another notable former contestant to receive a villain edit was Jaremi Carey, who performed as a drag queen with the name Phi Phi O'Hara. Carey is of Filipino and Portuguese descent, and he ultimately decided to stop doing drag altogether. In a tweet on August 6th, when asked whether he could be persuaded to do another season of *RPDR All Stars*, he responded via quotetweet, "For a lousy few hundred bucks an episode…and a million death threats PLUS to my mother with a host and production crew doing nothing to help…. HAHA! Never."

32. It's worth noting here that while The Vixen's catchphrase was used to demonstrate the ways in which she was combative before, during, and after the series, white queens with violent entrance phrases upon arriving into the workroom are not asked to link their language and their behavior. For example, Chad Michaels arrived on the set of *RPDR All Stars* season 1 and proclaimed "Happy hunger games, bitches!" evoking Suzanne Collins' famous young adult franchise in which the arena that pits child against child in a battle to the death is televised to citizens across the nation of Panem, directly referencing not just the Roman gladiatorial games but the modern-day spectacle of reality television.

33. Henry, Phillip. "Why We Needed to See The Vixen Fight Aquaria on Drag Race." *Them.*, https://www.them.us/story/the-vixen-fight-aquaria-drag-race. Accessed 15 Aug. 2020.

34. Treiber, Guilel. "Lip Sync for Your Life," *RuPaul's Drag Race and Philosophy: Sissy That Thought*, edited by Hendrik Kempt and Megan Volpert, Caris Publishing, 2020, pp. 136–139.

35. "Grand Finale."

36. Lenton, Patrick. "The Vixen Is The Drag Queen We Need In 2020." *Junkee*, https://junkee.com/longform/the-vixen-interview. Accessed 10 Aug. 2020.

37. *Ibid.*

38. @JustJaremi. "Rupaul is going exactly what she is calling Vixen out for….not listening and cutting off Asia. Look [I'm] done with the preachy drag bullshit, it is a family but it isn't either…it is a produced TV family, SOMETIMES you are lucky to have people who will stop and listen and not" *Twitter*, 21 Jun. 2018, 8:45 pm., https://twitter.com/JustJaremi/status/1009960425553911808?s=20

39. "Grand Finale."

40. *Ibid.*

41. *Ibid.*

42. Giroux, Henry A. "Public Pedagogy and the Politics of Resistance: Notes on a Critical Theory of Educational Struggle." *Educational Philosophy and Theory*, vol. 35, no. 1, Routledge, Jan. 2003, pp. 5–16.

43. Giroux, Henry A. "Neoliberalism, Corporate Culture, and the Promise of Higher Education: The University as a Democratic Public Sphere." *Harvard Educational Review; Cambridge*, vol. 72, no. 4, Harvard Educational Review, Winter 2002, pp. 425–63. Emphasis added.

44. Aitkenhead, Decca. "RuPaul: 'Drag Is a Big f-You to Male-Dominated Culture.'" *The Guardian*, 3 Mar. 2018. *www.theguardian.com*, https://www.theguardian.com/tv-and-radio/2018/mar/03/rupaul-drag-race-big-f-you-to-male-dominated-culture.

45. NSWP. "Street Transvestite Action Revolutionaries Found STAR House."

*Global Network of Sex Work Projects*, 4 Dec. 2015. https://www.nswp.org/timeline/event/street-transvestite-action-revolutionaries-found-star-house.

46. "RuPaul's Best Judy's Race." *RuPaul's Drag Race All Stars*, season 4, episode 8, VH1, 1 February 2019, https://www.amazon.com/gp/video/detail/B07KWPRZ5M/ref=atv_dp_season_select_s4.

47. Democracy Now. "Stonewall Riots 40th Anniversary: A Look Back at the Uprising That Launched the Modern Gay Rights Movement." *Democracy Now!*. http://www.democracynow.org/2009/6/26/stonewall_riots_40th_anniversary_a_look. Accessed 7 Aug. 2020.

48. In fact, RuPaul recently deleted his Twitter and Instagram accounts altogether, leaving fans confused. (RuPaul deleted his social media accounts on July 2nd, 2020, and then reactivated them after this hiatus on October 6th, 2020.)

49. "R/Rupaulsdragrace—Insider Tea: Gigi Tried to Cheat and Was Threatened with Disqualification and Legal Action by Production." *Reddit*. https://www.reddit.com/r/rupaulsdragrace/comments/gtncs6/insider_tea_gigi_tried_to_cheat_and_was/. Accessed 15 Aug. 2020; *Apparently Gigi Almost Got Disqualified during the Finale. | Fandom*. https://rupaulsdragrace.fandom.com/f/p/4400000000000001816. Accessed 13 Aug. 2020.

50. Wilde, Oscar. "The Decay of Lying." https://www.sscnet.ucla.edu/comm/steen/cogweb/Abstracts/Wilde_1889.html. Accessed 14 Aug. 2020.

51. Wilde, Oscar. "De Profundis." https://www.gutenberg.org/files/921/921-h/921-h.htm. Accessed 15 Aug. 2020.

52. "The love that dare not speak its name" is from the poem "Two Loves" by Lord Alfred Douglas and was famously quoted by Wilde himself during his trial for "gross indecency."

53. It was, in fact, Jaremi Carey who, on Twitter, alerted fans to the fact that *All Stars* season 6 contestants were in quarantine in order to film a new season during a global pandemic. Though RuPaul calls attention to the show's focus on safety in the reunion episode of season 12, the show must indeed, it seems, go on.

54. Other notable *RPDR* alumni have graduated to meaningful projects that tackle some of the more complicated and nuanced conversations about racism, queerness, transness, and drag, including Peppermint and Bob the Drag Queen's *Black Queer Town Hall* (in association with GLAAD) and HBO's new series *We're Here*, which sees Shangela, Bob the Drag Queen, and Eureka O'Hara travel to small, rural American towns to introduce residents to drag and invite selected community members to join them as entertainers in a drag show; each episode takes time, too, to identify and discuss systemic violence and oppression of members of the LGBTQ+ community, with a particular focus on the intersections of homophobia, racism, and misogyny.

55. Giroux, "Neoliberalism, Corporate Culture, and the Promise of Higher Education: The University as a Democratic Public Sphere," p. 455.

56. *Ibid.*, p. 441.

57. *Ibid.*, p. 452.

# Sashay Away

*Resources to Support Learners*

The editors of this collection would like to guide educators to some important resources to support LGBTQ+, BIPOC, and allied students in their "RuPedagogies" as well as for the community:

### APTLY OUTSPOKEN!—sites.google.com/view/aptly outspoken/who-we-be?authuser=0

A collective of anti-racist, cross-racial allies/accomplices who are disgusted and saddened by the senseless killing of Mr. George Floyd (1973–2020), another Black man, by police, and who are committed to using speech communication and writing to intervene into the daily and oppressive treatment of living Black bodies in the USA and Canada.

### Campus Pride—www.campuspride.org

Non-profit organization for student leaders and campus groups seeking support programs and services to create inclusive colleges.

### CPATH—cpath.ca

CPATH (Canadian Professional Association for Transgender Health) is the largest national multidisciplinary, professional organization in the world, working to support the health, well-being, and dignity of trans and gender diverse people.

### Family Equality Council—familyequality.org/

The council connects, supports, and represents parents who are LGBTQ+ in the U.S. as well as their children.

### Gay, Lesbian and Straight Educator Network (GLSEN)—glsen.org/

This advocacy network focuses on reaching out to public school students in the U.S.

## GLAAD—glaad.org/

This organization supplies resources about the history and advocacy of the community.

## Human Rights Campaign—hrc.org

An organization dedicated to advocacy and political lobbying.

## Immigration Equality—*immigrationequality.org/*

The largest LGBTQ+ immigration equality organization in the U.S.

## Lambda Legal—lambdalegal.org/

A non-profit organization dedicated to providing legal services to promote civil rights and promote public policy for the community.

## National Center for Transgender Equality—transequality.org/

This transgender advocacy group provides services throughout the U.S.

## OK2BME—ok2bme.ca

Operated by KW Counselling Services (Ontario, Canada), OK2BME is a set of free, confidential services including counseling and a youth group for kids and teens wondering about their sexuality or gender identity.

## PFLAG—pflag.org/

This advocacy group targets their services to parents, friends, and allies of the LGBT community with local chapters and events.

## Point of Pride—pointofpride.org

Entirely volunteer-operated, Point of Pride serves the international transgender community and works to support trans youth and adults who otherwise lack access through gender-affirming programs that empower them to live more authentically.

## Power On—https://www.poweronlgbt.org/

An organization that collects and redistributes old technology to individuals who wouldn't have access otherwise.

## Sage (Advocacy & Services for LGBT Elders)—https://www.sageusa.org/

An organization that provides educational resources, advocates on behalf of, and addresses policies relating to aging for LGBTQ+ elders.

## The Trevor Project—thetrevorproject.org

This organization provides a toll free and confidential suicide hotline for LGBTQ+ youth.

## TSER: Trans Student Educational Resources—transstudent.org

A youth-led organization dedicated to transforming the educational environment for trans and gender nonconforming students through advocacy and empowerment.

## Werk Those Pecs—werkthosepecs.com

A community-based organization whose mission is to help trans individuals pay for expensive and life-saving gender-confirming surgery. They also provide funds for other medical or basic living expenses as well as provided financial assistance for a Passport name change or gender marker changes.

# Spilling the Tea
## *Glossary*

**Back rolls**: refers to the fat on someone's back, particularly when it is accentuated by what they are wearing. Jade Jolie first made reference to this in season 5 regarding Alyssa Edwards.

**Beat**: to apply makeup.

**Busted**: when your appearance is messy, sloppy, unkempt, or poorly presented.

**Camp/Campy**: a type of hyper-real and/or over the top drag where the queen's priority is not on appearing feminine.

**Clock**: to identify someone's flaws and/or something that is being hidden.

**Condragulations**: a pun on *congratulations*, RuPaul uses this term when congratulating and awarding queens when they win a challenge.

**Drag Mother**: an experienced queen who is educating and fostering the talent of a younger and/or less-experienced queen.

**Fishy**: a queen who appears realistically feminine and/or resembles a cis-woman.

**Halleloo**: used to express excitement and joy, like a praise shout, that was brought into the vernacular of *RPDR* by seasons 2 and 3 and *All Stars* season 3 contestant Shangela Laquifa Wadley.

**House**: describes an alternative and/or chosen family within the LGBTQ+/drag communities. It came out of ball culture. They are usually named for the Drag "Mother" or "Father" who leads the house and supports the younger members. Many members will include their house's name in their drag moniker.

**KiKi**: another way of describing gossip or chatting amongst confidantes.

**Library**: a mini challenge on the show where the queens "read" each other; a play on the idea that you read in a library.

**Lip Sync for Your Legacy**: when the top queens of the week are challenged to lip sync together to determine the winner of a challenge.

**Lip Sync for Your Life**: when the bottom queens of the week are challenge to lip sync together to determine who will be eliminated.

**Mug**: another way of describing someone's face (e.g., You can beat your mug; you can apply makeup to your face).

**Padding**: foam or silicone cushioning used to create the illusion of a feminine silhouette.

**Pit Crew**: models who appear on the show to assist RuPaul or support the queens during mini and/or maxi challenges.

**PorkChop, The**: the first queen to be eliminated of the season. This title was derived from the first queen to be eliminated during season 1 of *RPDR*, Victoria "Porkchop" Parker.

**Reading**: indicating someone's flaws as a form of critique and/or humor. The term is a reference to the film *Paris Is Burning*.

**Rusical**: A pun on the word *musical* and is a more recent maxi challenge across the franchises where the queens put on a campy musical-inspired shows (often also referred to a "Unauthorized Rusicals" to take the shtick even further).

**Sashay Away**: a term that RuPaul uses to indicate when a queen has been or will be eliminated from the competition.

**Serve**: what inspires a queen that they hope to present to the judges.

**Shade**: when a queen insults another overtly or subtly.

**Shantay, You Stay**: a term that RuPaul uses to indicate when a queen has been selected to remain in the competition after a Lip Sync for Your Life.

**Slay**: a way of describing excellence and a strong showing.

**Tea**: another way of describing gossip or facts.

**Tuck**: describes when a queen is pulling their genitalia back to present a more feminine look. **Untuck**: describes when a queen is removing their garb and undoing a tuck. The show also uses the term to describe when the queens are waiting off the runway while the judges are filming their deliberations.

# Let's Have a KiKi

*Discussion Questions for the Class*

Here are some of the broader general questions that we have gotten and have ourselves asked to help instructors "break the ice" about *RuPaul's Drag Race* (*RPDR*), drag, queer studies, and the collection's work:

- Getting Started:
    - How did you first learn about *RPDR*?
    - When you think of drag, how would you define it?
    - Should "bio queens" and post-operative trans queens be allowed to compete on *RPDR*? Why, or why not?
    - How does the series normalize queer culture for its audience?
    - Who do you think is the target audience for the series today? Has it changed since it began?

- In "Start Your Engines: Critical Context into the Language and Influence of Drag":
    - How has *RPDR* changed or informed the way we perceive drag? Do you feel it does reflect a "heterotopia" as Kampouridou argues?
    - What do you feel is the purpose of the "makeover" episodes as a social experiment in gender and performance? How do the reactions of the participants inform the experience of viewers?
    - To what extent does the show effectively teach its audience the language of drag and queer culture?
    - What terms did Goetz-Preisner highlight that you feel have been rightfully "reclaimed" by queens, judges, and/or guests of the series?
    - Are there any terms that you feel should not be reclaimed?
    - What examples from the series stood out to you as applicable to Freire's theory of co-productive learning from Joy and McSweeney-Flaherty?
    - The series has taken on more of an overt political message in the last few seasons. Do you feel that that this can truly inform/influence young voters?
    - What do you feel is the purpose of connecting the nude form/body to drag? How do they develop our perceptions of sex and gender?

- ◊ Do you feel that sex and gender both truly are social constructs, as Mayberry argues?
- In "She Already Done Had Herses: When Drag Curates Culture":
  - ◊ What would you consider a missed opportunity for a broader conversation/lesson within *RPDR*? Was there one that you wish Martin had covered?
  - ◊ If you could add anything to the curriculum of *RPDR*, what would it be?
  - ◊ Would you consider the Indigenous dress of Raja and of Monét X Change to be of greater or lesser concern than Trixie Mattel (whose portrayer, Brian Firkus, is half–Ojibwe on his mother's side)? To what extent do you feel that all three performers are promoting ideologies that enable violence against Indigenous individuals, as Ward argues?
  - ◊ To what extent does your perception of their choices to wear Indigenous dress change based on whether it was required or not of a challenge (where their time and dress options are restricted)?
  - ◊ What is the power of dark affect in the classroom, and what is the balance of triumph and tragedy, as Fine positions them, in the stories we teach, tell, celebrate?
- In "May the Best Drag Queen Win: The Competitive Nature of Drag":
  - ◊ RuPaul presents the rubric of "charisma, uniqueness, nerve, and talent" for assessing the queens, and the Fantasy League presents another, as Workman shows, but what are aspects of the hidden curriculum by which competing queens are measured and assessed?
  - ◊ And how is this complicated in the *All Stars* seasons with the seemingly DIY curriculum and rubric against which they are left to measure themselves?
  - ◊ What is your favorite Snatch Game moment? Why? What is the popular and/or queer history behind it?
  - ◊ Piatkowski identifies and argues for layered nuance in Snatch Game performances when the queens take on feminized cismale celebrity figures—what are the layers and nuance when queens take on (as Trinity The Tuck did as Caitlyn Jenner and as Amanda Lepore, and Farrah Moan did as Gigi Gorgeous) transgender celebrity figures?
  - ◊ Zitzelsberger presents a clear case of digital drag as pedagogy as largely conceived, written, and argued pre–COVID-19—taking their work further in our pandemic times, what are best practices we can embody from these queens' example for teaching with technology, teaching remotely, and teaching pre-recorded?
  - ◊ How might our classrooms look differently if we adapted and adopted elements of this digital drag pedagogy for our online and remote classrooms?
  - ◊ How do you experience—even reconcile—your own fandom and "problematic faves," as Penney explores it, with watching and critically reflecting on *RPDR*?

- ◊ When you think about what you have learned from watching *RPDR*, and what the show has taught you, do the majority of the lessons (and/or the most impactful lessons) come from RuPaul or from the competing queens?

# Very Special Guest Judge
*Select Bibliography*

@chestersee (Chester See). "Hi," pinned tweet. Twitter, 30 May 2018, 1:13 a.m. https://twitter.com/chestersee/status/1001587237836898306.
@chestersee (Chester See). "We present to you... Miz Cookie!" Instagram, 25 May 2018, https://www.instagram.com/p/BjLNFWcHahs/?hl=en.
@fka_jayesimpson. "I'm just gonna publicly say it. I don't like the new Kent Monkman piece. I think it's inappropriate. Consent is first and foremost. Having restitution portrayed as sexual violence in with Indigenous women cheering it on is perverse and not subverting the narrative at all." *Twitter*, 15 May 2020, 8:46 PM, https://twitter.com/fka_jayesimpson/status/1261458086163648513.
@JustJaremi. "For a lousy few hundred bucks an episode...and a million death threats PLUS to my mother with a host and production crew doing nothing to help….HAHA! Never." *Twitter*, 6 Aug. 2020, 8:11 pm., https://twitter.com/JustJaremi/status/1291527253873098752?s=20.
@JustJaremi. "Rupaul is going exactly what she is calling Vixen out for....not listening and cutting off Asia. Look Im done with the preachy drag bullshit, it is a family but it isn't either...it is a produced TV family, SOMETIMES you are lucky to have people who will stop and listen and not" *Twitter*, 21 Jun. 2018, 8:45 pm., https://twitter.com/JustJaremi/status/1009960425553911808?s=20.
@RuPaulsDragRace. "Cultural appropriation! @monetxchange #DragRace." *Twitter*, 10 May 2018, 8:55 PM, https://twitter.com/RuPaulsDragRace/status/994742819116871681.
"#SUPERTUESDAY - MAKE YOUR VOTE COUNT, ELECTION MAKEUP TUTORIAL & DRAG RACE REVIEW | Kimora Blac." *YouTube*, uploaded by Kimora Blac, 3 Mar. 2020, https://youtu.be/-QIdPnDGPAY.
_bew1tched. "homage to his own heritage." *Instagram*, Feb. 2019, https://www.instagram.com/p/BtsWTFPgDZN/.
Abidin, Crystal. "Communicative Intimacies: Influencers and Perceived Interconnectedness." *Ada: A Journal of Gender, New Media & Technology*, vol. 8, 2015, http://adanewmedia.org/2015/11/issue8-abidin/.
Abraham, "Pink Runways & Strip Lighting: My First Time at Drag Con." *Refinery 29*, 30 May 2019.
Ahmed, Sara. *The Promise of Happiness*. Duke University Press, 2010.
———. "Queer Feelings." *The Routledge Queer Studies Reader*, edited by Donald E. Hall and Annamarie Jagose. Routledge, 2013.
———. *Queer Phenomenology: Orientations, Objects, Others*. Duke University Press, 2006.
———. "Strange." *Encounters: Embodied Others in Post-Coloniality*. Routledge, 2000.
Aitkinhead, Decca. "RuPaul: 'Drag is a big f-you to male-dominated culture.'" *The Guardian*, 3 Mar. 2018, https://www.theguardian.com/tv-and-radio/2018/mar/03/rupaul-drag-race-big-f-you-to-male-dominated-culture.
"Alaska Thunderfuck—The T (feat. Adore Delano) [Official]." *YouTube*, uploaded by Alaska Thunderfuck, 13. Oct. 2016, https://youtu.be/9Xw5VkCpxRg.

A_minus_call. "misrepresenting his Indigenous culture." *Instagram*, Feb. 2019, https://www.instagram.com/p/BtsWTFPgDZN/.

Anderson, Benedict. *Imagined Communities: Reflections on the Origin and Spread of Nationalism*. Verso, 2006.

Anderson, Kim. "The Construction of a Negative Identity." *A Recognition of Being: Reconstructing Native Womanhood*. Sumach, 2000, pp. 99–115.

Anthony, Libby. "Dragging with an Accent: Linguistic Stereotypes, Language Barriers and Translingualism." The Makeup of *RuPaul's Drag Race*: Essays on the Queen of Reality Shows, edited by Jim Daems. McFarland, 2014, pp. 49–66.

Anzaldúa, Gloria. *Borderlands/La Frontera*. Aunt Lute Books, 2007.

*Apparently Gigi Almost Got Disqualified during the Finale. | Fandom*. https://rupaulsdragrace.fandom.com/f/p/4400000000000001816. Accessed 15 Aug. 2020.

arela_haro. "I don't understand the problem." 10 Feb.2019. https://www.instagram.com/p/BtsWTFPgDZN/.

Auslander, Philip. *Liveness: Performance in a Mediatized Culture*. Routledge, 2011.

Austinj3500. "choice to represent her culture." Feb. 2019, *Instagram*, https://www.instagram.com/p/BtsWTFPgDZN//.

Baker, P. "Polari: The Lost Language of Gay Men," n.d, https://www.lancaster.ac.uk/staff/bakerjp/polari/home.htm. Accessed 8 Apr. 2020.

Barrett, Rusty. "Indexing Polyphonous Identity in the Speech of African American Drag Queens." *Identity as Improvisation*, edited by Mary Bucholtz, A.C. Liang, and L. A. Sutton, 1999.

Barry, Dan. "Giving a Name, and Dignity, to a Disability." *New York Times*. 8 May 2016. https://www.nytimes.com/2016/05/08/sunday-review/giving-a-name-and-dignity-to-a-disability.html. Access 17 Apr. 2020.

Bauman, Zygmunt. *Society Under Siege*. Blackwell, 2002.

Baumgartner, Jody, and Jonathan S. Morris. "The Daily Show Effect: Candidate Evaluations, Efficacy, and American Youth." *American Politics Research*, vol. 34, no. 3, May 2006, pp. 341–367. doi:10.1177/1532673X05280074.

Beard C., Wilson, J.P. *Experiential Learning: A Practical Guide for Training, Coaching and Education*. Kogan Page Publishers, 2018.

Bechdel, Alison. *Dykes to Watch Out For*, 1983, https://dykestowatchoutfor.com/. Accessed 8 Apr. 2020.

Bennett, Jeffrey, and Isaac West. "'United We Stand, Divided We Fall': AIDS, Armorettes, and the Tactical Repertoires of Drag." *Southern Communication Journal*, vol. 74, no. 3, Taylor & Francis, 2009, pp. 300–313.

Bersani, Leo. "Is the Rectum a Grave?" *October*, vol. 43, Oct. 1987.

Bimber, Bruce, and Richard Davis. *Campaigning Online: The Internet in U.S. Elections*. Oxford University Press, 2003.

Blankenship, Mark. "Mopping Drag Slang." *Out*, Here Media, 23 Apr. 2012, https://www.out.com/entertainment/2012/04/23/drag-queen-rupaul-race-language-slang. Accessed 1 Apr. 2020.

Bordo, Susan. *Unbearable Weight*. University of California Press, 2003.

Boyd, Jade. "'Hey, We're from Canada, but We're Diverse, Right?': Neoliberalism, Multiculturalism, and Identity on So You think You Can Dance Canada." *Critical Studies in Media Communication*, vol. 29, no. 4, 2012, pp. 259–274.

Brammer, John Paul. "How the Vixen Exposed the Racism of *RuPaul's Drag Race*." them, 22 Jun. 2018.

Brand, Dionne. "Whose Gaze, and Who Speaks for Whom." *Bread Out of Stone*, Vintage Canada, 1994, pp. 145–168.

Branum, Guy. "The Rules of Enchantment." *My Life As a Goddess: A Memoir Through (Un) Popular Culture*. Atria Books, 2018, pp. 207–231.

Brennan, Niall, and David Gudelunas. *RuPaul's Drag Race and the Shifting Visibility of Drag Culture: The Boundaries of Reality TV*. Springer, 2017.

Brooke, Zach. "Q & A: Trixie Mattel." *Milwaukee Mag*, 8 Sep. 2015. https://www.milwaukeemag.com/qa-trixie-mattel/.

## Select Bibliography 285

Brookes, Rod. "Introduction." *Representing Sports*. Oxford University Press, 2002, p. 8.
Brown, Alexis. "Being and Performance in *RuPaul's Drag Race*." *Critical Quarterly*, vol. 60, no. 4, 2018, pp. 62–73.
Bui, Long T., and Sabrina Strings. "She Is Not Acting, She Is." *Feminist Media Studies*, vol. 14, no. 5, 2014. p. 824.
Bullough, Robert V., Jr. "Teacher Vulnerability and Teachability: A Case Study of a Mentor and Two Interns." *Teacher Education Quarterly*, JSTOR, 2005, pp. 23–39.
Butler, Judith. *Bodies That Matter*. Routledge, 1993.
———. *Bodies That Matter: On the Discursive Limits of Sex*. Routledge, 2011.
———. *Gender Trouble: Feminism and the Subversion of Identity*. Routledge, 1990.
Cahill, Caitlin. "The Personal Is Political: Developing New Subjectivities through Participatory Action Research." *Gender, Place and Culture*, vol. 14, no. 3, 2007, pp. 267–292.
*Canada's Drag Race*, season 1, Saloon Media, 2020, *Amazon*, https://www.amazon.com/Canadas-Drag-Race-Season-1/dp/B08F3Y73MQ.
Carrera, Carmen (@carmencarrerafans). "Some of you guys asked me...." Facebook, 31 Mar. 2014, www.facebook.com/carmencarrerafans/posts/679959392050537. Accessed 14 Jan. 2019.
Carter, Franklyn. "Federal Judge Dismisses U.S. Women's Soccer Team's Equal Pay Claim." *NPR.org*, 2 May 2020, https://www.npr.org/2020/05/02/849492863/federal-judge-dismisses-u-s-womens-soccer-team-s-equal-pay-claim.
"Cartoons and Vodka—Official Music Video—Jinkx Monsoon." *YouTube*, uploaded by Jinkx Monsoon, 12 Jan. 2018, https://youtu.be/ejWnwVWuoCo.
Chachki, Violet. "Violet Chachki." *YouTube*, www.youtube.com/user/VioletChachki/about.
Chapman, Sam. "Local Drag Performers Often Don't Get Paid Enough to Even Cover the Cost of Their Outfit." *The Stranger*, 21 Sep. 2018, Thestranger.com/slog/2018/09/21/32646576/tip-your-local-drag-queens-they-need-it.
Charles, RuPaul. "A message to Mary Cheney from *RuPaul's Drag Race*." *Youtube*, 2015. https://www.youtube.com/watch?v=5G4-oatHs3A. Accessed 9 Jul. 2020.
———. "You can take performance enhancing drugs and still be an athlete." *Twitter*, 5 Mar. 2018, https://twitter.com/RuPaul/status/970709820364881920.
Chasin, Alexandra. *Selling Out: The Gay & Lesbian Movement Goes to Market*. St. Martin's Press, 2000, pp. 1–27.
Chaynes, Allysin. Personal interview, *Feel Your Fantasy*, Vol. 1, No.1, 2018. 16 Oct. 2017.
chaztrone. "O honey!" *Instagram*, Feb. 2019, https://www.instagram.com/p/BtsWTFPgDZN/.
cheokima. "Cultural Appropriation comments to someone." *Instagram*, Feb. 2019, https://www.instagram.com/p/BtsWTFPgDZN/.
Clarkson, Jay. "Contesting Masculinity's Makeover: Queer Eye, Consumer Masculinity, and 'Straight-Acting' Gays." *Journal of Communication Inquiry*, vol. 29, no. 3, 2005, pp. 235–255.
Connell, Raewyn. *Masculinities*. Polity Press, 1995.
———. "The Social Organization of Masculinity." *Exploring Masculinities: Identity, Inequality, Continuity, and Change*, edited by C.J. Pascoe and Tristan Bridges. Oxford University Press, 2016, pp. 136–144.
Connolly, Michael P., and Kathleen Lynch. "Is Being Gay Bad for Your Health and Wellbeing? Cultural Issues Affecting Gay Men Accessing and Using Health Services in the Republic of Ireland." *Journal of Research in Nursing*, vol. 21, no. 3, May 2016, pp. 177–96. *CrossRef*, doi:10.1177/1744987115622807.
"Conversation: Peppermint & Sasha Velour" *Youtube*, uploaded by Miss Peppermint, 15 Jun. 2020. https://www.youtube.com/watch?v=WWjBnDT9iQk.
Craig, Shelley L., et al. "Educational Determinants of Readiness to Practise with LGBTQ+ Clients: Social Work Students Speak Out." *The British Journal of Social Work*, vol. 46, no. 1, British Association of Social Workers, 2014, pp. 115–134.
Crath, Rory, and Cristian Rangel. "Paradoxes of an Assimilation Politics: Media Production of Gay Male Belonging in the Canadian 'Vital Public' from the Tainted Blood Scandal to the Present." *Culture, Health & Sexuality*, vol. 19, no. 7, Taylor & Francis, 2017, pp. 796–810.
Crenshaw, Kimberlé. *Mapping the Margins: Intersectionality, Identity Politics, and Violence against Women of Color*. Stanford Law Review, vol. 43, 1993.

Crookston, Cameron. "Passing the torch song: Mothers, daughters, and chosen families in the Canadian drag community." *Q2Q: Queer Canadian Theatre and Performance*, vol. 8, edited by Peter Dickinson, C.E. Gatchalian, and Kathleen Oliver. Playwrights Canada Press, 2018, p. 62.

Dam Bracia, Lillian. "Weighing in on Cultural Appropriation and Drag." *INDIE Magazine*, 30 Aug. 2017, https://indie-mag.com/2017/08/cultural-appropriation-and-drag/.

DasGupta, S., A. Fornari, and K. Geer, et al. "Medical education for social justice: Paulo Freire revisited." *Journal of Medical Humanities* 27(4). Springer, 2006, pp. 245–251.

"David Letterman and Jonathan Van Ness on Beard Trims, Self Care, Gender and LGBTQ Rights." *Youtube*, uploaded by Netflix, 27 Jun. 2019. https://www.youtube.com/watch?v=v_dHWI4CzUU.

Davies, Wilder. "*RuPaul's Drag Race* and What People Get Wrong About the History of Drag." *Time*, 9 Mar. 2018, time.com/5188791/rupauls-drag-race-history/.

Democracy Now. "Stonewall Riots 40th Anniversary: A Look Back at the Uprising That Launched the Modern Gay Rights Movement." *Democracy Now!*, http://www.democracy-now.org/2009/6/26/stonewall_riots_40th_anniversary_a_look. Accessed 7 Aug. 2020.

Denny, Simon, et al. "The Association between Supportive High School Environments and Depressive Symptoms and Suicidality among Sexual Minority Students." *Journal of Clinical Child & Adolescent Psychology*, vol. 45, no. 3. Taylor & Francis, 2016, pp. 248–261.

de Vries, Elma, et al. "Debate: Why Should Gender-Affirming Health Care Be Included in Health Science Curricula?" *BMC Medical Education*, vol. 20, no. 1. Springer, 2020, pp. 1–10.

Dewey, J. *How We Think. A Restatement of the Relation of Reflective Thinking to the Educative Process, Boston Etc.* DC Heath and Company, 1933.

"Divine | Violet Chachki's Digital Drag." *Youtube*, uploaded by Violet Chachki, 27 Jun. 2019, https://youtu.be/xkT6jtpCjtE.

Dodds, Sherril. "Embodied Transformations in Neo-Burlesque Striptease." *Dance Research Journal*, vol. 45, no. 3, 2013, p. 77.

Douglas, Lord Alfred. *Two Loves by Lord Alfred Douglas—Poems | Academy of American Poets*. https://poets.org/poem/two-loves. Accessed 15 Aug. 2020.

D'Silva, B. "Mind Your Language." *The Observer*, Guardian News and Media, 9 Dec. 2000, https://www.theguardian.com/theobserver/2000/dec/10/life1.lifemagazine3. Accessed 17 Mar. 2020.

Dubois, Luna. "Now that I have your attention…" *Facebook*, 3 Jun. 2020, www.facebook.com/misslunadubois/posts/283282076179622.

Duggan, Lisa. "Equality Inc." *The Twilight of Equality: Neoliberal Cultural Politics, and the Attack on Democracy*. Beacon Press, 2003, p. 50.

Edgar, Eir-Anne. "'Xtravaganza!': Drag Representation and Articulation in *RuPaul's Drag Race*." *Studies in Popular Culture*, vol. 34, no. 1. JSTOR, 2011, pp. 133–146.

efxir. "Come on casino queen." *Instagram*, 10 Feb. 2019, https://www.instagram.com/p/BtsWTFPgDZN/.

The EMMYS. "Nominations." *Academy of Television Arts and Sciences*, 2020, https://www.emmys.com/awards/nominations. Accessed 14 Aug. 2020.

Epstein, Steven. "Sexualizing Governance and Medicalizing Identities: The Emergence Of State-Centered' LGBT Health Politics in the United States." *Sexualities*, vol. 6, no. 2. Sage Publications, 2003, pp. 131–171.

"Eureka O'Hara—The Big Girl (Official Music Video)." *YouTube*, uploaded by Eureka O'Hara, 28 Jun. 2018, https://youtu.be/QUhEl-LSw5Q.

Fahnestock, Jeanne. *Rhetorical Style: The Uses of Language in Persuasion*. Oxford University Press, 2011, p. 123.

"FASHION PHOTO RUVIEW: Frozen Eleganza." *YouTube*, uploaded by WOW Presents, 8 Apr. 2020, https://www.youtube.com/watch?v=HlK6DKeFvsA.

Felski, Rita. *The Limits of Critique*. University of Chicago Press, 2015, p. 41.

Ferlatte, Olivier, et al. "Using Photovoice to Understand Suicidality among Gay, Bisexual, and Two-Spirit Men." *Archives of Sexual Behavior*, vol. 48, no. 5. Springer, 2019, pp. 1529–1541.

Figueroa, Kenneth. "Haunted: The Intersections of Queer Culture and Horror Movies,"

*Wussy*, https://www.wussymag.com/all/2017/10/6/haunted-the-intersections-of-queer-culture-and-horror-movies. Accessed 28 Jun. 2020.

"The Final Three, Hunty." *RuPaul's Drag Race*, directed by Nick Murray, performances by Alaska Thunderfuck, Roxxxy Andrews, Jinkx Monsoon, season 5, episode 13, 2013.

Fine, David, and Emily Shreve. "The Prime of Miss RuPaul Charles: Allusion, Betrayal, and Charismatic Pedagogy." *The Makeup of RuPaul's Drag Race: Essays on the Queen of Reality Shows*, edited by Jim Daems. McFarland, 2014, p. 168.

Firkus, Brian (Trixie Mattel). "Can people please stop HARPing on this costume?" *Instagram*, 12 Mar. 2019, https://www.instagram.com/p/Bu7UaiPg2sQ/.

\_\_\_\_\_. "Nude delusions." *Instagram*, 10 Feb. 2019, https://www.instagram.com/p/BtsWTFPgDZN/.

Fischer-Lichte, Erika. *The Transformative Power of Performance: A New Aesthetics*. Translated by Saskya Iris Jain. Routledge, 2008, p. 32.

Fischman, Gustavo E., and Peter McLaren. "Rethinking Critical Pedagogy and the Gramscian and Freirean Legacies: From Organic to Committed Intellectuals or Critical Pedagogy, Commitment, and Praxis." *Cultural Studies? Critical Methodologies*, vol. 5, no. 4. Sage Publications, 2005, p. 426.

Fiske, John. "The Cultural Economy of Fans." *The Adoring Audience: Fan Culture and Popular Media*, edited by Lisa A. Lewis. Routledge, 1992, p. 35.

"The Five Perspectives." *Teaching Perspectives Inventory*, Teachingperspectives.com/tpi/.

Fleischmann, Alice. *Frauenfiguren des zeitgenössischen Mainstreamfilms*. Springer Fachmedien Wiesbaden, 2016.

Foucault, Michel. *The History of Sexuality Volume 1: An Introduction*. Allen Lane, 1976, p. 37.

\_\_\_\_\_. "Of Other Spaces." *Diacritics*, translated by Jay Miskowiec, vol. 16, no. 1, 1986, p. 24.

\_\_\_\_\_. "Of Other Spaces: Utopias and Heterotopias," translated by Jay Miskowiec. Architecture/Mouvement/Continuité, no. 5, Oct. 1984.

Freire, Paulo. *Pedagogy of the Oppressed: New Revised 20th-Anniversary Edition*. The Continuum Publishing Company, 1993.

freyaviney. "U can't appropriate." *Instagram*, 10 Feb. 2019, https://www.instagram.com/p/BtsWTFPgDZN/.

Gemini, Raja. "I need to say something." *Facebook*, 24 May 2015. https://www.facebook.com/RajaOfficial/posts/i-need-to-say-something-those-who-accuse-me-of-cultural-appropriation-are-those-/1099553886727638/.

Genette, Gérard. *Paratexts: Thresholds of Interpretation*, translated by Jane E. Lewin. Cambridge University Press, 1997, p. 2.

Gerbaudo, Paolo. "Cahiers de doleance 2.0: Crowd-Sourced Social Justice Blogs and the Emergence of a Rhetoric of Collection in Social Media Activism." *Media Activism: Charting an Evolving Field of Research*, edited by Victor Pickard and Guobin Yang. Routledge, pp. 139–150.

Gillota, David. "'Cracker, Please!': Toward a White Ethnic Humor." *Ethnic Humor in Multiethnic America*. Rutgers University Press, 2013, pp. 76–103, JSTOR, https://www.jstor.org/stable/j.ctt5hjctg.7.

Giroux, Henry A. "Cultural Studies, Public Pedagogy, and the Responsibility of Intellectuals." *Communications and Critical/Cultural Studies*, vol. 1, iss. 1, 2004, pp. 59–79.

\_\_\_\_\_. "Neoliberalism, Corporate Culture, and the Promise of Higher Education: The University as a Democratic Public Sphere." *Harvard Educational Review*, vol. 72, no. 4, Winter 2002, pp. 425–63.

\_\_\_\_\_. "Public Pedagogy and the Politics of Resistance: Notes on a Critical Theory of Educational Struggle." *Educational Philosophy and Theory*, vol. 35, no. 1. Routledge, Jan. 2003, pp. 5–16, doi:10.1111/1469–5812.00002.

\_\_\_\_\_."Teachers as transformative intellectuals." *Social Education*, vol. 49. No. 5. 1985, pp. 376–79.

"GIVEAWAY!! JEFFREE STAR X SHANE DAWSON CONSPIRACY PALETTE & FIRST IMPRESSION | Kimora Blac." *YouTube*, uploaded by Kimora Blac, 5 Nov. 2019, https://youtu.be/mDQbgBKI3GM.

Godrej, F. "Spaces for Counter-Narratives: The Phenomenology of Reclamation." *Frontiers:*

*A Journal of Women Studies*, vol. 32, no. 3, Sep. 2011, p. 114, https://muse.jhu.edu/article/461367. Accessed 14 Apr. 2020.

Goldmark, M. "National Drag: The Language of Inclusion in RuPaul's Drag Race." *GLQ: A Journal of Lesbian and Gay Studies*, vol. 21, no. 4. Oct. 2015, pp. 501–520.

González, Jorge, and Kameron Cavazos. "Serving Fishy Realness: Representations of Gender Equity on *RuPaul's Drag Race*." *Continuum: Journal of Media & Cultural Studies*, vol. 30, no. 6. 2009, pp. 659–669.

Grace, D., M. Gaspar, and D. Lessard, et al. "Gay and Bisexual Men's Views on Reforming Blood Donation Policy in Canada: A Qualitative Study." *BMC Public Health* 19(1). Springer, 2017, p. 772.

Grace, Meghan, and Corey Seemiller. *Generation Z*. Routledge, 2019, p. 11.

Grant, Stuart. "The Essential Question: So What's Phenomenological About Performance Phenomenology?" *Performance Phenomenology: To the Thing Itself*, edited by Stuart Grant, Jodie McNeilly-Renaudie, and Matthew Wagner. Palgrave Macmillan, p. 23.

Gray, Jonathan. "Texts." *Keywords for Media Studies*, edited by Laurie Ouellette and Jonathan Gray. New York University Press, pp. 199–200.

Green, Rayna. "The Pocahontas Perplex: The Image of Indian Women in American Culture." *The Massachusetts Review*, vol. 14, no. 2. 1975, pp. 698–714.

———. "The Tribe Called Wannabee: Playing Indian in America and Europe." *Folklore*, vol. 99, no. 1. 1988, pp. 30–55.

Grosz, Elizabeth. "Bodies and Knowledges: Feminism and the Crisis of Reason." *Space, Time, and Perversion: Essays on the Politics of Bodies*. Routledge, 1995.

Gudelunas, David. "Digital Extensions, Experiential Extensions and Hair Extensions: *RuPaul's Drag Race* and the New Media Environment." *RuPaul's Drag Race and the Shifting Visibility of Drag Culture*, edited by Niall Brennan and David Gudelunas. Palgrave Macmillan, 2017, p. 240.

Halberstam, Jack. *Trans\*: A Quick and Quirky Account of Gender Variability*. University of California Press, 2018, p. 23.

Hancox, Donna. "Transmedia for Social Change: Evolving Approaches to Activism and Representation." *The Routledge Companion to Transmedia Studies*. Routledge, 2019, pp. 332–339.

Hanson "Teaching Shame." *Gay Shame*, edited by David M. Halperin and Valerie Traub. University of Chicago Press, 2009, pp. 132–164.

Harmony. Personal interview. 8 Aug. 2019, 14 Jul. 2020.

Hartman, Ann. "In Search of Subjugated Knowledge," *Feminism, Community, and Communication*, edited by Mary E. Olson. The Haworth Press, Inc., p. 200, par. 22.

Hauke, Alexandra, and Florian Zitzelsberger. "Subscribe to My Empire: Jeffree Star and Self-Branding on YouTube." *The Power of Makeup: Evolving Commerce, Community, and Identity in the Modern Makeup Tutorial*, edited by Clare Douglass Little. Lexington Books, forthcoming, p. 61.

Haver, W. *The Body of This Death. Historicity and Sociality in the Time of AIDS*. Stanford University Press, 1996.

Henn, Ronaldo, Felipe Viero Kolinski Machade, and Christian Gonzatti. "'We're All Born Naked and the Rest is Drag': The Performativity of Bodies Constructed in Digital Networks." *RuPaul's Drag Race and the Shifting Visibility of Drag Culture*, edited by Niall Brennan and David Gudelunas. Palgrave Macmillan, 2017, pp. 287–303.

Henry, Ben. "Black 'RuPaul's Drag Race' Queens Discuss the Racism They've Experienced from Fans of the Show and How It Affects Their Success," *Buzzfeed News*, 22 Nov. 2019, https://www.buzzfeed.com/benhenry/rupauls-drag-race-fandom-racism.

Henry, Phillip. "Why We Needed to See The Vixen Fight Aquaria on Drag Race." *Them.*, https://www.them.us/story/the-vixen-fight-aquaria-drag-race. Accessed 15 Aug. 2020.

Hickey-Moody, Anna, et al. "Pedagogy Writ Large: Public, Popular and Cultural Pedagogies in Motion." *Critical Studies in Education*, vol. 51, no. 3. 2010, p. 227.

Hills, Matt. "Transmedia Paratexts: Informational, Commercial, Diegetic, and Auratic Circulation." *The Routledge Companion to Transmedia Studies*, edited by Matthew Freeman and Renira Rampazzo Gambarato. Routledge, 2019, p. 290.

Hodes, Caroline, and Jorge Sandoval. "*RuPaul's Drag Race*: A Study in the Commodification of White Rule-class Femininity and the Etiolation of Drag." *Studies in Costume & Performance*, vol. 3, no. 2, p. 158.
Hollibaugh, Amber, and Margot Weiss. "Queer Precarity and the Myth of Gay Affluence." *New Labor Forum*, vol. 22, no. 3. 2015, p. 22.
hooks, bell. "Agent of Change: An Interview with bell hooks," by Helen Tworkov, *Tricycle*, 1992, par. 2 for what hooks characterizes as "Tina Turner Buddhism."
\_\_\_\_\_. "Is Paris Burning?" *Reel to Real: Race, Sex and Class at the Movies* [e-book]. Routledge, 2008.
\_\_\_\_\_. *Teaching to Transgress: Education As The Practice Of Freedom*. Routledge, 1994.
Huba, Jackie, and Shelly Stewart Kronbergs. *Fiercely You: Be Fabulous and Confident by Thinking Like a Drag Queen*. Berrett-Koehler Publishers, 2016, p. 169.
Imj5000. "No! People can't stop harping." *Instagram* Mar. 2019, https://www.instagram.com/p/Bu7UaiPg2sQ/.
Iyengar, Shanto, and Donald R. Kinder. *News That Matters: Television and American Opinion*. Chicago University Press, 1987.
Jay, Sarah. "Jean Paul Gaultier Married Kent Monkman to Apologize for Cultural Appropriation. Here's Why It Matters." *Fashion*, 13 Nov. 2018. https://fashionmagazine.com/style/jean-paul-gaultier-cultural-appropriation/.
jbrentstamper. "Oh honey, half breed honey?" *Instagram*, 10 Feb. 2019, https://www.instagram.com/p/BtsWTFPgDZN/.
Jenkins, Henry. *Convergence Culture: Where Old and New Media Collide*. New York University Press, 2006, p. 3.
\_\_\_\_\_. "The Revenge of the Origami Unicorn: Seven Principles of Transmedia Storytelling (Well, Two Actually. Five More on Friday)." *Confessions of an Aca-Fan*, 12 Dec. 2009, henryjenkins.org/blog/2009/12/the_revenge_of_the_origami_uni.html.
Jenkins, Sarah Tucker. *Hegemonic "Realness": An Intersectional Feminist Analysis of* RuPaul's Drag Race. MA Thesis, Florida Atlantic University, 2013, p. 84.
Johnson, E. Patrick. "Strange Fruit: A Performance about Identity Politics." *TDR* (1988–), vol. 47, no. 2, Summer 2003, pp. 88–116.
Jotanovic, Dejan. "What Do We Do With Bad Drag?" *Into*, 10 Oct. 2018. https://www.intomore.com/culture/what-do-we-do-with-bad-drag.
Joy, Philip, and Matthew Numer. "Queering educational practices in dietetics training: A critical review of LGBTQ inclusion strategies." *Canadian Journal of Dietetic Practice and Research*, vol. 79, no. 1, 1 Jun. 2018, pp. 1–6.
Justice, Daniel Heath, Bethany Schneider, and Mark Rifkin. "Heaven and Earth." *GLQ*, vol. 16, no. 1–2, 2010, pp. 1–3: p. 1.
Katz, Naomi, and Eli Katz. "Tradition and Adaptation in American Jewish Humor." *The Journal of American Folklore*, vol. 84, no. 332, Apr.–Jun. 1967, pp. 215–220.
Kellner, Douglas. *Media Spectacle*. Routledge, 2002.
Kent Monkman Studio. "Another Feather In Her Bonnet | Miss Chief Eagle Testickle & Jean Paul Gaultier." *YouTube*, 24 Jan. 2019. https://www.youtube.com/watch?v=8gMwwflxFpc.
Kidron, Beeban, director. *To Wong Foo, Thanks for Everything! Julie Newmar*. Universal Pictures, 1995.
Kight, Stef W. "The evolution of Trump's Muslim ban." *Axios*, 2 Feb. 2020, https://www.axios.com/trump-muslim-travel-ban-immigration-6ce8554f-05bd-467b-b3c2-ea4876f7773a.html. Accessed 1 Jun. 2020.
Knowles, M.S. *The Adult Learner: A Neglected Species*, 4th edition. Gulf Publishing Company, 1990.
Kumagai, Arno K., and Monica L. Lypson. "Beyond Cultural Competence: Critical Consciousness, Social Justice, and Multicultural Education." *Academic Medicine*, vol. 84, no. 6. 2009, pp. 782–787.
Kyungwon Hong, Grace. "'The Future of Our Worlds': Black Feminism and the Politics of Knowledge in the University under Globalization." *Meridians: feminism, race, transnationalism*, vol 8, no. 2. 2008, pp. 95–115.
Lakoff, Robin. *Language and Woman's Place*. Oxford University Press, 22 Jul. 2004, p. 4.

Lawson, Richard. "The Philosopher Queen." *Vanity Fair*, no. 713, Holiday 2019/2020, p. 80.
Lenton, Patrick. "The Vixen Is The Drag Queen We Need In 2020." *Junkee*, https://junkee.com/longform/the-vixen-interview. Accessed 10 Aug. 2020.
Levin, Sam. "Who Can Be a Drag Queen? RuPaul's Trans Comments Fuel Calls For Inclusion." *The Guardian*, 8 Mar. 2018, https://www.theguardian.com/tv-and-radio/2018/mar/08/rupaul-drag-race-transgender-performers-diversity.
Lim, Fidelindo, Donald V. Brown, and Henrietta Jones. "Lesbian, gay, bisexual, and transgender health: fundamentals for nursing education." *Journal of Nursing Education* 52(4), 2013, pp. 198–203.
Llayton, Chelsea K., and Lauren M. Caldas. "Strategies for inclusion of lesbian, gay, bisexual, transgender, queer, intersex, and asexual (LGBTQIA+) education throughout pharmacy school curricula." *Pharmacy Practice*, 2020, p. 1862.
Longman, Jeré, and Macur, Juliet. "Caster Semenya Loses Case to Compete as a Woman in All Races," *The New York Times*, 1 May 2019, https://www.nytimes.com/2019/05/01/sports/caster-semenya-loses.html.
Lorber, Judith. "Chapter 36: The social construction of gender" *The Inequality Reader: Contemporary and Foundational Readings in Race, Class and Gender*, edited by D. Gusky and S. Szelenyi. Routledge, 1994.
Lorde, Audre. "The Uses of Anger: Women Responding to Racism." *Sister Outsider*. Crossing, 1981.
Lotz, Amanda D. "Understanding Men on Television," *Cable Guys: Television and Masculinities in the 21st century*. NYU Press, 2014, pp. 19–51.
Love, Xtacy. "All drag is valid…" *Facebook*, 28 Jun. 2019, facebook.com/missxtacylove/posts/2318980471520852.
Luhmann, Susanne. "Queering/Querying Pedagogy? Or, Pedagogy Is a Pretty Queer Thing." *Queer Theory in Education*, edited by William F. Pinar. Lawrence Erlbaum Associates, 1998, p. 151.
Lynn, Sally. "'It is the Ugly That is so Beautiful': Performing the Monster/Beauty Continuum in American Neo-Burlesque." *The Journal of American Drama and Theatre*, vol. 21, no. 3., 2009, p. 16.
MacDonald, Baz. "A chat with Trixie Mattel—*RuPaul's Drag Race* star, Billboard charting musician and TV show host." *The Wireless*, 8 Mar. 2018. https://www.radionz.co.nz/news/the-wireless/375162/a-chat-with-trixie…rupaul-s-drag-race-star-billboard-charting-musician-and-tv-show-host.
Marlatt, Daphne. "Self-Representation and Fictionalysis." *Tessera*, vol. 8. 1990, p. 14.
Martin, Russ. "Monét X Change, Miz Cracker and The Vixen Get Real about Racism and *RuPaul's Drag Race*." *Flare*, 26 Jun. 2018, Flare.com/tv-movies/rupauls-drag-race-racism/.
———. "What's In Your Drag Bag." *Flare*, 21 Jun. 2019, Flare.com/tag/whats-in-your-drag-bag.
Massachusetts Commission on Lesbian, Gay, Bisexual, Transgender, Queer, and Questioning Youth. *Massachusetts High School Students and Sexual Orientation Results of the 2013 Youth Risk Behavior Survey*. 2013, http://www.mass.gov/cgly/YRBS13_FactsheetUpdated.pdf.
Maxouris, Christina. "Marsha P. Johnson, a [B]lack, transgender woman, was a central figure in the gay liberation movement." *CNN*, 26 Jun. 2019, https://www.cnn.com/2019/06/26/us/marsha-p-johnson-biography/index.html. Accessed 4 Jun. 2020.
McCormick Tribune Freedom Museum. "D'oh! More know Simpsons than Constitution. Study: America more familiar with cartoon family than First Amendment," *Associated Press*, Mar. 2006, http://www.nbcnews.com/id/11611015/ns/us_news-life/t/doh-more-know-simpsons-constitution/. Accessed 1 Apr. 2020.
McDonald, Michael David. *When the Government Apologizes: Understanding the Origins and Implications of the Apology to LGBTQ+2+ Communities in Canada*, 2019.
McIntyre, Joanna, and Damien W. Riggs. "North American Universalism in *RuPaul's Drag Race*: Stereotypes, Linguicism, and the Construction of Puerto Rican Queens." *RuPaul's Drag Race and the Shifting Visibility of Drag Culture*, edited by Niall Brennan and David Gudelunas. Palgrave Macmillan, 2017, p. 61.
McNeal, Keith E. "Behind the Make-Up: Gender Ambivalence and the Double-Bind of Gay

Selfhood in Drag Performance." *Ethos*, vol. 27, no. 3. Body, Self, and Technology, Sep. 1999, pp. 344–378.
McNeil, Elizabeth, James E. Wermers, and Joshua O. Lunn. "Introduction: Mapping Queer Space(s)." *Mapping Queer Space(s) of Praxis and Pedagogy*, edited by Elizabeth McNeil, James E. Wermers, and Joshua O. Lunn. Palgrave Macmillan, 2018, pp. 1–17.
Meân, Lindsey. "Sport, Identities, and Consumption: The Construction of Sport at ESPN.com." *Sports Media: Transformation, Integration, Consumption*, edited by Andrew C. Billings. Routledge, 2011, pp. 162–180.
Meyer, Jan, and Ray Land. *Threshold Concepts and Troublesome Knowledge: Linkages to Ways of Thinking and Practising within the Disciplines*. University of Edinburgh, 2003.
Mezirow, Jack. "Transformative Learning: Theory to Practice." *New Directions for Adult and Continuing Education*, vol. 1997, no. 74. Wiley Online Library, 1997, pp. 5–12.
Milner Adrienne N., and Jomils Henry Braddock II. "The Elimination of Sex Categories in Sport." *Sex Segregation in Sport: Why Separate is Not Equal*. Praeger, 2016, p. 112.
"Mimi Imfurst, Queens of Drag: NYC Ep8" *Youtube*, uploaded by Gay DotCom, 26 Oct. 2010, https://www.youtube.com/watch?v=nLS6q4Rnbns.
Mittell, Jason. *Complex TV: The Poetics of Contemporary Television Storytelling*. New York University Press, 2015.
Miu, Lucinda. Personal interview. 6 May 2019.
"Miz Cracker's Review with a Jew—S12 E06 Feat. Aiden Zhane." *YouTube*, uploaded by Miz Cracker, 5 Apr. 2020, https://youtu.be/u8n2NR_yS-k. "Pose—Naomi Smalls (Official Video)." *YouTube*, uploaded by Naomi Smalls, 16 Dec. 2018, https://youtu.be/-LnqdiACjdw.
Mogford, Elizabeth, et al. "Teaching Critical Health Literacy in the US as a Means to Action on the Social Determinants of Health." *Health Promotion International*, vol. 26, no. 1. Oxford University Press, 2011, pp. 4–13.
Molloy, Elizabeth, and Margaret Bearman. "Learning Practices Embracing the Tension between Vulnerability and Credibility: 'Intellectual Candour' in Health Professions Education." *Medical Education* vol. 53, iss. 1, 2019, pp. 32–41.
Monkman, Kent. "Biography." *Kent Monkman*. https://www.kentmonkman.com/biography.
\_\_\_\_\_. "Hanky Panky." *Instagram*. 16 May 2020. https://www.instagram.com/p/CARCAYogg7w/.
\_\_\_\_\_. *Nation to Nation*. 2020. https://www.kentmonkman.com/painting/nation-to-nation.
Monsoon, Jinkx. "Bio: The Making of Jinkx Monsoon," *Jinkx Monsoon*, https://jinkxmonsoon.com/bio/. Accessed 25 Apr. 2020.
Moore, Ramey. "Everything Else is Drag: Linguistic Drag and Gender Parody on *RuPaul's Drag Race*." *Journal of Research in Gender Studies* vol. 3, no. 2, 2013, p. 8.
Morris, Matthew, et al. "Training to Reduce LGBTQ+-Related Bias among Medical, Nursing, and Dental Students and Providers: A Systematic Review." *BMC Medical Education*, vol. 19, no. 1. Springer, 2019, p. 325.
Morris, Sean Michael, and Jesse Stommel. *An Urgency of Teachers: The Work of Critical Digital Pedagogy*. Hybrid Pedagogy, 2018.
Morrison, Josh. "'Draguating' to Normal: Camp and Homonormative Politics." *The Makeup of* RuPaul's Drag Race: *Essays on the Queen of Reality Shows*, edited by Jim Daems. McFarland, 2014, pp. 124–147.
"The Most Powerful Drag Queens in America." *Vulture*, 10 Jun. 2019, Vulture.com/2019/06/most-powerful-drag-queens-in-america-ranked.html.
Munzenrieder, Kyle. "Cardi B Will Trademark 'Okurrr'—Even if the Phrase Has a Long History Before Her." *W*, 21 Mar. 2019, https://www.wmagazine.com/story/cardi-b-trademark-okurrr-phrase-origin-rupal/. Accessed 9 Jul. 2020.
Murray, Garold. *Pop Culture and Language Learning: Learners' Stories Informing EFL, Innovation in Language Learning and Teaching*, 2:1, 2–17, first published 2008, Akita International University, Japan, http://dx.doi.org/10.1080/17501220802158792.
Nash, Catherine, and Andrew Gorman-Murray. "Queer Mobilities and New Spatial Media." *The Geographies of Digital Sexuality*, edited by Catherine Nash and Andrew Goman-Murray. Palgrave Macmillan, 2019, p. 30.

"Netflix's Queer Eye in Conversation." *Youtube*, uploaded by 92nd Street Y, 21 Jun. 2018, https://www.youtube.com/watch?v=noRolBwYkYQ.

Newton, Esther. *Mother Camp: Female Impersonators in America*. University of Chicago Press, 1972, p. 103.

Nicholson, Rebecca. "RuPaul: 'Drag is dangerous. We are making fun of everything.'" *The Guardian*, 3 Jun. 2015, https://www.theguardian.com/tv-and-radio/2015/jun/03/rupaul-drag-is-dangerous-we-are-making-fun-of-everything.

"Night 1: What Is Chanukah? - Jewtorials Chanukah Special." *YouTube*, uploaded by World of Wonder, 22 Dec. 2019, https://www.youtube.com/watch?v=5nDxKgUnwDk.

"NINA'S RPDR SEASON 12 SNATCH GAME RAWVIEW." *YouTube*, uploaded by Nina Bo'Nina Brown, 5 Apr. 2020, https://www.youtube.com/watch?v=VJtXXcFUmXE.

Nixon, Lindsay. *nîtisânak*. Metonymy, 2018.

Nolfi, Joey. "*RuPaul's Drag Race All Stars 3*: BenDeLaCreme on how Thorgy, aliens, and Wite-Out made a martyr." *Entertainment Weekly*, 2 Mar. 2018, https://ew.com/tv/2018/03/02/rupauls-drag-race-bendelacreme-on-how-thorgy-thor-aliens-and-wite-out-made-a-martyr/.

\_\_\_\_\_. "*RuPaul's Drag Race* Disqualifies Sherry Pie Over Catfishing Allegations." *EW*, 6 Mar. 2020. https://ew.com/tv/rupauls-drag-race-disqualifies-sherry-pie-catfishing-allegations/#:~:text=%E2%80%9CIn%20light%20of%20recent%20developments,air%20the%20season%20as%20planned.

NSWP. "Street Transvestite Action Revolutionaries Found STAR House." *Global Network of Sex*.

Oleksiak, Timothy. "When Queens Listen." *Reinventing (with) Theory in Rhetoric and Writing: Essays in Honor of Sharon Crowley*, edited by Andrea Alden, Kendall Gerdes, Judy Holiday, Ryan Skinnell. University of Press of Colorado; Utah State University Press, 2019, pp. 257–267.

"100% All Natural Soap for Men—Dr. Squatch" *Youtube*, uploaded by Dr. Squatch Soap Company, 18 Sep. 2019,https://www.youtube.com/watch?v=m_mF9MvksTU and "Dr. Squatch—Natural Soap for Men" *Youtube*, uploaded by Dr. Squatch Soap Company, 21 May 2018, https://www.youtube.com/watch?v=cjEK7qQKRDY.

Organization for Economic, and Co-operation and Development. *Society at a Glance 2019 - OECD Social Indicators—En—OECD*. 2019, http://www.oecd.org/social/society-at-a-glance-19991290.htm.

Page, Ruth. *Narratives Online: Shared Stories in Social Media*. Cambridge University Press, 2018.

Pandell, Lexi. "How *RuPaul's Drag Race* Fueled Pop Culture's Dominant Slang Engine." *Wired*, 2018, https://www.wired.com/story/rupauls-drag-race-slang/. Accessed 17 Mar. 2020.

Parameshwaran, Vishnu, et al. "Is the Lack of Specific Lesbian, Gay, Bisexual, Transgender and Queer/Questioning (LGBTQ+) Health Care Education in Medical School a Cause for Concern? Evidence from a Survey of Knowledge and Practice among UK Medical Students." *Journal of Homosexuality*, vol. 64, no. 3. Taylor & Francis, 2017, pp. 367–381.

*Paris Is Burning*. Directed by Jennie Livingston. Off-White Productions, 1989.

Parsemain, Ava Laure. *The Pedagogy of Queer TV*. Springer, 2019.

Patterson, Natasha. "Sabotaging Reality: Exploring Canadian Women's Participation on Neoliberal Reality TV." *Canadian Journal of Communication*, vol. 40. 2015, pp. 281–295.

Peck, Raoul. *I Am Not Your Negro*. Magnolia Pictures, 2016.

Phelan, Peggy. *Unmarked: The Politics of Performance*. Routledge, 1996.

Phillipson, Robert. "Linguistic imperialism." *The Sociological Quarterly*, vol. 39, no. 3. 1992, p. 514.

Potvin, Louise, et al. "Integrating Social Theory into Public Health Practice." *American Journal of Public Health*, vol. 95, no. 4. American Public Health Association, 2005, pp. 591–595.

Quenqua, Douglas. "They're, Like, Way Ahead of the Linguistic Currrrve." *The New York Times*, 28 Feb. 2012, https://www.nytimes.com/2012/02/28/science/young-women-often-trendsetters-in-vocal-patterns.html?pagewanted=all. Accessed 12 Apr. 2020.

"*RuPaul's Drag Race* Dictionary." *Fandom.com*, 2020, https://rupaulsdragrace.fandom.com/wiki/RuPaul%27s_Drag_Race_Dictionary.

## Select Bibliography

Razack, Sherene H. *Looking White People in the Eye: Gender, Race, and Culture in Courtrooms and Classrooms*. University of Toronto Press, 2001, p. 69.

Redmond, Sean. "Sensing Film Performance." *Performance Phenomenology: To the Thing Itself*, edited by Stuart Grant, Jodie McNeilly-Renaudie, and Matthew Wagner. Palgrave Macmillan, p. 167.

Reisner, Sari L., et al. "Mental Health of Transgender Youth in Care at an Adolescent Urban Community Health Center: A Matched Retrospective Cohort Study." *Journal of Adolescent Health*, vol. 56, no. 3. Elsevier, 2015, pp. 274–279.

"Reunited!" *RuPaul's Drag Race*, season six, episode 14, Logo TV, 19 May 2014, *Amazon*, https://smile.amazon.com/gp/video/detail/B00ICGYECE/ref=atv_dp_season_select_s6.

Rich, Adrienne. *Blood, Bread, and Poetry: Selected Prose, 1979–1985*. W. W. Norton & Company, 1994.

rickrichter. "Cultural appropriation is someone wearing costumes." *Instagram*, Feb. 2019, https://www.instagram.com/p/BtsWTFPgDZN/.

Riot, Tash. Personal interview. 10 Jun. 2019.

Rogers, Russell R. "Reflection in Higher Education: A Concept Analysis." *Innovative Higher Education*, vol. 26, no. 1. Springer, 2001, pp. 37–57.

Rose, Ava, and James Friedman. "Television Sports as Masculine Cult of Distraction." *Out of Bounds: Sports, Media, and the Politics of Identity*, edited by Aaron Baker and Todd Boyd. Indiana University Press, 1997, pp. 8–11.

"R/Rupaulsdragrace—Insider Tea: Gigi Tried to Cheat and Was Threatened with Disqualification and Legal Action by Production." Reddit, https://www.reddit.com/r/rupaulsdragrace/comments/gtncs6/insider_tea_gigi_tried_to_cheat_and_was/. Accessed 15 Aug. 2020.

RuPaul. "Born Naked." *Born Naked*. RuCo Inc., 2014.

———. "Each morning I pray to set aside everything I THINK I know, so I may have an open mind and a new experience. I understand and regret the hurt I have caused. The trans community are heroes of our shared LGBTQ movement. You are my teachers," 5 Mar. 2018, 3:57 pm. Tweet.

———. *GuRu*. Dey Street Books, 2018.

———. "Supermodel (You Better Work)." *Supermodel of the World*, 1993, Tommy Boy Records.

———. *Workin' It: RuPaul's Guide to Life, Liberty, and the Pursuit of Style*. It Books, 2010.

"RuPaul Charles: We're All In Drag." *Oprah's SuperSoul Conversations* from iTunes, 17 Jan. 2018, itunes.apple.com/us/podcast/oprahs-supersoul-conversations/id1264843400?mt=2.

"RuPaul/Justin Bieber," *Saturday Night Live*, created by Lorne Michaels, performance by RuPaul, season 45, episode 13, Broadway Video, 2020.

*RuPaul's Drag Race All Stars*, season 1, Logo TV, 2012, *Amazon*, https://www.amazon.com/gp/video/detail/B009VB83GW/ref=atv_dp_season_select_s1.

———, season 2, Logo TV, 2016, *Amazon*, https://www.amazon.com/gp/video/detail/B01KGB99VI/ref=atv_dp_season_select_s2.

———, season 4, episode 6, VH1, 2019, *Amazon*, https://smile.amazon.com/gp/video/detail/B07KWPRZ5M/ref=atv_dp_season_select_s4.

*RuPaul's Drag Race*, season 1, Logo TV, 2009, *Amazon*, https://www.amazon.com/gp/video/detail/B001RGOIWW/ref=atv_dp_season_select_s1.

———, season 3, Logo TV, 2011, *Amazon*, https://www.amazon.com/gp/video/detail/B004JGWASG/ref=atv_dp_season_select_s3.

———, season 4, Logo TV, 2012, *Amazon*, https://www.amazon.com/gp/video/detail/B007142CFE/ref=atv_dp_season_select_s4.

———, season 5, Logo TV, 2013, *Amazon*, https://www.amazon.com/gp/video/detail/B00B45B4X2/ref=atv_dp_season_select_s5.

———, season 6, Logo TV, 2014, *Amazon*, https://www.amazon.com/gp/video/detail/B00ICGYECE/ref=atv_dp_season_select_s6.

———, season 7, Logo TV, 2015, *Amazon*, https://smile.amazon.com/gp/video/detail/B00TG0HXVE/ref=atv_dp_season_select_s7.

———, season 8, Logo TV, 2016, *Amazon*, https://www.amazon.com/gp/video/detail/

B01BZGNENC/ref=atv_dp_season_select_s8.

———, season 9, Logo TV, 2017, *Amazon*, https://www.amazon.com/gp/video/detail/B06XK36FZS/ref=atv_dp_season_select_s9.

———, season 10, VH1, 2018, *Amazon*, https://www.amazon.com/gp/video/detail/B07B68P55J/ref=atv_dp_season_select_s10.

———, season 11, VH1, 2019, *Amazon*, https://smile.amazon.com/gp/video/detail/B07P5GN25J/ref=atv_dp_season_select_s11.

———, season 12, VH1, 2020, *Amazon*, https://smile.amazon.com/gp/video/detail/B06XK36FZS/ref=atv_dp_season_select_s9.

"*RuPaul's Drag Race* (2009–) Awards." *IMDB*, 2020, www.imdb.com/title/tt1353056/awards?ref_=tt_awd.

"*RuPaul's Drag Race: All Stars Four* official fantasy league," VH1/Viacom, Dec. 2018–Feb. 2019, Vh1dragracefantasyleague.com.

"RuPaul's DRAG RACE Season 12 Episode 6 Review w/ Chester Lockhart | Shot With Soju LIVE!" *YouTube*, uploaded by Soju, 5 Apr. 2020, https://youtu.be/9yHpS3MLCZo.

*RuPaul's Drag Race: Untucked*, season 4, Logo TV, 2012, *Amazon*, https://www.amazon.com/gp/video/detail/B0073PR0VW/ref=atv_dp_season_select_s4.

———, season 10, VH1, 2018, *Amazon*, https://www.amazon.com/gp/video/detail/B07B68P55J/ref=atv_dp_season_select_s10.

———, season 12, VH1, 2020, *Amazon*, https://www.amazon.com/gp/video/detail/B0859PL9Z5/ref=atv_dp_season_select_s12.

*RuPaul's Drag U*, season 1, Logo TV, 2010, *Amazon*, https://www.amazon.com/Tomboy-Meets-Girl/dp/B003WZZKGE/ref=sr_1_1?dchild=1&keywords=Drag+U&qid=1596308611&sr=8-1.

"RuPaul's DragCon LA." *Wikipedia*, Wikipedia Foundation, 30 Jan. 2020, https://en.wikipedia.org/wiki/RuPaul%27s_DragCon_LA. Accessed 20 Mar. 2020.

"RuPaul's Recipe for Success: Be Fabulous, Sing and Bring People Together (Guest Column)." *The Hollywood Reporter*, 15 Jun. 2018, https://www.hollywoodreporter.com/news/rupaul-his-recipe-success-guest-column-1119261.

*RuPaul's Secret Celebrity Drag Race*, season 1, VH1, 2020, https://www.amazon.com/RuPauls-Secret-Celebrity-Drag-Season/dp/B087MW4ZY7.

"RuPocalypse Now." *RuPaul's Drag Race: Untucked*, season 4, episode 1, Logo TV, 30 Jan. 2012, *Amazon*, https://www.amazon.com/gp/video/detail/B0073PR0VW/ref=atv_dp_season_select_s4.

Russell, Stephen T., and Jessica N. Fish. "Mental Health in Lesbian, Gay, Bisexual, and Transgender (LGBT) Youth." *Annual Review of Clinical Psychology*, vol. 12. Annual Reviews, 2016, pp. 465–487.

Ruti, Mari. *The Ethics of Opting Out*. Columbia University Press, 2017, p. 6.

Sandlin, Jennifer A., et al. "Mapping the Complexity of Public Pedagogy Scholarship: 1894–2010." *Review of Educational Research*, vol. 81, no. 3. 2011, p. 336.

"Sasha Velour Quotes." *BrainyQuote.com*, BrainyMedia, Inc., 2020, https://www.brainyquote.com/quotes/sasha_velour_940546. Accessed 9 Jul. 2020.

Schacht, Steven P. "Beyond the Boundaries of the Classroom: Teaching About Gender and Sexuality at a Drag Show." *Journal of Homosexuality*, vol. 46, no. 3–4, p. 225.

Schottmiller, Carl. "'Excuse My Beauty!': Camp Referencing and Memory Activation on *RuPaul's Drag Race*," *Sontag and the Camp Aesthetic: Advancing New Perspectives*, edited by Bruce E. Drushel and Brian M. Peters. Lexington Books, 2017, pp. 111–130.

———. "Reading *RuPaul's Drag Race*: Queer Memory, Camp Capitalism, and RuPaul's Drag Empire." Dissertation, University of California, Los Angeles, 2017, https://escholarship.org/uc/item/0245q9h9.

Scott, Lindsay D. "Prisons, Pedagogy, and Possibilities: An Application of Freire and Hooks' Educational Philosophies." *Dialogues in Social Justice: An Adult Education Journal*, vol. 2, no. 2. 2017.

Scotto, Miss. Personal interview. 2 Sep. 2019.

Scudera, Domenick. "The Professor Is a Drag Queen," *Chronicle of Higher Education*, vol. 61, no. 16, 2015, p. 1.

Sedgewick, Eve. "Reality and Realization." *The Weather in Proust*, edited by Jonathan Goldberg. Duke University Press, 2011, pp. 206–215; p. 208.
———. "Teaching/Depression." *The Scholar and Feminist Online*, vol. 4, no. 2, Spring 2006, par. 6.
Sega, Lauren. "The Philanthropy of Nina West—ColumbusUnderground.Com." *Columbus Underground*, 3 Oct. 2017, https://www.columbusunderground.com/the-philanthropy-of-nina-west-ls1.
"Shallow—Belfast - 2.23.19." *YouTube*, uploaded by Alaska Thunderfuck, 24 Feb. 2019, https://youtu.be/99uByxN-ts4.
"Shangela, Shea Couleé, & Aja Discuss Racism in the 'Drag Race' Fandom." Mikelle Street. *Billboard*, 4 May 2018, https://www.billboard.com/articles/news/pride/8289680/shangela-shea-coulee-aja-racism-drag-race-fandom. Accessed 20 May 2020.
Siebler, Kay. *Learning Queer Identity in the Digital Age*. Palgrave Macmillan, 2016, p. 16.
Silberman, Seth Clark. "Why RuPaul *Worked*: Queer Cross-Identifying the Mythic Black (Drag Queen) Mother." *Territories of Desire in Queer Culture: Refiguring Contemporary Boundaries*, edited by David Alderson, Linda R. Anderson. Manchester University Press, 2000, pp. 166–182.
Silencia. Personal interview. 2 Jul. 2019.
Simmons, Nathaniel. "Speaking like a Queen in *RuPaul's Drag Race*." *Sexuality & Culture*, 18, New York, 7 Dec. 2013, p. 631.
Simpson, Jaye (jaye_simplson). "this gross misrepresentation." *Instagram*, Feb. 2019, https://www.instagram.com/p/BtsWTFPgDZN/.
Skeggs, Beverley, and Helen Wood. "Introduction: Reacting to Reality Television," *Reacting to Reality Television: Performance, Audience and Value*. Routledge, 2012, p. 12.
Smith, Daniel R. "Persona." *Comedy and Critique: Stand-Up Comedy and the Professional Ethos of Laughter*. Bristol University Press, 2018, JSTOR, https://www.jstor.org/stable/j.ctv56fgq1.9.
Smith, Miriam. "Homophobia and Homonationalism: LGBTQ+ Law Reform in Canada." *Social & Legal Studies*, vol. 29, no. 1. 2020, pp. 65–84.
Smith, Nigel, M. "Bianca Del Rio: 'I would gladly do my comedy without drag'" *The Guardian*, 17, Dec. 2016, https://www.theguardian.com/culture/tvandradioblog/2015/dec/17/bianca-del-rio-comedy-drag-queen-rupaul-rolodex-hate.
Snipes, Jeremy T., and Lucy A. LePeau. "Becoming a Scholar: A Duoethnography of Transformative Learning Spaces." *International Journal of Qualitative Studies in Education*, vol. 30, no. 6. Taylor & Francis, 2017, pp. 576–595.
"Social Media Kings into Queens." *RuPaul's Drag Race*, season 10, episode 10, VH1, 21 Apr. 2014, Netflix app.
Spanos, Brittany. "RuPaul on 'Drag Race' Success, Being and Introvert, Survival Playlist." *Rolling Stone*, 19 Dec. 2017.
Spark, Muriel. *The Prime of Miss Jean Brodie*. HarperCollins, 2009, p. 5.
Spender, Dale. *Man Made Language*. Routledge & Kegan Paul, 1980.
"'Spilling The Tea': The Queens Kiki on Gay Dating Apps & Lady Gaga's 'Born This Way.'" *YouTube*, uploaded by *Billboard*, 27 Jun. 2017, https://www.youtube.com/watch?v=yBtji0rAFC8.
Stalling, L.H. *Funk the Erotic: Transaesthetics and Black Sexual Cultures*. University of Illinois Press, 2015.
Stavrides, S. *Towards the City of Thresholds*. Ellinika Grammata, 2002.
Stewart, Kate, and Pauline O'Reilly. "Exploring the Attitudes, Knowledge and Beliefs of Nurses and Midwives of the Healthcare Needs of the LGBTQ+ Population: An Integrative Review." *Nurse Education Today*, vol. 53. Elsevier, 2017, pp. 67–77.
Stommel, Jesse. "Designing for Care: Inclusive Pedagogies for Online Learning." *Jesse Stommel*, 19 Jun. 2020, https://www.jessestommel.com/designing-for-care/.
Story, J. *An Introduction to Cultural Theory and Popular Culture* (2nd ed). University of Georgia Press, 1998.
Strangelove, Michael. *Watching YouTube: Extraordinary Videos By Ordinary People*. University of Toronto Press, 2010, p. 87.

Straw, Will. "Systems of Articulation, Logics of Change: Scenes and Communities in Popular Music." *Cultural Studies*, vol. 6, no. 3, 1991, p. 369.
Strings, Sabrina, and Long T. Bui. "'She Is Not Acting, She Is': The Conflict between Gender and Racial Realness on *RuPaul's Drag Race*." *Feminist Media Studies*, vol. 14, no. 5. Taylor & Francis, 2014, pp. 822–836.
*Suspiciously Large Woman*. Directed by Cheyenne Picardo, performance by Bob the Drag Queen, Producer Entertainment Group, 2017.
theskylestrasser. "*begin beating Indian drums frantically*." *Instagram*, Feb. 2019, https://www.instagram.com/p/BtsWTFPgDZN/.
Thezachberge. "I have no reservations about this and it's a trail of white tears." *Instagram*, Feb. 2019, https://www.instagram.com/p/BtsWTFPgDZN/.
"Transgender Queens on Rupaul's Drag Race | GIA GUNN." *YouTube*, uploaded by Gia Gunn Entertainment, 6 Mar. 2018, https://youtu.be/la9QHkzID4M.
Treiber, Guilel. "Lip Sync for Your Life," *RuPaul's Drag Race and Philosophy: Sissy That Thought*, edited by Hendrik Kempt and Megan Volpert. Caris Publishing, 2020.
Trinity the Tuck. Interviewed by Bianca Guzzo. *IN MAGAZINE*, 17 Apr. 2019, http://inmagazine.ca/2019/04/interview-catching-up-with-trinity-the-tuck/. Accessed 10 Jun. 2020.
Trixie Mattel. "The Most Powerful Drag Queens in America. Ranking the new establishment." By the editors. *Vulture*, 10 Jun. 2019, https://www.vulture.com/2019/06/most-powerful-drag-queens-in-america-ranked.html. Accessed 5 Jun. 2020.
tsistsistas. "just bc she is native." *Instagram*, 10 Feb. 2019, https://www.instagram.com/p/BtsWTFPgDZN/.
Tuhiwai Smith, Linda. "Imperialism, History, Writing and Theory." *Decolonizing Methodologies: Research and Indigenous Peoples*. Zed Books Ltd., 2013, pp. 33–35.
Tylez, Porcelain. Personal interview. 7 Aug. 2019.
"UNHhhh Ep 57: "The 90s" w/ Trixie Mattel & Katya Zamolodchikova," *YouTube*, uploaded by World of Wonder, 14 Aug. 2017, https://www.youtube.com/watch?v=z3OnRH5YXu8&list=PLhgFEi9aNUb2BNrIEecCGXApgeX7Yjwz8&index=76.
Upadhyay, Nishant. "'Can you get more American than Native American?': Drag and Settler Colonialism in *RuPaul's Drag Race*." *Cultural Studies*, 2019, pp. 1–22; p. 13.
"Valentina @Allaboutvalentina." *Instagram*, 2020, www.instagram.com/allaboutvalentina/?hl=en.
"Valentina—[Official]." *YouTube*, uploaded by Alaska Thunderfuck, 13 Oct. 2017, https://youtu.be/7SKkkfn2zLc.
Van Ness, Jonathan, and Margaret Cho. Interviewed by Kaitlin Reilly. *REFINERY29*, 15 Jun. 2018, https://www.refinery29.com/en-us/2018/06/201908/margaret-cho-jonathan-van-ness-gay-pride-month. Accessed 10 Jun. 2020.
Van Sluys, Katie, et al. "Researching Critical Literacy: A Critical Study of Analysis of Classroom Discourse." Journal of Literacy Research, vol. 38, no. 2. SAGE Publications, 2006, pp. 197–233.
Vary, Adam. B. "Inside the Wondrous Expansion of—and Biggest Threat to—the 'RuPaul's Drag Race' Brand (EXCLUSIVE)." *Variety.com*, 29 May 2020, https://variety.com/2020/tv/news/rupauls-drag-race-international-all-stars-celebrity-sherry-pie-1234619728/.
Vaughn, Lisa M., and Raymond C. Baker. "Psychological Size and Distance: Emphasising the Interpersonal Relationship as a Pathway to Optimal Teaching and Learning Conditions." *Medical Education*, vol. 38, no. 10. Wiley Online Library, 2004, pp. 1053–1060.
Vesey, Alyxandra. "'A Way to Sell Your Records': Pop Stardom and the Politics of Drag Professionalization on *RuPaul's Drag Race*." *Television & New Media*, vol. 18, no. 7. 2017, pp. 589–604.
Vyle, Selena. Personal interview. 8 May 2019.
Wang, Grace. "A shot at half-exposure: Asian Americans in reality TV shows." *Television and New Media*, vol. 11, no. 5. 2010, p. 405.
Warner, Michael. *The Trouble with Normal*. Harvard University Press, 1999, p. 36.
"The way Miz cookie was so effortlessly prancing in those heels really was a gag," posted by u/RVulcanz. Reddit, 25 May 2018, 21.05. https://www.reddit.com/r/rupaulsdragrace/comments/8m3tzf/the_way_miz_cookie_was_so_effortlessly_prancing/.

"We, the NFL, condemn racism and the systemic oppression of Black People. We, the NFL, admit we were wrong for not listening to NFL players earlier and encourage all to speak out and peacefully protest. We, the NFL, believe Black Lives Matter. #InspireChange," *Twitter*, 5 Jun. 2020, 6:31 p.m. https://twitter.com/NFL/status/1269034074552721408.

Weaver, Caity. "Trixie Mattel Is for Men (and Women and Kids)." *GQ*, 29 Nov. 2017. https://www.gq.com/story/rixie-mattel-is-for-men-and-women-and-kids.

Weil, Simone. *Waiting for God*. HarperCollins, 2009, p. 132.

Weldes, Jutta, and Christina Rowley. "So, How Does Popular Culture Relate to World Politics?" *Popular Culture and World Politics: Theories, Methods, Pedagogies. E-international Relations Publishing*, edited by Frederica Caso and Caitlin Hamilton. Bristol, 2005, p. 15.

Wellard, Ian. *Sport, Masculinities and the Body*. Routledge, 2009.

Whitford, Emma. "Hundreds of Colleges Walk Back Fall Reopening Plans and Opt for Online-Only Instruction," *Inside Higher Ed*, https://www.insidehighered.com/news/2020/08/12/hundreds-colleges-walk-back-fall-reopening-plans-and-opt-online-only-instruction. Accessed 15 Aug. 2020.

Whitworth, Colin. "Sissy That Performance Script! The Queer Pedagogy of *RuPaul's Drag Race*." *RuPaul's Drag Race and the Shifting Visibility of Drag Culture*. Springer, 2017, p. 148.

"WHO | The Ottawa Charter for Health Promotion." *WHO*, World Health Organization. www.who.int, http://www.who.int/healthpromotion/conferences/previous/ottawa/en/. Accessed 12 Apr. 2020.

Widdicombe, Lizzie. "Can 'RuPaul's Drag Race' Save Us from Donald Trump?" *The New Yorker*, 4 Mar. 2020, https://www.newyorker.com/culture/culture-desk/can-rupauls-drag-race-save-us-from-donald-trump. Accessed 21 Mar. 2020.

Wierlemann, Sabine. "Political Correctness in den USA und in Deutschland." *Philologische Studien und Quellen, Band 175*. Erich Schmidt Verlag, 1 Sep. 2002, p. 2.

Wilde, Oscar. "De Profundis." https://www.gutenberg.org/files/921/921-h/921-h.htm. Accessed 15 Aug. 2020.

_____. "The Decay of Lying." https://www.sscnet.ucla.edu/comm/steen/cogweb/Abstracts/Wilde_1889.html. Accessed 14 Aug. 2020.

Wilson, Julie A. "Enterprising Democracy: Neoliberal Citizenship and the Privatization of Politics," *neoliberalism*. Routledge, 2018, pp. 199–202.

_____. "A New Hegemony," *neoliberalism*. Routledge, 2018, p. 22.

Wolfe, Patrick. "Settler Colonialism and the Elimination of the Native." *Journal of Genocide Research*, vol. 8, no. 4. 2006, pp. 387–409.

*Work Projects*, 4 Dec. 2015, https://www.nswp.org/timeline/event/street-transvestite-action-revolutionaries-found-star-house.

Young, Danielle. "RuPaul Attempts to Answer Diversity Question." *Essence.com*, 23 Sep. 2019, https://www.essence.com/videos/rupaul-drag-race-diversity-emmys/.

Yudelman, Julia. "The 'RuPaulitics' of Subjectification in *RuPaul's Drag Race*." *RuPaul's Drag Race and the Shifting Visibility of Drag Culture*. Springer, 2017, pp. 15–28.

Zhang, Eric. "Memoirs of a GAY! Sha: Race and gender performance on *RuPaul's Drag Race*." *Studies in Costume & Performance*, vol. 1, no. 2. 2016, p. 65.

Žižek, Slavoj. *The Ticklish Subject: The Absent Centre of Political Ontology*. Verso, 1999, p. 329.

# Charisma, Uniqueness, Nerve and Talent
## About the Contributors

Lindsay **Bryde** is the Education Technologist—Long Island at SUNY Empire State College. She is a proud alumna of Fredonia State University (MA in English, BA in English, BA in theatre arts) and Adelphi University (MFA in creative writing). Her experience as an educator includes teaching in face-to-face, online, and hybrid courses at myriad institutions. She has taught courses in composition, literature, speech, business writing, education, creative writing, dramatic writing, and film.

David J. **Fine** is a Ph.D. and an assistant professor of English at the University of Dayton. His research focuses on secularization and ethics in the modern British novel. He has published on issues of education, religion, and queerness and, with Emily Shreve, on RuPaul's pedagogy in *The Makeup of RuPaul's Drag Race* (2014). He teaches courses in feminist theory, LGBTQ+ literature, and community engagement and holds a master's degree in curriculum and instruction.

Ricarda **Goetz-Preisner** is a political scientist with a strong focus on popular culture. She researches questions of equality at the interface of politics, culture, and education. She has published papers on the herstory of sports, gender, and gaming, and the power of popular culture. She is also an expert speaker about gaming and the depiction of women in film. She is employed as an officer for basic research and international affairs for the City of Vienna Women's Department.

Phillip **Joy** holds a Ph.D. and is an assistant professor in the Applied Human Nutrition Department at Mount Saint Vincent University. His research interests include the health and nutrition of LGBTQ+ communities, body image, and arts-based methodologies. He is a co-editor of *Rainbow Reflections: Body Image Comics for Queer Men* (2019). He views teaching and learning as a co-productive experience and thrives to create safe spaces for all within his learning environments.

Vicky **Kampouridou** was born and raised in Greece. She studied civil engineering (with a specialty in public transportation) at Aristotle University of Thessaloniki. She holds a Master's in urban planning from National Technical University of Athens where she worked in feminism, gendered space, threshold bodily situations, the narration of the "other" bodies, culture of the margins and culture of phantasmagoria. She is a Ph.D. candidate at the Laboratory of Gender and Space at the National Technical University of Athens.

Russ **Martin** (he/him) is a writer, editor, and scholar. He completed his master's degree in popular culture at Brock University. His journalism has been featured in the *Toronto Star*, *Flare*, the *National Post*, *Xtra*, and *The Walrus*. He contributed to *Canadian Theatre Review*'s drag-themed issue and a forthcoming volume on monsters. He is an event producer with the Circus and its Other research project and a producer and in-house researcher for Toronto's online drag bar, Speakeasy TV.

Tommy **Mayberry** (he/she/they) is the Executive Director of the Centre for Teaching and Learning at the University of Alberta and is finishing their Ph.D. in English language and literature at the University of Waterloo. They work and research from an embodied standpoint to explore, individually and collectively, gender, pedagogy, performance, language, social media, and reality TV (to name a few) and have presented work and research across Canada and internationally in Oxford, Tokyo, Washington, D.C., and Honolulu.

Jill Marie **McSweeney-Flaherty** has a Ph.D. in interdisciplinary studies, where she examined the impact of space and place on health and well-being. She teaches Dalhousie's Certificate in University Teaching and Learning, supports faculty and staff in engaging in ethical and robust scholarship, and explores the development of learning spaces that encourage the co-creation of knowledge and understanding.

Mandy **Penney** (she/her) is a white, cis, queer settler and academic living on Treaty 6 territory in Ontario, Canada. She works as the Coordinator of Writing Services at Huron University College, and her most recent research interests are developing anti-racist and decolonizing policies and praxis in writing center contexts.

Peter **Piatkowski** is a London-based writer. He studied at the University of Illinois, Chicago, earning his BA before getting his MA from DePaul University in English literature and his MFA in creative writing from Roosevelt University. He has published in a variety of journals, anthologies, and websites, including *Off the Rocks*, *The View from Here*, and *Bright Wall/Dark Room*. His focus is mainly film, television, literature, and music.

Maggie **Ward** is a white settler Ph.D. candidate in English and cultural studies at McMaster University, which occupies the territories of the Haudenosaunee and Mississauga nations within the land protected by the Dish with One Spoon Wampum agreement. Her previous work has appeared in the *Canadian Review of American Studies*.

Nathan **Workman** is a Ph.D. student with the University of Wisconsin–Madison's Communication Arts Media & Cultural Studies program, focusing on contemporary queer media, intra-community dynamics, and transmedia branding practices. This framework was informed by his tenure as a humanities graduate at Old Dominion University and his work with Norfolk, Virginia's Tidewater Queer History Project. He enjoys learning about regional queer histories.

Florian **Zitzelsberger** is a Ph.D. candidate at the University of Passau, Germany, whose research focuses on queer theory, performance studies, and musicals on stage and screen. He has published on queer cinema, environmentalist metafiction as well as desire and queer failure. As part of the interdisciplinary project SKILL. de, his teaching addresses questions of representation as well as AIDS and the COVID-19 pandemic. He is working on a project examining "Post/Human Drag."

# The Library Is Open
## The Index

"Absolut Drag Ball" (season 1, episode 6) 74
Act, Courtney 24, 222
*The Adventures of Priscilla, Queen of the Desert* 41
Ahmed, Sara 21, 166, 170–171, 177, 233, 234, 235
Aitkenhead, Decca 5, 190*n*38, 263*n*44
*A.J. and the Queen* 15
Aja 237, 258
Akira 127, 223–224
*All Stars* 6, 11; season 2 74, 236, 238; season 4 196, 218, 221–222, 238–239, 246, 264; season 5 96, 214
*America's Next Top Model* 5
Anderson, Deborah 91–93, 95–96
Andrews, Roxxxy 10, 102–103, 223–224
Angel, Buck 110–111*n*39
Aquaria 27–28, 77, 80, 123–124, 164, 229, 261
Arbuckle, Fatty 208

B, Cardi 45
Baby bel-Bel 136
backrolls 8, 10, 277
Bailey, Jim 207, 220
bald 45, 96, 100, 101, 112*n*65, 112*n*72, 112–113*n*79, 222
Balenciaga, Mariah Paris 220
ball 1, 10, 37, 38, 40, 73, 93, 97, 110*n*36, 157*n*10, 183, 185, 199*n*3, 205–206, 225, 277
"The Ball Ball" (season 12, episode 4) 185
Banks, Tynomi 136
Barry, Derrick 73–74, 214
Bechdel test 39
Bell Bundy, Laura 45–46
Benet, Bebe Zahara 82–83, 134–135, 223
Berle, Milton 207–208
Betty, Acid 101
Beyond, Lashauwn 13, 99
*Big Mouth* 41
*The Birdcage* 41
Blac, Kimora 240–242
Black-eyed Leonora 1
Black Lives Matter 119, 193, 215, 251
Bloom's Taxonomy 8

Bob the Drag Queen 30, 67, 99, 121–122, 133, 135, 206, 209, 212–216, 266, 271*n*54
*Bob the Drag Queen: Suspiciously Large Woman* 212–213
*Bodies That Matter* 2, 234
Bonet, Trinity K. 211
Bordieu, Pierre 43
"Born Naked" (season 7, episode 1) 93–94
Bottoms, Dusty Ray 74–75, 170, 176, 263
Boxx, Pandora 206, 209, 219–220
*Broad City* 45
"The Broke Queen" *see* DeVayne, Chi Chi
Brown, Nina Bo'Nina 237, 242
Brown, Tammie 206
Bubois, Luna 136
Burdick, Jake 3, 91
Busch, Charles 207
Butler, Judith 19, 31, 40, 43, 105–107, 114*n*97, 146, 167, 234, 236; *Bodies That Matter* 2, 234; *Gender Trouble* 106, 119, 114*n*97

*La Cage Aux Folles* 40
Cain, Shuga 70, 123
Camp Wannakiki 128, 202*n*46
Canada 60, 63, 83–84, 108–109*n*1, 122, 148, 254, 273, 274
*Canada's Drag Race* 6–7, 9, 118–119, 121, 126–128, 130, 136, 200*n*16, 258
Carey, Jaremi 262, 266, 268–269*n*10, 270*n*31, 271*n*56; *see also* O'Hara, Phi Phi
Carlisle, Carlotta 129
Carrera, Carmen 3*n*10, 93, 97, 263, 266, 268–269*n*10
Chachki, Violet 95–96, 122, 228, 245
charisma, uniqueness, nerve, and talent (C.U.N.T) 48, 262–263
Charles, James 229, 231
Charles, RuPaul as drag mother 24–27, 59–61, 66, 76–81, 120, 190–191; as host 15, 32, 40–43, 66, 100–101, 146–148, 185–186, 208, 219, 252; on race 68–69, 148, 169–171, 189, 192–194, 260–263; as teacher 2, 4–5, 53, 66, 69, 72–73, 83–85, 91–96, 161–173, 177,

205–206, 257–265; trans controversy 47, 81, 189–190, 246–247, 263–264
Chaynes, Allyson 119, 127, 133
Cheney, Mary 40
"Cher: The Unauthorized Rusical" (season 10, episode 8) 146
Chi, Kim 63, 73–74, 80, 229, 254
"Choices 2020" (season 12, episode 9) 68
Closet, Heidi N. 191, 202n49, 260
code-switching 44
Cookie, Miz *see* See, Chester
Couleé, Shea 103
Covid-19 7, 225, 248, 249n4, 252–253, 255–256, 258–260, 268n6, 267, 280
Cox, Jackie 68
Cox, Laverne 97, 110n39
Cox, Sofonda 136
Cracker, Miz 30, 77–78, 123, 131, 164, 174, 206, 209, 212–215, 218, 222, 242, 261
Crews and Tangos Drag Race (CTDR) 118, 121, 126–129, 131, 134

*The Daily Show* 38
Davenport, A'Keria 70, 126
Davenport, Honey 126
Davenport, Kennedy 126, 222
Davenport, Sahara 126
Davenport family 126
*Death Becomes Her* 217
Dela Creme, Ben 26, 183, 206, 209–210, 215–218, 221–222
Delano, Adore 122, 229, 239
DeLarverie, Stormé 207
Del Rio, Bianca 23, 122, 135, 205–206, 209–212, 216, 218, 221
Derrida, Jacques 43
Descartes, René 18
Detox 190
DeVayne, Chi Chi 20–21, 63, 80, 229
*Diagnostic and Statistical Manual of Mental Disorders* (*DSM*) 83
dialogue (learning through/learning with) 72–76, 82, 84, 85, 161, 174, 265
The Diet Ghosts 122
Diore Fierce, Jaidynn 95
Divine 1, 112n55, 228, 245
"Divine Intervention" (season 7, episode 9) 115
D-Lite, Venus 93, 186, 202n50
drag kings 105, 111n40, 130, 137, 138, 201n39, 202n46, 222
drag mother 59, 74, 191, 214, 277
"Drag My Wedding" (season 6, episode 10) 16, 23–26
"Drag on a Dime" (season 1, episode 1) 163
"Drag on a Dime" (season 10, episode 1) 163–164
*Drag U* 163, 168, 257
DragCon LA 3, 53, 166, 204n83
DragCon NY 3
DragConUK 4

*Dragula* 128, 196, 202n46
The Duchess of Devonshire 1
The Duchess of Gloucester 1

Edwards, Alyssa 126, 220, 229, 277
Eichner, Billy 147
*Ellen* 211
Emmy Awards 4, 15, 163
Envy, Scarlett 70
ESPN 194
Estranja, Laganja 126, 133
"Evil Twins" (season 10, episode 11) 77–78, 173–174
extravaganza 38, 49, 101, 185

"Face, Face, Face of Cakes" (season 3, episode 7) 91–93, 95–96
Fahnestock, Jeanne 103–106, 113n91
fandom 3–4, 5, 30–31, 120–121, 127, 133–137, 204n83, 268n9, 280–281
*Fashion Photo RuView* 195
Ferrah, India 202n51
Filter, Brita 191, 202n49, 256, 258, 270n30
Firkus, Brian *see* Mattel, Trixie
fishy 50–51, 277
flazéda 49
"Float Your Boat" (season 4, episode 6) 69
Flowers, Nina 61, 74, 101
Floyd, George 203n58, 215, 255, 273
Fontaine, Cynthia Lee 190
Foucault, Michel 1, 18, 47, 232
Fox, Joslyn 23–24, 27
France, Tan 18
Freire, Paulo 8, 59, 65, 167, 169; *Pedagogy of the Oppressed* 168
"Frock the Vote!" (season 4, episode 9) 67–68

*Game of Thrones* 37
Garland, Lucy 228–229
*Gender Trouble* 106, 114n97, 119
Ginsberg, Merle 100
Giroux, Henry 3, 65–66, 73, 92, 107, 118–119, 257, 263, 266–267
Glasscock, Rebecca 82
Goode, Gigi 201n34, 258, 265
"Grand Finale" (season 12, episode 14) 254–255, 259–260, 266
*Grease* 70
Grosz, Elizabeth 19, 22
Gunn, Gia 51, 246–247, 263, 268–269n10
*GuRu* 72, 165–167, 174, 202n55

Hadid, Gigi 98
Halberstam, Jack 98, 105–106, 110–111n39
Hall, Jaida Essence 256–258, 265
hallelloo v, 8, 277
Harmony (research participant) 122, 134, 136
Heart, Monique 131, 164, 176, 266
Hickey-Moody, Anna 3, 91, 107
Hillz, Monica Beverly 263

*Hocus Pocus* 217
hog body 5
Honard, Justin *see* Thunderfuck 5000, Alaska
hooks, bell 76, 158n14, 171, 175, 176, 177, 212
*House of Cards* 41
*House of Drag* 128
House of Edwards 125
House of Kings 119
House of Lix 121
Hudson, Jada 136
Hytes, Brooke Lynn 122, 124, 132

Imfurst, Mimi 186, 202n51
Indigeneity 108n1, 129, 142–160, 255, 268–269n10, 280

Jeffreys, Joe E. 1–2, 118
Johnson, Marsha P. 69, 81, 203n60, 207, 264
Jolie, Jade 277

Kaepernick, Colin 193, 197
Katya 63, 95, 115, 206, 209, 218, 231, 239
Kressley, Carson 109–110n30, 260, 269n27
Kyne 258

LaBeija, Crystal 1
La Chapelle, David 93
Lady Bunny 1
Lady Gaga 94, 105, 236–237
Lady Godina 1
Larue, Danny 207
Laurel and Hardy 208
Lemmon, Jack 208
Leyva, James *see* Valentina
library 37, 205, 256, 277
lingerie 98, 111n48
*Little Women L.A.* 19
Lorde, Audre 170, 225
Love, Kylie "Sonique" 264
Love, Priyanka 127, 136
Love, Xtacy 128
Lovelock, Michael 2
Luzon, Manila 135, 144, 220
Lypsinka 207

"Madonna: The Unauthorized Rusical" (season 12, episode 7) 69
Marlatt, Daphne 94
*Match Game* 207, 219, 221
Mateo, Alexis 92–93
Mateo, Vanessa Vanjie 70, 134
Mattel, Trixie 20, 95, 115, 142–143, 149–152, 153, 155, 156, 206, 209, 212, 217–218, 228–229, 231, 239, 280
Matthews, Ross 185, 257
Matthews, Stacey Layne 92–93, 201n41
Max 95
McQueen, Laila 99
Methyd, Crystal 201n39, 258, 265
Michaels, Chad 67–68, 190–191, 270n32

Michaels, Kameron 27
Michaels, Kenya 201n41
Michelle, Alexis 152, 157n10, 220
Michelson, E. 19
microaggressions 254, 268–269n10
Midler, Bette 215–218
Milk 222
Minj, Ginger 206, 223, 239
mirror moment 22, 24, 30
Miss Chief *see* Monkman, Kent
Miss Fame 123
Miss Fiercalicious 124–**125**, 136
Miss Scotto 123
Miss Sweet Lips 1
Miu, Lucinda 122–124, 134
Moan, Farrah 123, 229, 237, 280
Monkman, Kent 143–144, 153–155, 156, 159n65, 160n69
Monsoon, Jinkx 10, 122, 206, 217, 220–221, 223–224, 239
Montrese, Coco 240
Morton, Mark 1
Mother Ru *see* Charles, RuPaul
*Mrs. Doubtfire* 108, 185, 208
Murphy, Eddie 212–213

Needles, Sharon 67–68
Netflix 15
NFL (National Football League) 197, 203n58

Ocasio-Cortez, Alexandria 69
Oddly, Yvie 124
O'Hara, Asia 28, 77, 134, 168–170, 202–203n56, 261–262, 266
O'Hara, Eureka 28, 77, 164, 170, 192–193, 202n52, 238, 261, 266, 271n54
O'Hara, Phi Phi 67, 102, 268–269n10, 270n31; *see also* Carey, Jaremi
O'Hara, Ra'Jah 126
Ojibwe 142, 149–150
O'Malley, Michael P. 3, 91
Ongina 63, 82–83, 96, 100, 101
Oprah 94
Oteri, Cherie 98

*Paris Is Burning* 37–38, 40–41, 49, 60, 185, 205, 211, 225, 278
Parker, Victoria "Pork Chop" (drag queen) 278
Pearl 49, 95, 191
*Pedagogy of the Oppressed* 59n3, 168
Peppermint 32–33, 263, 266, 271n54
Peru, Coco 207
Pie, Sherry 7, 270n30
Pierce, Charles 207
*Pit Stop* 194
The Pork Chop (first eliminated queen of a season on *RPDR*) 10, 278
presentation moment 22, 24
*Prêt-à-Porter* 95, 109–110n30
Pretty Harriet 1

*The Prime of Miss Jean Brodie* 43, 168, 171
Project Runway 5
public pedagogy 3, 92, 119, 137, 138, 224, 252–253, 255, 257

*The Queen Who Mopped Xmas* 186
Queer Eye 18, 45
queer pedagogy 161–181, 229–230, 233–235, 238, 239–241, 244–245, 247, 251n62

Raja 122, 135, 143, 145, 148–149, 155–156, 158n18, 191, 195, 242, 280
Rannells, Andrew 147
Raven 98, 195, 242
reading 37, 48–49, 196, 205–206, 225, 256, 278
*Reality TV and Queer Identities* 2
"Reunited: Alone Together" (season 12, episode 13) 254–256, 259–260, 265–266
Rice, Santino 101, 148–149, 216
Rickles, Don 211
Riot, Tash 123–124, 129
Ritz, Dida 67
Rivera, Sylvia 69, 81, 264
Rivers, Joan 210
Rojek, Chris 243, 251n59
Roy Haylock *see* Bianca Del Rio
Royale, Latrice 67
Ruiz, Mike 100
RuPaul (drag persona) *see* Charles, RuPaul
"RuPaul Book Ball" (season 8, episode 8) 73
RuPaul Fashion Photo Ruview 258
"RuPaul Roast" (season 7, episode 5, *RPDR*) 2, 102
*RuPaul's Drag Race (RPDR)* 2–5, 15–18, 32, 38, 43, 53–54, 59–63, 67, 79, 81–82, 85, 96, 102–103, 107, 117–125, 137–138, 161, 197–198, 206–208, 211, 215, 224–225, 228–230, 233–235, 237, 239, 243, 248, 254–255, 259, 262–263; family 125–128; fandom 131–134, 208–209; format 37, 39–42, 66, 72, 196; gender 144, 146, 187–189; language 45–52; race 135–136, 143–145, 156, 170–171; season 1 101; season 2 209, 219–220; season 3 91–93, 186; season 6 23–26; season 7 95, 150; season 8 19–22, 73, 80, 98–99, 101; season 9 67–68; season 10 21–31, 75–78, 146–149, 163–164, 174–176, 192–193, 262; season 11 6; season 12 69–70, 185, 252–253
*RuPaul's Drag Race Holi-Slay Spectacular* 264
*RuPaul's Drag Race U.K.* 6, 74
*RuPaul's Drag Race: Untucked* 13, 69, 170, 237, 257, 261
*RuPaul's Secret Celebrity Drag's Race* 6
"RuPocalypse Now" (season 4, episode 1) 13
RuPologize 4, 8
Rusical 5, 69, 70–71, 146, 277
RuVeal 4, 70, 72, 77–78
RuVS 4

St. Clair, Blair 176
Salah, Trish 97, 108, 110n38
Sanchez, Tyra 135
Sanders Pierce, Charles 104
Sandlin, Jennifer A. 3, 91
*Saturday Night Live* 205
Savage, Dan 67–68
Savage, Glenn C. 3, 91
Savage, Lily 207
Sedgwick, Eve 162, 172–173, 175, 176
See, Chester 30–31, 35n43
shade 5, 45, 46, 48–49, 99, 196, 205, 206, 278
Shangela 93, 126, 202n50, 206, 266, 271n54, 277
Shannel 102, 113n80, 131
Shannon, Lori 207
*Sibling Rivalry* 121
Silberman, Seth Clark 269n16
Silencia 121
simpson, jaye 150, 160n69
*The Simpsons* 38
Sin, Dahlia 270n30
Smalls, Naomi 20–21, 80, 98, 123–124, 125, 238
Snatch Game 5, 168, 207, 209–210, 216, 219–223, 224, 242, 280
"Snatch Game" (season 10, episode 7) 75–77
"Social Media Kings Into Queens" (season 10, episode 10) 16–17, 27–31
Socrative Circle 34
Soju 242
*Some Like It Hot* 40, 207–208
Sparks, Lineysha 222
*SportsCenter* 195
Starr, Jeffree 229, 241, 243
Stommel, Jesse 260
Stonewall Riots 60, 69, 203n60, 207, 264
storytelling 2, 29, 66, 71, 73–6, 77, 100, 174, 192–196, 198, 201n34, 201n39, 207, 215, 222, 230, 243–244, 246–247, 250n38
"Supermodel (You Better Work)" 41

Taylor, Trinity "the Tuck" 20, 190, 206, 222–223, 280
Thor, Thorgy 99, 222
Thunderfuck 5000, Alaska (drag queen) 109–110n30, 191, 220, 222, 223–224, 236–238, 239, 240, 251n59
Tiara, Plastique 126, 229
*To Wong Foo, Thanks for Everything! Julie Newmar* 41, 98, 108, 120, 199n4, 217
*Tootsie* 208
Trudeau, Justin 64
Trump, Donald 68, 70, 162, 167, 170
"Trump: The Rusical" (season 11, episode 4) 70–71
Turner, Robbie 21–22, 99, 222
Twitter 41, 102–103, 147, 217, 221, 262, 271n48, 271n53
Tylez, Porcelain 132–133

*UNHhhh*  10, 218, 231
Upadhyay, Nishant  145, 148, 158*n*17

Valentina  123, 229, 237–238
Van Ness, Jonathan  18
Velour, Sasha  32, 45, 96, 100, 101, 102–103, 131, 220, 229, 237
Vere Street  1, 11*n*4
Verley, Ilona  129
VH1  230, 242
*Victor/Victoria*  41
*Violet Chachki's Digital Drag*  10
Visage, Michelle  11, 25, 109–110*n*30, 147, 195, 222, 257
The Vixen  75–76, 169–171, 176, 192–193, 196, 202–203*n*56, 260–263, 266, 268–269*n*10, 270*n*32
Vyle, Selena  121–122, 129

*We're Here*  266
West, Nina  67, 206, 223

*Whatcha Packin'*  195
*What's the Tee*  258
Wilde, Oscar  265–266
Wilder, Billy  207–208
*Will & Grace*  211
Willam  99, 206, 207, 209, 239
Wilson, Flip  207–208
Windle, Joel  3, 91
Winters, Ivy  220
*The Wizard of Oz*  19
"Wizards of Drag" (season 8, episode 6)  16, 19–22
Work, Delta  93
*Workin' It!*  32*n*46, 91, 94, 99, 130*n*45, 164
World of Wonder (WOW)  9, 132, 194, 230, 242

X Change, Monét  28, 75, 121, 126, 134–135, 143, 147–149, 158*n*27, 176, 280

Zhane, Aiden  191, 202*n*49, 220, 258
Žižek, Slavoj  104–105, 113*n*91, 113–114*n*92

www.ingramcontent.com/pod-product-compliance
Ingram Content Group UK Ltd.
Pitfield, Milton Keynes, MK11 3LW, UK
UKHW010807100625
2148IPUK00007B/21